CLOUD STANDARDS

AGREEMENTS THAT HOLD TOGETHER CLOUDS

Marvin Waschke

technologies
PRESS

apress®

Cloud Standards: Agreements That Hold Together Clouds

ISBN-13 (pbk): 978-1-4302-4110-2
ISBN-13 (electronic): 978-1-4302-4111-9

President and Publisher: Paul Manning
Acquisitions Editor: Robert Hutchinson
Developmental Editor: Jeffrey Pepper
Technical Reviewer: Efraim Moscovich
Editorial Board: Steve Anglin, Mark Beckner, Ewan Buckingham, Gary Cornell, Morgan Ertel, Jonathan Gennick, Jonathan Hassell, Robert Hutchinson, Michelle Lowman, James Markham, Matthew Moodie, Jeff Olson, Jeffrey Pepper, Douglas Pundick, Ben Renow-Clarke, Dominic Shakeshaft, Gwenan Spearing, Matt Wade, Tom Welsh
Coordinating Editor: Rita Fernando
Copy Editor: Kim Wimpsett
Compositor: Bytheway Publishing Services
Indexer: SPi Global Inc.
Cover Designer: Anna Ishchenko

To Christopher and Matthew

Contents

Foreword

It's often said that to know where you are going, you must know where you have been. I think of this phrase often. It wards off knee-jerk reactions, especially when faced with the temptation to jettison due diligence and dive into the latest technology wave. Today, cloud computing is a cresting wave crashing through its "hype cycle." Experience brings perspective, healthy skepticism, and a vision of technological advances as a continuum.

The evolution to the cloud is just that—an evolution. From mainframes to distributed systems to personal computers to the Internet and now to the cloud: each computing wave took hold because of the demands of business were served by the advances in technology. The wave progression left a trail of standards, and successful standards have made it possible for IT to advance by building each technology on top of the one that came before. With the adoption of each new technology, business leaders took increasing control of their IT destinies in order to obtain their business services.

Cloud computing is the latest development in a trend toward understanding IT as a provider of services to business. Historically, technology planning and investment drove many IT decisions. This meant that IT investments did not always align accurately with business strategy, and IT projects were shaped as much by available technical resources as by business requirements and benefits.

Cloud computing distances IT services from the technical infrastructure. Cloud technical resources and attendant costs dial up and down to match the demand for services. This places IT planning and investment on a different footing from IT implemented on consumer premises. Enterprise IT professionals are free to focus on business service costs and benefits; cloud providers take on the task of predicting and investing in the technical infrastructure. Enterprise IT professionals can concentrate on designing and implementing innovative services tailored to the needs of the business instead of the infrastructure investment.

IT professionals need to embrace the potential of the cloud and prove themselves to be valued partners to business leaders looking for their cloud solutions. They must become influencers whose expertise is sought after by business service consumers who are otherwise only a click away from making independent technology decisions that may or may not be optimal for the enterprise. Conversely, cloud service providers can focus on implementation and technology rather than on creating and maintaining business services. Each entity—the cloud service providers, the IT professionals, and the business service consumers—becomes more efficient by concentrating and managing investments in what they do best.

Still, IT professionals cannot abdicate their responsibility for the technical infrastructure stability of an enterprise and must be prepared for what a colleague termed the *boomerang effect*, whereby prodigal business professionals, mired in technical details such as backups and security that still plague the cloud environment, enthusiastically relinquish control back to IT professionals.

For all the focus on the cloud's potential for comparatively swift implementations and dynamic business service composition, the importance of a solid technical foundation cannot be overstated. The potential of the cloud is possible only because of that foundation, which relies on tried and true technologies and standards.

Jacob Lamm
Executive Vice President
CA Technologies, Inc.

About the Author

Marvin Waschke is a senior principal software architect at CA Technologies. His career has spanned the mainframe to the cloud. He began his study of computer science as a mathematics major at the University of Chicago. His interest shifted to Chinese history and philosophy, but eventually he returned to computers at the beginning of the distributed era in computing. Since then, he has coded, designed, and managed the development of many systems, ranging through accounting, cell  tower management, enterprise service desks, configuration management, and network management.

For his entire career, he has maintained an interest in the role of standards in the development of computing and has served on numerous standards groups. He represents CA Technologies on the DMTF Cloud Management Working Group, DMTF Open Virtualization Format Working Group, DMTF Common Information Model REST Interface Working Group, OASIS Topology and Orchestration Specification for Cloud Applications (TOSCA) Technical Committee, DMTF Cloud Auditing Data Federation Working Group (observer), DMTF Configuration Database Federation Working Group, W3C Service Modeling Language Working Group, and OASIS OData Technical Committee (observer).

He is the editor-in-chief of the *CA Technology Exchange* (an online technical journal), and he designed, coded, and managed the development of the CA Service Desk Manager product.

About the Technical Reviewer

Efraim Moscovich is a senior principal software architect in the office of the CTO at CA Technologies. He has more than 25 years of experience in IT and software development in various capacities.

Moscovich's areas of expertise include virtualization and cloud computing, automation, event management/complex event processing, internationalization and localization, performance management, Windows internals, clustering and high availability, large-scale software architecture, continuous integration, automated testing, scripting languages, and diagnostics techniques.

He is an active participant in OASIS TOSCA technical committee and DMTF Cloud Management Working Group.

Moscovich has a master's of science degree in computer science from New Jersey Institute of Technology.

Acknowledgments

I must acknowledge two teachers from long ago: first, Robert Ashenhurst. Professor Ashenhurst taught my first formal course in computing at the University of Chicago. He implanted the idea in me that there is nothing cooler than writing a program. My second teacher was Herrlee Creel, also of the University of Chicago, a writer and specialist on ancient Chinese civilization. Professor Creel taught me to respect clear and simple language. I hope this book would have made him proud.

After I received degrees in Far Eastern area studies from the University of Chicago, I went to Western Washington University for a computer science degree. There, I learned about data structures and databases from Professor James Johnson and about IT projects from Professor Martin Osbourne.

I have been an employee of CA Technologies for close to 20 years, and I must credit CA with a great deal. CA gave me the opportunity to work with large-scale mission-critical systems. Without the customers and colleagues from these projects, this book would be shallow indeed. Above all, computing is about solving practical problems in a messy and contradictory world. Remove the mess and the contradictions, and it is all easy. Sincerely, I thank you all for messing me up and contradicting me at every turn.

Among my immediate colleagues, I must acknowledge, above all, my friend and colleague, Efraim Moscovich, who served as technical reviewer for this book. If there is anything good here, Efraim shares the credit both from his comments on the manuscript and from the stream of e-mails and instant messages we exchange. I must also acknowledge Donald F. Ferguson, former CTO of CA Technologies. On my watch, Don is the smartest man in any room he enters. He was the original sponsor and inspiration for this book.

I also want to acknowledge my old friend and manager, Jacob Lamm, who wrote the foreword. Jacob and I have had a long association in delivering service management to CA's customers, and I am in debt to his guidance and insight.

I have so many other colleagues: Mitch Engel, my current and long-suffering boss; my friends, Peter and Sal Lazarro, who understand IT systems on a level that few equal; David Tootill, whose talent at system building is incomparable; Greg Bodine, system architect par excellence; Mark Richardson, who can spot a bug in code from across the room; Cheryl Morris, who always has my back on the CA Technology Exchange; Chuck Jimmerson, who has never failed to inject reality into a technical discussion; and Paul Lipton, who so aptly manages the CA standards program. This list has no end. My colleagues at CA are wonderful.

Then there are the folks at CA Press and Apress. Karen Sleeth, director of CA Press, planted the idea of a book, and I will be forever grateful. Jeff Pepper and Robert Hutchinson were what I always imagined editors to be: correcting, prodding, and inspiring. Jay Harrison, another CA colleague, prompted, cajoled, and generally improved the book. Rita Fernando is always helpful and obliging.

Finally, a word about my family. My wife, Rebecca, supports me in every way; my son and daughter are there for me whenever I need them; but my twin grandsons, Matthew and Christopher, are the stars. At 10 years old, the cloud is their playground.

Introduction

This book is about the technology that supports the cloud and the standards that have made the cloud possible. It combines several subjects: computing, standards, and business. Information technology (IT) clouds are both a business arrangement and a collection of computing technology. As technology, a cloud is the power of large datacenters made accessible through a far-reaching network. As a business arrangement, a cloud separates responsibility for physical computing equipment and operations from the consumers of computing services, much as electrical utilities separate the responsibility for generating electricity from the consumers who use it.

Just as small and large electricity users benefit from efficient and reliable electrical utilities, both individuals and enterprises can benefit from the cloud.

The technology behind cloud implementations is vast and complex, but this technology did not appear from nowhere. It has risen from innovation and development that has accumulated since computing began. The technology came from many individuals and organizations. Without standards that hold these technologies together, the cloud would not be possible.

Standards make it possible for components and technologies from many different sources to work together. These standards are the product of an engineering community working together to forge ties that promote innovation and flexibility instead of continual reinvention of the same wheels.

Beginning in the mainframe era, businesses have assumed that to benefit from IT, they had to own and operate computing equipment. There was a period between mainframes and distributed computing when some businesses avoided owning large computers through time-sharing, but that practice declined as the cost of distributed desktop computers decreased and their capabilities increased. Time-sharing holds the kernel of the idea of the cloud and has resurfaced in a new form as computing has progressed.

The same forces that elevated the desktop computer to prominence have also heralded its decline. Desktops were dramatically smaller than mainframes and could do many of the same things. Today, handheld devices have capabilities similar to desktops, but they slip into a pocket and run wirelessly. Some of these tiny machines store as much data as a respectable datacenter of not too long ago. Datacenters now regularly hold hundreds of thousands of miniature equivalents of the most powerful desktops, all harnessed together to perform tasks that would have been inconceivable even ten years ago. Add the fast and ubiquitous global Internet to these capacities, and you have a cloud with nearly limitless IT resources available everywhere.

Tapping into the cloud, a farmer with a cell phone in Africa and a corporate executive in New York City access IT resources with equal ease. This is a playing field with vast new possibilities for innovation and growth, but to understand and use both the capabilities and limitations of the cloud, you must understand the underlying engineering revealed in its standards. The standards discussed in this book are the key to this understanding.

Setting the Scene

A Brief and Informal History and Introduction to the Cloud

Cloud computing is at the zenith of the hype curve. Everyone is talking about it. Cloud enthusiasts are enthused, marketing has a new hot topic, but skeptics dismiss it as an old idea from forty years ago rewarmed. These views are all justified.

What is *the cloud* that everyone is talking about? Here is a short and rather dry working definition:

The cloud is remote computing resources provided as a service.

Service is an often-used term that has many meanings, but here it is being used with a precise meaning derived from publications of the Information Technology Infrastructure Library (ITIL), an organization that will be discussed in a later chapter. In this definition, a *service* means a consumer–provider relationship in which the provider delivers value to the consumer and the consumer avoids designated costs and risks they would have incurred if they had delivered the value themselves (Figure 1-1). When an automobile owner takes her car to an oil changing service, for example, she is avoiding the costs, trouble, and risks of acquiring tools, learning the correct procedures, and so on. When the owner makes the decision to subscribe, she presumably has decided that the benefits of the service justify the charge for the service.

An IT cloud service is similar. Consumers avoid the cost and risk involved in providing the service themselves by paying the provider. On a technical level, the provider of service is strictly separated from the consumer of the service. This strict separation differentiates other architectures. The service relationship can take many forms, as can remote computer resources, so it is not surprising that cloud computing also takes many forms.

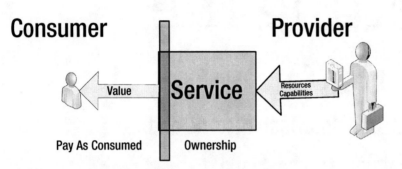

Figure 1-1. The service consumer and provider relationship

COMPUTING RESOURCES

The following are generally considered *computing resources.* (The occasionally used term *compute resources* generally refers to processing time rather than storage or network.)

- CPU time

- Memory

- Non-volatile storage (disk)

- Network

- Electrical power

- Peripheral devices

The two important things to note are that the computing is remote and is usually used in a limited and explicitly described way; and the provider takes responsibility for the cost and risk of delivering the service. The consumer and provider remain distinct, even when the provider is part of the same organization as the consumer, as is often the case. The consumer usually has to pay for the service, but there are a surprising number of free cloud services available. The costs and risks that the provider assumes are usually costs associated with setting up and running computers and the risks of failures, disasters, or losing money on the investment in computing equipment.

Our definition of the cloud as a service focuses on the business side of cloud computing, which may be surprising for a book that is about technical standards. In IT, technology and business are intertwined in a complex and intricate relationship. New technical capabilities cause new business opportunities and challenges, but at least as often, business challenges and opportunities inspire technical solutions. The rise of cloud computing was the result of movement in both directions. In later chapters, the business aspect of the cloud will shift into the background, but it will never disappear because business inevitably affects technology and standards.

Many of the standards which we will examine in this book help maintain the separation between the consumer and provider of cloud services. That separation is the source both of value and of complication—even loss of efficiency.

This may seem trivial and scant justification for the brouhaha that cloud computing has generated. But as we explore cloud computing, you will see that cloud computing is much more significant than it may seem from the bare bones of this definition.

History: Evolution of the Cloud

The significance of cloud computing is partially revealed in its history. It was not invented yesterday. Although the term *cloud computing* came much later, it is an idea from the '60s and '70s when computing power was expensive and hard to come by. In those days, the next big thing was *time-sharing*, a new idea that promised to break computing away from the batch-processing model. Whereas batch processing runs computing jobs in batches, one job at a time in sequence, the time-sharing model runs many jobs at the same time (*multitasks*) while users work concurrently, sharing the computer time. Although there are significant differences, the old notion of time-sharing is very similar to what we now call cloud computing. The common concept is to provide computing from a remote central source instead of locally. Both cloud computing and time-sharing are tied to the notion that computing power can be a utility that is dispensed as a service like electricity or water.

In the '60s and '70s, time-sharing was inspired by the expense and paucity of computer resources. Computers with what would now be called modest capacities occupied whole rooms and required massive power supplies and cooling systems. Large enterprises were able to set up computer systems, but many smaller enterprises clamored for computing power. In business, computers of that era were used mainly for back office jobs: accounts receivable, billing, and payroll all were efficiently computerized to yield speed and accuracy that could not be equaled by manual systems. Smaller organizations had similar needs and could reap similar benefits from this type of functionality, but in smaller volumes that would not justify a large computer. Time-sharing ameliorated this situation by providing simultaneous remote access to a central computer. Organizations could purchase computer time for their needs without the overhead of owning and managing an entire system that they could not fully utilize. Organizations that had a computer installation could recoup some of the costs of underutilization by selling time to other organizations.

Minicomputers began to appear at the same time time-sharing became popular. As the name implies, minicomputers were smaller than mainframes and cost less. Advances in technology soon began rapidly to increase the capacity of minicomputers to the point that they began to rival recently produced mainframes. Examples are the PDP-8 and the VAX, both from Digital Equipment Corporation, and models from some the great names in computing in the '70s and '80s such as Data General, Prime, and Wang Laboratories. Most minicomputers had multitasking operating systems and were able to support time-sharing.

Time-sharing and minicomputers evolved into *distributed systems*. Distributed computing is closely associated with the personal computer (PC). PCs appeared on the scene during the heyday of time-sharing and were rapidly accepted as office appliances, not unlike the typewriters they replaced. These appliances were usually owned and administered by ordinary office workers instead of computer professionals.

This turnabout in the proprietorship of computing power had far-reaching consequences. Instead of going into lengthy and difficult negotiations with corporate IT, individual office workers and managers could take the initiative and purchase and deploy relatively cheap off-the-shelf software to make their jobs more efficient.

Personal computers were transforming computing from something that existed only in the rarified atmosphere of the "glass house," the corporate datacenter, to a household commodity.

The Network and Distributed Systems

Almost as soon as PCs began landing on every desk and word processors replaced typing pools, PCs began to be connected together in networks. The initial impetus toward networks was often the need to share a single printer among several desks, but users soon discovered the advantages and convenience of being able to share documents and information over the network instead of passing data around manually.

Network technology had already been developed for remote access to time-sharing systems. Networks make *servers* possible. Servers function like the single printer that prints for all the computers in a group. Instead of translating digital signals into physical paper and ink, servers provide information and processing to other computers. Just as a single financial department can serve an entire enterprise, a single server might provide accounting data and processing to an entire enterprise. The server and its clients, typically PC desktops, all communicate on a single network.

In its simplest form, a server is connected to a relatively small number of interconnected computers in what is called a *local area network* (LAN), usually limited to a small geographical area (Figure 1-2). LANs can be connected together in an ever larger hierarchy (Figure 1-3), culminating today in the Internet. The Internet is the ubiquitous network of networks that connects most of the computing resources on the planet.

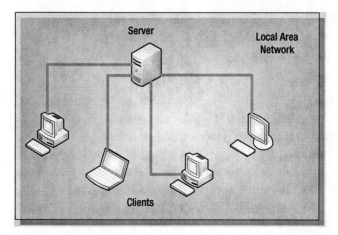

Figure 1-2. A simple LAN

Initially, the Internet was used mainly for sharing data in the form of documents linked together with hypertext. However, that is only one use of the Internet. Document sharing is still the primary activity on the World Wide Web, but the Internet also makes it possible, through *web services* and other mechanisms, to share remote computer processing. The Internet sets computing free from location. The laptop in front of me can interact with another computer in Australia or Mumbai more easily than I can get a cup of coffee at the nearest

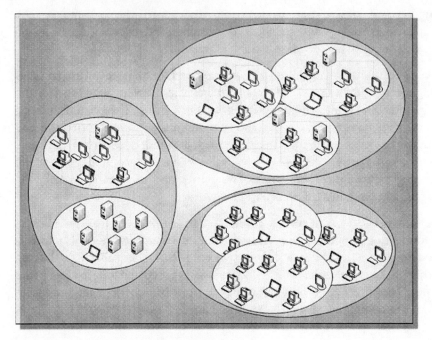

Figure 1-3. Interconnected LANs

Starbucks. This ubiquity and ease of access is an important aspect of cloud computing.

PCs and servers have been growing in power in accordance with Moore's law, not so much a law as a remarkably prescient prediction that computing power on a chip would double approximately every two years. Moore's prediction has been correct for the last thirty years, and many believe it is likely to continue for at least another decade, perhaps longer, since pundits have been forecasting the end of Moore's law in the next decade practically since the day Moore formulated it. The increase in the power of the PC meant that it became possible that the cake box on someone's desk was capable of serving an application to an entire department, even an entire organization.

Network connectivity and powerful distributed servers grew together hand in hand. Departmental LANs were connected into enterprise wide networks. Increased connectivity inspired more servers to act as resources to the entire network. As distributed servers became more powerful, they were able to take over more and more services that were formerly provided only by the powerful mainframe computers in the datacenter. The potential for uniform services for the entire enterprise causes more interconnected networks to be built out.

The stage in the evolution of distributed systems in which many servers sat on or under individual desks and in departmental closets was also characterized by an avalanche of new computer functionality that tumbled into business and industry through the '90s, often purchased with departmental budgets and without the benefit of corporate planning. This period might be described as the nadir of managed computing. The basics of IT management, like backup, security, and disaster recovery plans, were often neglected in this rapidly expanding milieu. The ad hoc administrators of these systems maintained the systems and installed new releases in the best way they knew how, but they were seldom trained in IT best practices, and their technical knowledge was often spotty. Consequently, the results were often mixed. Rumors circulated of entire enterprises crippled by the failure of an un-backed-up disk on a "power user's" desk.

The network and its servers were becoming enterprise assets, even mission-critical assets, whose stewardship could not safely be left to well-intentioned amateurs at their desks. Servers were moved from dusty closets and corners under desks to datacenters where they were backed up and maintained systematically. Gradually, the IT departments returned to a central role in administering distributed systems as well as centralized mainframes.

This was an interesting period. Moore's law was operating in the datacenter as well as on the desktop. Ever more powerful mainframes were decreasing in size at the same time distributed systems were increasing in power. Departmental servers that were hidden throughout the organization were moved into the datacenter, perhaps in space freed up by shrinking mainframes.

In the early '90s, John Gage at Sun Microsystems came up with the slogan "The network is the computer."[1] During the dot-com rush of the late 90s and the turn of the 20th century, the truth of that slogan came into its own. The Internet may have been over-hyped during that period, but the frenzy of the bubble served to introduce many people to the benefits of the World Wide Web and connection to the global network. This helped drive the build-out of a high-speed network infrastructure in a surprisingly short time.

The migration of commercial software installation to the network is a sign of the growing ubiquity of the network. Network installs, installing software from a remote server instead of distributing physical media, have been possible for a long time. Network installs began to be used within enterprises as soon as enterprise networks were established because they are quick and effective, but commercial software vendors cannot afford software installation methods that cannot be used by a significant portion of their market. In the '90s,

[1] Stefanie Olsen, "Sun's John Gage Joins Al Gore in Clean-tech Investing," CNET, June 9, 2008, http://news.cnet.com/8301-10784_3-9964131-7.html.

software installs were generally from media such as CDs, tapes, and even floppy disks because high-speed network connections were not common enough to make remote installation practical. These physical media-based installations were plagued with a host of unsatisfactory installs due to user errors, defective media and media-reading hardware, and media which were difficult to keep up-to-date with the latest features and fixes. Today, installation by download from the network is the rule rather than the exception. Although installation is still one of the more difficult aspects of software distribution, the result is at least that when you install, you are installing what the software vendor has designated current. The frequency of downloaded installations is an indication that high-speed network access has become close to a foregone conclusion.

Technology has placed staggering computing power into our hands each time we pick up a laptop or tablet. We now measure storage in terabytes, memory in gigabytes, and processor speed in gigahertz, having invented new names for numbers too large to manage with the vocabulary familiar when distributed systems began. A new laptop today may have two or more multi-gigahertz processors, at least two gigabytes of memory, and a terabyte or two of storage. It was not too long ago that these terms would describe a fair-sized datacenter.

One would expect that with all this storage and processing capacity, the result would be independence. A single user can carry all the computing capacity of an entire datacenter in their briefcase. But the exact opposite has happened. Instead of becoming more independent, we have become more dependent because we have discovered the value of being connected. With the advent of wireless connections and support for Internet connection via the cellular networks, many people have high-speed connection to the Internet not just some of the time but *all* of the time. On a personal level, we expect to read email all the time, post and read the latest chatter on Twitter, and track a host of friends on Facebook. The Internet extends everywhere, and everyone is continuously connected. In the enterprise, the same level of personal connection applies to the enterprise worker as well as the individual. In addition, the enterprise has discovered the value of distributed applications that instantly aggregate data from all over the organization and allow collection and mining of unprecedented quantities of data.

The presence of a reliable high-speed network everywhere makes cloud computing possible. Cloud services can be valuable only when they are accessible. The presence of a fast and reliable network opens cloud services to their users.

Virtualization

Networking has transformed the way we use computers in business and at home, but another technology also is actively shaping the current evolution of computing environments. This technology is called *virtualization*, a word that appears all the time today in computer circles but is not yet defined in standard dictionaries.

To explain virtualization, the concept of *layering* in computer architecture is an easy starting point. Almost everything in computing is built in layers. In a simplified form for explanation, a typical application running on a standalone PC can be seen as three layers:

- At the bottom is the physical hardware consisting of chips, circuit boards, and peripheral devices such as hard drives.

- Next is the operating system layer, which interacts with the hardware through well-defined interfaces and provides services such as management of multitasking and coordinating interaction with storage devices.

- The top layer is the application, which interacts with the operating system to obtain raw services such as input and output and transform them into useful services tailored to the tasks of the end user.

The rule in a layered architecture is that one layer interacts only with the layer directly beneath itself and the layer directly above itself. The application interacts only with the operating system, never directly with the hardware. The hardware interacts only with the operating system, never with the application directly.

Layering makes design and implementation easier, although strict layering is occasionally criticized as a barrier to optimization.[2]

The disciplines required for each layer in the application stack described earlier are rather different. The hardware layer requires the expertise of an electrical engineer who understands the physical characteristics of the components and electrical signals they work with. An operating system programmer needs some of the expertise of the hardware engineer in addition to skills in writing code to manipulate data at a highly granular level. An application programmer must understand the intricacies of user interfaces

---

[2] RFC 3839, "Some Internet Architectural Guidelines and Philosophy," http://tools.ietf.org/html/rfc3439#, page 7, discusses some issues with layering. These considerations do not apply to the discussion here.

and business logic and how to implement them in software with the functionality offered by the operating system. Although an occasional IT star masters all these levels at once, most of the time developing expertise in all layers and keeping all that information intact in one's head while working on a project is a formidable if not impossible task. A system that clearly differentiates between layers makes working on each layer more manageable and increases the likelihood that the total system will perform correctly.

The sequence of layers that make up an application is often called the *application stack* (Figure 1-4). Application stacks are often articulated much more finely than the rough approximation discussed here, but all are based on the principle of layering.

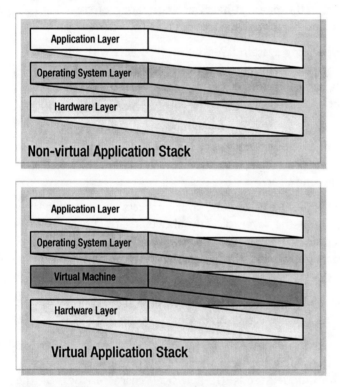

Figure 1-4. Non-virtual and virtual application stacks

Layering also makes possible virtualization. If layers are well separated and cleanly executed, a completely different implementation can be substituted for one layer without affecting the output of the layers above or requiring changes in the layers below. Virtualization substitutes a layer of software for hardware layers in an application stack.

A *virtual machine* is a computer that is simulated with software so that it can occupy the bottom layer in an application stack while running on an independent hardware layer that is independent of the originally intended hardware. Applications running on a properly implemented virtual machine behave identically or very nearly identically to the same applications running on real hardware.

Emulation of the hardware layer of the application stack is the most relevant to cloud computing, but there are other forms of virtualization. For example, virtual memory has been part of computer hardware for many years. Especially before semiconductor *random access memory* (RAM) took over, high-speed memory was one of the most expensive parts of a computer system.[3] Virtual memory substitutes cheaper, but slower, disk memory for expensive RAM. Virtual memory still plays a role in systems, but cheaper RAM has made it much less significant than it once was.

Other forms of virtualization include the inverse of virtual memory, using RAM to emulate disk drives. Storage and networks also can be, and often are, virtualized.

Virtualization may seem like a needless complication to implementation stacks. Why add the extra layers? Isn't that only extra development and complication? Actually, virtualization has proven quite valuable for a long time. IBM began researching virtualization in the mid-'60s. The term *virtual machine* began to be used in IBM labs around 1965. [4]

One of the basic problems in time-sharing is keeping users from interfering with each other. Users want to prevent their data and activities from being seen or tampered with by other users. Even more important, execution of programs must be kept strictly separate. Most time-sharing system use a technique known as *time-slicing*. One program executes a few instructions, and then another program executes instructions for a short time. Control

---

[3] Ferrite core memory was the prevalent form of RAM in the 1960s and early 1970s. In ferrite core memory, each bit was represented by a donut-shaped magnet. Several wires ran through each magnet in an elaborate pattern. The wires were woven in manually at great expense. Lucien V. Auletta, Herbert J. Hallstead, Denis J. Sullivan, Ferrite Core Planes and Arrays: IBM's Manufacturing Evolution, IEEE Transactions or Magnetics, Vol. Mag. 5, No. 4, December 1969, www.ibm-1401.info/IBMCoreArraysIEEEMagnetics1969.pdf, provides a fascinating description of the hurdles involved in automating the manufacture of ferrite core memory.

[4] Melinda Varian, VM and the VM community, past present, and future, SHARE 89 Sessions 9059–61, 1997; http://web.me.com/melinda.varian/Site/Melinda_Varians_Home_Page_files/25paper.pdf. This is a history of the development of IBM's virtualized operating system for S/360 and beyond. The paper is remarkable for both its technical content and its personal anecdotes from the author.

passes from program to program so that each gets its share of the central processing unit. If my program processes your data or your program starts executing my program's instructions, the results are a confused mess. Virtualization is an elegant solution to this challenge.[5] Give each user their own virtual machine to separate them from other users. This was one of the original reasons IBM engineers developed virtualization in the '60s: to provide a simple-to-implement method of separating users of a time-shared system.

IBM engineers used the term *hypervisor* for the program that coordinates virtual machines and interfaces them to the underlying layer. The term is still used today. Some hypervisors interface directly to the hardware layer; others interface to an operating system or even a higher layer.

Cloud providers face a problem similar to that of the early time-share developers. A cloud provider has a large store of computing power to divvy up among users. Giving users virtual machines is one way of dividing up computing resources without allowing users to intermingle resources. This problem is not entirely solved by virtual machines, but it results in a useful simplification. At the same time, offering consumers a virtual machine for their use provides them with a familiar environment for their work.

Prevention of user intermingling is not the only advantage conferred by virtualization. Virtual systems are much more flexible than real systems. Today, among operating systems, if we ignore the mainframe for a moment, a big dichotomy exists between Linux and Windows. The contest between the two operating systems is heated, but the important fact is that depending on the task and the preference of the implementers, both are used frequently. How does a cloud provider that wants to appeal to the largest possible user base accommodate this? Virtualization provides a ready answer.

In theory, at least, a virtual machine can be created with any operating system the user wants and that machine could be run on any hardware. That provides a great deal of flexibility. There are practical limits on this flexibility. Emulating a Windows 2008 server on a Motorola 6809 processor from 1978 might be possible.[6] However, such emulation would require an impractical amount of coding, and performance would be impossibly poor. Nevertheless, most of

---

[5] Virtual machines are not the only way to separate users. Most multiuser architectures segment memory into a separate address space for each user, but it is interesting that one of the early motivations for virtual machines was time-sharing.

[6] The 6909 instruction set is much different from the Intel instruction set that the Windows operating system is built on and the capacity of the 6809 operating at a single megahertz (a million instructions per second) is dwarfed by chips that operate at several gigahertz (several billion instructions per second). At that rate, since the 6809 had 8-bit registers and most Intel chips now have 32-bit registers, a rough calculation says that it would take a 6809 an hour to perform the calculation an Atom processor does in one second in a tiny netbook.

the operating system variants that are practically required can be emulated on virtual machines today.

Often, a legacy program will require an operating system that has not been ported to current hardware. Rather than attempt to port the application to a new operating system or the old operating system to new hardware, a virtual machine running the old operating system is often an easier solution. This means that a cloud provider can offer a wide selection of operating systems on virtual machines with relative ease to accommodate a wide range of requirements.

There are other uses for virtualization. Cloud computing services using physical hardware directly are possible. For instance, a consumer requests a machine with certain specifications, and the provider powers up the machine and physically connects it to the network. The provider gives the consumer instructions for accessing it, and the consumer is up and running. When the consumer is finished with their work, the provider takes the system down.

Blade systems make this process easier. In a blade system, each server's hardware is stripped down to its minimum and placed on a single board that plugs into a rack. A rack holds many servers at one time with power supply and mass storage separate. Assigning a blade to a cloud consumer is much simpler and more flexible than rolling out a new independent computer and bringing it online.

However, virtualization can improve on this process. A non-virtual blade system is basically limited by the granularity of the blade. The provider delivers computing a blade at a time. A virtualized system separates the computing power allocated to the user from the underlying hardware. Several virtual machines can run independently on a single blade, breaking the fixed granularity. Now, three users who need only a third of a blade can all run on the same blade without interfering. Even more interesting, hypervisors are capable of shifting virtual machines from physical machine to physical machine. This means that if a consumer's virtual machine begins to work harder and require more capacity, the hypervisor can move the virtual machine to a new blade that has more free capacity. This optimization is one of the great advantages of the cloud provider. A provider with a large number of consumers can take full advantage of the hardware in his datacenter by continuously handing over spare capacity available when a user decreases their load to another user with increasing load. Since electricity is one of the raw materials and key costs of running a cloud datacenter, the provider can also curb costs by shutting down unused systems automatically when demand goes down.

This doesn't even take into account the processing necessary to convert one instruction set into another. Virtualization does have its limits.

The Need for Clouds Today

One might think that with the tremendous computing capacity made available through the ever-increasing density of computer chips that continue to fulfill the predictions of Moore's law, there is a glut of computing power. Perhaps there should be little need for tapping into giant clouds of computing capacity because the computing power available to the average laptop user is so great. This has not proven to be true.

The needs of the individual user and the enterprise are different, and the cloud provides different potential for each. For an individual user, sheer computing power is usually not the issue. Individual users browse the Internet, do some word processing, work with a spreadsheet or two, follow social media, stream video, and play a few computer video games. Of those activities, playing computer games is almost certainly the most capacity stretching, and not surprisingly, the gamers are the ones pushing hardest for faster processing, more RAM, and faster secondary video processors.

But individuals do have needs that the cloud meets. One of the most basic is the need, or desire, to be independent of a single device. Email is a good example of this. Email has always had some cloudlike characteristics. Most often users receive email through a remote service such as Microsoft Hotmail or Google Gmail. Many of us have a collection of laptops, desktops, and smart phones that we use at one time or another. But we want our email when we want it, no matter which computer we are using at the moment. An answer to this need is to make email a self-contained cloud service. A user of a service like Gmail interacts with a service in the cloud rather than a service implemented on a local computer. Users do not download email to their local hard drives. Instead, it stays in the cloud, and the user can access it from anywhere. Consequently, the user can expect a similar experience from each device that connects to the cloud email service. In other words, the user can read his email no matter which device he is using. In fact, they can also use public computers in a hotel or an airport or can even use a computer borrowed from a friend. The connection to the cloud matters, not the computer.

Enterprises have different needs. Whereas individual users are not, at least now, particularly pressed for computing capacity, enterprises have become much more dependent on computing, and computing is being done on a much more intensive scale than ever before. Thriving enterprises are always strapped for computing capacity. When they are not strapped, good management dictates that they should shed capacity until they are strapped. Why? Because computing capacity is an investment and unused capacity is an idle investment, especially if it continues to consume electricity. A good manager liquidates idle investments and replaces them with active investments.

The problem for enterprises is that computing capacity is not liquid. It cannot be sold quickly and conveniently on an open market. More often, after computing capacity is acquired, unneeded capacity degrades and becomes obsolete before it can be liquidated. This is unfortunate in many ways. An enterprise is stuck with an investment in capacity that they cannot use. Consequently, when an opportunity arises where additional capacity is needed, the enterprise may be hesitant to invest in new capacity and thereby pass up valuable opportunities. In addition, computing capacity is not only computer hardware. There are also maintenance and staff costs that must be accounted for.

Enterprises are very good at discovering uses for additional computing capacity, but more than anything else, they need more flexible and manageable capacity in order to respond quickly and well to rapid change. This is exactly what the cloud promises to deliver.

Cloud Scenarios

This section contains some specific scenarios that cloud computing supports today. In later chapters, these scenarios will illustrate the use of the standards under discussion.

Scenarios for Individuals

Scenarios for individuals are less technical and easier to understand for most people, but the underlying implementation is not necessarily simple at all. In fact, the simplest appearing services may be the most complex to implement. In this introduction, however, we will concentrate on the service scenario, not the implementation.

Backing Up

One of the simplest and easiest things an individual can do to make use of clouds is to use a cloud backup service, and the payback for the investment can be enormous. Some backup services available now are even free if you do not have too great a volume to back up.

The advantages to cloud backup are easy to understand. Backing up your data is a tedious job that is easy to neglect—one of those jobs you put off for "just one day." The next thing you know, your hard drive has died, and you realize that "just one day" has stretched into six months, which means you have lost every photograph, every video clip, every audio clip, every document, and every spreadsheet you stored during that long six-month day. What good are those gorgeous terabytes of storage if you lose all your treasures anyway?

And then there is the question of where to back up. Enterprises often have whole groups devoted to backups. Backups are performed regularly, and the backup media is stored off-site in special facilities that are designed to withstand fires, flood, havoc, and mayhem. When magnetic tape was the primary backup medium, the storage rooms were specially climate controlled to preserve the tapes.

This kind of elaborate protection is usually out of the question for an individual. Most of us are doing well to back up onto a CD or DVD and put it in the bottom drawer of our desk. If you store JPEGs and MP3s and large video files, the number of DVDs required for a backup quickly becomes cumbersome. In addition, DVDs in a desk drawer may be good for a disk meltdown, but they are not much help after a fire or a tornado. I did an informal survey with some of my more knowledgeable (and cautious) friends and found that the really wary computer user stores his off-site backups either in the trunk of his car or at his mother's house. This increases the odds of surviving a catastrophe.

Of course, multi-terabyte external disk drives are easy to use and available at reasonable prices, so backup storage does not have to be bulky, but if you do use external drives, to be safe, you ought to have two drives. Back up, take the drive to your mother's, and back up next week on a second drive and exchange it with the one at your mother's. Did I say next week? What if the flood occurs the day before you backed up and you lose that video you shot two days ago of your daughter's first steps? Not so good! And don't think about storing that external drive in the trunk of your car in the winter: condensation destroys drives.

What the individual needs is a backup team to take over the cost and risks involved in setting up a backup center with secure and redundant storage and protect it against all the dangers that threaten individual backup systems.

From the user's standpoint, a cloud backup service works quite simply. The user designates certain sets of files for backup, which could be as extensive as all the files on the computer to as narrow as one or two critical files. From that point on, the backup service takes over. The files to be backed up are uploaded to a location that only the backup service provider needs to know. Future uploads can be on-demand, whenever a file changes, or on a schedule, say, every four hours. How this is set up is dependent on the provider. Typically, if a backed-up machine goes offline, the service will catch up when the machine goes back online. There is usually a small application installed on the backed-up machine to detect file changes and manage schedules and offline catch-up.

Exactly how data is stored and protected is the responsibility of the service provider, but the provider will usually guarantee the user of the backup service some kind of compensation if data is lost.

IMPORTANT STANDARDS FOR CLOUD BACKUPS

- TCP/IP for data transport

- CDMI storage standards

- COBIT data storage audits and controls

- Cloud Security Alliance, Security Guidance for Critical Areas of Focus in Cloud Computing for identification of critical security and governance concerns

---

Sharing Documents

Suppose that you and several colleagues have been assigned a research project. You each have a unique contribution to make to the project, and you are remote from each other, with perhaps one in London, one in Boeblingen, another in Shanghai, and one in Seattle; your team spans the world. You expect to write a single paper that you will all review and contribute to.

You and your colleagues could work together by exchanging documents via email, but that can easily become confusing. You would all have to agree on a word processor and make sure you all have compatible versions. Anyone who has worked in this kind of scenario knows that most word processors are more or less compatible but almost never completely compatible. Modifying a file with a word processor that is not identical to the processor that created the file will often cause something to change that was not supposed to change. This is at best annoying and, at worst, destructive.

Suppose you get past the compatibility hurdle and are using tools that work together. You still have to coordinate among yourselves. You usually have to keep track of which version of the document is the current definitive version and who is in control at a given time. When the contributors are widely separated and in different time zones, perhaps widely different time zones, coordination can become quite problematic and somebody always loses track.

A cloud document service like Google Docs can simplify collaboration. Google Docs consists of two major parts. One part is an online word processor. The user does not need to install anything on her machine. In fact, the individual's computer has almost no role working with documents in the Google Docs system. The work processing actually takes place on Google servers somewhere in the Google cloud. If the Google Docs word processor meets the needs of everyone in the group, compatibility is no longer an issue, and the members of the group do not need to go through the trouble and expense of acquiring and installing compatible word processors.

The other part of Google Docs is cloud storage of the documents. This is similar to using the cloud for backup, but it adds an element of sharing and collaboration. Any member of the group can edit documents shared within a group. This simplifies the whole collaboration process. Instead of each member of the group having a copy of the shared document, all have access to a single shared copy of the document. Members of the group can collaborate in real time, seeing each other's changes as they are made.

These advantages come from both sharing storage on the cloud and an application that runs on the cloud.

IMPORTANT STANDARDS FOR
CLOUD DOCUMENT SHARING

- HTTP

- OAuth

- OpenID

Cloud Scenarios for Enterprises

Enterprise computing differs from individual computing in many ways. Individuals are far less concerned about auditors and regulators than businesses are. Enterprises are far more likely than individuals to need programs and other forms of processing that are tailored to their own business needs. The sheer volume of computing done by enterprises dwarfs that of any individual. Enterprises are also likely to require, and have the influence to demand, a higher level of reliability and performance than individuals.

Cloud Service Models

The range of uses for the cloud for businesses is much wider than for individuals. There are three main classifications of cloud computing provided today, corresponding roughly to the application stack described earlier:

Infrastructure as a Service (IaaS)

IaaS is like the hardware layer of the application stack. An IaaS provider supplies the user with a virtual machine, virtual storage, and a virtual network. An operating system is usually also supplied.

Platform as a Service (PaaS)

PaaS providers provide a platform for building applications. A PaaS provider will supply infrastructure, but in addition, they supply the tools and building blocks for applications, such as an operating system, source code control tools, compilers, integrated development environments (IDEs), and data management tools.

Software as a Service (SaaS)

SaaS providers deliver a finished product to users. Similar to the Google Docs word processor that runs on a server in the cloud, a SaaS application runs entirely in the cloud. The end user accesses the application through a browser, and the use of the application is not dependent on the computer from which the user accesses the application.

Testing in the Cloud

Someone must test whenever software is written or revised. Sometimes software testing is automated, but the testing has to take place before the software can be deployed to real users. Software developers work hard to minimize the problems, which testing will discover, but there is always a need to test under realistic conditions. Testing can be difficult financially for software development organizations because equipment for testing can be expensive. A thorough test of an internal application that is used throughout an organization could require acquiring a complete duplicate set of the organization's hardware. Almost no one ever does this. Tests are devised that simulate the real environment and testers make do with a minimum of equipment, but the temporary need for equipment is still onerous, and testing is sometimes forced to be compromised.

Cloud IaaS has proven to be a boon to testing organizations. They can quickly deploy the virtual equipment they need to perform a test and equally quickly return the equipment to the provider's virtual pool. They are charged only for the actual computation they use. They no longer have to fit their temporary equipment needs with strategic acquisition plans of the organization, and they avoid the expense and hassle of physically deploying, undeploying, and returning purchased or leased equipment.

STANDARDS IMPORTANT TO TESTING IN THE CLOUD

- DMTF CIMI
- OMG OCCI
- Amazon EC2
- SNIA CDMI

Developing In the Cloud

At the next step up in the cloud service stack is development in cloud. This can take different forms. For software start-ups, one of the largest capital investments is in a development environment for their developers. This includes machines for developers to write and compile code, servers for storing and managing source code, and build servers for bringing together code from a team of developers into an integrated application for testing.

For example, Microsoft's Azure platform combines various services that a developer of an enterprise application might need in a convenient form for development and deployment. By making use of this cloud platform, a development organization acquires a ready-made environment that is the equivalent of an environment developed over time by a large software development lab. This is an opportunity for a start-up or an existing development organization moving into new territory to leapfrog ahead with a minimal investment.

Customer Relations Management in the Cloud

Among enterprise management applications today, customer relationship management (CRM) occupies a core position. The goal of CRM is to manage the relationship between the customer and the enterprise from end to end, from the customer's first encounter with a salesperson or tool through billing and customer support. Typically, managing the relationship between customers and sales gets special emphasis. This is not a simple task. Data must be collected from many sources and coordinated into a single representation of the customer relationship. CRM applications tend to be sprawling and complicated, typically involving large and difficult to administer databases and multiple servers. Maintaining and upgrading CRM applications can be notoriously difficult.

SaaS has proven to be an effective approach to taming the maintenance of these complex applications. Vendors such as Salesforce.com offer to their customers a CRM application hosted entirely in the cloud. The enterprise using a cloud CRM does not need to know where the data is stored or whether a table needs to be re-indexed, they do not need to understand what version of software is being run, and they never have to worry that the version of software on their laptop does not match the version on the server. All that is in the cloud and out of their hands.

STANDARDS IMPORTANT TO CRM IN THE CLOUD

- SAS 70 for evaluating providers
- ISO/IEC 27001 for establishing security and governance
- Cloud Security Alliance, Security Guidance for Critical Areas of Focus in Cloud Computing for identification of critical security and governance concerns

Standards
What and Why

Standards are everywhere, but what exactly are they? How do they come about? What do they accomplish? This chapter will answer these questions in depth. Using the information in this chapter, product managers and developers will be able to understand what kinds of standards apply to their cloud projects and how the standards can contribute to the success of the product. Managers and executives will be able to help their engineers make the right decisions in evaluating the applicability of a given standard to their projects.

What Are Standards?

Most often, when people think of standards, they think of a thick, difficult-to-read document with an acronym for a title and branded with the logo of a prestigious organization, and not much more about it. That is a good description of the appearance of many standards, but as a definition, it is inadequate for anyone who must use standards in their work. The dictionary is a good starting place. Different dictionaries use different wordings, but an apt working definition of a *standard* is that it is a "recognized object, example, or document accepted by authority or consensus as a model to which others should conform or criteria by which others should be judged."

This synoptic definition touches on the essential characteristics of all technical standards. Unlike a scientific treatise or an engineering specification, a standard does not stand on its own. Its value derives from the agreements that underpin the standard. Ordinarily, when evaluating an engineering specification, the first task is to read the specification and decide whether it makes sense, is technically correct, meets its deliverable requirements, and so on. When evaluating a standard, usually the first task is to determine where the standard derives its authority. Did it come from a *standards-developing organization* (SDO)? What kind of SDO? If not from an SDO, is it from a commercial organization? Or is it a common practice?

Technical correctness is clearly important in a standard, but how widely a standard is accepted and who follows the standard are at least, if not more, important. The usage and provenance of a standard will often reveal more about the technical quality of the standard in less time than a detailed technical review. More importantly, the standard development process of the SDO reveals the rigorousness of the review the standard went through. The kinds of interoperability and compliance testing the standard went through—and often much more—will be available for public scrutiny.

Why Are Standards Hard to Read?

Although clarity and ease of understanding are always desirable qualities in a standard, lack of ambiguity is paramount. A standard that means different things to different people will cause no end of problems when developers try to create systems that comply with the standard. If two development teams follow the same standard carefully but come up with divergent and incompatible results, the standard did not do its job, and the projects may be a failure.

Standards are different from other kinds of guidance, like handbooks or manuals. A handbook or a manual fails to meet its purpose if it is not clear and understandable to its audience. Standards should be clear and understandable, but those goals are secondary to avoiding ambiguity, which is not the same as achieving clarity. Eradicating ambiguity is a goal that often forces prose to be repetitious and difficult to read. Standards use special vocabularies that appear stilted and unnatural, but they are necessary to differentiate fine shadings of meaning, such as between *shall*, *may*, and *should*.[1] This language often requires concentration and study to understand.

Standards also can be hard to understand because explanations in a standard are often brief or not included at all. Just before publication, standards writers sometimes edit out explanations that were helpful to themselves in the early stages of developing the standard. They apply a sort of Occam's razor, paring away the inessential. This is not to torment the poor readers. The more said in the standard, the more opportunity for ambiguity to creep in. Therefore, the writers tend to remove explanations from the standard itself.

Another reason for the terseness of standards derives from the standards development process. The working group or committee examines and debates alternatives at length before they choose between them. After the

---

[1] Always check the glossary in the standard you are reading, but usually, *shall* (often all upper-case) means an implementer must do something. If they do not, they are out of compliance. *May* means that an implementation will be in compliance if they do it, but they will not be out of compliance if they do not. *Should* means that the standard encourages implementers to do something, but doing it or not doing it does not affect compliance.

working group makes its decision, the rejected alternatives are irrelevant to the standard, even though the deliberation that preceded rejection of an alternative may have significantly influenced the content of the standard. Discussions of the rejected alternatives are usually not included in the standard document because they lead to confusion.

Standards writers are as concerned about technical ambiguity as lawyers are concerned about legal ambiguity. *Normative* is an important and frequently used term in standards. Normative in the standards context means authoritative or prescriptive. Standards documents are careful to indicate which parts of the document are normative. These parts determine compliance with the standard. Non-normative sections help developers build compliant systems, but they do not determine compliance. They may be informative, they may be explanatory, or they may provide examples of the application of the standard.

Standards writers are not intentionally obscure or unsympathetic to the users of the standard, but they must make compliance clearly determinable, which is not the same as easily understood. Standards working groups often issue white papers and other materials such as primers and FAQs to provide the kind of explanatory material that the standard lacks. These documents can be more useful than the standard itself to readers interested in the content and significance of the standard rather than constructing a system that complies with the standard.

The Scope of Standards

Standards are usually exactingly explicit about their scope, the situations in which the standard applies, and the situations where it does not apply. Standards documents often devote as much space to describe what is not in the scope of the standard as what is in the scope of the standard. By defining the scope meticulously, the standards writers avoid another source of ambiguity. When standards are applied outside their scope, situations may occur that the standards writers have not considered. Those situations could alter the meaning of the standard itself.

For example, the *User Agent Accessibility Guidelines*, issued by the W3C as a recommendation, has a large "limitations" section.[2] *User agents* in this guideline are softwarelike web browsers or media players that deliver web content to users. The guidelines help developers build user agents that are usable by people with a wide variety of impairments. The authors of the guideline are careful to point out that there are impairments that the guidelines cannot

---

[2] www.w3.org/TR/2002/REC-UAAG10-20021217/intro.html#limitations

address and are therefore out of scope. Leaving this careful scoping out of the guidelines might lead developers to attempt to use the guidelines in ways that are inappropriate. For example, the guideline declares braille renderings to be outside the scope of the document, even though braille might appear to be part of the guidance. Without that scoping advice, developers would be tempted to make invalid assumptions about braille input and output based on what is said about nonbraille input and output.

The reason for all this concern over precision and avoidance of ambiguity is to make compliance to the standard a black-and-white decision. When asking whether a piece of software complies with a standard, the answer should be a clear yes or no. The value of a standard diminishes if there are situations where compliance with the standard is unclear. If, for example, a hardware manufacturer builds an Ethernet network interface card, the manufacturer must build a card that will interact properly with all equipment that complies with the Ethernet standard. A card that complies with the Ethernet standard "most of the time" or "75 percent complies" will not perform acceptably. An engineer who gets an answer like that must go back to the lab and make changes until compliance is clear and definitive. If the Ethernet standard were written imprecisely so that what is required and not required were not spelled out or if important use cases within the scope of the standard were not addressed, a definitive answer could never be given, and the standard would have little value to the manufacturer.

Technical standards apply to technical systems, and for our purpose here, we are talking about technical information technology (IT) standards that apply to computers, storage, networks, and software. Peripherals, such as printers, sensors, and components of automated manufacturing systems, are related to the IT standards that are the subject of this book, but they won't be part of the discussion here. For the purposes of this book, the word *standard* will mean a technical IT standard.

CHARACTERISTICS OF TECHNICAL STANDARDS

- Established by
  - ○ Custom
  - ○ General consent
  - ○ Authority
- Widely followed
- Usually documented with great precision

- Compliance can be decisively determined

- Scope and applicability are well understood

De Facto and De Jure Standards

Standards come from different sources. The first task is to identify the authority standing behind the standard. The technical correctness of the standard is important, of course, but a technically perfect document is far from a standard. This is because the unique value of a standard comes from it being followed consistently by many users.

An important distinction among standards is *de facto* vs. *de jure*. De facto is Latin for "in practice," and *de jure* means "in law." Legal language as well as standards discussions use both terms with somewhat different meanings. Their usage when describing standards varies, but in general, a *de facto* standard is one that has arisen from practice and an acknowledged standards group has not published an authoritative statement of the standard. A *de jure* standard is one that is supported by an acknowledged standards body, usually by publishing an authoritative version of the standard. Obviously, *de facto* standards can and often do become *de jure* standards when an SDO publishes an endorsed version of the *de facto* standard.

De Facto Standards

Generally, a *de facto* standard comes from practice. Someone, usually a company, builds a system in a certain way, and it works well. Another company emulates the first builder, perhaps improving the system. Then someone builds another system. This goes on until eventually practice evolves to the point that the majority of systems are built in this same way, and a *de facto* standard exists. Sometimes, a company is so successful with a practice that the practice becomes a *de facto* standard, even though the systems are always developed by the original owner who exercises patent rights and owns the *de facto* standard.

The IBM PC

The Intel processor-based personal computer that we know today is an example of a *de facto* standard. In the early 1980s, several non-IBM desktop computers were gaining interest in the market. IBM responded to their success with the 5150, which became the archetype for the PC. The interoperable PCs now produced by a wide range of manufacturers all evolved from the 5150 original design even though no standards organization has published a standard for the PC design. In other words, the IBM PC became a de facto standard.

Some special circumstances aided in establishing the PC de facto standard. IBM used off-the-shelf standard components, such as choosing the Intel 8088 as the processor instead of using a proprietary IBM chip. In addition, IBM engineers designed the original PC so users could extend it with third-party cards that would plug into the data bus. The architecture was open so that third parties could supply peripherals without obtaining a license, and IBM published a technical reference manual that described many details of the construction and specifications of the machine.

The open and accessible 5150 PC design and its descendants became the standard for personal computers. There was no standards body, but starting with Compaq, many manufacturers were able to successfully clone the first PC. MS-DOS would boot, the software would run, and most of the cards designed for the IBM PC would work in the clones. That was enough for the market. The de facto standard design became the basis for 30 years of evolution of desktop computing into a large and thriving industry, and it went beyond the desktop to become the basis for servers, clusters, and blade systems that approach and even match mainframe capacities.

The IBM PC experience is an example of a standard that began as a proprietary design and that was then taken over by the rest of the community without ever becoming a de jure standard.[3] The IBM PC de facto standard has held up and spawned a flourishing industry, but IBM eventually stepped away from PC manufacturing.

Windows Operating System

PC standard grew rather differently than another important de facto standard, Microsoft Windows. IBM relinquished ownership and control of the PC standard almost as soon as the PC appeared on the market. This allowed other vendors, such as Compaq, Gateway, and Dell, to step in and begin to compete on features and cost, which contributed to the vigor of the entire industry.

---

[3] I should point out that although a PC standard was never published by an SDO, many standards went into the PC. For example , many hard disks use the Serial Advanced Technology (SATA) interface. The Serial ATA International Organization (SATA-IO), an international open standards organization, publishes the SATA standard. However, there is still no overall standard for the PC.

The success of the PC is tied closely to the Windows operating system, another example of a successful *de facto* standard. Not everyone will agree that Windows is a standard since it is also a proprietary product. However, Windows and its precursor, MS-DOS, have all the characteristics of a standard. Windows is used everywhere. A developer who wants to write a program that will run on as many computers as possible will almost certainly choose to write for the Windows operating system. It is always easy to determine whether an operating system conforms to the Windows standard because all genuine Window operating systems come from Microsoft.

Unlike the IBM PC design, Windows remains Microsoft's closely managed intellectual property. Microsoft holds patents on many parts of the Windows system. Developers cannot write their own Windows operating system and sell it. A developer cannot take a piece of Windows and write it into their own code without reaching a legal agreement with Microsoft over rights and licenses.

Windows is Microsoft's possession, and it exercises control. Microsoft changes it when it wants to change it, and Microsoft is not constrained to consult with anyone on how they make changes. It may keep parts of it secret and demand that their licensed users keep it secret also. They may ask developers to sign nondisclosure agreements pledging secrecy when they are trained to work with Windows. Using Windows without a license from Microsoft may result in legal penalties. These are all ways in which the Windows standard differs from open standards supported by standards organizations.

In the case of Windows, this kind of *de facto* standard has worked well. PCs and servers running Windows are everywhere. Personal computer users have voted with their dollars for the effectiveness of this *de facto* standard and the way it works.[4] Although some may differ in this opinion, it is unlikely that computing would be where it is today without the investment that Microsoft has placed in Windows—an investment that would not have been made without the benefits that Microsoft accrued from ownership.[5]

---

[4] The *de facto* Windows standard is largely expressed in the WIN32 API. This is the documented programmatic interface that programmers use when interacting with the Windows operating system. Microsoft has developed numerous technologies to aid developers in using WIN32. These include .NET Framework, Dynamic Data Exchange (DDE), Common Object Model (COM), Microsoft Foundation Classes (MFC), and others. These technologies also have the flavor of a *de facto* standard. WIN32 followed WIN16. WIN64 is now used for 64-bit processors.

[5] Microsoft's ownership of its operating system standard is not the only pattern for operating systems standards that has been successful. Unix and Linux, derived from the Unix operating system, have also been successful in many ways. Unix's history is similar in some ways to that

Amazon.com EC2

Today, in cloud computing, Amazon.com's Elastic Compute Cloud application programming interface (EC2 API) is an important *de facto* standard. Amazon.com has published extensive documentation on the EC2 API for interacting with its IaaS cloud offering. The API has become a *de facto* standard for managing IaaS because Amazon.com is a successful pioneer in providing an IaaS service and Amazon Web Services (AWS) has a large body of users. Consequently, EC2 is used quite frequently, and some consider the EC2 API to be the *de facto* standard for IaaS management.

No standards body has yet sanctioned the use of the EC2 API. That is not a criticism of the EC2 API. We have just looked at what may be the two most successful computing standards of the past 30 years, the IBM PC and MS-DOS/Windows, and neither has the sanction of a standards body.

IBM and Microsoft took very different routes with the *de facto* standards that they originated. The important point is not that one scenario is better or more effective than another. Rather, successful standards vary widely and dismissing one approach over another is likely to be unwise. Where EC2 will go is not known. It could follow either the Microsoft pattern, the IBM pattern, or a completely different pattern of its own.

Regardless of how the EC2 scenario plays out, Windows and the basic PC design are very different from each other and from what we usually think of as a standard. In the case of the PC standard, PC manufacturers are free to innovate on the basic design in any way they want. The only limitation they face is whether the result works, and "working" means anything the market will accept.

Representational State Transfer

The PC standard benefited from documentation supplied by IBM at its inception. Unfortunately, that is not always the case with *de facto* standards. *Representational State Transfer* (REST) is an example of this. REST is unique among the standards discussed so far because it does not address the usual subjects of standards. REST is not a language, protocol, or interface; it is an architectural style.

Nevertheless, REST has the characteristics of a *de facto* standard. The REST style is a pattern for building applications that use remote services, most

---

of the IBM PC architecture. Unix was originally developed by AT&T, but AT&T released the Unix source code to academic institutions, and it evolved into an open standard maintained by the Institute of Electrical and Electronic Engineers (IEEE) and the Open Group.

often using the Internet. The entire World Wide Web is an example of a vast interoperable REST application.[6] The interoperability of the diverse sites of the World Wide Web is dependent on following rules that stem from REST. Here is an example of REST standard requirements: when Hypertext Transfer Protocol (HTTP) is used, REST principles require that HTTP operations be used in very specific ways. The scalability and resilience of the World Wide Web come in part from complying with these principles.

Unfortunately, REST is ambiguous. The definitive document on REST is Roy Fielding's dissertation[7] in which he describes and explains the principles that underpin REST. The dissertation is an explanation, not a normative document that describes the exact scope and requirements for compliance to a REST standard. Explanations are valuable, but they are often hard to transform into a compliant system. In addition to the dissertation, a collection of blogs and forums on the World Wide Web explain and clarify the principles, but these are not normative either.

The result of this situation is confusion. Architects and developers strive to follow the canon accurately, but each REST system has its own set of idiosyncratic interpretations. The unfortunate result is APIs that could have been more compatible than they are and time wasted on repeatedly debating the same decisions that could have been saved by referring to a standard document. This is an example of a situation where the documentation and normative guidelines of a standard specification would solve problems for developers.

On the other hand, Fielding describes REST as a set of architectural constraints, which are higher-level abstractions than standards usually address. Therefore, it may be more appropriate to provide standards for systems that are built on REST principles rather than REST. An example of this is the Cloud Infrastructure Management Interface (CIMI) from the Distributed Management Task Force (DMTF). The CIMI standard specifies a model and protocol for IaaS management based on REST, which can be tested for interoperability. You'll find more on CIMI in Chapter 11.

---

[6] Just how big is difficult to determine. One measure is the number of top-level domains (TLDs). As tracked by Daily Changes (www.dailychanges.com/), there are more than 130 million TLDs just with the six most popular postfixes (.*com*, .*net*, .*org*, and so on). Most of those TLDs represent REST applications that serve documents to browsers all over the world. Conservatively, that is 100 million interconnected REST applications, although many of these application would have to be described as very simple applications of REST principles, and some, such as SOAP-based web services, are not REST-based at all.

[7] www.ics.uci.edu/~fielding/pubs/dissertation/top.htm

DE FACTO STANDARDS CHARACTERISTICS

- No standards body involved.

- Often very effective because backed by experience.

- May be tied to a particular vendor.

- Documentation may be proprietary, ad hoc, or nonexistent.

- Patents and royalties may be involved.

De Jure Standards

An environment that encourages experimentation and innovation also encourages rapid progress and vigorous competition. However, there are also disadvantages to a freewheeling atmosphere. Some projects require cooperation by their very nature. PC architectures require some compatibility on interfaces with other computers, but they are actually islands unto themselves most of the time. The PC succeeded, at least in part, because there was a rich offering of software to run on it, but that richness derived from the ease of programming and the popularity of the PC, not from its compatibility with other machines.

Standards that deal with compatibility and interoperability between systems differ from standards that govern independent systems. When the goal is to bring together disparate systems, as in the case of the World Wide Web, the systems designers have to come together in some way. When those designers are from competing corporations with obligations to their stakeholders, coming together without a set of ground rules for sharing intellectual property is problematic. The World Wide Web Consortium (W3C), the Internet Engineering Task Force (IETF), the Internet Society (ISOC), and other bodies provided forums in which progress was possible.

De jure standards are standards that are sanctioned by standards bodies. There are degrees of *de jure* standards. Some standards are sanctioned not only by standards bodies but also by governments and have the force of law. For example, in the United States, government regulations with the force of law enforce standards for the purity and safety of pharmaceuticals. You can argue that these standards backed by law are the only true *de jure* standards, but the term is usually used more broadly for any standard that is sanctioned by some standards body. Most of the standards discussed in this book are endorsed or sanctioned by standards organizations, but none has the force of law.

De facto standards can become *de jure* standards. For example, the C programming language was documented by the authors of the language, Brian Kernigan and Dennis Ritchie, in a book, *The C Programming Language*, published in 1978. This book was the authoritative source for the rules of the language for a number of years. The Kernigan and Ritchie book was well received and became a classic of technical writing. Both compiler writers and programmers consulted it. The C language flourished and eventually captured the attention of the American National Standards Institute (ANSI). Consequently, in 1989, ANSI published a C language standard. The ANSI specification became the *de jure* standard for C.

De facto standards that become *de jure* standards are sometimes held up as superior to standards that are written directly by standards bodies. There certainly are many examples of *de facto* standards that have become excellent *de jure* standards and eventually become pillars of technical development. The C language is one of them.

Another example is the Ethernet standard. It began as a proprietary *de facto* standard at Xerox-PARC in the early 1970s. In 1983, the IEEE released the 802.3 Ethernet standard, which has gone through many versions and still has a working group continuing to enhance the standard.

Proponents of standards that start as *de facto* and evolve into *de jure* argue that until a standard has been implemented many times and gained many adherents, there is no assurance that the standard is well designed and will ever become widely adopted. Some of these *de facto* standards proponents go on to argue that standards working groups are seldom creative, innovative environments and are unlikely to generate useful standards.

It is tempting to argue that the painstaking meticulous work of writing unambiguous standards is not conducive to creativity, but there is more to consider. Producing a well-designed and usable standard requires a special kind of creativity. Although brilliant technical insights may underlie and inform standards, successful standards represent consensus and display unambiguous clarity more often than they advance new ideas. Innovation in a standard can even be detrimental if it provokes controversy. Standards working groups must have members who will not accept a misplaced word, even a slight ambiguity, a broken link, or a citation to a non-normative document in a normative section, and they light up when they find a hidden assumption. This kind of creativity is often underappreciated, but a working group without members who penetrate the standard to that level has a hard time achieving the level of clarity and precision required for a standard that can be applied with consistent good results.

De Jure Standards Administration

SDOs usually administer standards carefully. That involves several practices.

Clear Sources

The first is a clearly designated source for the standard. For example, if you want a W3C standard, you go to the W3C web site. There you can find previous versions of a standard, the current accepted version, and even drafts of future versions. This is much different from some *de facto* standards like REST, where there is no clearly designated source for the standard and those who want to implement a REST-compliant service surf the Web for Roy Fielding's dissertation, his blogs, and discussion groups that debate the fine points of REST.

Version Control

De jure standards almost always have clear versions of the standard. This is important for a number of reasons. If a version of the standard has faults or deficiencies, it may be tempting simply to fix the problem by correcting the standard. However, that is not the practice of most SDOs because users of the standard must be able to distinguish between corrected and uncorrected copies of the standard.

Version control is even more important when differentiating between major releases of a standard. A major release of a standard may mean a modification of the scope of the standard, a significant change in the data structures used by the standard, or other substantial modification. Users must be able to distinguish between versions in order to recognize these major changes.

Compatibility Rules

SDOs typically also maintain compatibility rules. A typical rule is that "zero-point versions maintain backward and forward compatibility, point versions maintain only backward compatibility, and full versions may be incompatible." Backward compatibility usually means that an input that worked with an earlier version will work with a later version. Forward compatibility means that an input that works with a later version will also work with an earlier version (although the older version may not show features that are present in the later version). See Figure 2-1 below.

Compatibility rules are important because predictability is important to users. Working groups often agonize over maintaining compatibility rules. A desired feature is often deferred to a later release to prevent compatibility rule

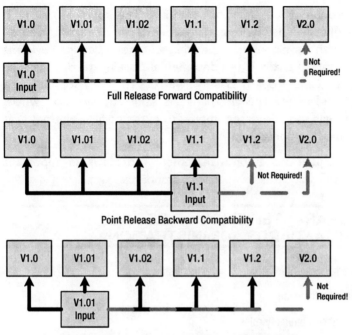

Figure 2-1. Release compatibility rules vary. This is one example.

violations. Without attention to compatibility practices, releases of the standard will whipsaw users into changing implementations without good reason. Users of standards look to the SDO to avoid the version whipsaw.

Error Management

Error management is an important part of the function of most SDOs. No standard is perfect. Working groups are careful, but as careful as they are, issues still can appear when a standard becomes widely implemented. Some of these issues will be trivial: a misspelling, a misstatement, or an error that has an obvious correction. These, a standards user can reasonably correct by exercising good judgment. The standard must be corrected, but the correction is simply an errata entry, not a real change. Other issues are more significant and require consideration by the working group to identify an appropriate solution. Still others might be major lapses that require substantial revision to the standard.

These errors must be managed. As they are discovered, errors must be triaged and classified for their significance. A critical error might require an immediate bulletin to warn the standard's user base. Others must be placed on the working group's agenda for consideration. The solutions must be released in a controlled manner. Releasing revisions of the standard too often will wreak havoc with development schedules, but not releasing revisions when there are substantial errors is also detrimental. Striking the right balance for errata and revision and properly classifying errors require a sophisticated process and good judgment. The alternative is a chaotic situation where corrections are unclear and users are tempted to extemporize solutions that lead to unpredictable interoperability.

A sophisticated and judicious error management process is an important reason to favor *de jure* standards over *de facto* standards.

CHARACTERISTICS OF *DE JURE* STANDARDS ADMINISTRATION

- Clearly designated source for copies of standard
- Controlled version
- Explicit compatibility rules
- Error management

Open Standards

Most *de jure* standards are also open standards. *Open* is a term that is often applied to standards, and it has to do with the accessibility of the standard and the process under which the standard is prepared for release. There is no formal definition for openness in standards, but there is general agreement around some fundamental principles.

OPEN STANDARDS PRINCIPLES

- Participation in the standards group is not restricted.
- Development follows a transparent and fair process that encourages full participation.
- The resulting standard is unencumbered.
- The standard is free or available at nominal cost.

Open Participation

Developers sometimes fear that standards are an opportunity for large companies to dictate the rules and consequently make it easier for them to dominate the market. Open standards restrain that possibility by insisting that participation in standards development is open to all. The exact interpretation of what constitutes open is subject to interpretation. For some standards bodies, openness means anyone interested may participate in the writing of the standard. Other standards organizations are open in the sense that anyone can join the organization, but the dues are substantial. Only dues-paying members are invited to participate in writing standards. Both approaches have merit. The wide-open approach gives access to a vast pool of talent, but the pool of talent may be unfocused and unable to concentrate on the important requirements. Groups with heavy entrance fees are in some sense elitist, but those big entrance fees also weed out members without a serious desire to produce relevant and high-quality standards. There is also a desire to preserve the investment in fees with an equal investment of high-level expertise and skill.

Which approach is better? Frankly, the answer to that question probably depends more on who is asking the question than standards themselves. From the standpoint of a company that invests in membership to the board of a prestigious standards organization, a well-funded organization with member companies that are willing to lend the time of their best engineers, the vote is clearly for the efficiency, organization, and commitment that the big-fee organization provides. To a developer in the trenches from a small start-up, the grassroots approach, such as an open source group that accepts contributions from anyone who meets the expected level of quality, is by far the best. In fact, both approaches can produce reliable standards. The quality of the standard depends more on the quality of the standards process than the gateway to participation.

Transparent Process

A transparent process ensures that open participation carries on through the development process. A transparent process means properly announced meetings that exclude no members. Working groups conduct meetings in an open manner following Robert's Rules of Order[8] or a similar systematic meeting protocol. Proper minutes record all decisions accurately and clearly, so decisions are a matter of record, not recollection. Meetings follow an

---

[8] Henry M. Robert, III, et al., *Robert's Rules of Order Newly Revised, 11th ed.*, (Philadelphia: Da Capo Press, 2011). The bylaws of a given group may specify other editions.

agreed-upon agenda so members can prepare properly. The point of all the formality is to be certain that the group gives every opinion full recognition and the resulting standard represents the best contributions of all the participants. Although there are usually rules about quorums and percentages of votes required to pass motions, most groups work toward unanimous consent on all important points. In an atmosphere of mutual respect, the assumption is that a single dissenting view can point to a potential flaw that must be identified and resolved. Missing that flaw is to no one's advantage.

From the viewpoint of the individual participants in a working group, all the rigmarole of minutes review and agendas, motions and seconds, and all the complication of meeting protocols often appear to be a tedious waste of time. However, standards group meetings are often contentious with high stakes. A transparent process is one way of assuring a high-quality result.

Unencumbered Standard

The Windows operating system is the opposite pole from an open standard. Windows belongs to Microsoft. If you want to use Windows, you must be prepared to obtain licenses from Microsoft and follow Microsoft's rules. That is a perfectly valid business model for Microsoft, but it is a closed, not an open, standard. Microsoft uses its ownership of Windows to generate profits for its investors. Open standards also generate profits but via a different route. Open standards work as tools for constructing software that can generate profit for the builders. The Windows standard is not a tool for constructing Windows; it is the result of Microsoft building the Windows operating system. Developers choose to use a particular standard because they think the standard will make their product better and appeal to a wider user base. Often that comes from the product being able to work with other products. Proponents of open standards maintain that standards, unlike the closed Windows standard, should never require anyone to pay fees or royalties to use a standard. Many standards organizations take this stance and have careful and extensive rules to guarantee that all intellectual property in their standards is unencumbered with embedded proprietary property.

Effectively, this is a patents issue. Most SDOs have rules and procedures related to the inclusion of patented intellectual property in a standard, or a standard is written in such a way that patented mechanisms must be used. Depending on the SDO, patented material may be prohibited, the royalties may be restricted, or the patents are merely disclosed. Usually, when an organization joins an SDO, it enters into an agreement regarding intellectual property. Often, that takes the form that members relinquish all intellectual property rights to contributions to the standard.

The care that an SDO takes over intellectual property is important to the user of the standard because it provides some assurance that the standard can be used without fear of a patent infringement suit in the future. One of the dangers from standards from less organized SDOs is that patented intellectual property may inadvertently be included. This can cause trouble long after a system based on the standard is deployed.

Freely Accessible

A standard that charges enough for access to the standard to be a profitable enterprise in itself is not open. In most cases, this is a self-defeating practice. This model has many problems. Going back to our definition of a standard, the value of a standard lies in the ubiquity of its acceptance. Putting a financial barrier in front of the use of a standard is a barrier to implementing the standard. Most standards organizations make their standards public and freely available, perhaps with a nominal fee that reflects the cost of making the standard available, not the cost of developing the standard.

DE JURE OPEN STANDARD CHARACTERISTICS

- Sanctioned and administered by a standards body

- May begin as a *de facto* standard and then adopted by a standards organization or may begin within a standards organization

- Precise and unambiguous documentation

- Clear and usually limited intellectual property rights

- Freely accessible

- Clearly designated versions

- Version compatibility set by policy

Public Standards Organizations

Public standards organizations, often called SDOs, are the backbone of IT standards.

National and International Standards Organizations

SDOs form a sort of hierarchy. Above individual SDOs are national standards bodies (NSBs). In the United States, the NSB is the American National Standards Institute (ANSI). The next level in the hierarchy is the international standards organizations. The International Organization for Standardization (ISO), the International Electrotechnical Commission (IEC), and the International Telecommunication Union (ITU) are all the sponsors of many international standards. The ISO and the IEC work together and often release IT standards jointly under the designation the ISO/IEC. See Figure 2-2 below.

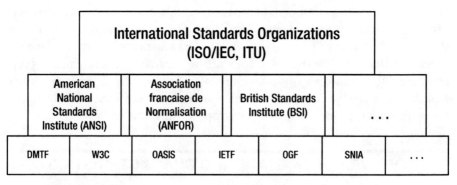

Figure 2-2. Standards organization can be arranged in international and national hierarchies.

The Open Virtualization Format (OVF) provides a good example of the progress of a standard from a *de facto* proprietary specification to an international standard. OVF began as the proprietary format developed by a single vendor. The vendor donated the format to an SDO, the DMTF. OVF then went through the DMTF open process. A working group was formed that represented several vendors that were interested in using the specification. The work group modified the proprietary specification to reflect the interests of the larger group. The working group then passed the standard through the DMTF technical hierarchy and eventually to the vote of the DMTF membership, where it was accepted as a DMTF standard. Subsequently, the DMTF presented OVF to ANSI, the United States NSB, even though the DMTF is an international organization that happens to be based in the US. ANSI accepted OVF as a U.S. national standard. From ANSI, OVF went on to ISO and the IEC. The ISO/IEC Joint Technical Committee also accepted OVF, and it became an international standard. After acceptance by the DMTF, most of the examination of standard was focused on the quality of the DMTF process, the rules followed in handling intellectual property, and the form and language of the specification rather than the technical details of specification.

The hierarchical progression from SDO to NSB to international standards organization is, in reality, not clear-cut. Most SDOs are in fact international groups. In the OVF example, the DMTF is based in the United States, but its membership is international, covering 40 countries. Typical DMTF working group meetings have to accommodate members in time zones ranging from Shanghai to London to San Francisco. There are other SDOs in a similar position. The World Wide Web Consortium (W3C) and the Internet Engineering Task Force (IETF) are similar to the DMTF in having international memberships. In fact, the memberships of most IT SDOs are international. With the ease of teleconferencing and electronic exchange of documents, the standards development process spans borders effortlessly. In addition, many SDO member companies are also international. A single member company may have working group members from several countries. The consequence is that most IT standards are international in the sense that experts from many nations have contributed to them.

Standards bearing the imprimatur of the ISO/IEC are important because the ISO/IEC is an international organization of organizations whose sanction is highly respected, but, oddly, its sanction no longer indicates that a standard has international origins. Most standards today are written internationally from the beginning.

Cloud SDOs

There are countless SDOs. They crop up whenever groups of engineers or companies get together with an idea for a new standard. Sometimes the group will go to an established SDO; often they will form a new SDO to address the area where they see a need for standardization. Some of these groupings are temporary and exist only for the duration of the idea. Other SDOs take on an enduring life of their own.

The following sidebar lists some of the most prominent SDOs in cloud standards. These organizations will be discussed in subsequent chapters in the context of each of the standards they have produced.

CLOUD STANDARDS DEVELOPMENT ORGANIZATIONS

- Cloud Security Alliance (CSA)
- Distributed Management Task Force (DMTF)
- Internet Engineering Task Force (IETF)

- Organization for the Advancement of Structured Information Standards (OASIS)

- Open Grid Forum (OGF)

- Storage Networking Industry Association (SNIA)

- World Wide Web Consortium (W3C)

- TM Forum

Cloud

Architecture in the Stratosphere

Cloud architecture is architecture written large. If cloud computing fulfills its promise, it will touch nearly every aspect of computing as we know it today, use every component of current computing technology, and inspire the development of untold new technologies. It will change the way individuals conduct their daily lives and how businesses, corporations, and government agencies execute their business. It presents an unparalleled challenge to software and hardware engineers that are comparable to putting a man on the moon or building a national electrical power grid.

These changes are already underway. We see them in the construction of massive Internet search engines and vast online libraries. Cloud architecture also lurks in the background of the slim lightweight tablets that have captured the imagination consumers and the smartphones that do everything from find the nearest dry cleaners to stream videos of remote catastrophes before the news media arrive.

In this chapter, we will look at the cloud more technically, concentrating on the architecture of the cloud. Much of this chapter will rely on publications by the National Institute of Standards and Technology (NIST) on cloud architecture.[1] It also relies on work done by the DMTF Open Cloud Standards Incubator reported in their white papers.[2]

---

[1] Peter Mell and Timothy Grance, "The NIST Definition of Cloud Computing," NIST, September 2011, http://csrc.nist.gov/publications/nistpubs/800-145/SP800-145.pdf; Fang Liu, Jin Tong, Jian Mao, Robert Bohn, John Messina, and Dawn Leaf, "NIST Cloud Computing Reference Architecture, Version 1," NIST, March 30, 2011, http://collaborate.nist.gov/twiki-cloud-computing/bin/view/CloudComputing/ReferenceArchitectureTaxonomy;

[2] DMTF, "Interoperable Clouds," DSP-ISO101, November 11, 2009 http://dmtf.org/sites/default/files/standards/documents/DSP-ISO101_1.0.0.pdf; DMTF , "Architecture for Managing Clouds," DSP-ISO102, June 18, 2010, http://dmtf.org/sites/default/files/standards/documents/DSP-ISO102_1.0.0.pdf; DMTF, "Use Cases and Interactions for Managing Clouds," DSP-ISO103, June 18, 2010, http://dmtf.org/sites/default/files/standards/documents/DSP-ISO103_1.0.0.pdf.

Architecture

Software architecture is the computing equivalent to the blueprint of a building. It describes the components of the system and how the components fit together. It also describes the function of the system when all the pieces are connected and the requirements that the system must meet to serve its purpose. Like a building blueprint with a structural view, a view of the plumbing, a view of the electric wiring, and a view of the heating and air conditioning, the architecture of the cloud is decomposed into several views.

Service-Oriented Architecture (SOA)

SOA is the architecture that has dominated enterprise architecture discussions for at least the past ten years.[3] SOA is an element of cloud architecture. Although cloud and SOA are not the same thing, it is hard to imagine cloud architecture without SOA, and every system based on SOA shares some characteristics with the cloud.

SOA applies the service principle of separation of consumer and provider to interaction between programs. The idea of separating consumers from providers is not new. Client-server architectures are almost synonymous with network computing. Clients and servers are just other names for consumers and providers. As the applications running on servers became more complex, software engineers began to realize that monolithic applications were generally not a good idea.

There are a number of reasons for this. Large applications with massive quantities of code are difficult to maintain. The mantra of software engineering, "loose coupling and high cohesion," becomes harder to enforce as applications increase in size.[4] Small, single-purpose modules that are linked together are

---

[3] Ali Asanjani, "Service-oriented Modeling and Architecture," IBM, November 9, 2011, www.ibm.com/developerworks/webservices/library/ws-soa-design1/.

[4] *Loose coupling* means to minimize the interdependence of sections of code so an error in one place will affect only the immediate section of code. *High cohesion* means each section coheres together to accomplish a single purpose.

I recall working with a colleague on an accounting program that had suddenly began to behave erratically. We were both experienced programmers, but neither of us had worked with the application long enough to know it well. The system was from the days before debuggers that allow you to follow a program step by step, and all we could do to identify the problem was to execute the program in our heads by looking at the code. We sweat bullets over the erratically behaving section of code, but we could not find any errors, which was predictable since the code had not changed for several years.

This was toward the end of the transition from keypunch cards, and the language the application was written in still had vestiges of its keypunch card origin. Digits or blanks in

much in favor. Small modules that are hooked together into large complex systems are like Lego blocks. Each block is simple, but they can be put together into complex structures and the same blocks can be rearranged into new structures.

With the desire for small, focused modules comes the need for a way of hooking the blocks together. Service-oriented architecture is a way of hooking together modules and an approach to designing applications that use loosely coupled and highly cohesive services as basic building blocks. Most SOAs rely on Hypertext Transfer Protocol (HTTP) as the communications link between their building blocks. This is the same communications infrastructure as used by the World Wide Web. This means that when needed, SOAs are able to connect over the Internet using the same infrastructure that has been in use for the World Wide Web.

A miniature example of SOA is the temperature gadget that many people have on their computer desktop. The United States National Weather Service has a web service that can be called with a ZIP code or a latitude and longitude. The call returns local weather data that is updated every hour.[5]

Behind the simple weather gadget is a data-gathering network of thousands of weather stations and weather-forecasting offices. Placing the temperature on your computer screen is nice, but that is not the main purpose of the service. The service is not only designed to output the temperature in human readable form. It is primarily designed to be consumed programmatically. For example, ideal harvest time for a crop is determined by hours of sunlight, amount of rain, and temperature. An agricultural harvest management application could

---

several far-right columns were the equivalent of keypunches. Some of these punches could cause the program to branch in surprising ways, and they were easy to miss if you were not accustomed to looking for them.

After several hours, one of us noticed a punch off at the right, and we realized that the control branched and set in motion a procedure in a completely unrelated area. Off we went to a module that logically had nothing to do with the problem as we saw it. That code was untouched also, but now we had our eyes on the pesky far-right columns, and we found the problem. An inexperienced programmer had removed a control punch about three jumps away from the starting point. Luckily, by then, it was after midnight, and the culprit was safely out of the building.

This experience was my introduction to the importance of coupling and cohesion. In a loosely coupled system, a missing control punch would affect only a single module, not cause a remote and apparently unrelated module to change its execution. In a cohesive system, modules do not wander off to perform unrelated tasks. If either of these principles had been followed, the problem either would never have occurred or would have been easily and quickly fixed.

[5] http://graphical.weather.gov/xml/ provides excellent documentation of the service including the XML to call it.

use the output of the weather web service to schedule equipment to harvest crops for optimum yields. An application like this uses SOA and web services to create an efficient system.

Typical interactions between SOA web service providers and consumers are often not examples of cloud computing because they are not implemented with clouds. Frequently, the servers in an SOA are conventionally administered on-premise machines sitting in a data center. However, cloud computing would not be nearly as attractive today without the experience of the last decade with SOA. Developers have become familiar with implementations that separate consumers and providers and the decomposition of applications into SOA services that can easily be implemented in a cloud. The standards that are used in SOA, like SOAP, play a huge role in cloud computing.[6]

Service Models

Clouds can be classified by the types of services they provide to their consumers. NIST defines three types: Infrastructure as a Service (IaaS), Platform as a Service (PaaS), and Software as a Service (SaaS).[7] These three were discussed briefly in Chapter 1. They are not the only cloud services that have been proposed. Storage as a Service, Data as a Service, and Security as a Service have all been proposed and have their advocates. For the most part, these are variations on the basic three and do not need special treatment.

IaaS and PaaS are architecturally very similar, although the consumer experience is somewhat different. In IaaS, the consumer describes and requests a piece of infrastructure, such as a computer or a storage device, from the provider. The provider creates and gives the user access to the specified infrastructure. This is often a virtual computer the consumer can log on to using telnet[8] or Secure Shell (SSH),[9] perhaps with a LAMP stack[10]

---

[6] Originally, SOAP was an acronym for Simple Object Access Protocol. The SOAP standard is maintained by the World Wide Web Consortium (W3C), www.w3.org/TR/soap12-part1/. The 1.2 version, published in 2004, dropped the acronym because the working group felt that SOAP was not limited to accessing objects and "Simple Object Access Protocol" was therefore misleading. See http://lists.w3.org/Archives/Public/xmlp-comments/2005Sep/0003.html.

[7] Peter Mell and Timothy Grance, "The NIST Definition of Cloud Computing," NIST, September 2011, http://csrc.nist.gov/publications/nistpubs/800-145/SP800-145.pdf.

[8] J. Postel, J. Reynolds, "Telnet Protocol Specification," May 1985, http://tools.ietf.org/html/rfc854. Telnet is insecure. Telnet does not encrypt and passwords are easily sniffed. SSH supplants it.

[9] SSH is defined in www.ietf.org/rfc/rfc4251.txt. There are numerous RFCs in the full corpus on SSH, but this one is at the center.

[10] A LAMP stack is a common open source software configuration for an all-purpose web server. It consists of a Linux, Apache, MySQL, and Perl/PhP/Python.

installed. Much more complex combinations of machines, network, and storage are possible. The consumer then proceeds to access the infrastructure over the Internet, installing whatever software they need and using it as they want.

The primary activities for the IaaS cloud provider are to respond to the users' requests for new provisioning and eventual deprovisioning;[11] to keep the infrastructure available and performing to agreement between the consumer and provider, which may involve expanding and contracting the computing infrastructure in response to consumer demand; and to track usage for billing.

A PaaS provider offers a more elegant product that includes a development environment and a smooth path from developing an application to deploying it from the provider's cloud, but the underlying activities of creating and deploying infrastructure are similar to those of an IaaS provider.

SaaS is somewhat different. A SaaS service offers to the consumer software installed and running on the provider's cloud. Thus, the SaaS provider is concerned with the development and maintenance of a software service such as CRM or e-mail and less concerned with quick and flexible infrastructure deployment.

Unlike IaaS, which offers each consumer independent instances of machines, storage, and network, SaaS providers may have instances of their software that are used by many consumers simultaneously. In this context, consumers subscribing as a group are often referred to as *tenants*, and supporting multiple tenants with a single running instance of software is called *multitenancy*. A battle rages over the efficacy of multitenancy vs. isolated virtual environments as the best way to support SaaS. In Chapter 1 we discussed the invention of virtualization as a way of separating users in a time-sharing environment. This is analogous to the current discussion of virtualization vs. multitenancy for SaaS.

Deployment Scenarios

Deployment scenarios represent the basic patterns in which a system is made available to its users. The architecture of deployment is concerned with where components are placed, how they are connected, and how they are accessed. The NIST architecture consists of four variations.

---

[11] The terms *deployment* and *provisioning* can be used interchangeably although the current trend is to use *provisioning* more often. The two terms are sometimes distinguished. In its limited sense, *provisioning* is preparing a server for service. *Deployment* often is limited to software. Standing up services on a cloud usually involves both virtual hardware and software, so either term applies, but *provisioning* seems to be more frequently used.

Private Cloud

A *private cloud* is operated by an organization for its own benefit. Ordinarily, a private cloud is accessed only by members of the organization that owns the cloud. The reasons for operating a private cloud are similar to those of public clouds, but the privacy of a private cloud results in significant differences.

Consumers and providers are still distinct in a private cloud deployment, although they are members of the same organization (see Figure 3-1). Usually an IT team will be designated as the cloud provider. The provider group will configure hardware to power the cloud and deploy software for cloud management. In a private cloud, activity usually occurs within the safe haven of the corporate firewall. When a private cloud is hosted by an external cloud provider for the exclusive use of a single enterprise, a corporate firewall may not be present, although the contract between the provider and the consumer enterprise may include firewalls and private networks (perhaps virtual) that provide protection similar to a private cloud hosted by the enterprise.

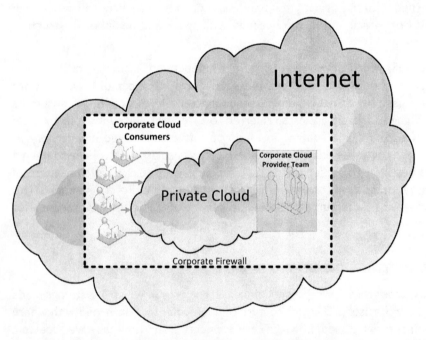

Figure 3-1. Corporate private clouds generally are protected by a firewall.

In many ways, private clouds are less challenging than public clouds. Security for private clouds within the firewall is simpler. Private cloud consumers are usually authenticated in the corporate network and granted access to the private cloud via their corporate credentials. In contrast, public cloud consumers may have to log in and authenticate with the cloud provider. This is an additional security system for the corporate security officer to fret over, and this one is under the control of the third-party cloud provider, swelling the reasons to fret.

Within a corporate firewall, the attack surface, the points at which an unauthenticated user can gain access, shrinks because malevolent outsiders are excluded by the firewall, although malevolent insiders must still be guarded against. A big concern for corporate use of public clouds is that a second or third party becomes a custodian of corporate processes and data. Since there are no second or third parties involved in a private cloud, concerns over the safety of data and processes are covered by familiar on-premise rules of governance. Internal governance may even improve within a private cloud because the distinct separation of responsibility between cloud consumers and providers clarifies roles and simplifies enforcement of divisions of responsibility.

The advantages to a private cloud primarily stem from more efficient use of resources. A cloud pools compute, network, and storage resources and parcels them out on demand to the services supported by the cloud. Servers and other resources that are only partially utilized by one service are dynamically assigned to support other services that need extra capacity. When properly implemented and managed, pooling results in increased utilization without decreased performance. In traditional, nonpooled configurations, systems are sized for acceptable performance at peak loads. A typical IT service may operate at peak load less than a third of the time. When these systems are sized for peak load, the systems typically operate at far less than capacity well over half of the time in order to maintain performance levels during the peaks. Cloud resource pooling presents an opportunity to recover some of the unused capacity and transfer it to other services. The amount of unused capacity that can be recovered is dependent on the mix of services supported by the private cloud.

Public Cloud

Public clouds externalize support of services by separating the consumer of the service from a public provider. In a private cloud, the cloud resource pool is a set of private resources that is set aside to be treated as a pool. The architecture of a public cloud is the same, but the pool of resources is shared between all the customers of the cloud provider (see Figure 3-2). The efficiency of private clouds in reclaiming unused resources is limited by the mix of services that the cloud supports. If an organization has a mix of services that all peak at 11 on Monday mornings, the cloud will have to be provisioned to support adequate performance during the peak, even though the cloud may be over-provisioned for rest of the week.

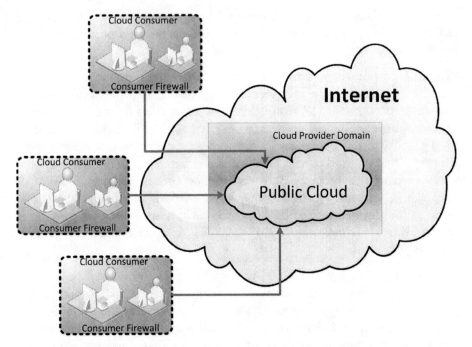

Figure 3-2. Public cloud consumers typically communicate with a public cloud through the Internet.

Scale gives a public cloud an advantage over a private cloud for resource utilization. With a widely varying consumer base that covers many time zones, usage peaks have a much better chance of evening out, meaning that public providers have a much greater chance for optimum utilization of their hardware and facilities.

Large data centers use staff more efficiently. The staff required to administer a small hundred-server data center can manage many more blades on a rack. Racks installed in cargolike containers designed to be shuffled with a forklift are orders of magnitude more readily reconfigured than rooms of individually cabled boxes. Energy and cooling expenses are significant parts of data center costs. A giant roofless data center in a cool climate next to a hydroelectric dam is likely to reduce both cooling and energy costs in meaningful increments.

There is also an advantage to public clouds in the ownership structure. It is a classic rent vs. own decision. Usually, if an asset can be used completely, it is cheaper in the end to purchase the asset outright rather than leasing or renting it. However, an asset that is used for only relatively short periods, sitting idle for a substantial time, is likely to be cheaper to rent. Many IT assets fall into this category.

A common example in software development is test equipment that may be used for only a few weeks and then sit idle for months. The on-premise solution is to lease equipment for testing. The problems with leasing are the facilities for running the equipment are still required and the time and trouble involved in receiving, provisioning, and then decommissioning and shipping the equipment back is substantial. A public cloud is a tidy solution. Its on-demand computing is quickly set up, requires a minimal on-premise facility, is billed in proportion to use, and can be taken down with a few commands.

Finally, purchasing on-premise equipment is usually a capital expenditure, while a public cloud is usually an operating expense. Converting capital expenditures to operating expenses is often attractive because operating expenses are generally more flexible than capital investments. If the business climate improves, cloud operating expenses are more easily dialed up to take advantage of new opportunities. Conversely, when business turns down, cloud expenses can be more easily adjusted downward to maximize profits. This freedom to respond to changing conditions can be very attractive to CEOs and CFOs struggling to balance priorities in a volatile business environment.

With all these advantages, why bother with private clouds? In the future, private clouds—even private computing—may disappear because the advantages to public clouds are real. Seventy or eighty years ago, every community had their own electric power company with its own sources of electrical energy. However, these small sources have largely disappeared because they cannot compete with the efficiency of regional utilities. Private clouds may go the same way of small electric utilities.

Nevertheless, private clouds are not likely to go away for a while. It may be nothing more than the pains of transition, but the fact that operating a private cloud is under the same governance and security as traditional on-premise computing is very attractive to many enterprises. Undoubtedly, these issues will eventually be resolved, and later chapters will describe some of the standardization and best-practice efforts that have already begun to address some of these problems.

Community Cloud

Community clouds are shared among a limited set of partner organizations or enterprises (see Figure 3-3). They are semiprivate and have some of the characteristics of both public and private clouds. Usually, community clouds are established because the participating organizations have shared goals or requirements that make a shared architecture desirable. Combining their effort and resources into a single shared cloud may be more efficient and produce superior results. For example, a group of hospitals may band together in a consortium to manage patient referrals or their supply chains. A community cloud is an efficient way to provide the needed services while avoiding the redundancy of duplicate implementations and equipment at each participating hospital while realizing economies of scale.[12]

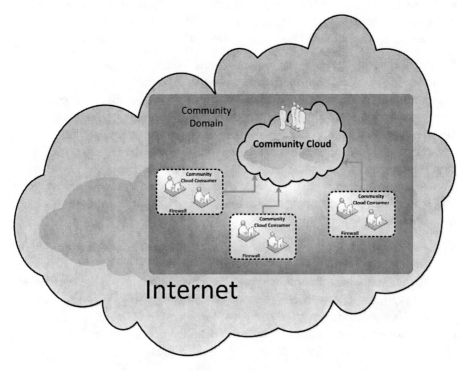

Figure 3-3. A community cloud is an intermediate between a private and public cloud.

Hybrid Cloud

A *hybrid cloud* is a combination of private, public, and community clouds that remain distinct entities but are used in combination. Hybrid clouds are often proposed as a way of providing elasticity that goes beyond the capacity of a private cloud. An organization may ordinarily operate using only a private cloud, but during a peak season or other extraordinary situation their needs may exceed their capacity. In hybrid architecture they would transparently and automatically begin to use a public cloud. In Figure 3-4, the organization has two clouds available for overflow. The software enabling the overflow could contain policies that automatically choose the public cloud with the

---

[12] www.cloudbestpractices.info/3SO-case-study is a discussion of a community cloud for a consortium of hospitals.

lowest rate at that moment or use other criteria such as available network bandwidth or other considerations.

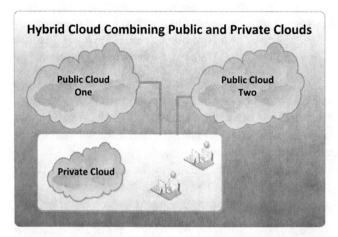

Figure 3-4. Hybrid clouds combine cloud deployment scenarios.

Roles

Roles in computer architecture describe the people or agents that that interact with the system or perform tasks in the system. Roles are usually characterized as humans, but they are often played by a computer program that takes the place of a person. For example, the first role we will discuss here is the cloud consumer. Although the consumer is usually thought of as a person, in the enterprise, the consumer is more often than not a system like an inventory control system or a transaction surveillance system that is gathering data or executing work in a cloud rather than on premises. Roles are logical, not absolute. A person or agent may be both a consumer and a provider at the same time, consuming from one cloud and acting as a cloud provider to a second consumer.

Consumer

In Chapter 1, we talked about the provider and consumer roles in a service. A cloud consumer receives the benefits of cloud services. When you as an individual use cloud services—for example, accessing your electronic books or music collection in a cloud—you are the cloud consumer. When you want to retrieve a book, you go to the web site of your supplier and log in with your user name and password. Before you enter your credentials, if the site has a secure encrypted transport, your browser will verify that the site is the site it presents itself to be. Assuming these security checks are passed, you then have access to the service and can download your book.

In the enterprise, the scenario is much the same. The user of the service, however, is much more likely to be another computer program rather than a person, and the cloud may be private or a community cloud, in which case the provider is a group in the same organization or a shared-cloud group among a group of organizations.

Although it may not be explicit, there is a business relationship between the cloud consumer and the cloud provider. One purpose of authentication and login of cloud consumers is to establish the existence and acknowledgment of a proper business relationship. This is important even when the effective consumer of the service is a computer program. In that case, the program is an agent of the consumer in the business relationship, but the terms of the contract still apply, and the program will authenticate just like a person.

Service level agreements (SLAs) are usually an important part of cloud service business relationships. An SLA is an agreement between a provider and consumer on the details of service delivery. It describes the service and spells out the responsibilities of the consumer and provider. SLAs usually have technical and contractual components. ITIL calls the technical component of an SLA a service level objective (SLO) or a service level target (SLT). An SLO is typically a threshold, like "Five nine uptime" (system up 99.999 percent of the time), that can be objectively measured. In an SLA, an SLO has penalties and incentives associated with it. For example, the SLA may specify that for every day there is an outage exceeding the five-nines-uptime threshold, the consumer can deduct a certain amount from their bill, but the customer will pay a premium each month that the five-nine requirement is met for the entire month.

Architecturally, SLOs are important to cloud system designers because the design must support measuring the SLOs and the process penalties and incentives may be automated. An SLA based on SLOs that the system cannot measure cannot be enforced effectively. Therefore, cloud system architects should be aware of the range of SLOs that are likely to be needed for consumers to be comfortable with the business relationship between provider and consumer. Although the cloud consumer is always the beneficiary of the service, his actions change with the type of service. With IaaS, the consumer typically installs software and runs applications on the infrastructure they receive as a service. This is analogous to an IT technician in a data center setting up equipment, installing software, and administering applications for customers within the corporation. For PaaS, the consumer uses the platform supplied by the provider to develop applications and deploy applications like a developer in a development lab. SaaS consumers use applications made accessible and kept running by the SaaS provider. SaaS consumers are like the customers of the data center, except the hardware, software, and administration are supplied by the SaaS provider instead of a corporate IT department.

Provider

The *cloud provider* has many responsibilities (see Figure 3-5). The cloud provider has the responsibilities of a data center manager on the consumer premises for acquiring, deploying, and managing the physical infrastructure as well as the data center facilities. The provider installs and maintains the software that makes the services available to the consumer. For IaaS, the provider must supply virtualization software that emulates the infrastructure that the consumer requests. PaaS providers provide development environments for creating and deploying applications. This often requires the same ability to provide virtualized infrastructure as an IaaS provider. SaaS providers offer software implementations to their consumers and maintain and administer the software they provide.

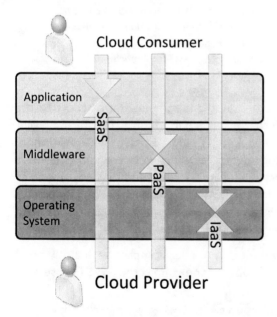

Figure 3-5. The responsibilities of the consumer and provider change with the service model.

In addition to the infrastructure and software, providers are responsible for the security and privacy of the service users, and they manage the offered services to maintain compliance with the SLAs with the consumers.

Auditor

The *cloud auditor* assesses and verifies the availability, integrity, and confidentiality of a cloud system and its information. Whenever a service plays a significant role in a system that affects the safety of human life or investments, the service is likely to be audited. Government regulations, such as the Sarbanes-Oxley Act, also often require audits.[13]

The auditor looks for controls: rules and mechanisms that prevent or reveal significant mistakes or anomalies in a service. The Cloud Security Alliance (CSA) has published "Cloud Controls Matrix," a list of example controls for auditing a cloud provider.[14]

Some CSA-recommended controls are administrative. Control IS-03, for example, states: "Management shall approve a formal information security policy document which shall be communicated and published to employees, contractors and other relevant external parties . . . ." The control goes on to describe the scope of the policy and to whom it applies.

Other CSA controls are highly technical. For example, IS-20 states:

> Policies and procedures shall be established and mechanism implemented for vulnerability and patch management, ensuring that application, system, and network device vulnerabilities are evaluated and vendor-supplied security patches applied in a timely manner taking a risk-based approach for prioritizing critical patches.

To evaluate controls such as IS-20, a cloud auditor must have access to the cloud provider's implementation that will make it possible to determine that such procedures are in place. A typical IT audit involves examination of reports, examination of policy documents, review of software, and interviews of personnel. The range of subjects included in a cloud audit include review of security software and checks on its effectiveness, examination of data privacy controls, assessment of data integrity checks, and examination of data retention and disposal rules and procedures.

An audit will often determine whether a provider complies with a published security standard such as ISO/IEC 27001.[15] For example, the AWS EC2 service

---

[13] ISACA, "IT Control Objectives for IT," September 2006, www.isaca.org/Knowledge-Center/Research/ResearchDeliverables/Pages/IT-Control-Objectives-for-Sarbanes-Oxley-2nd-Edition.aspx. A good summary of the applicability of Sarbanes-Oxley to IT.

[14] Cloud Security Alliance, "Cloud Controls Matrix, V. 1.2," August 26, 2011, https://cloudsecurityalliance.org/wp-content/uploads/2011/08/CSA_CCM_v1.2.xlsx.

[15] www.27000.org/iso-27001.htm provides a summary of the standard. The text of the standard itself can be purchased at webstore.iec.ch/preview/info_isoiec27001%7Bed1.0%7Den.pdf

has ISO/IEC 2001 certification.[16] The consumer is left with the responsibility for determining whether ISO/IEC 27001 certification meets the needs of their use of the service.

Cloud software architecture must consider the auditor role or risk developing a cloud that cannot be audited acceptably. Auditors exercise a tremendous influence on how systems can be used. Often, particularly with mission-critical systems, an auditor's approval determines whether a project will proceed.

Broker

The *cloud broker* is a forward-looking role defined in the NIST cloud architecture. NIST anticipates that cloud interactions may become so complex that there will be a role for intermediaries between consumers and providers. A cloud broker could offer value-added services as an intermediate between consumers and a provider such as supplying enhanced security, or it could act as service aggregators and bundle cloud services from various providers into service packages. Cloud brokers might provide services that dynamically change providers to obtain the best service at the best rates. At present, cloud brokers do not play a large role in most implementations, although brokers exist, and their role may increase as clouds evolve.

Carrier

Clouds depend on network connections between the provider and consumer. In private clouds, provider-consumer communication usually occurs almost exclusively on a corporate network behind a firewall. The *cloud carrier* for a private cloud is usually the IT department responsible for the corporate network. Public clouds use public networks for communication. These public network providers are the cloud carriers for the public cloud. Often a public cloud provider or their consumers will establish a relationship with public network providers to establish suitable SLAs to assure appropriate performance for the cloud consumer. In this "post-PC era," communication with clouds is not limited to desktop computers wired to a network. The reach of cloud carriers extends to wireless laptops and other handhelds and mobile devices that use the cellular network.

Developer

Cloud developers create services to be deployed on a cloud. One of the potential benefits of cloud computing is packaged services that can be

---

[16] http://aws.amazon.com/security/#certifications

purchased and deployed more easily than traditional software packages. The cloud developer differs from a traditional software developer because she designs and develops both the software and the virtual infrastructure that will support the service. Traditional developers only develop the service software and installation scripts and programs that will place the software on hardware which the customer supplies. Cloud packaged services are often easier for both the developer and the consumer. The near total control of the infrastructure enjoyed by the developer in cloud deployment reduces the seemingly endless range of possible infrastructure that a traditional installation has to cope with. At the same time, the consumer no longer has responsibility for configuring the environment for the installation.

There are many variations on this role, and it will undoubtedly change as cloud computing evolves. Cloud developers can be independent, a member of the cloud provider organization, a cloud consumer developing their own services on IaaS or PaaS, or a third-party organization.

A cloud developer scenario that appears to be growing in importance is a catalog of services offered by a provider. Cloud developers build services that are placed in the catalog for consumers to choose and deploy.[17] These developers could be from the provider organization, consumers, or third parties.

Amazon AWS has a form a cloud service catalog in which users select preconfigured Amazon Machine Images (AMIs) to install on the Amazon cloud.[18] Some of these AMIs are free; others require paid licenses.[19] Other

---

[17] Cloud services from a catalog are a form of virtual appliance, which is itself a form of software appliance. Software appliances have been around for a long time. The earliest software appliance I know was a firewall system that ran on an early Linux release with a kernel hacked to optimize network packet inspection. The hacked and stripped-down Linux was installed with the firewall software on a low-cost generic PC and sold as a complete unit. We used to joke that the PC was the delivery media for the software. Later versions of software appliances left out the PC and put the software and operating system on a single CD that would install both the operating system and software. Virtual appliances install as virtual machines. Cloud services are distinct from software and virtual appliances in several ways. They are built as services following the consumer-provider pattern. They tend to be more complex than appliances, often involving many separate virtual machines preconfigured to work together. Finally, they are specifically designed to be deployed on clouds.

[18] http://aws.amazon.com/amis

[19] The formal ITIL definition of a *service catalog* is a database or structured document listing all IT services available for deployment. It is published to IT customers. The usage here is slightly different because a cloud provider is a specialized form of IT department, and a cloud catalog is usually limited to services available from the cloud. The purpose of an ITIL service catalog is to support the sale and delivery of IT services; usually the consumer of the service pays the publisher of the catalog. In the Amazon AMI catalog, some of the AMIs are free, others are free but require licensing, and others require payment to the developer via an

cloud providers, such as Microsoft Azure, have similar facilities, but Amazon is a good example. Amazon offers a number of AMIs developed by Amazon developers. In this case, the cloud developers are part of the cloud provider organization.

Amazon also offers AMIs developed by other organizations. An Oracle customer who wants to run an Oracle database on the Amazon cloud can use an AMI supplied by Oracle in the Amazon AMI catalog. The Oracle AMI contains a configured and installed Oracle environment. The consumer who installs the Oracle AMI saves the time and trouble of downloading the Oracle software and going through a tedious install of the database. In this case, a software vendor is supplying the AMI as a convenience to their customer who will pay license fees to Oracle for software on the AMI. Oracle developers are acting as cloud developers.

In another variation, the cloud developer may be the consumer who develops an AMI as an easily reproducible service. For example, a rapidly expanding retail business may have a specialized inventory service that they deploy for each store. By creating an AMI with the inventory service installed, the installation time for each new store can be greatly reduced.

Unlike providers and consumers, which have been around nearly as long as computers, the developer who specializes in developing for the cloud is a role in IT that appears to be growing in importance. They transform traditional programs into cloud programs. Their success or failure in developing cloud services will be one of the determinants of the success of cloud computing.

This chapter has addressed the high-level architecture of the cloud. In the next chapter, we will address the organization of cloud implementations and some of the technologies on which the cloud depends.

Amazon billing service. Amazon's primary financial stake is in the IaaS services that power the deployed AMIs, and the AMIs are there to facilitate the use of Amazon's services. This is more complicated than the usual service catalog of an IT department, but Amazon's AMI listing still meets the basic ITIL definition. To further complicate the situation, Amazon has a second service catalog distinct from the AMIs. This is the listing of services such as EC2, S3, and RDS. Consumers pay Amazon for these services. This catalog is closer to the typical ITIL service catalog.

CHAPTER

4

Security and Governance
Managing Risk

Without adequate security and governance, clouds have little business value. An IT service can be important in many ways. The continuous and efficient performance of the service can be vital to the profitability of the enterprise. An online business cannot be profitable if its web site is unavailable or cannot process orders. A manufacturer that depends on just-in-time inventory is in serious trouble if its cloud-based inventory system is unavailable. Unauthorized or malicious access to the service may cause substantial damage or expose the enterprise to legal penalties. We have all read news stories about businesses that have lost control of private information such as credit card numbers and the effects on their business. Regulatory compliance may require organizations to report regularly and accurately on artifacts such as the integrity and security of financial reports.

When any or all of these circumstances are present, security and governance are paramount. Services that are sensitive to security and governances are typically the most critical and vital services in business and therefore get the most attention and highest levels of investment.

These critical services are also likely to yield a good return on cloud implementation. However, there are barriers to a cloud implementation of critical services. There is a well-established discipline for measuring and managing risk in critical services with extensive guidelines and best practices. Unfortunately, cloud technology has progressed faster than the discipline of cloud risk management. This gap, which is closing rapidly, still can halt cloud service implementations, turn a well-engineered project into a fiasco, or even eliminate cloud projects from consideration.

An IT service implemented with cloud may not have more risks than a service on the consumer's premises, but clouds are less understood, and they introduce risks that locally installed services do not have. Most businesses are subject to some form of audit. Auditors look for controls that mitigate risk, and when they see unfamiliar risks that are not controlled or are controlled in unfamiliar ways, an auditor may raise concerns that can stop the implementation of the service.

The catch-up situation is unfortunate, but it is changing. An indication of the change shows in the Cloud Security Alliance (CSA) guidance. CSA is a coalition of industry practitioners, corporations, associations, and other key stakeholders in cloud security and governance. CSA issued the first version of its guidance in April 2009.[1] It issued version 2.1 in December 2009.[2] Version 3.0 appeared in November 2011.[3] Between the first and third versions, the guidance doubled in size. Many of the sections in version 1.0 were little more than warnings of possible vulnerabilities and dangers. Version 3.0 has matured to recommending specific steps to take to avoid or mitigate risks. Cloud governance and security have grabbed the attention of the security and governance community, and the catch-up gap is closing.

Governance

Governance is the complex combination of laws, regulations, institutions, policies, customs, processes, and technologies that assert the proper relationship between the stakeholders and goals of an organization. Governance maintains the rights of stockholders as the ultimate owners of the organization, and it defines the roles of the management and employees of an organization. Many types of organizations are subject to governance. Businesses, from a plumbing-supply partnership with a dozen employees to a multinational corporation with tens of thousands employees, all are subject to some form of governance. Nonprofit organizations and government agencies are also subject to governance.

Governance affects many aspects of an organization. One purpose of governance is to ensure that the corporate management and employees treat

---

[1] "Security Guidance for Critical Areas of Focus in Cloud Computing Version 1.0," Cloud Security Alliance, April 2009, https://cloudsecurityalliance.org/guidance/csaguide.v1.0.pdf.

[2] "Security Guidance for Critical Areas of Focus in Cloud Computing Version 2.0," Cloud Security Alliance, December 2009, https://cloudsecurityalliance.org/guidance/csaguide.v2.1.pdf.

[3] Paul Simmonds, Chris Rezek, and Archie Reed, "Security Guidance for Critical Areas of Focus in Cloud Computing Version 3.0," 2011, https://cloudsecurityalliance.org/guidance/csaguide.v3.0.pdf.

the investments of the stockholders honestly and follow sound business practice. Laws enforce some aspects of governance, and regulatory compliance is an important aspect of governance. For example, the Sarbanes-Oxley Act requires a level of financial transparency from management. Good governance requires that those regulations be followed. Governance also involves compliance with industry-specific regulations such as a pharmaceutical manufacturer complying with Food and Drug Administration regulations.

Above all, the purpose of governance is to manage risk. Managing risk does not eliminate risk. Rather, the first step in managing risk is to identify what the risks are and how they may affect the organization. The risk manager then looks for ways to reduce or eliminate the risk, but they also evaluate the cost of mitigation and balance these costs against the cost of the risk. Aware of the balance, management can act reasonably. They can decide to accept an unmitigated risk if it makes business sense, or they can mitigate it. Many business decisions, including stockholder decisions to buy or sell shares, depend on risk assessments.

IT governance is the governance that applies to IT. Understanding IT governance requires an understanding of IT assets. The IT physical infrastructure certainly is an asset, but it is no different from other enterprise assets. The unique IT assets are data and process.

Data consists of the records and other information that the organization has generated or collected. Value accrues to stored information in several ways. Some stored information may have no obvious value until an innovative data mining operation extracts nuggets of value, perhaps of great value like purchasing patterns for selective marketing. Other items of data may not have value in themselves, but their loss may still be detrimental. For example, in U.S. courts, litigants must share relevant documents with their adversary. These documents could be old e-mails with no value until a lawsuit requires them.

Other data has intrinsic value. Business records, production logs, and customer records all are necessary for running the business. Their value increases as data analysis gets better at extracting information that leads to a business advantage.

IT processes include applications, systems, and services that carry out the business of the organization. Interruption to these processes interrupts business. Interruptions can result from the process stopped by something like a malicious flip of a power switch, but there are other causes. A system may be running fine, but the users are not able to communicate with it because the network is at fault. More insidious, a service can become corrupted and perform erratically or produce false results. All of these represent risks that may result from process failures. The magnitude of the risk is measured by the impact on the business.

There are two important sources for cloud governance that cloud consumers and providers should be aware of. The first is from the Cloud Security Alliance (CSA) mentioned earlier. The CSA has published a Cloud Control Matrix[4] that is an adjunct to the ISO/IEC 27001 information security management standard, discussed later in this chapter. The CSA cloud control list is intended to be implemented following practices from ISO/IEC 27001, described shortly.

Another important source for cloud governance is from the Information Systems Audit and Control Association (ISACA).[5] ISACA addresses information systems security and auditing in many publications, including Control Objectives for Information and Related Technologies (COBIT),[6] which covers IT governance in general. Other, more specialized publications focus on cloud governance.

Security

Security is protection from harm. It is an important part of governance, although governance encompasses more than just security. In IT, harm can come in many ways. It can be a physical threat of damage to equipment. It can come from a few lines of malicious self-reproducing code that burrow their way through the Internet. A malefactor can guess or trick someone into revealing a password and gain illicit access to a system. A rogue employee can use privilege to damage data and processes.

Generalizations always have exceptions, but cloud installations are probably not much more or less secure than installations on the consumer premises. Securing a cloud is not much different than securing an enterprise computing system. They are subject to the same kinds of threats and have the same solutions. The viruses attacking a cloud datacenter are the same viruses that attack an individual PC.

However, there is an enormously important difference between the distribution of responsibility in a cloud consumer-provider implementation and an installation on the consumer's own premises. The cloud provider takes on many of the security responsibilities that consumers ordinarily would assume themselves. Redistribution of responsibility even occurs in private

---

[4] http://cloudsecurityalliance.org/wp-content/themes/csa/ccm-download-box.php

[5] www.isaca.org/about-isaca/Pages/default.aspx

[6] www.isaca.org/cobit/pages/default.aspx

clouds when an internal cloud provider takes over an installation previously deployed and managed by a department.

For example, a research group that moves their data storage from their own storage devices to a corporate private cloud may have to work through governance and security issues over data requiring special treatment. Data related to defense research contracts often requires special handling and security checks. Knowledge of these requirements and appropriate procedures has to migrate from the research group to the operators of the corporate cloud. The reallocation will be difficult because the research group loses direct control of activities that may jeopardize their department. As you will see later, the reallocation of responsibility for security is a major concern in cloud governance.

The problem goes back to risk management. Security is a method for mitigating certain kinds of risk. Like all mitigations, security has costs as well as benefits, and decisions must be based on those costs. When a corporate security officer decides to implement a level of encryption or add encryption where none existed before, she evaluates the cost of reduced performance and perhaps the cost of custom code for a special algorithm or application. Then she compares that cost to the threat to her corporation's business and makes a decision.

The security officer for a public cloud provider has to use a different equation. The cost of encryption will be the same, but he will balance the cost against the threat to the cloud provider business, not the consumer's business.

There is nothing inherently wrong with this. The threat to the cloud provider's business could be formidable and may correspond closely to his customer's threat. In this case, all is well because the provider is compelled to be as diligent as the consumer. But there may also be mismatch. For example, a cloud provider will probably not want to fund mitigations that are not of value to enough consumers to justify usage rates that compensate for the cost of enhanced controls. A provider decision that satisfies most consumers may be egregiously dangerous to some consumers. This means that the customer must be prepared to examine the cloud provider's decisions in the light of their risks, not rely on the cloud provider's assessment of risk.

This is the point where governance is important. For business, there must be transparency. For the corporate security officer to assert to her management and board that the cloud installation meets corporate governance, she, or the corporate auditors, must be able to audit the cloud provider to gain a correct understanding of the risk of the cloud installation. One of the ways to gain this understanding is through an information management security system.

The Information Security Management System (ISMS)

Security and governance is a process aided by technology, not a technology in itself. The structure and rules of conduct of an organization are a large part of security and governance. Many aspects of the process, such as maintaining plans for the management oversight of security incidents, are not inherently technical, and the only technology involved is the document management system that keeps the paperwork tidy. Nevertheless, especially in cloud implementations, the process also depends on security technology to reinforce policies and controls.

An approach to the security and governance process is described in the ISO/IEC 27001 standard, published in 2005. ISO/IEC 27001 is a general standard for IT security, and it is often used as the basis for information security audits. It is not specific to cloud implementations, but it applies to the cloud like it applies to all aspects of IT. Much of the work of the CSA has been to provide cloud-specific guidance within the framework of ISO/IEC 27001.

Cloud providers have begun getting certification in ISO/IEC 27001. This means that cloud consumers should familiarize themselves with ISO/IEC 27001. Understanding what it means to comply with ISO/IEC 27001 is likely to become crucial to understanding how safe a given provider will be for the consumer's business.

There are several documents in the ISO/IEC 27000 series. ISO/IEC 27000 is a short overview and introduction, published in 2009.[7] ISO/IEC 27002 is a code of practice for implementing information management security within the framework of ISO/IEC 27001.[8] ISO/IEC 27005, with the latest version published in 2011, is a more detailed discussion of the principles laid out in ISO/IEC 27001.[9] There are other documents in the series that address more specialized subjects. ISO 27001 is the central document and referenced frequently on cloud security.

The ISO/IEC 27001 Deming Cycle

ISO/IEC 27001 outlines a Deming cycle for IT security management. A Deming cycle (Figure 4-1) is a series of steps for continuous improvement of business processes. It is alternatively called a PDCA cycle, standing for Plan, Do, Check,

---

[7] www.iso.org/iso/catalogue_detail?csnumber=41933

[8] www.iso.org/iso/home/store/catalogue_ics/catalogue_detail_ics.htm?csnumber=54533

[9] www.iso.org/iso/home/store/catalogue_ics/catalogue_detail_ics.htm?csnumber=56742

Act.[10] The cycle begins with planning. In the Plan phase, objectives, processes, and targets are established. The next phase, Do, is the operational phase. The Do phase executes the plans from the previous phase. Execution generates data for the Check phase. The Check phase studies the generated data and compares the results to the targets and objectives from the Plan phase. The Act phase starts with the results of the check phase and acts on them with corrections. Then the cycle begins anew with a planning phase that builds on the experience of the previous cycle.

The phases of the Deming Cycle do not always occur serially. Although each builds on the previous phase, phases may run simultaneously. For example, Check phase studies often are done while the Do phase continues to generate data. The important thing is that when the cycle is in full operation, checking is based on data from doing, acting is based on checking, planning is based on acting, and doing is based on planning. Each phase can be and usually is in effect simultaneously after the cycle is going well.

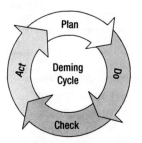

Figure 4-1. The Deming Cycle is a method for continual improvement in business.

Plan Phase

At the start of the Plan phase, the scope and policy of the ISMS are determined. This is largely an executive management decision and may be a board-level decision. The scope of the ISMS is an important decision that determines the parts of the enterprise the ISMS will affect. The scope may be limited to a single business unit or datacenter. Cloud consumers should be careful to

---

[10] Deming called his PDCA cycle the Shewhart Cycle, because Walter A. Shewhart, a pioneer in statistical industrial quality control, first formulated it. (See http://wikipedia.org/wiki/Shewhart for a short biography and description of his work.) In Deming's book *Out of Crisis* (MIT Press, 1986), Deming applied the cycle to the improvement of the production of products and service. Chapter 2, "Principles for Transformation of Western Management," is especially relevant. Because Deming used the PDCA cycle extensively, his name is attached to the cycle, in spite of Shewhart's prior invention.

examine the scope of the certification and verify that the certification covers everything important to them. This information may not be easy to find or interpret. Amazon, for example, provides security and compliance certification information in its AWS Security and Compliance Center.[11] The documentation is extensive. However, the consumer must be aware that their requirements may be unique, and simply noting that Amazon Web Services AWS has obtained several certificates is not enough to assure security and compliance.

AWS has also published a growing collection of white papers on security and compliance.[12] Consumers will find these papers helpful, both for applying Amazon's support of security and compliance and for evaluating other providers. Other providers are also responding to consumer requests for better support of security and compliance.

There are other parts to the Plan phase. The entire ISMS must be planned and documented. The risks must be identified and assessed, and decisions must be made on how to mitigate them. Risk mitigation is often accompanied by controls. (See the "Controls" sidebar.) In the Plan phase, controls are chosen and implemented.

CONTROLS

Controls are important in any business or organization. They are processes to assure the achievement of goals. They can take many forms. Double-entry accounting is a classic example of financial control. Balanced books help assure that all funds are properly accounted for. Unbalanced books signal questionable accounting. Financial controls are only one form of control. The familiar password challenges that control entry to computer systems are another form of control. When a password expires and the user is prompted to enter a hard-to-crack mixture of letters and digits, it acts as a control on the password challenge to assure that the password is strong. Controls are often manual procedures that auditors check to verify that personnel follow them. These procedures can be as straight-forward as a question on an audit, such as "Is critical IT equipment physically secure?" The effort to assure achievement of management directed objectives distinguishes controls from other processes.

Do Phase

The Do phase places the ISMS into operation. This includes deciding who will fund and take responsibility for executing each part of the plan. The controls

---

[11] http://aws.amazon.com/sec

[12] See http://aws.amazon.com/security/#background for a list of current papers.

chosen in the Plan phase are implemented, often as forms that must be filled out regularly and regular verification that security software is working properly. Security incident reporting and processing are other key functions in the Do phase. Security issues, which are typically detected by controls, must be recorded, responded to, and analyzed. In addition to controls and incidents, tools for measuring and reporting on governance must operate in the Do phase. These reports provide the raw input for the next phase.

Check Phase

In the Check phase, the effectiveness of the risk mitigations and controls is monitored. The ISMS is monitored for violations and errors in data processing and for security lapses. Effectiveness reviews, risk assessments, internal audits, and management reviews occur.

Act Phase

In the Act phase, the ISMS team takes the Check phase results and enacts improvements, corrections, and preventative measures. General reports to all stakeholders maintain transparency.

As the cycle returns to its beginning, the Plan phase engages with plans for future changes and possible expansion of the ISMS.

Statement on Audit Standards No. 70 (SAS 70)

SAS 70 is an auditing standard from the American Institute of Certified Public Accountants (AICPA).[13] It is 70th in a series of auditing standards from the AICPA. No. 70 applies to auditing service organizations. Other SAS standards apply to other types of organizations and subjects. SAS 70 applies to all types of services, and IT services often are subject to SAS 70 audits. SAS 70 guidance is directed toward communication between auditors of service provider organizations and auditors of service consumer organizations. It does not specify control objectives or activities that a service organization must maintain or perform. Instead, it provides guidelines for verifying that a service organization has designed and implemented their controls properly and operates them effectively.

---

[13] http://umiss.lib.olemiss.edu:82/record=b1038093 provides the text of SAS 70. http://sas70.com/sas70_overview.html provides a useful overview.

The SAS 70 Audit

A SAS 70 audit is performed by a qualified certified public accountant. The audit report has several sections including a formal description of the provider's controls and the auditor's evaluation of the effectiveness of the controls in operation. A Type I report contains only the auditor's evaluation of the design of the provider's controls and their suitability for achieving their goals. A Type II report includes a Type I report and goes on to state the auditor's opinion of the effectiveness of their operation over a review period. Often, a SAS 70 audit begins with a Type I report followed by periodic Type II reports.

Service consumers often insist on SAS 70 audits because the consumer's own executive management, auditors, or regulators require a SAS 70 audit of the consumer's essential external services. Deploying mission-critical service on a cloud may trigger such requirements. Public cloud providers often participate in SAS 70 audits. Declaring successful SAS 70 audits help assure consumers of the integrity of the provider.

However, a provider that passes a SAS 70 audit does not imply that the use of the provider will pass the consumer's own audit. A SAS 70 audit assures that the information in the audit will permit the consumer's own auditor to make a decision on the suitability of the provider's controls. A SAS 70 audit is a positive indication, but it does not guarantee that a service provider is suitable for all purposes.

SAS 70 Example

For example, a service consumer may require that a certain class of confidential files must be irretrievably destroyed when they expire, not simply deleted. To trust those files to cloud storage, this consumer must have assurance that the files on the cloud, including all their backups and secondary and temporary copies, can be irretrievably deleted, not just made difficult to access. The consumer's auditor, regulators, or executive management may deem this requirement critical. A SAS 70 audit will help them determine that this requirement is met.

A SAS 70 audit on the provider may report on controls that support the consumer deletion requirement, but the requirement is specialized, and the provider may not have controls that support irretrievable deletion. Whether the provider has the required controls or not, their SAS 70 audit is still valid if it was conducted according to SAS 70 guidance.

The value of the SAS 70 audit appears when the consumer or their auditor evaluates the provider. Instead of a disruptive visit to the provider and an expensive audit of the provider's controls by the user auditor, the user auditor can determine the adequacy of the provider's controls by examining the SAS 70 audit. The SAS 70 guidance assures the consumer auditor that the report is a complete description of the provider's controls.

Consumers must realize that a SAS 70 audit is not a required item to check off. It is a report prepared according to acknowledged auditing standards on the provider's controls, but it is up to the consumer and their own auditors to decide whether those controls apply to their situation.

Cloud and ISMS

When applied to cloud security, the planning phase ISMS cycle begins with the identification of assets and risks. The assets in the cloud fall into two broad groups: data and processes. Data is the information that is stored in the cloud. Processes are the business processes implemented with cloud services.

Data

Data is subject to unavailability, corruption, and loss. It is also subject to undesired exposure. These threats are the same threats that menace services installed on the consumer's premises, and many of the same protections that work in local installations apply to cloud implementations, but there are important differences. These differences affect what controls are possible and how they can be applied.

Loss

Data may become unavailable through failures or malfunctions, in which case the consumer is temporarily unable to access the data entrusted to the cloud. For example, a network partition caused by a failing router or a broken cable can separate the consumer from the cloud provider. This can happen with private, community, and public clouds. Any time data is stored remotely, a network partition can prevent access to the data. Possible failures are not limited to the network. Other vulnerabilities include failures in a datacenter such as a storage unit that temporarily switches offline or a disk fault. An entire datacenter can go offline because of a power failure or other disaster.

Or data can become unavailable for nontechnical reasons. A cloud provider can go out of business and shut down. Or data may be sequestered for legal reasons. There are many ways that data can become unavailable.

All of these threats can and usually are mitigated. Failover, redundant systems, and formidable physical security are all characteristic of cloud datacenters, but the customer is always faced with a question: does this adequately mitigate my risks?

The difficulty with the cloud is in implementing controls. For example, CSA data governance control DG-03 dictates that policies and procedures must be established for handling and security of all data and objects that contain data.[14] In a completely local ISMS, the need for a suitable control like this would be identified in the Plan phase of the ISO/IEC27001 process. In the Do phase, a group, most likely in IT operations, would accept responsibility for the control, the cost of implementing the control would go on their budget, and they would write up an operational plan or tailor a plan that was already specified for them. Then they would get management approval for the operational plan. Finally, the team would begin to execute and provide regular management reports on their activity in accordance with their plan.

In a cloud implementation, this would happen differently. The control is equally important to both a local and remote implementation. Data can be lost, destroyed, or exposed both on and off-premises, especially when procedures and policies for handling and security are weak. But in an off-premises implementation, the procedures and policies for the physical objects that contain the data are in the possession and control of the cloud provider, not the owner of the data.

The specific risks are similar both on and off-premises. The theft of a disk containing credit card numbers will be damaging, and the extent of the damage will have nothing to do with whether it was stolen from an enterprise data center or some other location. But the implementation of the controls that will mitigate the risk is quite different. It is possible that the provider will be so obliging as to go into an ISMS Do phase with approvals, reports, and reviews like those supplied by the local IT department, and it is even likely that large enterprises will have contracts with cloud providers that amount to this. However, that kind of relationship is closer to outsourcing than what we usually think of as a cloud implementation and will most likely be available only to the largest cloud consumers.

The most likely way to establish an off-premises control is in the contract between the consumer and the provider. There are several approaches to risk mitigation in cloud contracts. One approach is for the cloud provider to be certified as compliant to a security standard like ISO/IEC 27001. Certifications are reassuring and helpful, but consumers still have to enter the cloud carefully.

---

[14] "Cloud Controls Matrix, Version 1.2," Cloud Security Alliance, August 2011, https://cloudsecurityalliance.org/research/ccm/

Risks

Cloud implementations often rely on contractual provisions to take the place of direct control of the physical infrastructure. This heightens the need for a careful evaluation of the risks involved in an implementation *before entering into the contract*. Failure to do so can result in a contract that does not protect against important risks. This is especially important when the customer enters the contract through a clickwrap.[15]

As the success of Amazon AWS has shown, clickwrap access to cloud services is an attractive business model for cloud providers. But without an adequate level of security, risk mitigation, and regulatory compliance built into the cloud services that the clickwrap makes available, the service will be unacceptable for many business purposes. In addition, the consumer must beware of the reliability of the provider itself. The best certification and policies are not adequate if a consumer blithely clicks through into a contract with a provider that is not prepared to support the SLAs in the click through contract.

De-perimeterization

Enterprises have been bedeviled recently by the rapid decay of two pillars of enterprise security: the impenetrability of the enterprise network and the locked doors of enterprise facilities. Traditionally, anything inside an enterprise network or behind a locked door on the enterprise premises was safe. But recently these defenses have begun to erode. Use of cloud resources is just one example of moving resources outside the traditional perimeter. Viruses and other malware question the impermeability of the ramparts. Bring your own device (BYOD), working from home, and similar trends have expanded the workplace beyond the old clear limits. Security has new challenges and needs new tools.

De-perimeterization is a strategy that does not depend on a cloud provider's security and compliance practices or a contract or SLA between the consumer and provider. It does not take the place of diligent provider selection and thoughtfully prepared contracts and agreements, but de-perimeterization can increase security and aid in governance of IT. Although it applies to more than cloud installations, it is an important strategy for effective cloud usage.

---

[15] Also called a *click-through* or a *browse-wrap*. It refers to agreeing to a contract by clicking a web page.

De-perimeterization is a concept developed by the Jericho Forum of the Open Group.[16] It is both a condition and a strategy.

Network perimeter defense is a traditional strategy for defending IT. The limits of the corporate network and the corporate facility are a perimeter that separates IT from dangerous outside influences. The network perimeter is protected with defenses such as firewalls, proxies, and password challenges. Locked doors and guards physically secure the corporate premises within the perimeter. The emphasis is on blocking external threats from penetrating the defensive perimeter. The zone inside the perimeter is safe. Although access to sensitive resources within the perimeter may be limited to those with proper authorization, the system assumes that anyone inside the perimeter has some legitimate purpose and some level of trust.

The traditional enterprise network perimeter is dissolving in several ways. Work patterns are changing, and a growing number of employees work outside the traditional workplace. Instead of inhabiting a cubicle in a corporate office, workers telecommute from home, work from airports and coffee shops, and even work from the beach or a ski run. This has expanded both the network and physical corporate perimeters and opened new vulnerabilities. Security officers can no longer be certain that resources are physically protected or that activity is behind an impermeable firewall.

The network perimeter is becoming more porous in other ways. Viruses and worms enter via e-mail and the Internet. Business transactions tunnel through firewalls. Employees working in the office use social media such as Facebook and Twitter and engage with customers and other businesses over the Internet. With the explosion of smartphones and tablets, private devices have crept inside corporate walls and onto enterprise networks.

The cloud is also a contributor to the weakening of the perimeter. Public and shared SaaS, PaaS, and IaaS services extend corporate computing beyond the enterprise premises to cloud provider facilities. Connection to these clouds is often via public networks. This further obscures traditional boundaries. Not only is data passing through the perimeter, data and processes may be stored and executed outside the perimeter and outside corporate control.

Because of these trends, the traditional perimeter has lost much of its defensive efficacy. A strong perimeter defense can even appear to inhibit business instead of protect it from threats, although the threats have by no means disappeared. The Jericho Group calls this general trend toward a weaker perimeter *de-perimeterization*.

---

[16] https://www.opengroup.org/jericho

De-perimeterization as a Strategy

However, de-perimeterization is a solution strategy as well as a problem. The de-perimeterization strategy embraces the thinning of the perimeter and attempts to turn the disappearance to an advantage. The strategy is to shrink the defended perimeter down to the assets themselves.

For example, consider a file. On a desktop in an office, the lock on the front door and the network firewall form a perimeter that protects the file. But store the file on a laptop and allow an employee to take the laptop home on the subway; the perimeter is gone. To provide protection, the perimeter must travel with the laptop and the file. One way to accomplish this is to require a password on the laptop. Even better is to encrypt the file in addition to a password. Then, the aspiring information thief would have to break the laptop password. If the thief breaks the password, he meets a second perimeter and has to decrypt the file. The chance of losing data from exposed personal devices decreases when a perimeter barrier stands at each level around each asset. A defensive organizational perimeter is still useful, but it becomes only one line of defense in a robust proliferation of perimeters.

Following a de-perimeterization strategy, all applications, processes, and resources are made secure with perimeters in themselves. Like our encrypted file, an application secured with a password is not dependent on a secure organizational perimeter. By securing the application itself, its secure perimeter is limited.

De-perimeterization strategy is well suited to the cloud. When cloud services are implemented off-premises in either a private or public cloud, the implementation distorts the traditional perimeter. As a result, traditional governance and security controls do not apply. A consequence is that the consumer must rely on contractual assurances of governance. Shrinking perimeters to protect each asset individually yields a higher level of security, but it requires new and perhaps unfamiliar approaches.

Cloud Security Practice

Cloud consumers must be cautious. There is no rote formula or instant solution to cloud security and governance. Governance and security must be tailored to business requirements and risks, which vary with each organization. A good policy is to follow a framework like ISO/IEC 27001. That means a process of continual scrutiny and improvement. But these assurances may not be easily obtained, particularly with the clickwrap contracts used by many providers. When the assurances are not present, the consumer must sort through the documentation offered by the provider and determine what controls are in place.

IaaS Practice

The provider will implement some controls. Which controls the provider will implement depends on the type of service offered. An IaaS provider will implement the fewest controls. They will probably assert that the equipment will be physically secure and protected from natural disasters, assert that a level of failover will be provided, offer a guarantee of service levels and other similar controls. An IaaS provider may also assert that the infrastructure of one consumer will be separated and mutually invisible to other consumers. They probably will not assert that an application running on the infrastructure will be secure from malicious attacks from the network, because factors under the consumer's control, such as firewall settings, Internet accessibility, and operating system patch levels, affect vulnerability. It will most likely be the responsibility of the consumer to install and maintain a properly designed and secured application.

Cloud providers are generally diligent about external vulnerabilities that they can control. They are especially diligent about problems that may arise between consumers. In this context, consumers are often called *tenants*. Cloud providers usually assert that a consumer's data and processes will never be accessible to another tenant. They maintain the separation in various ways, usually at an architectural level below the application level. They use facilities like the virtual internal network, the hypervisors instantiating and managing virtual resources, and the storage system. The rules concerning data and process access are usually spelled out carefully in the consumer contract and SLA.

PaaS Practice

PaaS is an intermediate between IaaS and PaaS and shares security issues with IaaS and PaaS. PaaS providers often instantiate infrastructure like virtual machines for their clients, but they also provide fundamental applications such as databases and development environments. Consequently, PaaS providers usually offer more controls that touch on the integrity of the platform, and they may provide security services that they will control. For example, the provider will be responsible for securing and keeping up the patch level of databases that are part of the platform. An IaaS service, on the other hand, probably would not provide these security services a database system installed by the consumer on the provided infrastructure.

SaaS Practice

SaaS providers provide the most controls. A SaaS service can be guaranteed to be designed and operated securely with a specified quality of service because it retains more control than IaaS or PaaS providers. SaaS providers can make many additional assertions about the application, and they take over more responsibility for the responsibility and integrity of the system.

SaaS providers can assert that their application is free from interference and not visible to other tenants. Any cloud consumer can be called a tenant of the cloud provider, but the term is used most often for SaaS.

There are two basic patterns for SaaS tenancy. One pattern instantiates and provisions a complete application for each subscriber. Following this pattern, partitioning tenants is similar to IaaS, and similar techniques are used, although the consumer may be less aware of the implementation of the partition. This pattern has the advantage that is usually easier to implement securely, but it is less flexible when tenants overlap, such as when two tenants are two departments in the same enterprise and may want to share some data.

The other important patterns for multitenant SaaS applications are similar to strategies used by managed service providers. Instead of installing separate instances of each application for each tenant, the provider has a limited number of installations of the application and assigns several tenants to each.

This strategy has advantages for the provider. Fewer installations can reduce application administration. If the provider supplies more than the bare application, for example, providing technicians to respond to incidents as well as the service desk application, jobs can be streamlined if technicians can work several tenants at once from a single application installation. Sometimes, sharing data between tenants is supported more easily in a single application installation. Subtenants are also more easily supported.

The downside to this strategy is that partitioning tenants becomes an application-specific job that can be complex. Depending on the application architecture, data from one tenant may be physically stored contiguously with data from another tenant. In relational databases, this can present subtle problems when data from two tenants are on the same page and held by a page lock or can present not-so-subtle problems when legal authorities confiscate a disk. In many cases, single-instance multitenancy is application specific and highly detailed.

Nevertheless, a cloud consumer has to realize that cloud governance and security depends more on their own scrutiny and diligence than any other factor. A public cloud is not inherently less safe than a private cloud or an implementation on the consumer's premises, particularly as cloud providers are becoming more sensitive to security and governance. Amazon's public documentation of AWS security and controls is an example of this sensitivity.[17]

The important thing is that documentation and certification does not mean that a cloud implementation will properly mitigate the risks to any particular organization. A software developer may not be concerned about a high level of security and precise governance over routine product testing records, but a pharmaceuticals manufacturer may have to treat similar routine testing records with great care because they contain confidential patient information. What is appropriate for one consumer is not appropriate for another.

Governance and Security Standards

This section contains descriptions of some of the security standards that are important in securing and governing the cloud. These are tools that developers have available to make the cloud secure and mitigate security risks. The set of standards discussed here does not answer every question about cloud security, but it is intended to give a taste of what is being done with standards to secure the cloud. Most of the focus, as is to be expected, is on interoperability—how cloud sites can work together securely without driving users to distraction with too many passwords and too many challenges. Most of familiar applications of these standards are for SaaS sites like Google and Facebook, but these standards also often have a role behind the scenes in more technical realms.

Basic Authentication

Basic Authentication (RFC 2617)[18] is usually discussed more for its insecurity and inadequacies than for its virtues. It was included in the HTTP 1.0 specification, and it was once a common way to secure sites on the Internet. Basic Authentication is still occasionally used, and the browsers and HTTP servers all support Basic Authentication, but the protocol has fallen into disfavor because it is not secure. Nevertheless, Basic Authentication is important because other, more secure forms of authentication derive from Basic Authentication. Features were added to the protocol to fix Basic

---

[17] http://aws.amazon.com/security/#certifications has on overall view or 2011's "Amazon Web Services: Overview of Security Processes." http://d36cz9buwru1tt.cloudfront.net/pdf/ AWS_Security_Whitepaper.pdf has more detailed information.

[18] 1999. "HTTP Authentication: Basic and Digest Access Authentication." http://tools.ietf. org/html/rfc2617 RFC 2617 replaced RFC 2069 (http://tools.ietf.org/html/rfc2069) . The HTTP 1.0 standard (http://tools.ietf.org/html/rfc1945) and 1.1 standard (http://tools.ietf.org/ html/rfc2616) also discuss Basic Authentication.

Authentication flaws, and understanding the flaws provides insight into other designs.

Users see Basic Authentication in action when a browser requests a password for entry to a web site (see Figure 4-2). In the background, the browser has sent an HTTP request to the site and has received a 401 No Authorization reply, which is the HTTP status code that indicates access to the area of the site that requires a user name and password and there is none presented or the pair presented is not acceptable. The reply will contain a "realm" identifier that marks the segment of the site that the challenge applies to. If the browser does not have a user name and password cached for the realm, the browser will request a name and password from the user. The user types in the requested user name and password. The browser concatenates the name and password into a single string with a colon separator, base64 encodes[19] the string, places it into a new request, and sends it to the server. If the server recognizes the name and password, it grants access. Since HTTP is stateless, each request to the server requires a name-password string; the browser takes care of this without user input after the initial challenge.

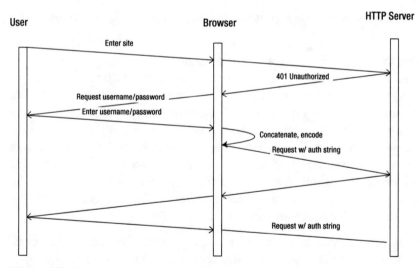

Figure 4-2. Basic authentication sequence diagram

---

[19] Although base64-encoded text is difficult for humans to read, it is not encrypted; the encoded text converts easily back to ordinary text without requiring shared secrets or special knowledge. Without going into a full explanation, base64 encoding simply converts ASCII text into base 64 digits. This kind of encoding prevents the contents of a block of text from damage as it passes through different media that might interpret special characters and perform unwanted transformations, like truncating a string at an embedded quotation mark.

As everyone points out, Basic Authentication passes the user name and password in clear text over the Internet, which is an insecure transport. In other words, bad actors easily intercept HTTP requests and read off the user name and password from the authorization field. The base64 encoding is no barrier.

Using "naked" Basic Authentication on a public network has dangers because the packets can be intercepted on the wire and the user name and password extracted. Even a site with no valuable resources to protect that tracks only site usage with Basic Authentication endangers their users with naked Basic Authentication. People tend to assume that passwords are secret, and they use the same password for leaving comments at a hobby site as they do when making withdrawals from their bank account. Whenever passwords are exposed in clear text on a network, there is a danger.

Fortunately, there are some easy solutions to passing clear passwords in Basic Authentication. One is to use the HTTPS protocol instead of HTTP. When HTTPs is used, all the messages are encrypted in a secure way. Chapter 10 discusses HTTP and HTTPS, so I will not go into it here.

Another solution is to use Digest Authentication, which is discussed in the next section.

However, there are still issues with Basic Authentication that neither HTTPS nor Digest Authentication solves. A system that requires each service provider or site owner to maintain a secret list of user names and passwords places a burdensome responsibility on the provider, and users of the system are placing trust in the provider, possibly more trust than they would if they were aware of the dangers involved. The service provider must keep the list up-to-date and secure. From the governance perspective, if a user name and password controls access to consumer assets, the consumer may require audits of the security provisions of the keeper of the passwords. This places requirements on a service provider that they may not care to take on.

Shared secret passwords themselves are an issue. For some purposes, passwords give too much power to the service provider. In traditional Basic Authentication–like security, both the service provider and the service consumer have access to the secret password and therefore access to the consumer's assets. A consumer may want an arrangement where the service provider has only restricted access to their assets or information without the consumer's permission. The situation is comparable to the traditional bank safety deposit box that will not open without both the bank's key and the customer's key.

Digest Authentication

Digest Authentication was introduced in 1997. It is an addition to the 1996 HTTP 1.0 specification. It addresses some, but not all, security issues in Basic Authentication.[20] The RFC 2617 authors point out that Digest Authentication is safer than Basic Authentication, but it still has challenges. Although it provides the encryption that Basic Authentication lacks, it is still a password challenge system, and there is no special provision taken for initial password exchange.

CRYPTOGRAPHIC HASHES AND NONCES

A hash is a function that will transform an arbitrary-length string (called the *message*) into a fixed-length string (called the *digest*). An ideal cryptographic hash will easily generate a digest for any message. It will be difficult to construct a message that will produce a given digest, and it will not be feasible to construct two different messages with the same digest. Finally, a small change in a message will produce a decidedly different digest. A hash with these characteristics has many uses. By sending a digest along with a message, the receiver can verify that the message did not change in transmission. If the sender and receiver have a shared secret, the sender can send the digest of the secret to the receiver to prove the identity of the sender to the receiver.

To secure the secret further, the server sends to the client a random "nonce" value with the challenge, which the client adds to the message, computes the digest, and returns it to the server along with the nonce. Thus, the digest changes whenever the nonce changes, and therefore no one can use the digest from an intercepted packet to gain illicit access.

As a default, Digest Authentication uses the MD5 cryptographic hash algorithm with a nonce to avoid sending the password in clear text in response to a challenge from the server. Troubling news on MD5 appeared in 1996. A collision was discovered. In other words, researchers found a way to generate two messages with the same digest.[21] The first discovery led to a series of

---

[20] HTTP 1.0 appeared as RFC 1945 (www.ietf.org/rfc/rfc1945.txt). Shortly thereafter, RFC 2069 (www.ietf.org/rfc/rfc2069.txt) was published, which covered both Basic Authentication and Digest Authentication. RFC 2617 (www.ietf.org/rfc/rfc2617.txt) replaced RFC 2069 in 1999. RFC 2617 was published along with HTTP 1.1, RFC 2616 (www.ietf.org/rfc/rfc2616. txt).

[21] Dobbertin, Hans. 1996. "The Status of MD5 After a Recent Attack." ftp://ftp.rsasecurity. com/pub/cryptobytes/crypto2n2.pdf

discovered weaknesses in MD5. Subsequently, NIST took MD5 off the list of recommended cryptographic hashes.[22] Although MD5 is no longer recommended, it is still used and has been involved in some security incidents fairly recently.[23] Consequently, systems that rely on MD5 are more secure than Basic Authentication, but MD5-based Digest Authentication is not considered strong security. However, most browsers and some HTTP servers still support MD5, and it is still used.

RFC 2617 specifies a mechanism for servers and clients to negotiate a hash algorithm; consequently a more secure hash algorithm, such as one of the SHA series, might be chosen.[24] However, that requires both the browser client and the server to support the more secure algorithms.

Open Authorization

Open Authorization (OAuth, RFC 5849)[25] is an open specification that defines a "resource owner" role. Open Authorization is an alternate approach that has advantages over Basic Authorization or Digest Authentication in some circumstances. Using OAuth, a resource owner can securely grant temporary and limited privileges to a client for access to a service where the resource owner has deposited resources without revealing the resource owner's credentials to the client.

For example, the owner of a group of digital photographs stored in a cloud photo-management service might want use a photo-printing service, also in the cloud, to print some special photos. Using OAuth, the owner authorizes the print service to access the photos for printing, but the owner does not have to reveal credentials for the photo management site to the printing service. The less often and the fewer places credentials are revealed, the stronger they remain.

In OAuth terminology, the *server* service is a custodian of resources of the resource owner. The *client* is a service to which the resource owner might want to grant constrained and temporary access to a limited set of resources.

---

[22] www.nsrl.nist.gov/collision.html

[23] http://web.nvd.nist.gov/view/vuln/detail?vulnId=CVE-2004-2761

[24] Secure Hash Algorithm. NIST lists several approved algorithms. MD5 is not on NIST's list, and some questions have been raised regarding the collision resistance of SHA-1. See Quynh Dang's 2011 "Recommendation for Applications Using Approved Hash Algorithms" at http://csrc.nist.gov/publications/drafts/800-107/Draft_Revised_SP800-107.pdf.

[25] http://tools.ietf.org/html/rfc5849 is OAuth 1.0. It is likely to be soon replaced by 2.0, which is in draft http://tools.ietf.org/html/draft-ietf-oauth-v2-23. http://hueniverse.com/oauth/guide/history/ provides excellent background from the perspective of the early authors of the specification.

In Figure 4-3, the photo storage service is the server, and the photo-printing service is the client.

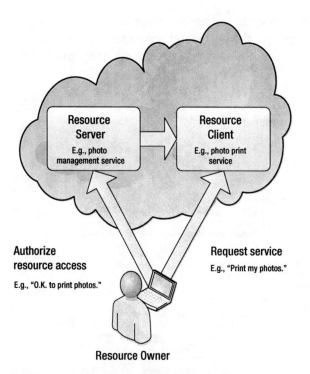

Figure 4-3. Using Open Authorization, a resource owner obtains third-party services without revealing credentials to the third party.

An OAuth transaction begins with the establishment of a relationship between a server and a client. A resource owner cannot grant privileges to a client that does not have credentials with the server. OAuth calls these *client credentials*.

The resource owner initiates the transaction by entering the client site and requesting that the client do something with a resource from the server. The client uses its previously obtained client credentials to request a non-resource-specific *temporary credential* from the server. The client then directs the resource owner to the resource server OAuth authorization URL with the temporary credential just obtained. The resource owner then signs into the resource server with their resource server credential.

Note that at this point, the resource owner has not presented any credentials to the client. The resource owner has only privately presented credentials to the resource server.

The resource owner chooses the resources and access granted to the client. The server returns the temporary credential to the client marked as resource-owner-authorized.

The client can then use the authorized temporary credential to obtain access tokens from the server for getting the permitted resources. The temporary credential and the access tokens are valid for an appropriately short time (Figure 4-4).

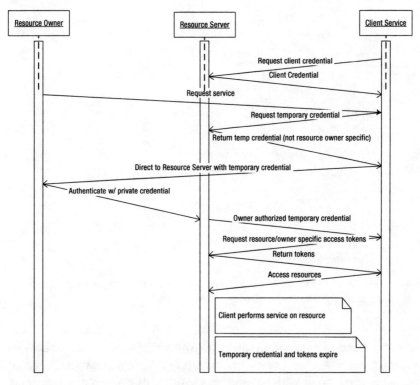

Figure 4-4. OAuth describes the exchange of client credentials, private credentials, and resource tokens.

When a server and a client offer OAuth, a resource owner's relationship with the client and her relationship with the server are strictly separated. This means that the resource owner is not obliged to trust the client for anything more than the service requested.

OpenID

OpenID[26] is a protocol based on OAuth that addresses a related but different use case. OAuth lets a resource owner securely grant access to a resource without revealing credentials to the client gaining access to the resource. OpenID lets a user securely log in to many sites using a single credential while sharing the credential only with a single authenticating site.

These two problems may seem different, but they are actually quite similar. Both cases involve a *user*, who authenticates with a *provider*, and a *client*, who relies on authentication with the provider rather than sharing the credentials of the user.

In OAuth terminology, the user is the resource owner. In OpenID terminology, the user is the end user. The provider in OpenID is the OpenID provider, which corresponds to the resource server in OAuth. The OAuth client corresponds to the OpenID relying party.

Similar to OAuth, relying parties (clients) register with OpenID providers (resource servers). End users register with OpenID providers and establish some form or credential, such as a shared secret user name and password.

When an end user wants access to a relying party (client), rather than offering credentials to the relying party, the end user offers indicates an OpenID provider to the relying party. The relying party sends the end user to the OpenID provider, and the end user authenticates with the OpenID provider. The OpenID provider then supplies a signed certificate to the relying party, and the end user is authenticated with the relying party. Like OAuth, the end user's credentials with the OpenID provider are never revealed to the relying party.

The only credential supplied by the end user is supplied to the OpenID provider. An interesting aspect of OpenID is that the method of authentication is not specified. It could be Basic Authentication, Digest Authentication, or some other form, such as biometry like a retinal scan or other type of certificate. This places some of the choice of the strength of security on the end user who chooses the OpenID provider.

---

[26] The OpenID Foundation publishes the OpenID standard in several separate documents that are available at http://openid.net/developers/specs/.

Security Assertion Markup Language (SAML)

OASIS approved SAML version 2 as a standard in March 2008.[27] SAML is a language designed to facilitate the exchange of security information between online business partners. Security information exchange makes life easier for cloud consumers and providers. Like OAuth and OpenID, SAML decreases the need for users to enter credentials to repeated sites.

SAML is a language as well as a protocol. Unlike OAuth and OpenID, SAML can be a tool for addressing more than one use case. The key SAML use case is related to the OAuth and OpenID use cases, but it also differs. The SAML authors consider web single sign-on (SSO) to be the most important use case for SAML.[28] SSO is an important user convenience. Using SSO, a user signs on and authenticates only once. Then the authentication is saved and reused so federated sites do not compel the user to sign on again. Everyone is familiar with SSO implemented for a single site. A user authenticates with a site, typically by entering a user name and a password. These credentials are stored in a cookie in a directory on the user's machine. The next time the user enters the site, the cookie is read, and the user signs on automatically.[29] That is fine for sites in a single DNS domain, but it does not allow for SSO among different DNS domains because DNS domains do not share cookies. SAML supports multidomain single sign-on (MDSSO), usually just called SSO.

Assertions are the heart of the SAML language. Most assertions assert something about a *subject,* which is some entity like an authenticable user or agent. An *asserting party* makes an assertion to a *relying party*. The asserting party is sometimes called a SAML *authority*. A SAML *requester* requests something from a SAML *responder*. A requester can be either an asserting party or a relying party.

In the SSO use case, SAML identifies an *identity provider* (idP) and a *service provider* (SP).

In a simple SSO scenario, an idP has partnered with an SP and has established a trust relationship. That means the SP is willing to accept the idP's assertions. In the scenario, a user authenticates with the idP and then is directed to the

---

[27] The official version of the standard is available for download on the OASIS site. See http://saml.xml.org/saml-specifications.

[28] "Security Assertion Markup Language (SAML) V2.0 Technical Overview" at www.oasis-open.org/committees/download.php/27819/sstc-saml-tech-overview-2.0-cd-02.pdf provides an excellent introduction to SAML including a discussion of the driving use cases. "SAML V2.0 Executive Overview" at www.oasis-open.org/committees/download.php/13525/sstc-saml-exec-overview-2.0-cd-01-2col.pdf is less detailed, but it provides a quick introduction.

[29] Of course, if someone other than the owner of the machine gets on, say some guy who picks up a laptop left in in a coffee shop, that person has access to all those sites.

partner SP for some service. The idP asserts to the SP that the user is authenticated and has certain properties, like special membership status with the idP. Since the SP trusts the idP, it accepts the assertion and creates a session for the user without requiring a login or authentication. This is called an *idP-initiated* SSO scenario.

SP-initiated scenarios are possible also. In that case, the user begins a conversation with the SP site. To authenticate the user, the SP will send the user to the idP with an authentication request, similar to sending the user to an OpenID provider in an OpenID scenario. The user authenticates with the idP, and the idP generates an assertion that the user is authenticated for the SP and the user is ready to enter the SP site.

SAML scenarios can become complex, involving several sites, and SAML can use both pure HTTP protocol or SOAP protocol for assertions and other communications. For privacy, SAML supports pseudonyms and transient, one-time identifiers, which are intended to minimize a service provider's knowledge of authenticated users. Also, when authentication is requested, the level of authentication can be indicated so that a user is not forced to go through all of the factors in a multifactor authentication or other strong authentication to access a less significant resource.

Security is also important in SAML. How does an SP know that an assertion is from the idP and not from an imposture that has intercepted an assertion and reused or spoofed it? SAML recommends using Public Key Infrastructure and HTTPS to prevent these kinds of attacks.

PUBLIC KEY INFRASTRUCTURE

Public Key Infrastructure (PKI) uses asymmetric encryption to send sensitive information safely over an insecure public network. Symmetric encryption uses the same key to both encode and decode a message. Asymmetric encryption uses a different key to encode and decode. One key is called a *public key*, and the other is the *private key*. Public and private keys are created in unique pairs. A message encoded with the public key can be decoded only with the matching private key. A message encoded with the private key can be decoded only with the corresponding public key. Ordinarily a user keeps his private key secret and posts his public key in a universally accessible place.

If someone wants to send a message that only the recipient can read, they can encode it with the recipient's public key, and only the recipient can decode the message with his private key. On the other hand, if someone wants to send something and she wants to ensure that the recipient is certain that the message is from her, she can encode it with her private key. Her recipient will know that if he can decode it with her public key, only she could have sent it. The two techniques can be combined into a message that is decodable only by the recipient and bears a signature that could come only from the sender.

The beauty of this arrangement is secret keys never have to be exchanged.

There is a network of commercial purveyors of public-private keys that support protocols like HTTPS that use PKI. These are called *Certificate authorities* (CAs).

Conclusion

Security and governance are important factors in cloud deployments. Business requires certainty and reliability. I have covered the application of governance standards and practices to cloud deployment and security standards that make the cloud safer and easier to use. These are challenges that the cloud must meet if it is to fulfill its promise of more efficient, convenient, and reliable computing.

Cloud Implementation
Implementation Architecture and Cloud-Related Technologies

The implementation of a cloud is not simple. In this chapter, I will cover building a cloud and examine some of the technologies and concepts used. Most of the attention will be on the concerns of the cloud provider. The discussion applies equally to private, public, community, and hybrid clouds. It also applies to IaaS, PaaS, and SaaS, although some aspects of implementation differ between types of service offerings.

The cloud offers simplicity, but the cloud is not at all simple. It may be the single most complicated construction in human history. The moving parts of the cloud are the electrons, pulses of light, and electromagnetic waves coursing through computers, metal cables, glass fibers, and space. These parts are as near to uncountable as anything created by human beings. The number of engineers building the cloud, the lines of code, and the dollars eventually spent on building out the cloud is unknown, probably unknowable, but is unquestionably immense.

At the same time, the construction of the cloud depends on simplicity. It is too complicated to grasp as anything but an abstraction. The cloud is usable and effective because it hides its complexity. It is called the *cloud* because, for decades, when designers wanted to show a network made up of many interconnected nodes, instead of drawing each node and each connection, they scribbled a cloud. The scribble was an abstraction to hide all the nodes and connections that were present in reality but were distractions from the discussion.

The cloud abstraction has acquired great power. The notion that one can connect to the cloud and accomplish work without knowing what it is, where it is, or how it works has great attraction, but underneath the simple abstraction, there is a lot to be explained.

Cloud implementation is the root of complexity. The most significant differentiator between cloud implementations is scale. Although the implementations share similar architectures, a SaaS application with millions of users like Google's search engine will not be implemented in the same way as a specialized service expected to have only a few hundred subscribers. Despite enormous differences, all cloud implementations follow the same general patterns.

Functional and Management Interfaces

Every cloud service has two kinds of interfaces. Sometimes services combine the two into a single interface, blend them in various ways, or even further subdivide them, but logically separating the interfaces helps analyze what they do and what is required of them.

All computer users are familiar with one kind of interface to services, cloud or not cloud. This is the interface they interact with as they type into word processors and spreadsheets, read and write e-mail, surf the Net, play games, watch videos, and do their jobs by interacting with various applications—in other words, the interface they use to do all the usual things that are done with computers.

However, users do not interact with computers only in this way. Computers must be set up, monitored, and maintained as well as used. Users upgrade their video cards, add memory or a new disk, install service packs, upgrade the operating system, and perform many other tasks that divert them from the work and entertainment for which they acquired the computer. These tasks control, maintain, and improve the operation of the computer, but they are not services themselves. They only facilitate the real services.

The functional and management interfaces represent these two modes of interaction with a computer. The management interface consists of all the ways that we interact with our computers to prepare them for use and later for maintenance and tuning. Often, the management interface to a PC uses mechanisms that differ from the usual functional interface tools such as keyboards, mice, touch pads, and screens. Managing a PC can involve opening the case and plugging in cables and cards, perhaps extracting and replacing chips, and even heating up a soldering iron and reattaching a broken connection.[1] Other times, management is similar to the functional interface when it involves running programs such as disk defragmenters or memory checkers. The distinction is not in the artifacts that implement the interfaces. The functional interface is for performing computing work. The management interface is for preparing, maintaining, maintaining, and monitoring the computer for its intended work.

The management and functional interface distinction applies to any service.

Think of an automobile as a service that transports the consumer (driver) from place to place. The steering wheel and pedals that the driver uses to drive the auto (consume the transportation service) are elements of the auto's functional interface. When mechanics raise the hood and make adjustments or replace parts, they use the management interface of the auto.

Consumers usually want the functional interface to be as rich and deep as possible to maximize the value of the service, but the management interface is another story. Although some drivers enjoy lifting the hood and doing their own maintenance, most prefer leaving the wrenches to the mechanics. Consumers typically want to see as little of the management interface as possible.

Cloud services also have functional and management interfaces (Figure 5-1). Ordinarily, the functional interface is the exclusive province of the consumer. The consumer may even insist that the provider have restricted access to the functional aspect of the service for security or governance. It should not be

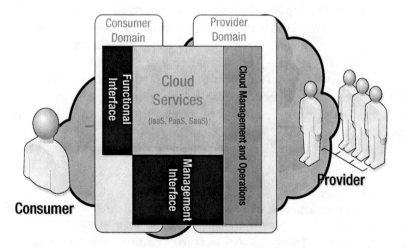

Figure 5-1. The consumer uses both the functional and management interfaces.

[1] Soldering irons really are still used occasionally. For example, instructions for re-soldering a laptop power port appear on YouTube. See www.youtube.com/watch?v=wTQcy6TVH80.

surprising that functional cloud interfaces are very similar to the functional interfaces of on-premises systems. Cloud providers often strive to supply the same user experience and deliver services identical to those that users get from the functional interfaces of on-premises systems.

Cloud management interfaces often are quite different from their on-premises equivalent. The cloud provider supplies a management interface to the consumer for requesting and modifying services. For SaaS, the management interface can be simple. At its simplest, there may be no management interface at all. Although we may not often think of the Google search engine as a SaaS service, it is a software service that we do not pay for directly. There is no contract or authorization. Google does all the maintenance behind the scenes, and the user interface is through a browser that users already have installed on their computers. There is nothing for the management interface to do, and most consumers are happy about it.

Other SaaS applications may have more elaborate management interfaces. If the SaaS service is unavailable to outsiders, the consumer will have to use the management interface to designate in some way the users who are to have access. They may need to have passwords or other credentials issued. Billing and service level agreements (SLAs) may have to be agreed to.[2] Perhaps consumer-specific policies have to be established. Databases sometimes need to be populated. These are all parts of the management of the system.

However, since consumers often subscribe to SaaS services to avoid the maintenance associated with on-premises applications, SaaS providers usually make an effort to minimalize and simplify management requirements. One way of doing this is to design the management interface so that the consumer only submits a business description of the demands, specific features, and policies needed for the service. The service provider takes it from there, translating the business description into technical requirements and implementing an appropriate system. For example, the consumer might request a 100–500 user service desk, all user information stored within Swedish national boundaries, and user authentication based on the consumer's LDAP directory.[3] The user interface for this could be a form with a few check

---

[2] A service level agreement (SLA) is an agreement between a service provider and consumer that sets targets and thresholds for delivering the service. Service level agreements usually state penalties and incentives for meeting or missing these targets and thresholds.

[3] Lightweight Directory Access Protocol (LDAP) is a standard for storing and maintaining a distributed directory of information. Usually, organizations use LDAP to store user account names, e-mail addresses, desk locations, and the like. LDAP is an IETF standard; RFC 4510, http://tools.ietf.org/html/rfc4510, is the latest version, published in 2006. LDAP is a simplified version of the X.500 directory standard from Comité Consultatif International Téléphonique et Télégraphique (CCITT). Active Directory is the Microsoft implementation of LDAP.

boxes and blanks to fill in. The provider translates this high-level information into numbers of servers, amounts of memory, database configurations, and so on. As long as the provider chooses a technical implementation that meets the consumer's performance, governance, and security requirements, SLAs will be met, and the consumer will be satisfied.

At the other end of the spectrum, IaaS providers have a somewhat different challenge. Simplicity is desirable in any interface, but simplicity may trade off with power to address the users' requirements. IaaS consumers have precise technical requirements with complex representations, and their decisions derive from engineering analysis. Their engineers have translated business requirements into technical implementations. Therefore, IaaS consumers want management interfaces that will instantiate the infrastructure precisely as they have specified it. An IaaS management interface would not satisfy many IaaS consumers if it fulfilled a request for a server running Red Hat Linux version 4 (RHL4) with one running Windows 2008. The IaaS consumer probably chose RHL4 to meet a specific requirement. In comparison, a SaaS or PaaS consumer probably will not care which operating system underpins a service as long as the functionality is right. Consequently, IaaS management interfaces are naturally more complex and low-level than SaaS interfaces, although they may be simpler for the provider to build because detailed specifications require less automated intelligence to implement.

NIST Cloud Implementation Architecture

NIST divides the architecture of a cloud implementation into the service, resource abstraction, and physical layers.[4] This architecture will be the basis for the rest of this chapter.

Service Layer

In the NIST cloud architecture, the service consumer interacts with the service layer through functional and management interfaces. The service layer represents the layer in which the service provider exposes services to its consumers (Figure 5-2). Depending on what those services are, the exposure will be different.

Cloud providers often build SaaS services in their own independent clouds. Alternatively, they can be built on a PaaS service or directly on an IaaS service.

---

[4] National Institute of Standards and Technology (NIST) is an agency of the United States Department of Commerce. NIST is charged with promoting innovation through metrology, standards, and technology.

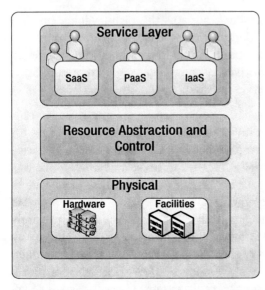

Figure 5-2. The provider architecture is divisible into three layers.

Similarly, a PaaS service can be independent, or it can use an IaaS service for its physical implementation. The SaaS, PaaS, and IaaS distinctions are not strict. A predominantly PaaS service such as Windows Azure can provide IaaS-like services to host applications developed on the Azure platform. Amazon's EC2 IaaS service assumes a platform-like role when service consumers instantiate Amazon-supplied Amazon machine images (AMIs) that contain development stacks.

IaaS Service Layer

The functional interface to an IaaS service is analogous to interacting with the physical infrastructure. Individual machines, storage units, and networks are all visible to the service consumer. The visible entities are usually virtual; that is, virtualization simulates devices that are not physical devices in a datacenter. However, in some circumstances, the service consumer may interact with real rather than virtual entities. An arrangement like this forgoes the flexibility and opportunities for efficiency offered by virtualization but may occasionally be necessary. For example, governance or security may require physical separation of resources used by certain processes. In this case, the service provider could offer a management interface that is uniform for both physical and virtual entities, although the behind-the-scenes activity may be quite different.

The functional interface to IaaS is the operating system of the machine and whatever applications are installed on the instantiated virtual entities. The functional interface to the service is largely dependent on installation decisions of the consumer.

Amazon EC2 has several options for managing its service, including both SOAP and REST APIs and a command-line interface (CLI). Of these, the AWS Management Console is the simplest to use. The management console is a graphic browser interface that supports creating instances of a wide variety of images ranging from a stripped-down Linux image to elaborate development and application stacks. From the console, the user can launch new instances and start, stop, and terminate existing instances.[5] Other management activities include setting up security and preparing for access to the instantiated entities. From the same console, the user can perform similar management activities for other Amazon services such as its Relational Database Service (RDS) and S3 storage service.

The functional interface to EC2 will be familiar to on-premises computer users. For example, if you create a simple instance of a Linux machine in Amazon EC2, you can connect to the instance via a secure telnet session such as Secure Shell (SSH). SSH uses asymmetric encryption with public and private key pairs. If the user does not have a cryptographic public-private key pair, the user can request a key pair from the management console before launching an instance. EC2 records only the public half of the key pairs it generates. The private half belongs to the consumer. When the consumer launches an instance from the management console, the console requests a public key before instantiating the instance. Later, when the consumer wants to work with the instance, the user supplies a private key to SSH before connecting. If the private key matches with the previously submitted public key, the user is given access to the instance.[6]

Note the intricate exchange between the management interface (the console) and the functional interface (SSH). The consumer passes a public key to the management interface. The management interface has no knowledge of the private key. No one can unlock the instance without the private key, which the consumer keeps secret, even from the cloud provider. The private key–public key mechanism neatly isolates the functional interface from the provider.

Separation of managerial and functional cloud interfaces can aid the security and governance of cloud installations. A fundamental problem with cloud

---

[5] A stopped EC2 instance is not running but still exists and is restartable. A terminated instance no longer exists and is not restartable.

[6] You can think of the public key as a padlock and the private key as the padlock key. The consumer gives EC2 the open padlock but not the key. EC2 snaps the padlock shut on the instance. After the padlock is shut, only the holder of the padlock key can unlock the instance. Since EC2 does not have the key, it cannot get to the instance.

security and governance is that a cloud provider is an outside party. In a service on the consumer premises, the consumer has complete control of physical and network access to the infrastructure that supports the service. If necessary, the IT department can disconnect the network, shut down the machine, and even store it in a locked closet. In addition, enterprise management has control of IT personnel. Management can run background checks, obtain personal bonds, and exercise strict access controls. All this is to guarantee with near complete certainty that no one has tampered with critical systems.

For a cloud IaaS installation, that level of certainty is hard to attain because no matter how hardened the logical security, the cloud provider's organization and infrastructure are not under the same control as the consumer's own premises. One element in reducing the uncertainty is to separate management interfaces from functional interfaces.

Management interfaces are a conversation between the cloud provider and consumer and therefore must be open to the provider. The functional interface is a conversation between the consumer and the service from the cloud. Although there may be special occasions when the provider must have access to the functional interface, there is no general reason for the provider to access the functional interface. Thus, cloud services in which the consumer controls the provider's access to the functional interface shield the consumer's business from the provider.

The EC2 public key–private key mechanism reduces the opportunity for mischievous provider-side access to the instance. In on-premises computing, operating systems lack security when first installed, which the administrator later sets up. Starting without security is acceptable within the safe haven of an enterprise datacenter, but it is not acceptable in an environment where the instance may be exposed to a world of intruders, worms, malware, and the unverified reliability of provider personnel.[7]

The telnet session is a typical Unix/Linux command-line session. The experience is the equivalent of signing on to a computer with a Linux operating system on your desk. At that point, if you have root privileges, you can access most of the resources of the system. If you instantiate an instance with a Windows operating system, the experience is different but equivalent. Instead of a telnet session, you would probably launch Windows Remote Desktop to log into the instance. The Remote Desktop interface is a graphic rather than

---

[7] This does not imply that cloud providers have been irresponsible or unreliable. The point is that a cloud implementation has vulnerabilities that are not present in systems implemented by the consumer on the consumer premises.

a telnet command-line interface, but the functional interface is the same: access to the resources typically exposed by the operating system.

For IaaS, the functional interface to an infrastructure instance is typically the operating system of the instance. This applies to entities like virtual switches or virtual disk volumes as well as virtual computers. An IaaS service is usually a means for delivering other services. In that case, the functional interface of an IaaS instance is likely to be used to manage a service that is implemented by the IaaS instances. An example of this is a SaaS service implemented on an IaaS service from another provider (Figure 5-3). Managing the SaaS service may involve accessing the operating systems of the virtual machines that the SaaS runs on. This may not be the most elegant way of managing the SaaS service, but it may be expedient.

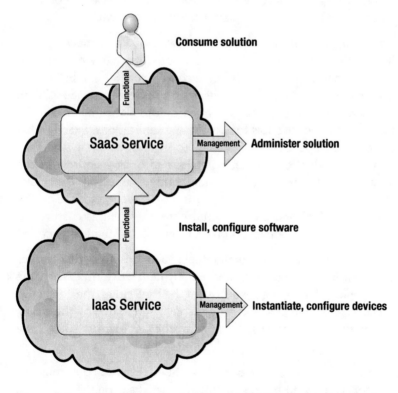

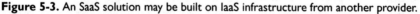

Figure 5-3. An SaaS solution may be built on IaaS infrastructure from another provider.

PaaS Service Layer

A PaaS provider exposes platform services to consumer, often in addition to the underlying infrastructure. A PaaS provider might provide a relational database service that consumers can configure and use to store and retrieve relational data. Unlike an IaaS consumer installing a relational database on a virtual machine in an IaaS cloud, the PaaS consumer is not aware of the virtual or physical machines that support a PaaS database. They may know very little about the database except how to access it. The PaaS provider may also supply inter-process communication buses, security, user interface modules, language stacks, HTTP servers, web services, and potentially many other facilities that consumers can include in their applications. The consumer has access to these services for applications, but they are spared the burden of installation and low-level maintenance and administration.

The consumer can usually create applications on their own site and upload them to the PaaS cloud. They might choose to use their own development tools, or the PaaS provider may provide a software development kit (SDK) that the consumer can (or perhaps must) use to develop applications on their own premises and upload to the PaaS platform for deployment.

In another variation, the consumer uses the PaaS cloud as a development platform. The functional interface of a PaaS service often exposes a graphic integrated development environment (IDE) such as Visual Studio, Eclipse, or the provider's proprietary tools. The consumer uses the supplied IDE to develop applications on the resources provided by the platform. Within the IDE, the consumer has a set of tools for developing applications. Exactly what the consumer can do depends on the set of tools and resources the PaaS provides, but typically, they can write, compile, and deploy entirely in the environment supplied by the cloud provider and running on the cloud provider's infrastructure. Often the applications developed in the IDE can be seamlessly tested and deployed on the cloud consumer's infrastructure, or the consumer downloads the application to run on their own infrastructure.

Using PaaS, the consumer can develop and deploy applications with a smaller up-front investment in a development and deployment platform. When the applications are deployed using the resources of the PaaS cloud, the consumer also avoids the overhead of maintaining the resources provided by the cloud, but, unlike SaaS, they still are responsible for the applications they have deployed.

Alternatively, the PaaS provider may provide an SDK that the consumer can use to develop applications on-premises, upload to the PaaS on the provider's platform, and deploy on-premises. All are possible platforms for deployment. In yet another variation, the consumer develops applications.

PaaS may be considered the most versatile of the cloud service models because it shares characteristics and capabilities with both IaaS and SaaS models. A PaaS service may expose some aspects of virtual infrastructure, and it also exposes platform elements such as relational databases that are very close to being full-fledged software applications.

SaaS Service Layer

For SaaS services, the functional interface is almost all that is visible. The service provider configures the platform and infrastructure. The consumer uses the application. In this way, SaaS functional interfaces are as varied as the services that SaaS provides. The managerial interface offered to the user varies also. One of the advantages offered by SaaS implementations is the reduction of management tasks compared to on-premises implementations. For example, the SaaS service provider applies patches and performs software upgrades. In addition, the user is not bothered with system maintenance and tuning in response to varying loads. Consequently, the consumer managerial interface can be limited to high-level management tasks such as adding new users, changing user roles, modifying workflows, and performing other business-oriented administration tasks.

Resource Abstraction Layer

Abstraction is at the center of cloud computing. It is a basic concept that makes cloud computing work. The cloud separates the consumer of a service from the implementation of the service. Users see the results delivered by the service but not the environment that produces the result they consume.

The resource abstraction layer isolates the user from the physical implementation. As you will see in later sections of this chapter, datacenters are complex entities filled with thousands and hundreds of thousands of individual computers and other devices connected into a single entity we call the *cloud*. But cloud consumers are exposed only to the abstraction that the cloud provider has chosen to expose. This may be the collection of virtual infrastructure exposed by IaaS, the platform exposed by PaaS, or the software exposed by SaaS.

In a traditional on-premises infrastructure, a hands-on CIO can go to the datacenter and count the servers in the room to gauge the activity of the department. If the IT department has moved to a virtualized model, the site uses logical entities that behave like servers but exist only as a collection of processes running on the physical servers in the datacenter. The number of virtual servers running applications may exceed the number of physical servers.

The hands-on CIO can still count physical servers, but she is likely to under-estimate the productivity of her department if she relies solely on her physical count. To true up her report, she must incorporate some abstract measure of department productivity that compensates for virtual servers. If the implementation further evolves to running on a public or private off-the-premises cloud, there will be few physical servers to count, and the CIO must develop reports that are based on abstract measures of productivity rather than the physical environment.

This increase in abstraction is a reason for relying on standards. Counting servers has direct and transparent simplicity because a count of physical servers is easy to check. Comparing this year's count with the count from last year is a reasonable way to check the growth of the department. As computing becomes more abstract, transparency tends to decline, and reports can become hard to verify and compare because abstractions shift easily and subtly differ.

For example, if there is a question about the number of physical machines in use in a local datacenter that does not use virtualization, the CIO can send someone to count them or go herself if she is so inclined. When virtualization enters the environment, there are no longer physical objects to count, and definitions begin to distort and overlap. A count of virtual machines could mean the number of running machines or the number of distinct images that could be instantiated or yet something else. And because virtual machines are so much easier to stand up and the resources are so much less than for physical machines, starting a virtual machine is not as significant as commissioning a physical machine. Some virtual instances are the equivalent of a physical machine but not all. Maybe counting services or running applications would be more meaningful, but exactly what is a running service? Or an application? IT departments acquire sophisticated management solutions to track services and applications. Even more complicated, in a cloud elastic computing environment, new virtual machines can be launched by the provider, not the consumer. Although the CIO may be happy with the ready access to resources at a desirable cost, an obvious inventory task has escalated into a project!

Undoubtedly, there are simpler ways to provide the CIO with a straightforward measure of her department, but the point is that managing a system that is no longer tied to a concrete set of on-premises devices requires equally abstract management techniques. Different people define abstractions like *running service* or *virtual machine* in different ways for different reasons. Without agreements on concepts like this, management is difficult. Standards help corral the shifting abstractions by limiting the possible variations and providing consistent terminology. Thus, standards become an important instrument for mutual understanding and transparent management.

Cloud computing places formal and often physical barriers between the consumer and the hardware that powers the service. The user is isolated from lower levels of the computing stack by an abstraction. The abstraction eliminates inessential elements from the user's view of and access to the service. The details of the abstraction depend on the type of service. An IaaS service abstracts the physical hardware out of the consumer's view and replaces it with an abstraction that describes an infrastructure that the provider has simulated to meet the consumers' requests. The simulated infrastructure usually is a set of formalized operating systems that behave as if they were operating on the hardware the consumer has requested.

PaaS abstracts away both the hardware and the operating system and discloses only the elements of the development platform that the service provider is offering to the consumer. SaaS abstractions are on an even higher level; the consumer sees only the user interfaces applications and none of the infrastructure. Everyone uses search engines like Google, but very few have any conception of the software behind those searches and the vast infrastructure that powers the searches.

Abstractions are beneficial to both the consumer and the provider. Abstraction simplifies and streamlines the user experience by eliminating distractions that are not central to the user's mission. What benefit would it be to the average user to know how Google executes a search or the hardware that powers it? On the provider side, abstraction gives the provider the flexibility to implement services efficiently. If an IaaS provider had to move in a physical server from the warehouse and plug it in to the network when a consumer requested it, cloud computing would be little more efficient than computing on the consumer premises, and becoming a cloud provider would not be the opportunity it is today.

The resource abstraction layer implements these abstractions. The requirement for the abstraction layer is to provide an interface to the consumer that is appropriate to the service offered, transform the requests from the interface to a form usable by lower levels, and pass the outputs from the lower levels back to the consumer.

Cloud providers often rely on virtualization for this flexibility. Virtualization decouples processes launched on the infrastructure from individual machines in the physical infrastructure. At the IaaS level, with proper configuration, a virtual machine created for a subscriber to the IaaS service can run on many different physical machines, and a single physical machine can host many virtual machines. Using this flexibility, the cloud provider is able to optimize the allocation of activity to the physical machines, usually blades in a rack. As processors approach their maximum capacity, virtual machines can be migrated to processors with spare capacity.

Virtualization presents flexibility in other ways. For example, the memory available in the underlying physical infrastructure limits the memory to a virtual machine. Let's say the physical machine has 32 gigabytes of memory. A virtual machine may be allocated a much lower number, say, 2 gigabytes. The 2-gigabyte limit is administrative, not absolute, if the virtual machine is able to address memory beyond 2 gigabytes and free memory is available. Administrative limits can be controlled programmatically. Providers can take advantage of this to provide services that expand automatically to meet needs.

This is dramatically different from a physical machine that is limited to the memory installed in the physical box. When the load dictates that a physical computer needs more memory, following good management practices, a person or process issues a request for a change. In the best circumstances, the change is pre-approved; in the worst circumstances, a change control board has to approve the change. After the change approval, a technician installs a new memory module. All this procedure is necessary because unless the box is a high-end enterprise server or mainframe, a technician will have to stop the physical machine and open the case to make the change. This disruptive activity has to be managed. In the best-run departments with expedited procedures, this is still a several-hour process. In contrast, a virtualized system can be designed to respond in milliseconds to a memory deficiency instead of several hours involving several people.

In a conventional, on-premises, nonvirtualized environment, services with high performance and availability requirements must run on hardware sized for peak loads with extra capacity to avoid slowdowns and outages. When hardware is sized for maximum load, resources are often idle more than half the total up time. This is an egregious waste.

Physical Layer

The equipment and facilities that execute cloud services make up the physical layer in the NIST cloud architecture and consist of computing units that execute instructions, communications gear and input and output channels that route messages between computers and connect the cloud to the outside world, and storage units that cache and preserve data. In a cloud datacenter, the equipment is both familiar and exotic. Clouds do little if anything that has not been familiar for decades, but they perform at a scale and level of performance that makes everything they do seem magnified and transformed into something foreign.

Cloud providers are building datacenters of staggering computing power using unique designs to gain efficiency and enable increasing size. The challenge to the cloud provider is simple: execute a huge number of instructions in as short a time as possible to run as many programs as fast as possible—the same problem that has faced every computing system designer since Charles Babbage.[8] Datacenters face several problems that go beyond executing more and more instructions in shorter and shorter times. But in pursuit of that goal, many other problems arise such as energy consumption, the closely related issue of cooling, network bandwidth and speed, and massive data management.

Energy

Executing all those instructions takes energy—enormous quantities of energy. The quantity of energy used by datacenters has been increasing every year. In 2007, the EPA reported that electricity usage for servers and datacenters had doubled since 2000 and had reached the point that it was similar to the amount consumed by the U.S. transportation manufacturing industry (the manufacture of cars, trucks, aircraft, and ships).

Cloud providers have pressing incentives to reduce energy consumption. Energy is a major cost that profoundly affects cloud datacenter profitability. In addition, for civic reasons, many of the large cloud providers are committed to green computing and reduced energy consumption.

Power Usage Effectiveness

Power Usage Effectiveness (PUE) is the measure commonly used today for determining the energy efficiency of datacenters. PUE measures the ratio of energy used for running computers, network equipment, and storage compared to the total energy consumed by the datacenter. If all the energy goes to running computers, the ratio would be 1.0. If the PUE exceeds 1.0, it indicates that some energy is going to overhead rather than computing. The EPA study mentioned earlier estimated the average PUE for U.S. datacenters to be 2.0. In other words, for every watt that powers computing gear in a typical datacenter, another watt goes to overhead.

---

[8] Babbage's writings on nineteenth-century manufacturing are a fascinating sidelight to cloud datacenters. Many of the problems and solutions Babbage proposed for Victorian manufacturing are analogous to the problems of computer architecture. From Babbage's analysis of factory procedures, it is no surprise that he invented the first programmable computer. As a software architect, I find his *Economy of Machinery and Manufactures* fascinating. Chapter 23 discusses what amounts to thread synchronization in needle manufacture. (Absolutely no pun intended.) Babbage's discussions on factory organization show many of the same modes of thinking that are required in cloud implementation design. See www.gutenberg.org/ebooks/4238.html.gen.

Recently constructed cloud datacenters have done much better. Google reports that its datacenters in the third quarter of 2011 had a trailing 12-month average PUE of 1.14, considerably better than the EPA projection of 1.2 for state-of-the-art facilities.[9]

Google's accomplishment is impressive, but it is not alone; many datacenters have made progress in energy efficiency by concentrating on several areas.

Cooling

Much of electrical energy that flows into datacenters escapes as heat, which is lost energy. If the heat is not properly dissipated, temperatures rise too high, errors begin to occur, operation becomes unreliable, and equipment can eventually be damaged. The traditional solution is to use computer room air conditioning (CRAC) systems and chillers.[10] These methods increase energy consumption.

A number of alternative approaches have appeared. The simplest step toward cooling efficiency is to cool less and let the temperature in the datacenter rise. Traditionally, datacenter managers cooled the center to a comfortable temperature for humans or even lower, expecting cool rooms would have fewer equipment failures and prolong equipment life. In the last five years, progressive datacenter managers have challenged these temperature guidelines and have allowed datacenter temperatures to increase without ill effect. The American Society of Heating, Refrigerating, and Air-Conditioning Engineers (ASHRAE) released guidelines in 2011 for datacenter temperatures that permit temperatures greater than 80 degrees Fahrenheit.[11]

Another technique for making the datacenter more energy efficient is to use the surrounding environment for cooling. In other words, open the windows and let in cooler air. Datacenters can be located and designed to take maximum advantage of climate and local features to reduce cooling requirements. An extreme example is a roofless datacenter where the computing equipment is in modular weatherproof units similar to shipping containers.

Another approach to efficient cooling is systems that pump water cooled by the environment through the datacenter to reduce the temperature in strategic locations like a chiller. The water can pass through heat exchangers

---

[9] www.google.com/about/datacenters/inside/efficiency/power-usage.html

[10] Chillers are cooling systems that use chilled liquid, often water, for cooling.

[11] ASHRAE Technical Committee (TC) 9.9 Mission Critical Facilities, Technology Spaces, and Electronic Equipment [2011]. http://tc99.ashraetcs.org/documents/ASHRAE%20 Whitepaper%20-%202011%20Thermal%20Guidelines%20for%20Data%20Processing%20 Environments.pdf

to reduce its temperature and be used again, and the recovered heat can be diverted to other purposes. A datacenter in Finland uses cold seawater as its cooling agent and uses recovered heat from the seawater to warm buildings and residential hot water.[12] Locations that do not have a ready supply of cold water use evaporation in cooling towers to cool the water. Datacenters are occasionally criticized for depleting fresh-water supplies. Some systems avoid excessive use of water by recycling the water so that the system is closed and water intake is minimal. In addition, the cooling water does not have to be potable, avoiding energy used for purification and decreasing fresh water depletion.

Power Conditioning

Another area where energy is lost in the datacenter is "power conditioning." The voltage of the electrical current that flows on computer circuit boards is much lower than the voltage in the transmission lines to the datacenter. A typical home computer has a power supply that steps down the 120-volt current in household circuits to 20 volts and rectifies the 60-hertz alternating current to 0-hertz direct current. Much of the heat radiating from a running desktop comes from this power supply. A simple step to managing this energy loss is to locate power supplies where they contribute least to the heat load for the air conditioning or chillers.

Typically, power is stepped down and conditioned in several stages before it arrives at the blades in the racks. Each transformation releases energy in the form of heat. Often, reducing the number of transformations helps reduce the energy loss.

Location

Cloud datacenters tend to be located in areas where energy costs are low. Perhaps more important, energy supplies must be stable as well as economical to support the level of reliability datacenters require. The decision to place a datacenter is complicated. The climate and thermal resources like cold seawater or moderate temperatures and steady winds for cooling are factors in addition to stable and cheap energy supplies. Proximity to consumers is a complex factor. Some jurisdictions, like some in the European Union, require that some types of data not cross national boundaries. For resiliency in the face of disasters that might disable or destroy a datacenter, centers are often

---

[12] Miller, Rich. 2011. Sea Cooled Data Center Heats Homes in Helsinki. Data Center Knowledge. www.datacenterknowledge.com/archives/2011/09/06/sea-cooled-data-center-heats-homes-in-helsinki/

geographically separated. The quality of the communications infrastructure is also important. Cloud datacenters must have a communications infrastructure that will support their bandwidth requirements. This means they must have high-bandwidth connections to the Internet backbones and to their customers with private connections. If this network infrastructure is not already present, it has to be built, adding to the cost of the center. All these factors must be balanced in choosing a datacenter location.

Cloud Datacenter as Computer

Cloud datacenters are built with hundreds of thousands of multicore servers, each core executing billions of instructions per second. The total number of instructions executed per second in a large datacenter is in the mind-numbing trillions. But amassing the capacity for trillions of instructions per second is only a single step toward powering a cloud. The trillions of instructions have to be coordinated and directed, and the processors must have access to data storage and network bandwidth. The resource and abstraction layer is charged with identifying tasks, starting programs to execute, and allocating the needed resources, but a lower layer is equally important. That layer is the plumbing that supplies the processors and other resources that execute instructions.

If we look at the problem from a high level, there are two basic stratagems for doing more in computing: do the job faster on a single processor, or chop the job into segments (a process known as *sharding*) and execute in parallel on many processors. The first method, executing a single thread faster, is the easier of the two strategies, but invariably, efforts to use faster and more powerful processors meet limits. Scaling up clouds requires processing in parallel, and lots of it. This can be done in various ways. It may involve a single operating system for many processors and many cooperating operating systems, each with a few processors.

Cloud Datacenter Loads

Parallelization is a key strategy in supercomputing. In fact, large cloud datacenters resemble supercomputers, although their loads differ and they function under different constraints.

The load on a cloud datacenter varies with the types of services. A homogeneous SaaS provider, a search engine for example, performs the same tasks repeatedly. They can optimize the search process to slice the job into many small pieces and efficiently engage an optimum number of processors. This is similar to a supercomputer that runs a limited set of programs to perform a specific task. A PaaS or IaaS provider will probably have a much more heterogeneous load. These providers have little control over the programs executed on their cloud, and the load will be less predictable. In this case, the design goal will be coarser grained: to pass virtual machines to and from different processors, vary the number of processors executing the virtual machines, and dynamically allocate resources such as storage, memory, and network bandwidth.

Datacenter Networks

The inevitable decision to pursue a parallel processing strategy in the datacenter implies that passing instructions and data from processor to processor will be critical in making the cloud perform. The time it takes to decide where to execute a job and how to get it there, and then to move the data through intermediate points, can easily overshadow the time to execute the instructions in the job. The ideal is to pass any job from any processor in the datacenter to any other processor in the datacenter nearly instantaneously. That ideal may seem relatively easy to accomplish when looking at two processors on the same motherboard, but optimizing connectivity between arbitrary numbers of nodes in a network is a classic networking problem. The solution to the problem is always a compromise based on the requirements and the capabilities of the available equipment. Choosing the best solution to this networking problem is as critical to success of a cloud implementation as the speed and number of processors in the datacenter.

Both supercomputers and cloud datacenters have to solve this problem. Cloud datacenters often act as if they are supercomputers, although datacenter nodes are not coupled as closely, and there are other differences in the implementation. The connections between processors in a single parallel computer are called the *interconnect* rather than a network. Supercomputer interconnect design has influenced datacenter network design. Consequently, in a cloud datacenter the distinction between networks and interconnects is blurred.

One of the differences between supercomputers and cloud datacenters has been that supercomputer interconnects are based on proprietary buses and protocols, designed specifically to meet supercomputer requirements for high performance and bandwidth. Datacenters reflect their origin as LANs and tend to use Ethernet equipment and protocols. However, in recent lists of the fastest supercomputers, close to half use Gigabit Ethernet–based interconnect protocols, further blurring the distinction between supercomputers and cloud datacenters. [13]

---

[13] http://i.top500.org/stats (November 2011 list). 100 Gigabit Ethernet is the fastest version of Ethernet, which will be discussed in a later chapter. The TOP500 statistics do not indicate whether Gigabit, 10 Gigabit, 40 Gigabit, or 100 Gigabit Ethernet was used.

Grids, Supercomputers, and Datacenters

Grids, supercomputers, and datacenters that act as a single computer are three different ways of managing and coordinating the processing power. Each has advantages.

Grids

Grids are also similar to cloud datacenters. Grids have been defined in different ways. Generally, grids are a mixed and loosely coupled set of independent computers harnessed to perform coordinated computing tasks. The computers in a grid may be geographically distant and in different administrative domains.

The SETI@home project, one of the first large grids, is a well-known example of one kind of grid.[14] The Search for Extraterrestrial Intelligence (SETI) project collects massive quantities of signal data from radio telescopes spread all over the world. The data is not purposely acquired for SETI research. Instead, it is gleaned and reused from the telescopes' regular research activities, which are seldom directed toward SETI.

The SETI@home project retrieves the telescope data for analysis, divides it into small packages, and distributes it to a grid. Each node in the grid searches its data package for patterns revealing extraterrestrial intelligence and returns its results to the central SETI@home system for further processing. The proverbial search for a needle in a haystack understates the scale of the task, but SETI@home confronts the scale problem by reducing it to many small jobs.

The SETI@home grid is composed of volunteer machines connected to the Internet. Volunteers download the SETI@home software, often to a home personal computer, and receive data for analysis from SETI@home. The SETI@home software runs only when the volunteer computer is idle. When the analysis is complete, the SETI@home software returns the results to SETI@home where it combines with analysis from a myriad of other home computers. Typical HTTP connections transfer the data.[15]

SETI@home is an example of a loosely coupled grid of heterogeneous systems. It harvests unused CPU cycles from thousands of volunteer machines to perform a difficult task at low cost and high speed. This is especially appropriate for a project like SETI, which might have difficulty securing backing

---

[14] http://setiathome.ssl.berkeley.edu/

[15] Hypertext Transfer Protocol (HTTP) will be discussed in much more detail later.

for a more conventional approach. A supercomputer or a cloud implementation might be faster and use less energy, but the cost for SETI is minimal. [16]

Not all grids are like the SETI@home grid. The Conficker botnet is a different example. Conficker is a malware worm that uses infected machines to perform questionable tasks like mass spam distribution and denial-of-service attacks.[17] The infected machines act as a loosely coupled grid. At one point, Conficker was described as the largest cloud service in the world.[18]

Commercial grids tend to be more tightly coupled than the ad hoc grids described previously. They are usually designed to harness the computing resources of an enterprise more effectively. New services can be rolled out on the grid and distributed over many physical devices. Tighter coupling transfers tasks from node to node in the grid. As coupling becomes tighter and resource allocation becomes more complex, grids and cloud datacenters are less distinguishable. Clouds can be implemented on grids without the full effort required for a large-scale cloud datacenter.

Generally, grids, datacenters, and supercomputers form a continuum. Grids are heterogeneous and loosely coupled. Datacenters are less heterogeneous and more tightly coupled. Supercomputers are most homogenous and most tightly coupled. Grids have distinct, separate operating systems on each node, and the grid software is minimally aware of the characteristics of the operating systems on other nodes. A cloud datacenter usually has separate operating systems on each node, but they operate in concert with other operating systems in the center and share resources like storage. Supercomputers resemble cloud data centers, but they have one operating system, and all the resources connect to a single high-speed fabric instead of a network. Even this distinction is blurry because supercomputers have begun to use high-speed network technology for their fabric and datacenters have begun to use networks that resemble supercomputer fabric.

---

[16] SETI@home has been criticized for its energy usage. http://setiathome.berkeley.edu/forum_thread.php?id=56450&sort=6 provides a taste of some of the controversy. It may use more resources than an energy-efficient data center performing the same job.

[17] A denial-of-service (DOS) attack bombards a site with input exceeding the capacity of the site. The overwhelmed site fails to respond to requests, denying service to legitimate requestors.

[18] www.networkworld.com/community/node/58829. Since that report in 2010, Conficker has been controlled, although it is estimated still to infect 1.7 million computers. See http://laws.qualys.com/2012/04/microsoft-sir-2012---new-confi.html.

Interconnect Fabrics

Switches and routers control the paths taken through networks.[19] The overall system of connections and switching between processors in a supercomputer is called the *interconnect fabric*. Supercomputing engineers have examined fabrics for connecting processors both theoretically and practically, evaluating the geometry and dynamics of efficient switching patterns. This research has been applied to the construction of interconnect fabrics in cloud datacenters.

The cloud datacenters reproduce supercomputer interconnect fabrics using commodity Ethernet switches and off-the-shelf blades in standard racks.

A LAN Compared to an Interconnect

A typical LAN is a tree (Figure 5-4). A message arrives and travels down the tree to the leaves that are usually endpoints such as personal computers and printers. The root of the tree and each subtree are switches. In datacenter jargon, messages from the root to leaves are *southbound* traffic. Messages from the leaves to the root are *northbound* traffic. Traffic between endpoints

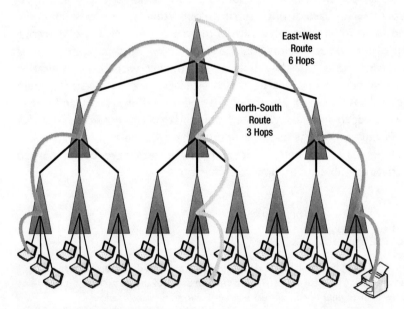

Figure 5-4. A typical LAN fabric is a tree.

---

[19] Routers route traffic between networks, and switches direct traffic within networks. Routers and switches were once distinct devices, but both have become more programmable, and each can be programmed to perform functions once reserved for the other.

within the LAN is *east-west* traffic. Simple tree fabrics handle north-south traffic well. If the LAN is a three-layer tree, incoming southbound data will reach its destination passing through a maximum of three switches. Northbound data finds its way out of the LAN equally easily. However, east-west traffic is another story. A message from a PC to a printer in another leg of the tree cannot travel directly east-west from node to node. Instead, it travels north, up the tree, to the first switch that is a parent to both the PC and the printer. This slows data movement because each path through a switch takes time. In the worst case, the number of passes through switches will double on east-west traversals.

If a LAN consists of personal computers that communicate with the Internet and perhaps a corporate datacenter, a deep tree fabric like this can be acceptable or even optimal. If east-west traffic is only an occasional print job and routing is optimized for communicating with the corporate center and the Internet gateway, users are likely to be satisfied with performance.

Trees like this are usually not adequate for a datacenter fabric. East-west traffic in a datacenter is critical. When a running virtual machine moves from one processor to another or when jobs are sharded and assigned to different processors, these are east-west transactions. A datacenter fabric must optimize these east-west transactions as well as north-south transactions. If not, cloud performance will suffer.

In a typical datacenter organization, servers are in standard 19-inch racks. The number of servers in a rack varies depending on the physical configuration and the manufacturer of the server, but 40 to 80 servers is common. Each rack has a switch that manages communication among the servers in the rack and acts as a gateway beyond the rack. Racks cluster in groups with a switch for each cluster. The number of racks in a cluster can vary, but having between 8 and 100 is typical.

In this arrangement, communication is fastest between servers in the same rack. Communication between servers in the same cluster will be slower than communication in the same rack but faster than communication between servers in different clusters. In other words, east-west transactions within the same rack are optimized over transactions between racks in the cluster. Transactions within the cluster are optimized over transactions that leave the cluster.

Although the arrangement shown in Figure 5-5 is likely to be typical, the fabric that connects the cluster switches can take various forms. The optimization of interconnect fabric is an important area of research that depends on how the resource abstraction layer distributes the workload as well as the load itself.

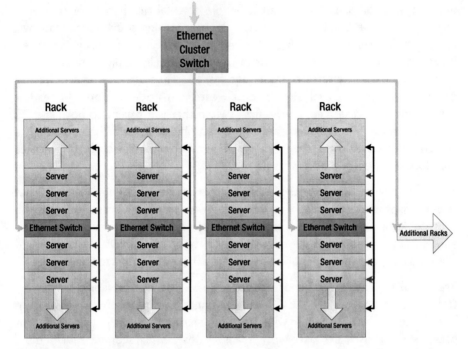

Figure 5-5. An Ethernet switch manages input and output to a datacenter cluster, which is further distributed by switches in the racks.

Both supercomputers and cloud datacenters consist of multiples of generic processors, often the same processors that power desktop PCs and stand-alone servers. The lists of top supercomputers show that many use exactly the same off-the-shelf processors. The interconnect fabric is one determinant of the overall performance of both datacenters and supercomputers (Figure 5-6).

Supercomputers aim at high performance and capacity. These goals are important to cloud datacenters, but cost-efficiency and reliability are equally important. Datacenters are willing to trade off performance for the lower cost of commoditized configurations like Ethernet switches and blades on standard racks supplied by competing vendors. They are also willing to compromise performance for reliability.

Physically, datacenters cover more area than supercomputers. Partly, this derives from the way datacenters have grown from a collection of servers to take on some of the characteristics of a supercomputer, but there are other reasons that they remain physically large. Cloud datacenters are more concerned with physical separation for reliability and disaster avoidance. An

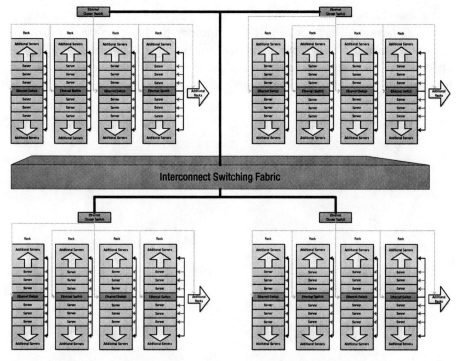

Figure 5-6. The interconnect switching fabric connects clusters of racks.

important part of datacenter design is to avoid single points of failure that can cripple the entire center, such as a single cooling system or one energy source. Spreading the datacenter over a campus or wider area is often sensible, even though there may be some performance impairment. Another reason is economic. Energy and cooling may favor a less dense distribution.

Processing Power in Cloud Architecture

With each chapter, I have gone deeper and deeper into the working of the cloud. This chapter has concentrated on processors and computing, but a cloud and its supporting datacenter are more than an optimized set of processors devoted to the efficient delivery of maximum computing power. The cloud sits on three pillars: computing, storage, and network. Future chapters will discuss the other two pillars in much more detail.

The cloud is a great simplifier, but simplification comes at a cost in complexity. This is paradoxical but true. It takes only a few minutes and simple commands to instantiate a virtual computer on a service like Amazon EC2. This machine appears as a familiar simple computer. It requires little more than basic computer literacy to set up and use. But as you have seen in this analysis of cloud services and datacenters, the technology behind that straightforward activity is formidable, in both complexity and scope. A simple cloud is the product of complex implementations. However, at every stage, standards have helped make complex implementations a reality.

CHAPTER 6

Cloud Storage and Cloud Network

Although the computing power of clouds is fascinating, never underestimate the importance of storage and network in cloud implementations.

Limitless remote storage is one of the most attractive features of the cloud. At the same time, storage is usually the slowest component in a computing system. Programmers are familiar with input and output to storage that takes orders of magnitude more time than other operations. Cloud implementations often rely on breaking up data into segments and processing all the segments at the same time on several processors.

Amdahl's law addresses the limits of increasing speed by adding additional parallel processors. [1] Amdahl pointed out that most tasks involve serial steps

[1] Gene Amdahl, "Validity of the Single Processor Approach to Achieving Large-Scale Computing Capabilities," 1967. Reprinted from the AFIPS Conference Proceedings, Vol. 30 (Atlantic City, N.J., Apr. 18–20), pp. 483–485. Reston, VA: AFIPS Press. Available online at turing.eas.asu.edu/cse520fa08/Alaw.pdf.

There is another side to Amdahl's law that is sometimes called Gustafson's law (see www.scl. ameslab.gov/Publications/Gus/AmdahlsLaw/Amdahls.html). Gustafson pointed out that Amdahl's use case was based on an unrealistic question: "How much will total execution time be decreased if a processor is added?" Seldom does anyone write a program and successively add processors to see how fast it will execute. Instead, a better use case is "What can this computer system do in *x* hours?" In practice, with each expanded computer system, problems are tailored to take advantage of added processors and reduce the fixed serial overhead. The serial overhead can be reduced by changing the algorithm, smarter data caching, or many

that cannot execute in parallel. For example, if a calculation cannot be performed until data is retrieved from storage, the calculation must wait for the retrieval. The retrieval and the calculation cannot execute in parallel unless the program is refactored in some way. The collection of steps that must be executed serially forms a fixed overhead that cannot be reduced by adding processors. When the number of processors is small, the serial overhead may be only a small fraction of the total execution time. As the number of processors is increased, the total execution time will decrease, but the serial portion will remain constant. Therefore, the total execution time can be reduced by adding processors, as long as there are additional steps that can be divided and executed in parallel. However, the speed gained by adding a processor will become negligible as the overhead of serial operations increasingly dominates the total execution time. Often, storage activity is a limiting factor in increasing cloud performance. This is one of the reasons why cloud storage is important in cloud design.

A cloud requires both an internal network inside the data center that supports a cloud as well as a network that connects the cloud to its consumers. If either is inadequate, the cloud will not satisfy its consumers. If the internal network is inadequate, the cloud implementation cannot harness the processors in the center for useful work. If the external network is slow or loses data, consumers are justifiably disappointed with the service.

Understanding what happens in the cloud requires some understanding of storage and networks, and some of the most important cloud standards apply to storage and networking. The standards themselves are discussed in Chapters 8 and 9. This chapter, which caps off the discussion of what the cloud is, describes how storage and the network work in cloud implementations.

Cloud Storage

Cloud storage operates on a different scale from the storage directly attached to a PC or server, but the hardware is similar. It all relies on technology introduced in the mid-1950s by IBM and extended by many vendors and researchers.[2] Like the hard drive in a PC, most cloud storage relies on spinning

---

other means. Thus, Amdahl's law holds, but the prediction that increasing processors has limited efficacy does not hold.

[2] See www-03.ibm.com/ibm/history/exhibits/650/650_pr2.html for a description of the first commercial hard disk. It held a whopping 5 megabytes of data and had a maximum seek time of a glacial 0.8 seconds. At the time, the only random access storage was punch cards; in addition, the data density of the Random Access Method of Access and Control (RAMAC), as it was called, was many orders of magnitude greater than cards, and access was much faster also. IBM touted RAMAC as the means for instantaneous update of accounts instead of

disks marked with magnetic blips. The spinning blips represent 0s and 1s that can be retrieved randomly and remain available when the power is shut off and turned on again.[3] These devices store information in the cloud as well as on personal computers and on-premises servers. There are other forms of storage, like solid-state disks, but they still emulate the behavior of a spinning disk.

Storage Device Networking

In a cloud datacenter, large-scale storage is often shared storage hardware rather than storage directly attached to the communications bus of a single computer like the familiar disk drives in personal computers and stand-alone servers. However, directly attached storage (DAS) still has a role.

There are advantages to local DAS. Some large datacenters include locally attached storage on each blade in the racks; others do not. DAS generally has a higher bandwidth and lower latency connection to the processor than storage that does not connect directly to the computer communications bus. The converse of this advantage is that comparatively DAS is slow to read or write from all but the directly attached host. DAS grants speed but only to the attached node. Network attached storage (NAS) and storage area networks (SANs) grant accessibility, flexibility, and efficient usage, at some cost in speed for writing and reading data that is not shared between processors. Sometimes, the benefits of sharing data via shared storage and flexible allocation of storage from a pool outweigh the advantages of a speedy DAS device. Other times not.

Network Attached Storage

Network attached storage (NAS) devices have evolved from file servers. File servers began as independent computers with relatively large disks. When networking became prevalent, users found advantages in sharing large disks among smaller machines. One large disk may be cheaper than several smaller disks of equivalent total size, and a single disk on a power user's desk is often easier to maintain and secure than smaller disks in PCs scattered through an office. In addition, north-south communication from a PC to a central disk

---

periodic batch updates. This may have been more significant than either the Internet or the cloud.

[3] Data center managers almost never power down disks intentionally. Some are almost superstitious about the consequences of powering down a disk that has been spinning continuously for several years. The theory is that continuous long-term spinning distorts the physical geometry of the disk gradually and can render the disk unreadable if it ever stops. This may be true, or it may be a datacenter myth.

may be faster than east-west communication between individual PCs. Above all, sharing data by retrieving it from a single source generates fewer mistakes and less work than trying to keep current and accurate copies on each PC.

These same advantages scale up in a cloud datacenter. Disks scattered in the racks require coordination to keep them backed up. When a disk fails on a blade, it may be more efficient to wait to replace the entire blade, or even the entire rack or cluster, rather than trifling with the failure of a single disk. Concentrating disk capacity in a small number of NAS devices can be a better solution.

File servers communicate with the rest of the PCs on the LAN via Ethernet and TCP/IP (Figure 6-1). File servers are general-purpose computers that deal with data using the same application-level data abstractions as other computers on the network. The file server reads raw data, structures it into abstractions like file systems, and furnishes the structured data to other computers. File servers use application-level protocols like Network File System (NFS) and Common Internet File System (CIFS).[4] Communicating with these protocols, networked computers mount remote file systems and use them as if they were local.

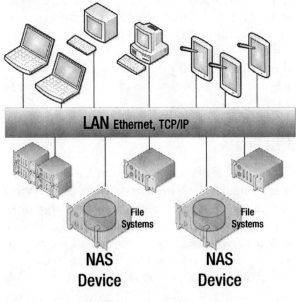

Figure 6-1. A NAS connected via a LAN

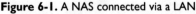

[4] CIFS, also called Server Message Block (SMB), is usually associated with Windows. The Microsoft specification for CIFS is at http://msdn.microsoft.com/en-us/library/ee442092.aspx. Sun Microsystems originally developed NFS for Unix in the mid-1980s. The IETF now maintains it. The version 4.0 standard is in RFC 3530 (http://tools.ietf.org/html/rfc3530). RFC 5661 (http://tools.ietf.org/html/rfc5661) defines version 4.1.

NAS devices take the place of file servers. They serve only files, and they usually do not supply general computer services. NAS device operating systems are typically ordinary operating systems stripped down to the minimum needed for file serving.[5] Their hardware is also specialized to support large quantities of storage and high-performance input and output.

Storage Area Networks

SANs are another approach to shared storage that are often used in cloud implementations and have significant advantages. The relationship between SANs and NAS can be confusing. Some partisans argue that NAS and SANs are contending approaches that cannot mix. Whether this is true depends largely on what you consider to be mixing. I will get back to this topic after discussing SANs.

A SAN is a high-performance network that connects storage hardware to servers and to other storage hardware. Unlike NAS, a SAN network is distinct from the LAN that connects servers to servers and clients (Figure 6-2). SANs can and are optimized for moving data to and from storage, unlike LANs, which are subject to broader requirements.

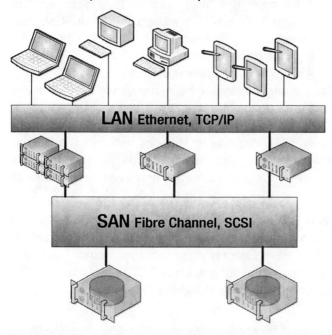

Figure 6-2. Two SANs connect servers to a storage bus.

[5] FreeNAS is an example. It is an open source project based on the FreeBSD version of Unix. See www.freenas.org.

SANs usually run on high-performance Fibre Channel networks.[6] The storage devices on a SAN are block devices. To the operating system on the connected servers, SAN devices look like raw disk drives. Data appears as fixed-size blocks. Like a DAS drive attached directly to a server, the server operating system manages the raw blocks and transforms them to appear as application-level abstractions like file systems. The data protocols used typically on a SAN are disk-level protocols like Small Computer System Interface (SCSI), the same protocols that computers use to communicate with attached disks. Typical SAN protocol stacks (Fibre Channel and SCSI) are simple and usually implemented in hardware, which is well suited to rapid high-volume data transfer. NAS protocols (Ethernet, TCP/IP, and CIFS) are more complex and usually run in software. Consequently, they easily deliver more complex application-level abstractions, but they are slower.

A noticeable difference between SAN and NAS is where application-level abstractions are created. On a SAN, the server, not the SAN device, creates the application-level abstractions. In contrast, a NAS device creates the application abstractions for the server.

There are advantages to both approaches. In terms of sheer throughput, a SAN running on Fibre Channel and SCSI with a hardware protocol implementation has advantages over a NAS reading a disk with SCSI, then using compute time for software transformation of raw data blocks into file systems, and finally trickling data back and forth with SMB over TCP/IP on an Ethernet LAN. On the other hand, the recipient of data from a NAS has the easy job of reading and writing customary file systems, and a NAS device tends to be easier to set up and plug into an existing system. A NAS device provides some of the benefits of a SAN without the cost and effort of setting up an independent data fabric. Depending on the jobs performed, delegating the overhead of transforming raw data to application abstractions to a dedicated NAS device may be superior to burdening servers with this extra task.

The Storage Networking Industry Association (SNIA) defines a SAN as a network primarily for communication between computer systems and shared storage devices.[7] Although Fibre Channel is the most commonly used SAN transport, other transports, such as Ethernet and TCP/IP, are possible. The most recent Ethernet versions support throughput that rivals Fibre Channel.

---

[6] Fibre Channel is a standard high-performance protocol that was originally developed for supercomputing. See www.fibrechannel.org. Despite the name, Fibre Channel can run on both optical fibers and copper twisted-pairs like Ethernet.

[7] SNIA is an important group for cloud storage standards. More will be heard about it. See http://snia.org. A SNIA discussion of what constitutes a SAN can be found at www.snia.org/education/storage_networking_primer.

The distinguishing characteristic of SANs is the separation of client-to-server and server-to-server communication from computer-to-storage and storage-to-storage communication. NAS built on an independent data fabric is a SAN. The tendency in datacenter design has been to converge on fast Ethernet as a transportation protocol.

Most current installations that combine SAN and NAS implement the NAS with SAN as the data source, rather than attempt to combine the NAS directly in a SAN fabric (Figure 6-3). This is a reasonable compromise. The NAS gets the benefits of hardware shared on the SAN fabric, and the servers get the benefit of the abstraction provided by the NAS device. The choice between NAS and SAN is not easy for an on-premises datacenter and equally difficult for a cloud provider. A SAN moves more data faster. If moving more faster is most important, a SAN is likely to be desirable. If processing on the server is critical, NAS or NAS combined with a SAN has advantages.

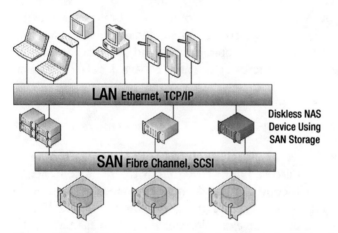

Figure 6-3. A NAS device can use a virtual device on the SAN as its physical storage.

Disk Arrays

The storage made available through a SAN or NAS usually exists physically as high-capacity storage devices that are composed of many individual disks, called *redundant disk arrays* or, more specifically, Redundant Independent Disk Arrays (RAIDs).[8] RAIDs make use of three techniques: striping, mirroring, and

---

[8] The concept of RAID was introduced by David A. Patterson, Garth Gibson, and Randy H. Katz in 1988 in their paper "A Case for Redundant Arrays of Inexpensive Disks (RAID)" (University of California Berkeley), available online at www-2.cs.cmu.edu/~garth/RAIDpaper/Patterson88.pdf. In the original paper, RAID was an acronym for Redundant Array of Inexpensive Disks. Subsequently, usage replaced "inexpensive" with "independent." The original paper is concerned with increasing storage reliability and performance at lower cost,

parity. Each technique yields special benefits. Different RAID configurations are called *levels*. The simplest level, level 0, straightforwardly mirrors data on two disks. As levels ascend, they include parity and striping in more complicated and specialized patterns.

In a RAID, resilience and speed trade off. For a given array, the number of disks that can fail without data loss depends on redundancy, but disks that are only mirrors help resiliency but not performance. The storage designer must choose the right balance of speed and reliability.

Striping

In striping, the RAID device shards sequential data into arbitrary blocks and writes each segment to a different disk in the array. Each disk is a data stripe. A striped write occurs in less time than the same sequence of data written stripe by stripe to a single disk. For example, a sequence of data written to four stripes simultaneously will take a quarter of the time it takes to write the four segments sequentially to a single stripe. When reading the data back, the RAID controller reads all the stripes simultaneously, and the data comes back four times faster. Thus, striped disks can store and retrieve data faster than an individual disk.

Mirroring

Continuously maintaining two or more disks as exact copies of each other is *mirroring*. At every instant, mirrored disks have exactly the same contents. In a RAID device, the RAID controller performs the mirroring, usually in hardware microcode. Mirroring increases the resilience of a RAID. If each write is mirrored to three disks, for example, four disks must fail before the data is lost. Mirroring reduces the vulnerability of data to many forms of disk failure, including the classic "disk crash."

Parity

Parity is a mathematical method for detecting errors and creating redundancy in binary data. The oddness or evenness of the number of set bits in a collection of bits determines the parity of the collection.[9] When the parity of a collection is known, any single missing element can be calculated based on the other values. For example, a triple like "101" has a parity of 0 or even

---

but the important breakthrough and subsequent interest was in the increase in reliability and performance that RAIDs made possible.

[9] In binary data, a 1 is called a *set bit*, and a 0 is called a *clear bit*.

because there is an even number of set bits (1s). This can be calculated quickly in hardware by performing a consecutive cumulative exclusive-or (XOR) in either direction. For this example, "((1 XOR 0) XOR 1)" results in 0. The resulting 0 is the parity for the triple. If one of the bits is lost, XORing the parity with the remaining elements will recover its value. In this case, if the 0 in the middle were lost, it could be recovered by performing "((1 XOR 1) XOR 0)," the left and right bits with the parity value. The result is 0, which is the original value for the middle bit. The three bits in 101 could each be stored on a disk in a RAID, and the parity bit could be stored on a fourth disk. Consequently, if any of the four disks in the array were to fail, the data on the remaining three disks could be fed into an XOR calculation to recover the contents of the missing disk.

This scheme uses fewer disks than mirroring to achieve the same goal. Using mirroring only, the RAID would mirror three disks in the example; the RAID would have six disks instead of four. The single parity disk replaces three mirrored. XOR calculations are implemented in fast hardware, so the speed difference is not great. The disadvantage to using a parity bit is parity cannot correct two errors at once. However, the probability of two simultaneous errors is usually low enough to permit the savings.

This is a simple example of the use of parity in RAIDs. More complex parity schemes exist. SNIA describes 20 parity schemes in its RAID technical position.[10]

Limitations

RAIDs provide excellent protection against classic "disk crashes." Unfortunately, there are forms of failure that RAIDs cannot protect against. A catastrophe, like a fire or flood, that affects the entire data center can destroy an entire RAID. In addition, RAIDs are no help against clumsy humans who inadvertently delete data, defective programs that go rogue and write bad data and corrupt existing data, and bad actors who malevolently damage and destroy data. Perhaps most insidious of all, there are well-intentioned but poorly designed systems that do not save, unwisely ruin, or inadequately protect their own data. For those kinds of problems, there are other strategies.

One such strategy is redundancy on much larger scale than disks in a RAID. Cloud implementations replicate petabytes or exabytes of data between distant datacenters. One reason for replication on this scale is to distribute data into locations that are geographically distant. This practice prevents a

---

[10] "Common RAID Disk Data Format Specification Version 2.0 Revision 19," SNIA, March 27, 2009, www.snia.org/sites/default/files/SNIA_DDF_Technical_Position_v2.0.pdf.

local catastrophe like an earthquake or a flood from destroying all copies of data or disabling access to the data.

Cloud Data Management

The most important characteristic of cloud storage is a global approach to data management. Clouds are large and rely on wide area networks. Management approaches that are reasonable for smaller installations often do not work at cloud scale. Therefore, cloud management over global networks presents special challenges. Principles that seem ironclad at on-premises scale must be reexamined and revised.

ACID

The principle of transaction integrity characterized by the ACID (atomicity, consistency, isolation, durability) properties must be reexamined in the cloud. A transaction is a unique, indivisible operation, in this case, data operation. The typical basic data transactions are create, read, update, and delete (CRUD). In applications, individual data transactions are aggregated into the application's transactions. Application transactions also follow the ACID principles.

ACID has governed data system designs for decades. Briefly, atomic transactions are

- **A**ll-or-nothing, never partially completed in the system. (For example, either you made that bank deposit or you did not— no half-in, half-out.)

- **C**onsistent systems always comply with all consistency rules. (If every debit must be matched with a credit, the system must never allow a debit without a credit.)

- **I**solated transactions never interfere with each other. (Your transactions never affect my transactions.)

- **D**urable results of committed transactions do not disappear from the system until changed by another committed transaction. (No backdoor modifications to the data.)

Systems with ACID properties exhibit the level of integrity that is associated with financial accounting.

ACID has been the gold standard of distributed data system design, but in cloud applications, the ACID standard is difficult, if not impossible, to meet.

To understand why this is so, we have to call in another concept with an acronym: the CAP theorem (Figure 6-4).

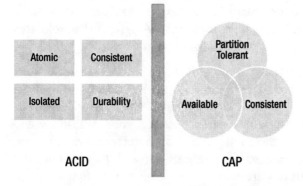

Figure 6-4. ACID and the CAP theorem can be opposing principles.

CAP

The Consistency Availability Partitioning (CAP) theorem addresses three characteristics of distributed data systems: consistency, availability, and partitioning. Consistent systems never break consistency rules. If a data element is set to a certain value in a complete transaction, that data element must have the set value no matter where the element is accessed. If the element is replicated, it must not be accessible until the set value is available from all the replicated systems. To a user, a consistent system appears to be a single system, although the actual system may be replicated among many geographically and logically distant storage units.

Availability is usually described as the ratio of the time a system is available to the time the system could be available. The availability ratio of a system down one hour in a week is 0.99404. A completely available system has a ratio of 1.0. For CAP, an available system appears to have 1.0 availability. That usually means that the system is available during declared business hours, which for cloud services often means available all the time.

Partitions and partition-tolerant systems refer to the consequences of lapses of communication between nodes in a system. When a communications lapse occurs, which is usually a network failure, the system is divided, or partitioned, into groups of nodes that can or cannot communicate with each other. If I disconnect my PC from the Internet, I have created a trivial partition. On one side of the partition is my PC. On the other is the rest of the Internet. The Internet itself is partition tolerant because it continues to operate even though a partition exists.

The CAP theorem states that of three characteristics of distributed systems—data consistency, data availability, and tolerance of network partitions—only two can ever be true simultaneously. A system that is always consistent and available cannot tolerate network partitions. A system that is always available and partition tolerant cannot always be consistent. A system that tolerates partitions and is always consistent cannot always be available.

Cloud implementers must always deal with these important trades-offs because network partitions are a fact of Internet life. Behind a firewall where an enterprise IT department controls every detail of the network, network partitioning is controllable, if not eliminated. Consequently, availability and consistency are all possible at the same time in an enterprise environment. However, when applications connect to data via a network that includes the Internet, uncontrolled partitions are part of the environment. Simultaneous availability and consistency become problematic (Figure 6-5).

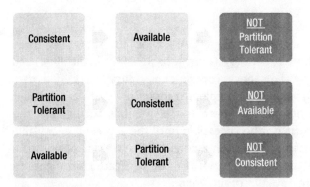

Figure 6-5. The CAP theorem describes three mutually exclusive properties of distributed systems.

A rigorous proof of the CAP theorem exists, but this is not the place to prove it.[11] Instead, I will work through an illustration in order to understand the theorem. Understanding the CAP theorem is more important than the formal proof.

The CAP notion of consistency differs in emphasis from the corresponding ACID concept. A CAP-consistent data source can be written from anywhere, and, until another write, a read from anywhere will yield an identical result.

---

[11] For a formal proof of the CAP theorem, see Seth Gilbert and Kathy Lynch's 2002 paper "Brewer's Conjecture and the Feasibility of Consistent, Available, Partition-Tolerant Web Services" at http://lpd.epfl.ch/sgilbert/pubs/BrewersConjecture-SigAct.pdf. It is heavy reading if you are not mathematically inclined, but for those of you with fond memories of honors math classes, the proof is quite interesting.

For example, if you subscribe to an online backup service that maintains consistency, it will not matter where or when you connect to the network to write a backup. The result will be consistent restores from anywhere. It will not matter if you are at home, at the Starbucks on the corner, or at a hotel on another continent when you restore the backup. If the storage is consistent, the result of the restore will be the same, always reflecting your latest backup. The location or access route will make no difference. In addition, if the system is consistent, and you wanted to, you could back up and immediately restore with assurance that you have restored the backup you just made. The backup and immediate restore operation will not change the data on your computer in any nontrivial way.

Now let's examine what might happen if a backup system does not maintain consistency in the CAP sense.[12] An illustration from the old days when tapes were manually mounted puts the consequences of inconsistency in human terms. With manually mounted tapes, a common problem occurred with backups when an operator carelessly fumbled and grabbed an old backup tape from the rack instead of the most current one. The old backup from a month ago will overwrite and destroy the data accumulated in the intervening month. This will, at the minimum, ruin an operator's lunch.

Lack of consistency in a cloud storage system can cause the equivalent of grabbing the wrong tape, with equally annoying results. In a consistent system, operations always appear as if the system is a single node and the results of the operation are instantly available throughout the system. That level of consistency is not easy to maintain on a widely distributed system.

Suppose you and your laptop were to fly from Australia to New York (Figure 6-6). On arrival, your finger slips, and you inadvertently delete an unknown number of important files. You check the backup record on your laptop and heave a sigh of relief. Your backup service automatically backed up your laptop yesterday in Sydney. Restoring from that backup will solve all your problems.

Signals in optical fibers theoretically move close to the speed of light, but traversing a network is more than signal transmission. Routers and other processing can slow data down with limited predictability, but generally greater distance means greater latency (the time a data packet consumes traversing the network from source to destination) and less throughput (the amount of data transmitted in a unit of time). To reduce the effect of network delays on latency and throughput, cloud providers often cache data regionally.

---

[12] These examples are simplified and exaggerated. Although they illustrate the principles, developers have been wrestling with these problems for a long time. As a result, the real-life examples are more subtle than these examples. For instance, mirroring a backup, even half-way round the globe, does not take a week in real life, but the example is clearer if the inconsistency is exaggerated.

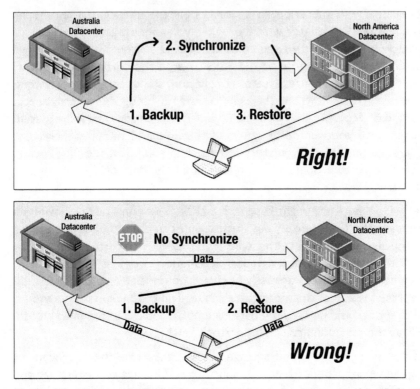

Figure 6-6. A backup system distributed between two datacenters can destroy data if the datacenters are not synchronized.

In this case, suppose the backup service has regional storage centers in Australia and North America. Backups taken in Sydney are stored in the Australia center for quick access in Australia. Backups taken in New York are stored in the North America center. The North America and Australia centers synchronize once a week. As long as no one writes data in Australia and then reads it in North America before synchronization, the system will appear consistent; but write a backup in Sydney and read it in New York before the centers synchronize, and you will see an old version of the backup. In other words, the backup operation in Sydney may not have the appearance of taking place simultaneously in Australia and North America. The backup available in New York could be as much as a week older than the backup written in Sydney. Instead of restoring the deleted files, a restoration from the North America server might wipe out a week of work. This level of data consistency in a backup service is inhospitable to travelers.[13]

---

[13] And unrealistic. I doubt that a real backup service would ever have such a pokey synchronization policy. I exaggerate for clarity.

One way of achieving consistency is to compromise availability, the second factor in the CAP theorem. Availability means that the system is always available for reading and writing. Transaction control and locking often compromise availability by placing locks on data until a transaction completes.

Suppose the backup service were to put an exclusive lock (no reading or writing) on any backup in the North America center that had been superseded by a backup on the Australia server and remove the lock only when the two centers become consistent. In other words, if you tried to restore in New York, you would get the error "Data inconsistent. Try later." Depending on your perspective, this may or may not be an improvement over losing data from lack of consistency, because the inconvenience of not being able to restore until the synchronization could be almost as bad as losing data.

This leads to the third factor in the CAP theorem, partition tolerance. A partition exists in a network when all the messages sent from one component to another are lost. A single message lost between two hosts is a trivial partition of short duration and scope. A more interesting (annoying) partition is a failure that blocks messages from many components for a long period. A partition-tolerant system permits an arbitrary number of messages between its components to be lost without ill effects. In our example, severing an undersea cable might create a partition between the North America center and the Australia center that lasts for some time.[14]

If our backup service could assert that a network partition would never occur, their system would not need to be partition tolerant, and the system could always be consistent and available. While the Australia center copy of your backup supersedes the North America center copy, the system could divert your restore requests from the locked North America center to the Australia center. Latency and throughput might suffer, but the data would be correct and available. This is great, but the backup service could not prevent a broken undersea cable from interrupting communication between Australia and North America and partitioning the network. Blocked by the partition, the North American backup, behind an exclusive lock, is not available, nor is the Australian center on the other side of the partition. Removing the lock violates consistency. Our backup system is in a dilemma that is a consequence of the CAP theorem. If it is to work properly during all network partitions, it must sacrifice either availability or consistency.

---

[14] In real life, partitions may be more subtle. Undersea cables are usually redundant, and there are always satellite links. Consequently, severing a cable may not completely cut off communication. But the break would cause many simultaneous partitions of short duration because routing over the alternate paths takes time, especially when the total available bandwidth is substantially depleted. In that case, the difficulties that arise from the partition would probably be as annoying, but they would occur on a more granular level.

The Internet is a wild land. Partitions large and small occur all the time, few as spectacular as a severed undersea cable; most are short-duration routing issues, but the network is partitioned in one way or another constantly. Therefore, cloud storage providers tend to assume that some measure of partition tolerance is a requirement. In fact, Internet designers usually assume that any given point in the network may be unreachable at any time. This assumption contributes to the resiliency of the Internet, but it causes headaches when designing for the cloud.

The character of the Internet forces cloud providers and application builders to compromise, often in the form of "eventual consistency." Those familiar with Domain Name System (DNS) probably have experienced eventual consistency. DNS uses distributed data servers to translate human-readable domain names to numeric IP addresses. When adding a new domain, it does not appear in the cache of every DNS server immediately. Instead, the change is propagated gradually as caches age. Given time, the new domain information replaces all the caches, and the system becomes consistent. Under eventual consistency, the system may be inconsistent immediately after a write, but the system guarantees eventually to become consistent.

DNS has been successful because eventual consistency fits with the service and expectations are clear. Domain name registrars warn that a new domain may take days to propagate everywhere, and users should plan that a new site may be hard to reach for a few days.

The cloud backup system that I discussed earlier exhibits a form of eventual consistency. Eventually the Australia and North America sites will be consistent, but a guarantee of eventual consistency does not solve the backup system's problem. To satisfy its users, the backup system has to compensate for the consequences of eventual consistency.

Useful constraints can be placed on eventual consistency. For instance, the backup system might guarantee monotonic updates; in other words, a backup will never be overwritten by a previous backup. That would give users some degree of confidence that their most recent data would never be lost. Although they could still overwrite data on their laptop by reading an old backup from the cloud, all would not be lost because eventually the most recent backup would appear. The backup system might further compensate by comparing the date and time of the last backup on your laptop with the date and time of the last backup on the server and warn you if there is a danger of overwriting. The backup system might have a third datacenter in Europe and replicate the data there also. If Australia is cut off, maybe the last backup made it to Europe. There are many ways to deal with eventual consistency, but CAP is a mathematical certainty that will have its way.

The CAP theorem implies that managing cloud storage is an art of compromise. The ACID criteria are impossible to meet in public clouds because of the unavoidable possibility of network partitions on the Internet. Carefully engineered private clouds may reduce the probability of partitions, but it is hard to imagine any network in which partitions are impossible. Yet with an understanding of the implication of the CAP theorem, reliable services can be built. The challenge, like so many challenges in computer engineering, is to provide reliable services in an unreliable environment.[15]

Storage in the Cloud

Storage in the cloud takes several forms. Amazon S3 (Simple Storage Service) is an example of low-level IaaS storage. Amazon charges for the volume of storage used by the consumer and for data access. S3 is designed for fast, reliable, high-volume storage. It supports only the most basic data operations: create, read, and delete with several interfaces for storing and accessing data (a forms-based graphic user interface and SOAP- and REST-style programmatic interfaces).[16] The consumer can designate the region in which their data will be stored to comply with data location regulations or to help manage network latency. In addition to S3, other services are available to support using S3 with EC2 virtual machines, mass import and export, and other functions.

The S3 service level agreement (SLA) guarantees a level of service availability enforced with payment credits for lapses in availability. Amazon also promises a high level of data durability—data stored in S3 is unlikely to be lost. Their storage facilities are designed to withstand simultaneous lapses of two facilities without loss of data. Much of this level of reliability stems from a data replication policy. When S3 writes data, the transaction does not complete until the data has been written to more than one facility.

S3 works well for backup and other mass storage applications; most users probably would not want to back up their laptop using the demanding S3 interface. Some cloud backup services, for example, use Amazon's high-volume S3 service for storage. These backup services concentrate on providing more sophisticated and easy-to-use features like automated backup and restore rather than maintaining a mass storage facility.

Although a mass storage service has many uses, more structured data services are also important. For more structured data management, Amazon offers other services that range from simple "attribute-value" storage to installations

---

[15] Werner Vogels, CTO of Amazon, has an excellent article on eventual consistency and the CAP theorem. See http://queue.acm.org/detail.cfm?id=1466448.

[16] Representational State Transfer (REST) and SOAP discussed in more detail in Chapter 10.

of a selection of popular relational database management systems. Other cloud providers offer services similar to Amazon S3 and other services. Like when subscribing to any service, consumers should compare service level agreements and features carefully before making a decision.

There are also storage services that are aimed at the consumer market. Some are designed for accessibility. Using these services, a subscriber stores their files with a cloud service. Then they are able to access the files from any desktop, laptop, tablet, or smartphone connected to the Internet. The files are typically accessed through a browser, although some services can be configured to automatically synchronize local copies of files with the copy stored in the cloud. Music, video, and photo services that store music and photos on cloud storage that is available from many different devices are variations on this theme.

Cloud Networks

Clouds are totally dependent on networks. With no effective way of communicating between the consumer and provider, either the separation between consumer and provider must be absolute or the two must meld together to communicate. Neither represents cloud services. In this section, I will examine in some depth the basis for cloud networks.

OSI Layers

The Open System Interconnect model is an influential description of network architecture and a good starting point for understanding the Internet. The International Standards Organization (ISO) developed and published the model in the early 1980s. The model is a seven-layer abstract architecture for connecting one application with another. This architecture is a blueprint for the communications network that has become the foundation of the Internet and the cloud. Its abstractions make it possible to design the sprawling Internet that connects widely separated consumers to providers. It is also the basis for connecting enterprise consumers to private clouds, and it plays a role in the fabric that links individual processors into warehouse-scale supercomputers in the datacenter.

Not all networks follow the OSI model. The Fibre Channel and SCSI protocols that often implement SANs have their own abstraction model that does not correspond to the OSI model. The TCP/IP protocol that is the foundation of Internet communications has layering that does not correspond exactly to the OSI model. Nevertheless, the two are close enough that the OSI model is useful for describing TCP/IP, if only by pointing out the exceptions. The OSI model can describe other protocols besides TCP/IP, but TCP/IP will occupy center stage here.

The seven layers of the OSI model are, from lowest level to highest, the physical, data link, network, transport, session, presentation, and application layers. Numbering begins with 1 for the physical layer and ends with 7 for the application layer. Often, the layers are referred to by numbering alone. For instance, second-layer routing refers to routing that occurs in the data link layer.

Sending a message starts at the application layer. Each layer takes data handed to it from the layer above, adds whatever is necessary to accomplish the layer's assigned task, and passes it down to the next layer until the message arrives at the physical layer. The physical layer converts the data to signals and transmits it. The physical layer signal is detected by a data link layer entity. Then the data goes up the layers, often reversing its course at the network layer and passing back down to the physical layer for further transmission. Finally, the message passes through the upper layers to the destination application.

As messages, or packets, go down the stack, each layer wraps the packet with the information needed by the next layer down, so the packet grows with each step. When a packet goes up the stack, the layer strips off the wrapping so that the upper layer gets only the information from its corresponding layer in the source stack. In this way, the layers logically communicate across the stack without needing to be aware of the lower layers of the stack.

OSI layering is extremely powerful. As long as an implementation maintains consistent interfaces between layers, each layer is independent. For example, we generally assume that Ethernet implements the data link layer, but that is not necessary. If a LAN implements the data link layer with token ring, as long as the data link has the proper interface to the network layer, the end-to-end network is not affected. This means that a token ring LAN connected to the Internet does not require changes to the network layer and above. In the same way, dissimilar LANs will bridge together. The OSI layer architecture is one of the keys to the broad compass and robustness of the Internet (Figure 6-7).

Physical Layer

The physical layer is responsible for signals on the wire and in the air. This layer defines the patterns of electrical signals that represent 0s and 1s in the physical connection. It is concerned with voltages and wave patterns, not the information that the patterns convey or where they come from or go to. The

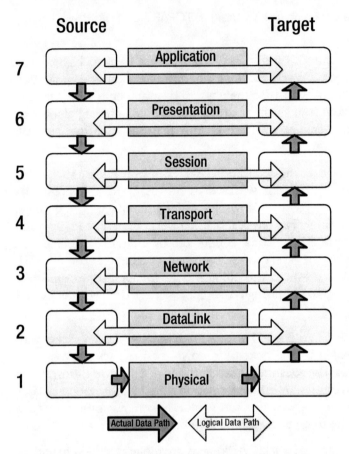

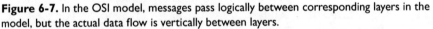

Figure 6-7. In the OSI model, messages pass logically between corresponding layers in the model, but the actual data flow is vertically between layers.

physical layer signals leave the source and begin their traverse to the target, but the physical layer does not discriminate. Its signals go to every device on its wire. The data link layer must sort out where signals go on which physical layer wire.

Only exceptionally does a signal from a host go directly to its destination. If it goes directly to its destination, the data link layer will identify the signal and move the packet up the destination stack. If it is directed out of the LAN, the data link layer of an intermediate node like a router will intercept the signal. The router's data link layer will pass the data up to the network layer. The network layer interprets the information in the data packet that points to the final destination of the packet and pushes the packet back down so that the physical layer can pass it to the next target.

Data Link Layer

The data link layer manages activity within a local area network, and its basic responsibility is to pass data to and from the network layer of the device identified in the destination address of the data link packet. Ordinarily, a local IT department is responsible for data link services. In home LANs, data link services are usually very simple and are supplied by a home router that connects to the network service provider's system and the wired or wireless network interfaces in the home computer.

Ethernet

The Ethernet standard (IEEE 802.3) applies data link activities. Other standards are candidates, but Ethernet is by far the most common. In the 1980s and 1990s there were three contending standards for LANs: Ethernet (802.3), token bus (802.4), and token ring (802.5). Ethernet is now the winner among the contenders, but both token rings and token buses have advantages and proponents and still prevail in some applications.

In its early days, Ethernet relied on an algorithm that theoretically allowed unbounded delays on a heavily loaded LAN. Token ring and token bus operate more efficiently under heavy loads, but they are not as efficient as Ethernet under light loads, and they are more difficult to install, requiring coaxial cables. They are also more subject to single point of failure than Ethernet. They were suitable for systems such as assembly line management that are sensitive to network breakdown from heavy loading.

The theoretical issues with Ethernet diminished with the appearance of full-duplex Ethernet and Ethernet switches. Early Ethernet was half-duplex, which meant a node could not send and receive at the same time. With full duplex, loads doubled. With Ethernet switches, which meant that the network interface on the connected device would only receive packets directed to it, loading became even less significant. While these implementations were going on, Ethernet equipment decreased in cost as greater quantities were produced. Token bus and token are rare now.

The Ethernet standard has advanced with additions to the standard almost every year. 802.3ba, published in 2010, supports 40 gigabit/second and 100 gigabit/second throughputs.

Medium Access Control Sublayer

The data link layer is divided into two sublayers: the Medium Access Control (MAC) sublayer and the MAC-client sublayer. The MAC layer encapsulates data into frames for passage to the physical layer. It uses MAC addresses, which are unique addresses that manufacturers permanently assign to hardware.[17] The network layer, above the data link layer, uses IP addresses, which point to the location of a host in the network rather than a specific piece of hardware. The Address Resolution Protocol (ARP) translates IP addresses to MAC addresses. ARP queries the local subnet and maintains a cache of IP address to MAC address mappings.

The MAC sublayer is also responsible for recovering from transmission failures. When parsing frames on reception, it can also detect some errors. The OSI model gives the MAC layer substantial responsibility for error detection and recovery. However, responsibility for error recovery has largely moved up the protocol stack over time.

Error detection and recovery has tended move up in the model for practical reasons. Error detection and recovery is often imperfect in the lower layers, so the upper layers still have to detect and recover from errors. If error cleaning repeats in each layer, performance can be improved by eliminating some of the error handling in the lower layers.

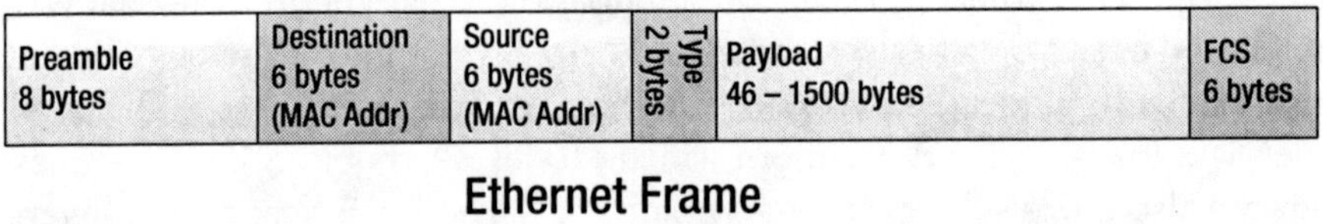

Preamble 8 bytes	Destination 6 bytes (MAC Addr)	Source 6 bytes (MAC Addr)	Type 2 bytes	Payload 46 – 1500 bytes	FCS 6 bytes

Ethernet Frame

Figure 6-8. The basic Ethernet frame here is augmented in later versions of the standard.

The Ethernet frame or packet layout displays the functionality of the data link layer (Figure 6-8). It consists of a preamble, an 8-byte bit pattern that marks the beginning of a frame. The destination is expressed as a MAC address. The source MAC address follows, then the type in two bytes, and then the payload. The payload contains all the data passed down from the upper layers. For example, the payload will contain IP addresses from the network layer and port numbers from the transport layer, although the data link layer is not aware of any of this.

The Ethernet source and destination MAC addresser are like not the same devices and the IP addresses received by the network layer. The source MAC

---

[17] MAC addresses are not as permanent as they once were. Devices that can change MAC addresses at will are useful for hot failover and virtualization. Consequently, many devices support changing MAC addresses in software. Mutable MAC addresses are also handy for man-in-the-middle schemes and other mischief.

address will be the MAC address of the current node. The destination will be the MAC address of the next node in LAN, perhaps another router. The next network layer will the source and destination IP addresses from the Ethernet payload and decide where the packet goes next.

As packets move down from layer to layer, each layer encloses the packet with its own prefix and suffix. The data that goes on the wire contains the packets from each layer, nested like a Russian doll. As packets move up the layers, each layer strips off its own prefix and suffix and passes up an upper layer packet. Thus, each layer always works with a packet in its own format.

Medium Access Control Client Sublayer

The client called Logical Link Control (LLC) is the interface with the network layer above the data link layer. The MAC client also has the job of bridging to other subnets. The bridge itself will vary with the complexity of the network. The bridge transforms a layer 2 packet from one subnet to the other. There may be routing functions performed at this layer also, choosing between several possible subnets.

Network Layer

The network layer is the layer that ties together the entire Internet. The main purpose of the network layer is to route packets between subnets. It is associated with the Internet Protocol (IP) in the Internet stack and supports communication from network node to network node over diverse subnets. Typically, an independent network service provider supplies network layer services, but the IT department of an enterprise with more than one LAN also provides network layer services to route messages within the enterprise to the rest of the network.

The network layer addresses point to the relative positions of hosts in the network rather than the MAC addresses used by the data link layer that point to devices. As mentioned earlier, manufacturers assign MAC addresses to devices more or less permanently when creating the device. This has nothing to do with where the device is located or what it is connected to. If a device moves from one LAN to another or one network to another, its MAC address does not change. IP addresses are hierarchical and point to relative positions in a network. IP addresses start with a high-level domain and successively refine the location. The same IP address may move to a different device, and the same device may have more than one IP address. The network uses the IP address hierarchy to make routing decisions.

The IP addresses of four dot-separated decimals that most people are familiar with are from the IPv4 version of the IP standard, which goes back to 1981.[18] The IPv4 address space contains more than 4 billion addresses. This space has become inadequate with the worldwide acceptance of the Internet and the practice of assigning addresses to devices such as cell phones and embedded monitoring devices. Only a fraction of the available addresses are now in use, but they are allocated in such a way that allocating new addresses has become increasingly difficult and will continue to become more difficult without a change.[19]

Engineers in the 1990s anticipated this depletion of available IP addresses and began work on a second IP standard. The result was the IPv6 standard. It addresses the address depletion problem with wider addresses that open a larger address space. IPv4 has 32-bit addresses, which makes available approximately 4 billion addresses. IPv6 widens addresses to 128 bits. The number of IPv6 addresses borders on incomprehensible: 340 billion billion billion billion, or 34 followed by 37 zeroes.[20] Perhaps more importantly, the address allocation agencies have gained experience from which to guide their policies.

The IPv6 standard addresses also addresses problems that have appeared in the network layer. The network layer is responsible for packet fragmentation. Not all subnets are equal. Larger packets transmit more efficiently than shorter packets, but not all subnets can support larger packets. When a large packet routes to a subnet that will not accept the large packet, the network layer in IPv4 is responsible for splitting the packet, creating new headers, calculating a checksum for each new packet, and routing the new packets to the next subnet. Fragmentation and checksum calculations slow down routers, decrease network throughput, and increase latency. IPv6 reduces these problems by eliminating checksums and fragmentation.

There are no checksums in an IPv6 packet to be calculated, and the network layer no longer fragments packets. The upper layers are responsible for determining the minimum transmission unit size from source to destination for the packet and sending only those packets that will travel all the way to the destination. If they send a packet that is too large, an IPv6 router simply drops it. There is no checksum in an IPv6 packet, which relieves the network layer of the tasks of calculating and verifying the checksums of incoming packets and calculating checksums of outgoing packets. This error checking is

---

[18] RFC 791, http://tools.ietf.org/html/rfc791.

[19] Stephen Shankland's 2011 article "Moving to IPv6: Now for the hard part (FAQ)" at http://news.cnet.com/8301-30685_3-20030482-264.html sums up the situation nicely.

[20] I do not intend to try to predict when the IPv6 address space will fill.

left to the upper layers, where it will not cause low-level bottlenecks and applications can decide what level of checking is worth the expense.

Network layer flows are another important addition. IPv6 flows are identifiers on sequences of packets that the network layer can route identically. For example, when the network transmits a large document, all the packets can be marked with a single flow identifier. Instead of reading and calculating a route for each packet, the router can cache the route for the first packet and only read the flow identifier for the rest of the sequence. This reduces the load on the router and helps eliminate network layer bottlenecks.

The primary impetus for implementing IPv6 has been address depletion. A milestone occurred in February 2011 when ICANN allocated the last top-level domains.[21] Technologies such as Network Address Translation (NAT), which translates a single registered IP address into many unregistered addresses hidden behind the registered address, have alleviated some of the shortage. Up to now, the address shortage has caused more predictions of disaster than real difficulties, but the pace of change always increases.

When the shortage reaches the tipping point and IPv6 is widely implemented, you will also see the effects of the optimizations of the network layer that IPv6 provides. As cloud computing increases its dependence on efficient network communication, the increase in network layer routing efficiency may prove more important than the expansion of the address space.

Transport Layer

The transport layer takes network communication to a higher level of specificity. The network layer transfers packets from host to host over the Internet. The transport layer connects applications to applications. Since a host can support more than one application at a time, simply transferring a message from one IP address to another is not adequate. The transport layer is also responsible for ensuring that data arrives in good condition. Since the network layer may have fragmented, reordered, or lost packets during transmission, the transport layer is responsible for reassembling the packets, putting them into the correct order, and rounding up missing packets. The transport layer also checks for errors inside the packets and may request retransmission of faulty packets.

Although some transport protocols are connectionless, many are connection-oriented. A connection-oriented service is like telephone service. The first

---

[21] Stephen Shankland, "Net Powers: IPv4 is over. All Hail IPv6!" CNET, February 3, 2011, http://news.cnet.com/8301-30685_3-20030520-264.html?tag=mncol;txt; Internet Corporation for Assigning Names and Numbers: www.icann.org

phase is establishing the connection, which is like dialing a phone number. The second phase is using the connection, which is the equivalent of talking on the phone. The final step is connection termination, which equates to hanging up the phone.

A connectionless service is more like a traditional mail system. A sender writes a letter, addresses an envelope, and drops the envelope into a mailbox. The sender does not know whether the addressee received the mail unless the addressee writes back.

Connectionless services can be the underlying transport for a connection-oriented service. Stretching our mail analogy to the breaking point, the mail sender and receiver could agree only to start a correspondence after they have exchanged an agreement to start and to mark each letter in the correspondence with a sequence number that identifies the series of letters in the correspondence. After receiving a letter, the recipient agrees to send an acknowledgment, and the original sender agrees not to send another letter until the acknowledgment arrives. Finally, the correspondence will not end until both parties have exchanged agreements to end.

As you might guess, connectionless services are generally faster because there is no setup, acknowledgment exchange, and takedown rigmarole. On the other hand, connection-oriented services are more reliable. There is no possibility of undetected lost, duplicate, or out-of-order messages.

The most common protocol used in the transport layer is the Transmission Control Protocol (TCP). TCP is connection-oriented. There is an alternate to TCP. User Datagram Protocol (UDP) is connectionless. It is simpler and has fewer delays than TCP, but it also is subject to the potential errors of a connectionless protocol. UDP is useful when speed is paramount. Voice over Internet Protocol (VoIP), for example, uses UDP because an occasional dropped packet is preferable to a delay. Many online games use UDP for the same reason.

TCP introduces the notion of connections and ports. Ports represent the external connection point of an application or process. Each side of a TCP connection has an IP address and a port associated with it. Ports are 16-bit unsigned integers ranging from 0 to 65535. Some ports are so-called well-known ports. For example, 80 is the port associated with a Hypertext Transfer Protocol (HTTP) service. Ports 20 and 21 are associated with a File Transfer Protocol (FTP) service. Other ports are used for more specialized services such as 3260, which is registered for use by iSCSI in SAN fabrics. Yet other ports have no registered purpose and are available for other uses.

Internet Assigned Number Authority (IANA) registers port numbers. Ports from 0 to 123 are reserved as official well-known ports. On Unix-like operating systems, only root-level processes can bind a socket to a well-known port. IANA maintains a registry for the range from 1024 to 49151 where enterprises and organizations publicly register ports for use by specific services. IANA suggests using 49152 to 65535 for dynamic or private ports. Dynamic (also called *ephemeral*) ports are usually used only for the life of a connection.

Most of the activity of the transport layer takes place in code on clients and servers. Unlike the network layer, the transport layer is completely unaware that a message may take a circuitous path through several subnets before it reaches its destination. The implementation of the layer is self-contained on the source and destination of the messages. This has some implication for cloud computing. Performance issues in the transport layer are easier to deal with in a distributed environment than network layer issues are. If a cloud provider has performance issues in the public network layer, unless the cloud provider happens also to be the network provider, the cloud provider will have to go to the network provider's organization to resolve the problem. If an issue is in the transport layer or above, the provider can address the problem directly. The resolution could involve recoding, adding hardware, or choosing a different protocol. These are not simple issues, but in-house issues are usually easier to resolve than issues that involve communication with third parties.

Consequently, protocol changes that move error checking out of the network layer and into the upper layers and simplification of network layer routing are important to the future of cloud computing. The most significant service level agreements in cloud computing are between the consumer and the cloud provider. Placing more responsibility for performance in the hands of the provider who is contractually obligated to meet performance goals will result in superior service. This is in addition to the network service itself, which promises to improve.

Session, Presentation, and Application Layers

The layers above the transport layer are important in the overall delivery of services to cloud consumers, but they are less distinct or clear-cut than the lower layers. This is partly because the OSI approach to these layers differs from the methodology that has evolved around Internet standards. The OSI approach to networked applications is to develop a toolbox of standard services specified in the upper-layer standards. For example, the OSI presentation layer is responsible for converting EBCDIC-coded text to ASCII-coded text.[22] The Internet application layer is a combination of the OSI

---

[22] Extended Binary Coded Decimal Interchange Code (EBCDIC) is an 8-bit character code used mostly on IBM mainframes, and it is seldom used anyplace else. American Standard

session, presentation, and application layers. It is simpler, is less formally defined, and does mention EBCEDIC to ASCII conversion in its model.

In general, the Internet approach to networking is practical rather than formal. The core Internet network protocols—Ethernet, IP, TCP, and UDP—developed without a closely defined layer model. A pragmatic "try it and see" attitude prevailed. The OSI conceived and designed the model first and wrote the protocols later.

There are deficiencies and strengths in both approaches.

In theory, the model should precede the protocol. The OSI protocols fit into the OSI model better than the Internet protocols fit the Internet model because the OSI protocol designers had a complete and exact model to follow. The Internet protocol designers made the model up as they went along and not always with perfect consistency. For instance, the interface between the network and transport layers is not as crisply defined as it could be, and the transport and session layer are mixed together some.

Nevertheless, the Internet protocols seem to have prevailed over the OSI approach. The OSI model designers did not have the benefit of experience when they designed their model. The Internet designers gained experience as they worked on their model and protocols. They ploughed their experience back into the project as they went along. Consequently, necessity and practice have shaped a set of Internet protocols that are relatively simple to implement. Experience with a wide range of conditions has forced the protocols to grow in robustness. Network operators have faced power surges, tsunamis, denial-of-service attacks, and many other calamities, all demanding resilience. The OSI approach that focuses on overall architecture has not had the benefit of the same scale of real-world experience, although the design-first approach may still excel in the long run.

Like the ascendance of Ethernet over token ring and token bus, as a technology is used more, the equipment manufacturers get better at building better gear for less money, the coders become better at coding to the standards, and general knowledge of the technology spreads. When this happens, it does not seem to really matter whether a technology is better or worse than another: the technology that is better known and has a wider choice of better and cheaper equipment prevails.

Code for Information Interchange (ASCII) is used on distributed systems and the Internet. Universal Character Set Transformation Format – 8-bit (UTF-8) is a far-reaching expansion of ASCII that can represent almost every existing alphabet, including East Asian ideographs. The IETF now requires UTF-8. The ASCII code table is part of the UTF-8 code table. Consequently, any document coded in ASCII is also coded in UTF-8.

Cloud and Networks

The cloud without a network that connects the consumer to the provider cannot exist. Sometimes, a private cloud uses only a private network. In other cases, a private connection is made over the facilities of a public provider; in yet other cases, the connection is at least partially over the Internet. In all these cases, the performance and security of the cloud depend heavily on the network component of the system. The networks of today are much faster than those in use when the Internet began, and its reach has increased immensely. High-speed, broadband connections are available almost everywhere, and wireless networking severed the tether to a wired connection. Without the increase in reach and performance, cloud computing would be slow and difficult to access. Nevertheless, the principles that are the foundation of networked computer communication have not changed while the network has become faster and more efficient.

In the cloud, the OSI distinctions between session, presentation, and application layers can be made, but they are not nearly as significant as they appeared when the OSI system was conceived. In the cloud, the most significant distinctions are determined by the provider of the service. In typical public cloud usage, some components to provide access to the service are implemented by the consumer on their equipment, on their premises. The transport of data and commands to and from the cloud is usually the responsibility a network provider, and the implementation of the service itself belongs to the service provider. As a result of these divisions, the architecture of cloud services tends to cleave along these lines also. The conventional network stacks, whether IETF or OSI, were well enough designed that software built following these stacks also fits into the requirements of the cloud.

The significant changes in networking for the cloud have occurred in the communications protocols used by the wide area network as networks have evolved to take advantage of the expanded network infrastructure. Routers and switches have become faster. Intelligent switches have almost eliminated slow single duplex communication within local area networks. Intelligent switches and routers have made virtual networks possible that operate at a layer above the physical infrastructure. This means that networks can be designed with less dependence on the physical infrastructure. Many of these advances are reflected in the standards discussed in Chapter 9.

Cloud architecture is built on a network stack like the OSI stack. The OSI stack is abstract, and it applies to the cloud as much as it applies to a conventional network on a consumer premises. The difference is where the application layer is implemented. In a cloud implementation, part of the application layer is implemented in the cloud, part is implemented in the high level communication layer (typically HTTP) between the consumer and the cloud, and part is implemented on the consumer site (typically a browser). In a non-cloud implementation, everything is on the consumer premises.

Conclusion

This chapter touched upon some of the techniques and challenges of storage and networking in the cloud. Both storage and networks are two of the most complex aspects of computing in general and cloud computing in particular. Not surprisingly, they are also areas in which standards play a large role. Much more detail on network and storage standards appears in Chapters 8 and 9.

A Map of Cloud Standards

Arranging the Standards

This short chapter introduces the standards that will be discussed in the next five chapters. These standards address many details, and it is easy to get lost in the minutia of their acronym jungles, losing a coherent overall view. Some readers will skip over many of these details, but it will be easier to understand why these details are important when you reference a large-scale map of these standards (Figure 7-1).

Previous chapters covered what the cloud is and how it is put together, and standards are part of this organization. There are several reasonable ways to organize cloud standards, and it is not necessary to declare one method as superior to the rest. Cloud standards can be classified by their place in the overall pattern of cloud computing. An alternative is to classify by their form—that is, whether they are languages, protocols, application programming interfaces, utilities, or other forms.

Cloud standards can also be sorted by the standards development organization that publishes them. The NIST cloud architecture could be used to divide standards by deployment model, classifying as private, public, community, or hybrid cloud-related standards.[1] The NIST architecture could also be used to divide cloud standards by service model, distinguishing between SaaS, PaaS, and IaaS applicable standards. All of these, and more, are valid.

---

[1] Fang Liu, Jin Tong, Jian Mao, Robert Bohn, John Messina, Lee Badger, and Dawn Leaf, *NIST Cloud Computing Reference Architecture*, NIST Special Publication 500-292, September 2011, www.nist.gov/manuscript-publication-search.cfm?pub_id=909505. This document describes the NIST architecture, which is also discussed in Chapter 3.

Each of these methods has its place. Here, I have classified standards by the areas of technical expertise that use them: storage, network, Internet, web services, and standards that apply specifically to clouds. I stipulate, however, that the cloud itself may be too new to have its own well-recognized engineering specialty.

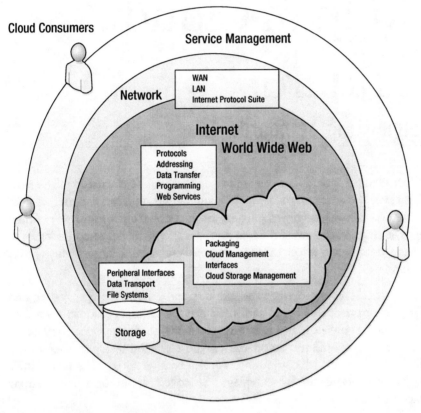

Figure 7-1. A map of cloud standards

Storage

A persistent theme in this book is that the cloud uses or extends existing technology at least as often it inspires new technology. Storage standards are as important to the cloud as they are to traditional implementations. Understanding the strengths and limitations of the storage standards used in on-premises distributed computing also sheds light on cloud computing.

Storage standards fall into three general categories associated with the nature of the storage, as mentioned in Chapter 6. These categories are direct attached storage (DAS), network attached storage (NAS), and storage in a storage area network (SAN). On-premises installations, even desktops, can use each of these types of storage, and they rely on the same standards on-premises as in the cloud. These standards also apply to structured storage like file systems and unstructured raw block storage.

The standards associated with DAS fall into two categories: the standard interfaces used to move data on and off storage devices and the standards for file systems. The device interface standards operate close to the hardware. They abstract the device interface from the hardware so that one interface will work with many different devices.

Without interface standards, someone would have to write and install different software for each make and model of storage device. When programming to a standard device interface, the programmer does not need to know, for example, that the inner cylinders on some disks have fewer blocks of data than the larger diameter outer cylinders, nor does she have to perform device-specific timing calculations to optimize reads and writes. This is the kind of programming that is best done by an expert in a disk manufacturer's lab, not by a general programmer trying to make a PC work. The standard interface hides these characteristics and many others of the device construction. The programming necessary to make the disk hardware work with the interface falls to the disk manufacturer that has the expertise to do it right.

Device interface standards impose little structure on the data. Instead, the interface handles the data as *blocks*, sequences of binary data of a known length but without a known organization. A storage device interface simply reads and writes blocks of data to locations on the storage device.

A few applications use raw block data, but most expect file systems that structure data into files with identifiers and properties such as owners, creation dates, and access control lists (ACLs). Most file systems group files into hierarchical directories. File systems standards define the familiar programmatic interface most programmers are accustomed to.

NAS is similar to DAS. It uses the same standards as DAS, both device interfaces and file systems. The difference between the two is the network that is inserted between the computing device and the storage device. NAS is concerned with accessing file systems remotely over a network. There are standards that address remote access, although they are not specific to NAS since hosts often remotely access file systems implemented on other hosts that are not NAS devices.

SAN systems do not deal with file systems, although the computers attached to a SAN may use the same file systems as DAS and NAS to structure data stored on a SAN. SANs use the interfaces DAS and NAS use on internal data buses, but they use them as network protocols on a data network, often with special data link layer network protocol for rapid transfer of large blocks of data.

The Storage Network Industry Association (SNIA) standard for cloud storage, Cloud Data Management Interface (CDMI), addresses management of storage of all types in the cloud. CDMI is one of the few standards that is specific to the cloud and is discussed in Chapter 11, rather than among the storage standards in Chapter 8.

Network

Network standards for the cloud are important because cloud computing is remote computing over a network. For the most part, network standards do not differ from the standards used in on-premises computing, although on clouds virtual networks implemented with virtual switches often appear. Also, increased reliance on remote computing increases the pressure for reduced latency and increased bandwidth.

The natural classification for network standards is to use the OSI network layers. In particular, standards for the data link, network, and transport layers are important.

Internet and World Wide Web

The Internet is the foundation of cloud computing. The public cloud dwells within the public Internet. Private and community clouds may not use the public Internet, but they use the same protocols on an internal intranet as the public cloud. Cloud-based applications use the same browsers and the same programming methods as noncloud Internet applications, so the same standards apply to cloud as to the Internet.

These include the basic protocol of the Internet, Hypertext Transfer Protocol (HTTP), and the closely related secure version (HTTPS). HTTP depends on a uniform convention for addressing locations on the network. As its name implies, HTTP is a protocol for document exchange. A set of standards has developed for structuring these documents, referred to as *markup languages*.

HTTP is the standard protocol of the World Wide Web, the collection of HTTP servers and applications that interact to provide the functionality that we access through the Internet.

Internet programming languages have also appeared. Some of these, such as JavaScript, were designed to be implemented as part of browsers.[2] Others such as PHP were built for use on back-end servers. Some such as Perl, Python, and Ruby began as programming languages for stand-alone systems and were conscripted for use on the Internet. Perhaps the most significant Internet programming language is Java. Java has become the language of choice for many large projects of all types, with a role similar to the role of C and C++ in the past. These languages have become important in moving the Internet from a passive displayer of remote documents to an all-purpose computing conduit. Unfortunately, a discussion of these language standards falls outside the scope of this book.

Web Services

An important step in the evolution of the Internet to cloud computing is the appearance of service-oriented architecture (SOA) and web services. Web services are an instrument for remote computing over the Internet. A program on one host uses web services to request and perform some computation or other action and return the results. A network, often the Internet, separates the web service requestor and server. Standards for web services involve the languages and frameworks for architecting web service servers, languages for serializing data for transmission over the network, and protocols for handling the serialized data. Cloud service consumers request services from servers running in the cloud. These requests and replies are almost always in the form of web services.

Cloud

Cloud-specific standards are emerging. There are three types of cloud-specific standards currently available: packaging standards, management interface standards, and storage management standards. The goal of cloud standards in development now is to make clouds, especially public clouds, interoperable. One of the promised benefits of cloud utility computing is a competitive marketplace where consumers can shop for the best service and change

---

[2] JavaScript was intended to be a lightweight alternative to Java applets executed in the browser. Java was seen as a language for professional programmers, with JavaScript being more suited to casual web developers. Since then, JavaScript has become popular and has evolved to use on servers also. Server-side JavaScript also appears on both cloud servers and servers on the consumer premises.

providers when they find an offer for a better alternative. A marketplace like that assumes that barriers to changing providers are low.

The situation is analogous to the days prior to standardized storage device interfaces. Someone had to write new software whenever disk drives changed. Until interfaces became standardized, this was a damper on competition among disk drive providers because consumers could not plug in a new drive without tricky software changes. Consequently, they were generally stuck with the decisions made by the PC manufacturers. Even the PC manufacturers could not change drives easily to take advantage of hardware improvements because the software rewrites got in the way. The situation changed when interfaces were standardized, and it became easy to plug in a new drive that may have a quite different hardware configuration without fussing with incompatible drivers and other software.

In the cloud, the standards focus has been on IaaS computing, perhaps because the management interface to IaaS is typically much more complex than the management interfaces of PaaS and SaaS, as discussed in Chapter 3. A more complex interface implies more code to change when switching interfaces. Also, there is a stronger perception that IaaS is a commodity crying out for fluid movement from provider to provider.

Standards to ease moving IT services from IaaS cloud to IaaS cloud have taken two directions. One direction is to define standard management APIs for IaaS. The other direction is to define standard packages that clouds with different APIs can still instantiate uniformly.

Packaging and management standards are not in competition, although they address similar high-level problems. Services in standard packages are not a substitute for a standard IaaS management API, and there will still be a place for standard packages if all IaaS management APIs were built to the same standard. Cloud providers will have to do more work to support standard packages if they do not have a standard API. Therefore, without a standard IaaS management API, standard packages are not as common if the providers have to put more work into supporting them.

Currently, competing package standards and competing interface standards are both evolving. This is also analogous to storage device interfaces. Several storage interface standards now define interfaces that do almost the same thing, but each prevails in its own area. Some argue that competition among standards is counterproductive, but for storage device interfaces, the market, the standards bodies, and engineering have come together to sort them out. It may work the same way for cloud standards.

The third type of standard specific to the cloud applies to storage and making cloud storage available in a standard way.

Other cloud-specific standards may appear in the future. Both SaaS and PaaS are ripe for standardized interfaces. There is no sign that consumers will quit clamoring for performance and bandwidth as entertainment media move to the cloud and new uses for cloud computing are discovered. The desire for bandwidth and performance has driven revisions to old standards and the development of new standards. There is nothing to indicate that those pressures will cease soon. Therefore, cloud-specific standards will undoubtedly continue to evolve rapidly.

Service Management

For business, cloud management is service management. Service management is a two-way street, and cloud service management goes both ways. From the service provider's point of view, the goal is to manage services for maximum return and minimum risk on services offered to consumers. From the consumer's direction, the goal is to realize maximum benefits from services consumed at minimum cost and risk.

Service management is not an engineering discipline like network management or Internet protocols. Service management standards do not have pass-fail test suites. Instead, there are best practices and guidelines that managers apply to their organizations to optimize their outcomes.

There are no cloud-specific management practices, but many IT management best practices apply to cloud. They generally fall into IT management practices and telecommunications service management.

From this point on, this book will focus on specific technical standards instead of on a high-level discussion of the context of the standards that make cloud computing possible.

CHAPTER 8

Storage Standards

Progress in the Datacenter

Storage comes in three forms in cloud systems: directly attached storage (DAS), network attached storage (NAS), and storage area networks (SANs). These types of storage share standards, but each uses the standards in different ways. This chapter will discuss three types of standards: peripheral interface standards, transport standards, and file system standards. This chapter will not discuss the Cloud Data Management Interface (CDMI) standard from the Storage Networking Association (SNIA). CDMI may seem an obvious choice for this chapter, but it fits with the other cloud-specific standards better than with these lower-level storage standards.

Storage forms a natural hierarchy. Physical devices are at the base. They are attached either remotely or directly to processing units that use and produce data. Many standards have been developed to manage the transformation of data on the communications bus to and from data on the storage media. These are the first group of standards examined here.

The next group of standards is concerned with the transport of data between processors and storage. These standards are also applied to the exchange of data between processors in supercomputers and datacenters.

The final group of standards focuses on structuring data for storage. With a uniform structure for stored data, data access methods do not have to be re-invented for each project, and data sharing becomes much easier. Early on, software engineers settled on the concept of the "file" as a convenient storage structure. File system standards are concerned with managing these file structures uniformly.

Peripheral Interface Standards

Peripheral interface standards establish protocols for transferring data to and from storage devices. Storage devices can be interfaced directly to a motherboard within a computer case or on a blade in a rack. They can be external, either as a simple remotely attached disk or as a NAS or as part of a SAN. All of these connections rely on a peripheral interface standard to communicate between the storage device and the host.

Advanced Technology Attachment (ATA)

ATA is the first of a series of standards that began in the early days of the personal computer. It is the simplest of the protocols and the least expensive to implement. Until recently, ATA was almost entirely limited to personal computers, and almost no one thought of ATA as a datacenter protocol.

ATA began as a parallel interface and eventually evolved into the serial interface. In its first incarnation, the interface was called Advanced Technology Attachment (ATA). The "Advanced Technology" is a reference to the IBM PC AT, the Advanced Technology personal computer.[1] ATA is often called IDE, but the standards consistently refer to it as ATA.[2]

Serial vs. Parallel Interfaces

Understanding why ATA evolved from a parallel interface into a serial interface requires some understanding of serial and parallel interfaces. The same reasoning applies to other interfaces.

Parallel interfaces use multiconductor cables, often flat ribbon cables, to send multiple bits simultaneously on separate conductors. An 8-bit parallel interface sends an entire byte at a time by placing each of the 8 bits on eight separate conductors and sending them all at once. In contrast, a serial interface sends 1 bit at a time over a single conductor.

---

[1] At the time, the AT really did represent advanced technology. The AT moved from the 8-bit Intel 8088 to the 16-bit 80286. That meant the AT had to have a 16-bit data bus. The ATA interface reflects the wider AT bus.

[2] It is not clear what IDE stands for. Integrated Drive Electronics, Imbedded Drive Electronics, and Intelligent Device Electronics have all been proposed. See http://ata-atapi.com/hiwfaq.html#T19. IDE is said to be someone's trademark. Western Digital is occasionally mentioned as the owner, but it does not claim IDE as a trademark in its documents that discuss IDE. For example, see http://wdc.com/wdproducts/library/other/2579-001037.pdf. IDE is often used in place of ATA. There is no standard for IDE, and the ATA standards do not mention IDE. To avoid confusion, IDE is not used here, even though it appears frequently in hard disk marketing literature.

At first glance, a parallel interface would seem to be inherently faster and higher bandwidth than a serial interfaces. Common sense says that if trucks all travel at the same speed, two trucks traveling abreast will deliver twice as much as one truck, and with the line speed of bits being equal, an 8-bit parallel interface ought to deliver eight times more data in the same time as a serial interface, but in practice, parallel interfaces have deficiencies.

Interference between signals on parallel conductors is a problem. The signal on one conductor gets confused with the signals on its neighbors. This is called *cross talk*. To compensate, the conductors in a parallel cable usually have ground conductors between each data conductor to help block interference between conductors. A parallel ATA cable has 40 conductors, but only 16 are data conductors. The rest are for operational control and signal interference suppression. Later, to support increased data speeds, the standard switched to 80-conductor cables for even more ground lines to increase cross talk suppression.

Cross talk stems from mutual inductance and capacitance between the conductors. As the frequency of the signal increases, the intensity of the inductance and capacitance interference also increases. The amount of interference also increases with the length of the cable. As the speed and length of a parallel cable increases, its performance decreases.

Also, parallel interfaces are subject to a form of Amdahl's law. If you recall, Amdahl's law says that a parallel calculation can never be faster than its slowest thread. A data unit passed in parallel can never be faster than the signal on the slowest conductor. This means that one delayed or garbled bit holds up the entire byte or bytes transmitted in parallel until the miscreant catches up.

Further, detecting bits in a data signal depends on precisely synchronized clocks on the sender and receiver. In a parallel interface, the signal must be synchronized across all the data conductors. The capacitance and inductance that cause cross talk also cause what is called *clock skew*, a measure of lack of synchronization. This too causes errors and delayed signals.

For these reasons, parallel interfaces become less and less practical as speed and distance demands increase. Serial interfaces are not subject to the same limitations, and they can transmit more data faster and over greater distances than parallel interfaces. Consequently, parallel interfaces, like the IEEE 1284 Centronics printer port that used to appear on every PC, have been replaced by faster serial interfaces like Universal Serial Bus (USB) and Serial ATA.[3]

---

[3] See Michael Schuette's 2002 article "Serial ATA and the 7 Deadly Sins of Parallel ATA" at www.lostcircuits.com/mambo//index.php?option=com_content&task=view&id=50&Itemid=46 &limit=1&limitstart=0 for a detailed discussion of parallel vs. serial at the transition from Parallel ATA to Serial ATA.

On the other side, the advantage to parallel interfaces for computers is that CPUs operate in parallel. A 16-bit processor has 16 parallel data lines that must all be set with meaningful values before they can be read. When data arrives serially, the bits have to be collected and the data lines set before the processor can use the data. One of the facts of life with computers is that performance depends on more than the width of the registers and the speed of the clock. A processor can operate no faster than the data bus that supplies it with data. When data is read from or written to storage, it requires less complicated electronics, and there is less delay if the data does not have to be converted between parallel and serial forms. Therefore, the choice between parallel and serial interfaces is a balance between transmission speed and the hardware and time required to marshal the bits to and from parallel.

This explains much of the early preference for parallel interfaces. Fast serial interfaces were not of much use without fast chips to convert serial to parallel. This issue crops up again in the form of zero-transfer interfaces. In these interfaces, an adapter places data directly into host memory from the peripheral without any other movement. This action requires efficient electronics to move the data correctly from the serial line.

The ATA interface was widely used by the late 1980s, but a standard was not released until the ANSI standard INCITS X3.221-1994 was published in 1994.[4]

An ancestor of the ATA standard was the proprietary interface for the ST 506 disk, one of the first hard disks used in PCs. The ST 506 was a 5.25-inch disk sold by Seagate and its predecessors in the early 1980s.[5] Smaller 3.5-inch disks were replacing larger 5.25-inch disks at that time, and the ST 506 interface was widely emulated by 3.5-inch disk manufacturers. IBM decided to use a hard disk emulating an ST 506 interface in the PC-XT and later the PC AT.

What eventually became the ATA interface connected the ST 506 interface with the IBM PC data bus.

The original IBM PC had an 8-bit wide bus to match its 8-bit 8088 processor. The bus was expanded to 16-bit for the 16-bit 80286 processor in the PC AT. IBM published the specifications for the PC AT bus and called the AT bus the Industry Standard Architecture (ISA) bus. The Advanced Technology Attachment interface began as a hard disk and controller plugged directly into the PC AT bus.

---

[4] See 2005's "Gene Milligan's History of CAM ATA" at http://ata-atapi.com/histcam.html for an early history of the ATA bus.

[5] "ST 506 412 OEM Manual," Seagate Technology, April 1982, www.bitsavers.org/pdf/seagate/ST412_OEMmanual_Apr82.pdf

IBM contracted Western Digital to supply the disk controller for the PC AT. Connecting directly to the ISA bus, the first manifestation of ATA was naturally parallel, but disks were slower, and parallel speeds were completely adequate.

One of the consequences of the parallel interface was an 18-inch limit on the length of the ATA ribbon cable connecting the disk to the motherboard or disk card plugged into the data bus. This meant that disks would remain inside the computer enclosure.

ATA Standards Groups

The ATA standard began as a proprietary interface used in the IBM PC AT, but it was soon in use by several manufacturers that imitated the PC AT architecture. Lacking a definitive standard, the interfaces were almost the same, but too often an edge or corner incompatibility surfaced, and a system would not work.[6] The industry needed an ANSI standard, but it had to be written by another group before it could be made a national standard by ANSI.[7] As mentioned in Chapter 2, ANSI does not write standards; it only approves them. A group of disk manufacturers and system designers formed the Common Access Method (CAM) committee to write up a consistent specification.

The CAM group took the results of their work to ANSI in 1990. ANSI referred the specification to the Accredited Standards Committee X3, Information Technology, later called the National Committee for Information Technology Standards (INCITS).[8] INCITS, or X3, published the first ATA standard as X3.221-1994 in 1994. It is called ATA-1.

ATA-1 (X3.221-1994)

ATA-1 standardized a number of features.[9]

Programmed I/O (PIO)

ATA-1 specified PIO modes 0, 1, and 2. PIO is a method of transferring data to and from the disk that is under the control of the device CPU. The modes

---

[6] Edge and corner cases come up frequently in standards discussions. The terms come from audio engineering. The edge of a room is a special case for sound propagation. Sound anomalies occur there that do not appear in the rest of the room. Corners are an even more special case. By analogy, edge cases occur when a standard applied in an extreme way. Corner cases occur when a standard is applied in two or more extreme ways at once.

[7] www.ansi.org/

[8] www.ncits.org/

[9] ftp://ftp.t10.org/t13/project/d0791r4c-ATA-1.pdf

refer to the speed in which the data is transferred. Pre-ATA-1, only mode 0 existed. The speeds of 0, 1, and 2 modes are 3.3, 5.2, and 8.3 megabytes/second respectively. These data transfer speeds are low by current standards. In addition to being slow, PIO has the additional disadvantage that it takes processing time from the main CPU. While the disk transfers data via PIO, other system activity must stop because the main CPU is busy with the transfer. Therefore, not only is the data transfer slow, the rest of the system must slow down also.

Although PIO has disadvantages, some systems still use it as a fallback mode. On PCs, the Basic I/O System (BIOS) contains PIO code. PIO is a method of data transfer that is also used by keyboards, mice, and similar basic input devices. Because the code is in the BIOS, no special drivers are necessary for PIO, just as a standard keyboard does not need a special driver. PIO continues to be maintained because there is no need to change for simple slow input devices. Keyboards and mice trickle data a few bytes at a time compared to disk drives, so PIO transfer speed and CPU interference are not issues for that kind of peripheral.

Also, PIO is still useful for disks. When a system is impaired, a device that does not need to load a driver may still operate when more complex and demanding devices stop. When drivers are missing, a disk can fall back to PIO and still boot the system. A machine that boots is easier to troubleshoot, and a machine only communicates through the beeps from the Power-On Self-Test (POST). Sometimes, trusty PIO saves the day. Because it is robust, if slow, it is still useful, and the standard has never deprecated it, although it is not normally used for significant data transfer.

Direct Memory Access (DMA)

In addition to PIO modes, ATA-1 supported several Direct Memory Access data transfer modes: single-word DMA modes 0, 1, and 2 and multiword DMA mode 0.

DMA addresses the problem of the involvement of the system CPU in data transfer. DMA is a method of transferring data directly from a peripheral to system memory. The PC AT had two DMA chips providing seven DMA channels. The peripheral device driver sets a memory location and size and starts the transfer. When the transfer is complete, the device driver sends an interrupt to the CPU.

ATA-1 specified 4 DMA transfer modes: three single-word modes (0, 1, and 2) and a multiword mode (0). The single-word modes had speeds of 2.1, 4.2, and 8.3 megabytes/second. The multiword mode transferred at 4.2 megabytes/

second. In single-word mode, a single word (two bytes) was sent at a time to the DMA channel. After each word, the DMA transfer was set up again. Setting up the DMA channel for each word was not efficient, but it still did reduce the load on the system CPU somewhat. However, multiword was better; instead of word-by-word transfers, large blocks of data could be sent in bursts. The speeds attained by DMA transfers are all about the same as the PIO speeds in ATI-1, but the decrease in interference with the main CPU offered by DMA, particularly multiword DMA, was an advance.

Logical Block Addressing

ATA-1 supported two modes of addressing data on a disk: disk geometry based and Logical Block Addressing (LBA). A disk drive is a stack of thin disks. Read-write heads access data in concentric rings on each disk. The rings, called *cylinders*, are divided into sectors, each of which usually holds 512 bytes of data. Each disk has a numbered read-write head devoted to reading and writing the data on that disk, so a head number designates a disk in the stack. The sector is a segment of the circular stripe of data laid down on a cylinder on a disk. A triplet of cylinder, head, and sector numbers can identify the

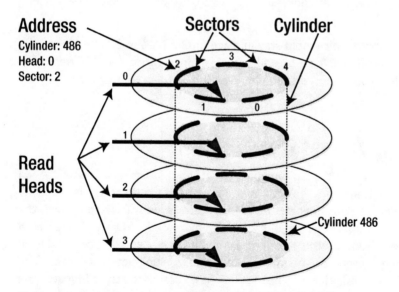

Figure 8-1. CHS hard disk data addresses were based on the geometry of the disk.

contents of any sector on the stack of disks. This is called Cylinder Head Sector (CHS) addressing (see Figure 8-1).

ATA-1 limited the CHS address space to 16.853 cylinders, 16 heads, and 63 sectors. The largest disk addressable using this address space is 137.4 gigabytes. The PC BIOS limited disks to 1024 cylinders, 16 heads, 63 sectors, and 528 megabytes. That meant that although an ATA disk could contain more, the PC could access only 528 megabytes of data on the disk. The BIOS influenced software design, and this limit crept into higher-level constructs.

It was not long before the physical size of disk drives began to approach the BIOS addressing limit. In addition, drive geometry no longer conformed to the simple CHS geometry, and circuitry on the drive was already translating CHS addresses to the real geometry of the disk, which involved innovations like placing more sectors on the larger outer cylinders, which ruined the neat uniformity of CHS.

Logical Block Addressing abstracts the disk geometry out of data addressing. A logical block address has no hint of cylinder, head, and sector numbers. It is a single number that has no connection with the physical layout of the disk. Translating logical sectors into physical disk locations is left to logic circuitry on the disk. ATA-1 allocated 28 bits for logical block addresses, which was larger than the 24-bit allocation in the unofficial practice that preceded ATA-1. A 28-bit address will address 137.4 gigabytes of data like ATA-1 CHM addressing.

The 137.4 gigabyte limit would stay in place until ATA-6 in 2003 widened the LBA address to 48 bits. A 48-bit address will address more than 128 petabytes of data, which is likely to be adequate even for cloud-scale storage.[10]

ANSI declared ATA-1 obsolete in 1999.

ATA-2 (X3.279-1996)

Manufacturers did not stop building larger and faster disks when ANSI published ATA-1. Instead, they continued to progress, increasing disk capacity and responding to consumer demands for greater speed. To keep up with the pace of innovation, the manufacturers extended ATA-1. Since each manufacturer extended the standard to match their own additions, usage of the interface began to fragment, and incompatibilities appeared. The community realized that it needed a new standard to eliminate the incompatibilities and guide the PC hard disk industry forward.

---

[10] For perspective, the Library of Congress is estimated to contain about a quarter of a petabyte of data.

ATA-2 followed the ATA-1 standard two years later in 1996.[11] Larger and faster disks needed more rapid transfer rates. Engineers were building more intelligence into the disk hardware. Disks could respond to higher-level commands that required less knowledge of the disk hardware architecture while increasing the speed of data transfer and supporting larger data volumes on the disk.

New Data Transfer Modes

ATA-2 added four new data transfer modes to the standard. PIO modes 3 and 4 supported transfers at 11.1 and 16.7 megabytes/second. Two multiword DMA modes were added. Mode 1 transferred data at 13.3 megabytes/second; mode 2, 16.7 megabytes/second. The transfer rates of multiword DMA did not exceed that of PIO, but multiword DMA had the potential to reduce host CPU overhead.

Block Transfer

Block transfer commands transfer blocks of data to and from the disk instead of transferring data a sector at a time. Block transfer is implemented with the READ MULTIPLE and WRITE MULTIPLE commands. The commands use the starting address and number of sectors to indicate the data to be moved. ATA-2 block transfer commands work together with multiword DMA to further reduce the overhead involved in moving large blocks of data. Instead of generating an interrupt to the system CPU after the read or write for each sector, the interface generates an interrupt after the block transfer is complete. This permits the transfer of large blocks of data, for example when a program is loading, without processing for each sector. This can yield much better performance.

Identify Device Command

Use of Logical Block Addressing, block transfer, and multiword DMA all are dependent on the ability of both the host and the device to support these advanced modes of operation. Therefore, hosts have to be able to query the device for information on its configuration and the features it supports. ATA-1 specified an IDENTIFY DRIVE command that provides much of this information. ATA-2 added the IDENTIFY DEVICE command that provided more information. The IDENTIFY DEVICE command was designed to meet the needs of more advanced PC BIOS implementations, which could configure themselves to use disk drive features.

---

[11] www.t10.org/t13/project/d0948r4c-ATA-2.pdf

ATA-2 was declared obsolete 2001.

ATA-3 (X3.298-1997)

ATA-3 was published in 1997.[12] The initial version of the document appeared in February 1995, before ATA-2 was published. The first draft of a revision of a standard frequently precedes the release of the original standard when development in an area is vigorous. In the light of future enhancements, it is interesting that the ATA-3 scope declaration specifically limits the specification to host systems that have storage devices within the processor enclosure. This is, no doubt, because of increased transmission speeds that made cable lengths and radio frequency containment more important. This was a limitation that would have to be removed before ATA could have a significant role in datacenters.

Data Transfer Modes

Single-word DMA modes were quietly dropped in ATA-3, and no new modes were added. This reflected the success of multiword DMA.

Self-monitoring, Analysis, and Reporting Technology (SMART)

The intention behind SMART is to provide warnings of adverse low-level conditions on disk drives. Responding to the warnings, users can make informed decisions on disk drive reliability and take steps to avoid data loss or corruption. SMART properties have two states: threshold exceeded and threshold not exceeded. Depending on the property, the indicator may mean that the drive is in peril. The ATA-3 SMART specification may be confusing because it specifies how to read SMART attributes, but it does not specify what SMART attributes are or how to interpret them. The metrics are left to the manufacturers.

APPARENT GAPS IN STANDARDS

Standards often have apparent gaps like the lack of specification of indicators for SMART. Manufacturers have many reasons for wanting to keep critical factors private. They may fear that revealing critical metrics will reveal too much proprietary information about their implementation. They may be afraid that publishing metrics as part of a standard will invalidate an important patent. Or they may fear that

---

[12] www.t10.org/t13/project/d2008r7b-ATA-3.pdf

requiring a metric may preclude innovative changes that would render the metric meaningless.

Whatever the reason, standards like ATA-3 specify how to determine whether the hard drive implements SMART, how to retrieve SMART indicator values, and how to enable and disable SMART, but the standard does not state the indicators that may be returned or hint at the meaning of the indicators.

This is frustrating but is superior to the alternative in which a diagnostic and predictive tool like SMART is completely outside the realm of standardization. With SMART, general software applications are available that offer access to SMART indicators. The indicators are manufacturer dependent, and the interpretation of the thresholds depends on documentation from the manufacturers. Nevertheless, there is some consistency in the indicators, and access is uniform, so SMART is useful to the user, although it is easy to imagine a more perfect world where SMART would be even more useful.

Security Mode

ATA-3 added six security commands to the ATA command set for setting up and using a password for disk access. According to the specification, manufacturers can set up a master password to unlock a disk if the user password becomes lost. However, requesting maximum security when resetting the user password will disable the manufacturer password.

Reliability

Transmission speed to and from a storage device depends on the speed the device can produce and consume data, the speed of the host, and the speed that data can be transmitted between the device and the host. By the time ATA-3 was being written, the speed of the device and the host had increased to the point that problems with "ringing" in the connecting cable were jeopardizing reliability in the higher-speed transmission modes. Ringing is unwanted voltage oscillations that occur when unintended capacitance and inductance begin to resonate at their characteristic frequency. The ringing voltages degrade signal detection. A step that can be taken to suppress ringing is to terminate cables with resistors that interfere with the ringing oscillations. A properly terminated cable suppresses harmonic reflections from the cable ends, which decreases the effect of the oscillations. The ATA-3 specification included new recommendations for terminating the cable and other ringing suppression steps. This was another step in the struggle with the parallel interface.

ATA-3 was declared obsolete in 2002.

ATA/ATAPI-4 (NCITS 317-1998)

ATA/ATAPI-4 was a major specification release.[13] The physical size of the specification nearly doubled in thickness. The formal title for ATA/ATAPI is Advanced Technology Attachment with Packet Interface Extensions. The extensions were added to support nondisk drive devices, mainly CD-ROM and tape drives. This resulted in a major addition to the capabilities of ATA.

80-Conductor Cable

ATA/ATAPI-4 includes a specification for an 80-conductor cable to replace the old 40-conductor cable. The 80-conductor cable is optional. ATA/ATAPI-4 also includes a provision so that the host can detect whether the cable is 40-conductor or 80-conductor and make decisions on which transfer modes to use. The problem described with "ringing" cables in ATA-3 was made worse by the increased speed of the UltraDMA modes specified in ATA/ATAPI-4. The 80-conductor did not add new signal lines. Every other conductor in the cable was grounded in an effort to decrease the capacitance and inductance between the conductors in the cable.

ATAPI

By the early 1990s, a typical business PC had a floppy drive and two hard drives. A single ATA cable would support two hard drives. CD-ROMs disrupted this stable situation. Early CD-ROM drives usually plugged into a sound card using proprietary interfaces, but business PCs ordinarily did not have sound cards. At that time, managers tended to think that the audio circuitry and speakers on the motherboard were adequate for business. But as software got larger and the number of floppy disks needed to install business software climbed into the double digits, CD-ROM drives, unlike sound cards, became necessities rather than luxuries.

A CD-ROM is a random access storage device similar to a disk drive and can be managed similarly. This made CD-ROMs a logical candidate to plug into an ATA connector and act like an ATA device; sound cards would no longer be needed to plug in a CD-ROM. The problem was that CD-ROMs and other similar devices like tape drives required more commands, such as Eject Disk or Rewind.

Until ATA/ATAPI-4, ATA commands were all exercised by loading the command parameters into a command block, a group of eight I/O registers, and then loading the command register with the command. This is a common and effective way of communicating directly with hardware, but it is terse and brittle. The entire sense of a command can alter when a single bit changes.

---

[13] www.t10.org/t13/project/d1153r18-ATA-ATAPI-4.pdf

The position of the bits of a parameter in the command block determines the parameter's significance.

The command register scheme can be blazingly fast, but it awkward and inflexible for more elaborate and extended commands of the kind used by the new devices. ATAPI adds an entirely different command method to ATA called *packet commands*. Instead of loading registers, packet commands are sent as packets. The packet is sent by loading a "packet" command into the command block. This signals the receiver that a command packet is about to be sent. Then the packet is sent as data under PIO control, that is, via the host CPU, not DMA. After receiving the packet, the device returns any return data, again via PIO, and the transaction is complete.

ATA/ATAPI-4 does not specify the commands to send via the packet command. Devices are free to define their own command set. These are outside the scope of the ATA standard. In practice, the ATAPI commands are usually SCSI commands for removable media.

Host Protected Area (HPA)

The HPA is created by setting a size for a disk that is smaller than the disk's real physical size. When a host starts to use a disk through ATA, it executes an "identify device" command that returns information on the geometry and state of the disk including a parameter called *max address*. Normally, the maximum address will be the last sector on the disk that can be read or written. ATA/ATAPI-4 adds a command to set the maximum address. If the maximum address is lowered, the disk size is effectively decreased, and the disk space from the lowered maximum address to the real maximum address is sequestered from normal commands. The sequestered area is the HPA.

HPAs are used in various ways. The most visible way is when manufacturers place restoration software in the HPA. If a disaster occurs but the HPA remains intact, the user can restore the system without a recovery disk, which is helpful with lightweight laptops that have shed traditional CD-ROM drives. An HPA is a handy place to hide nefarious data from exceptionally obtuse investigators and a convenient place for diagnostic tools that must be outside the normal boot disk. It's interesting that ATA/ATAPI-4 adds support both for CD-ROMs and for a feature that makes them less necessary.

CompactFlash Association (CFA) Feature Set

CompactFlash is a format for small solid-state cards used in portable electronic devices such as cameras. Hosts treat these cards like hard drives. However, CF cards have some issues that set them apart. These issues are similar to the issues of solid-state drives. The lifetime of a CF card depends on the number times the system writes data to an address on the card. If the system writes to a single address too many times, the entire card goes bad. Therefore, a card will last longer if the system distributes writes evenly over the physical address space. This is called *write leveling*.

ATA/ATAPI-4 CFA feature set contains six commands to support CF cards. These commands provide access to data stored on the card that is used for write leveling. They also support block erasure and writes without erasure, which enables a level of control that is needed for CF cards.

New Data Transfer Modes

Three new modes were added in ATA/ATAPI-4. These are called Ultra DMA (UDMA) 0, 1, and 3. Their speeds were 16.7, 25.0, and 33.3, respectively. In order to achieve the speed increase, UDMA uses a technique sometimes called *double clocking*. The earlier DMA modes transferred data on the leading edge of the square-wave clock signal. Ultra DMA transfers data on both the rise and the fall of the signal. It is as if the band began by playing notes only at the top of the stroke of the conductor's baton and then later started to play at both the top and the bottom of the stroke. The tempo would double without the conductor changing the beat of the baton. In the same way, UDMA doubles the transfer rate without changing the clock.

Error Checking

The speed of UDMA increased the danger of transmission errors between the device and host. To counteract this risk, ATA/ATAPI-4 added a Cyclical Redundancy Code (CRC) check value.

CRC CHECK VALUES

A CRC check value is similar to a cryptographic hash. A CRC check value calculated from a message will change decidedly with a slight change to the message. The device calculates a check value for the block of data it is about send, appends the check value to the block, and transfers it to the host. The host then calculates its own check value from the received data and compares it to the check value from the device. If the values match, the transmission was error-free. If they do not match, the host requests a resend.

A CRC check value is not suitable for protecting against intentional alteration. A message can be contrived to be altered in such a way that the CRC check value remains unchanged, although it is almost impossible that such an alteration would occur as a transmission error. The CRC check value is not encrypted. Therefore, a malefactor is not hindered from intercepting a message with a CRC check value, altering the message, recalculating its check value, and sending the message on its way.

However, a CRC check value reliably detects the types of alterations made to a message by transmission errors, and its simple algorithm executes rapidly in hardware, unlike complex cryptographic hashes.

Tagged Command Queuing

To read or write a sector of data, the disk controller moves the read head to the cylinder that the sector is on and waits for the sector to rotate under the head. When the sector arrives, the head reads or writes the sector. Then the controller moves the head to the cylinder of the next sector and waits again for the target sector to rotate under the head. Under the best circumstances, the sector arrives at the head at the instant the head has moved to the cylinder and there is no rotational delay, but that does not happen often enough. In the worst case, the controller has to wait for an entire rotation before the data can be read or written. Waiting for the sector to rotate under the head can easily be the slowest part of the transaction. If the order of the operations could be optimized to minimize the waits for rotation, data transfer speed would increase.

TCQ allows the controller to perform its reads out of order to avoid rotational delay. The feature is called *tagged* command queuing because the commands are tagged to flag commands that have not yet executed.

TCQ did not work out as well as expected. Although data comes off the disk faster, through an unfortunate combination, the queued commands caused the DMA control to fire off too many interrupts to the host CPU, and the improvements were canceled out.

ATA/ATAPI-5 (NCITS 340-2000)

ATA/ATAPI-5 was a minor release of the standard.[14] Two UDMA modes were added, 3 and 4. Speeds were 44.4 and 66.7 megabytes/second, respectively. For these modes, the 80-conductor cable introduced in ATA/ATAPI-4 was made mandatory. For other modes, either the original 40-conductor cable or the 80-conductor cable was allowed. The specification also included a reference to the connect defined in the CompactFlash Association's CF+ and Compact Flash Specification Revision 1.4.[15]

---

[14] www.t10.org/t13/project/d1321r3-ATA-ATAPI-5.pdf

[15] http://affon.narod.ru/CARDS/cfspc14.pdf

ATA/ATAPI-6 (NCITS 361-2002)

Released in 2002, ATA/ATAPI-6 was the last parallel ATA release.[16] It was replaced by Serial ATA three years later.

Expanded Logical Block Address (LBA)

ATA-1 allocated 28 bits to Logical Block Address. This was adequate at the time, but by ATA-6, 28-bit addresses were becoming an unacceptable limit on disk size. 137 gigabytes of data was a huge disk when ATA-1 expanded the limit from 24 bits to 28, but no longer. ATA-6 added an option to use 48-bit addresses. Using 48-bit addresses, drives holding 144 petabytes are possible. In addition to increasing the address space, commands using 48-bit addressing use a 16-bit sector count register for block reads and writes. In other words, the command can request about 33 megabytes of data be either read or written. 28-bit commands use only an 8-bit sector count register, which permits only about 130 kilobytes of data at a time.

Device Configuration Overlay (DCO)

The DCO is similar to an HPA. Both features set aside areas of the disk that are not accessible by ordinary commands. This makes forensic investigation of disks a bit more complicated because forensic tools have to be able to execute the special commands that make these areas accessible.

The stated reason for adding the DCO feature set to ATA/ATAPI-6 was to make it possible for a disk manufacturer to acquire batches of similar but not identical disks and, using the DCO feature, make them all appear identical. In addition to setting an artificial size on a disk, unlike HPA, DCO will turn off disk functionalities. The manufacturer uses DCO to configure all the disks in a mixed batch to the size of the smallest and activates only those features supported by all the disks. All the disks then appear to be the same and can be documented and used identically.

A disk can be configured to have both an HPA and a DCO. The DCO feature sets a maximum LBA address, reserving a portion of the disk. Then an HPA command sets a second, lower, maximum address. The difference between the DCO set maximum and the HPA set maximum is the HPA. The DCO is the area above the DCO set maximum. The operating system sees only the maximum set by the HPA and therefore has access to neither the HPA nor the DCO (see Figure 8-2).

---

[16] www.t13.org/Documents/UploadedDocuments/project/d1410r3b-ATA-ATAPI-6.pdf

Maximum Address

DCO Set Maximum
Address

HPA Set Maximum
Address

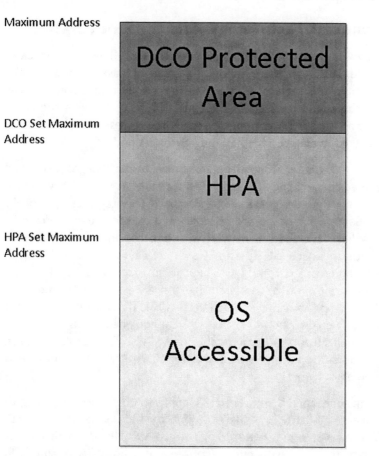

Figure 8-2. DCO and HPA areas are protected from the OS.

The DCO is somewhat more difficult to access and remove than the HPA. The usual methods for detecting and interacting with an HPA are inadequate. Another set of commands are used. This reflects the goal of the standards writers. The motivation for the HPA was to support a protected area that could be used under special circumstances, like system recovery. The DCO was originally intended to be completely inaccessible.

The relative difficulty of working with the DCO has generated flutters in the forensic community and, one would guess, among malefactors.[17]

---

[17] Alexander Krenhuber and Andreas Niederschick, "Forensic and Anti-Forensic on Modern Computer Systems," May 2008, www.fim.unilinz.ac.at/lva/SE_Netzwerke_und_Sicherheit_Comm_Infrastructure/forensic.pdf . It is interesting that six years after ATA/ATAPI-6 was published, the DCO remains mysterious.

Serial Advanced Technology Attachment (SATA)

In 2005, ATA took a new turn. SATA abandoned the old 18-inch parallel cable for a serial cable. Although there was not a great increase in data transfer speed over the parallel interface, revisions to the specification soon followed that increased the speed to 6 gigabits/second. (Note that unlike the older ATA specifications, the SATA community tends to express transfer rates in bits, not bytes. 6 gigabits/second is 750 megabytes/second.)

Without the move to a serial interface and a few other changes that were added to the specification, the ATA interface probably would not have a role in cloud computing. The designers of the Parallel ATA interfaces continually aimed for adequate performance and reliability at a reasonable cost. From its inception, ATA has developed in parallel with another interface, the Small System Computer Interface (SCSI). The SCSI interface, for reasons discussed in the next section of this chapter, has been the interface of choice for high-performance datacenter disks, mass storage appliances, and high-end Unix workstations. Although its name is "Small System," SCSI has been used almost exclusively on larger distributed systems. SCSI-equipped disks are more expensive to manufacture than comparable ATA disks. The result has been that ordinary workstations and home computers have ATA disks, but ATA is less common in datacenters.

SATA disks remain cheaper than SCSI disks, but SATA disks are beginning to appear in datacenters. Features in SATA permit SATA disks to intermix with SCSI disks in some ways, and features have been steadily added that make SATA more attractive in a datacenter. Consequently, both SATA and SCSI appear in cloud storage.

SATA Standards Groups

SATA began as an industry consortium convened by Intel at the same time the INCITS T13 group was working on ATA/ATAPI-6, which was released in 2002. The consortium presented the first SATA specification to the T13 group, where it was eventually published as INCITS 397-2005 in 2005 in three volumes. The T13 group called the specification ATA/ATPI-7.[18]

The role of the industry consortium passed to SATA-IO, a nonprofit, independent group of member companies. SATA-IO has taken over

---

[18] Volumes 1, 2, 3: www.t10.org/t13/docs2004/d1532v1r4b-ATA-ATAPI-7.pdf, www.t10.org/t13/docs2004/d1532v2r4b-ATA-ATAPI-7.pdf, www.t10.org/t13/docs2004/d1532v3r4b-ATA-ATAPI-7.pdf

responsibility for writing and publishing the SATA standard. It has published four versions of the standard, which are available for a fee at their site.[19]

Adoption of SATA

The true advance in SATA was the transformation from parallel to serial transmission. The parallel interface challenges to increased data transfer rates were discussed earlier in this chapter. SATA redesigned the electrical system of ATA while retaining the ATA command set. This meant that the hardware—the circuitry, chip sets, cables, and connectors—all had to be redesigned, but the software above the driver level would remain largely unchanged.

The first release of SATA improved data transfer rates only marginally. ATA-6 supported 133 megabytes/second transmission, and SATA 1.0 supported 1.5 gigabit/second, which is almost 200 megabytes/second, but this is a little misleading because SATA uses 8b/10b encoding. Each 8-bit byte of data on the wire is encoded in 10 bits. The encoding gives superior clock synchronization, error detection and correction, and electrical characteristics to the serial physical signal. With 8b/10b, faster transfer rates are possible, but it does add overhead. Consequently, 1.5 gigabit/second is really only 1.2 gigabit/second, about 150 megabytes/second. This is faster than ATA-6, but in practice, the increase is hard to detect.

Not surprisingly, there were issues rolling out SATA. The first SATA drives on the market were ATA drives disguised with bridge chips rather than designed in "native" SATA. Bridging added overhead and further reduced throughput. With any new technology, there are defects that slip through the testing process and mar performance. As a result, some disparaging voices were directed at the first wave of SATA.[20]

The SATA Cable

For the end user, the most visible change between Parallel and Serial ATA is the cable. A compact rounded cable replaced the ATA lasagna noodle-like ribbon cable. The 40 or 80 conductors of the PATA cable are reduced to seven—two pairs of data lines and three grounds. The SATA cable has several advantages over the old parallel cable. Physically, it is easier to handle inside a

---

[19] www.sata-io.org/

[20] You can find a negative view of SATA at http://ata-atapi.com/sata.htm. To balance the picture, you can find a more positive view with comparison testing here: www.lostcircuits. com/mambo//index.php?option=com_content&task=view&id=50&Itemid=46&limit=1&limitst art=0.

computer enclosure, and the connectors are easier to align and plug in. Also, the connectors are designed for hot-plugging. The ground pins in the SATA connector are longer that the data pins, so the ground always connects before the data lines connect. The thinner cables also interfere less with air circulation in the enclosure. The limit on cable length is 1 meter, which offers more flexibility than the 18-inch ATA ribbon cable.

Advanced Host Controller Interface (AHCI)

AHCI is an open specification for a host bus adaptor for a SATA disk. AHCI is designed as a Peripheral Component Interconnect (PCI) device.[21] The AHCI moves data from a SATA disk to host system memory. Intel developed and owns the specification but grants free licenses and periodically updates the specification.[22]

AHCI provides efficient DMA data transfer, and it provides support for Native Command Queuing (NCQ). NCQ addresses the same problem as TCQ. See the earlier section "Tagged Command Queuing." Combined with AHCI, NCQ solves problems that hindered TCQ from achieving its goals.

eSATA

eSATA is an extension to the SATA specification that supports external SATA drives maintained by SATA-IO.[23] eSATA specifies cables that have an extra layer of shielding against electromagnetic radiation and rugged connectors designed to tolerate frequent plugging and unplugging. The electrical specifications are also stricter. An external hard drive complying to eSATA is capable of transferring data at SATA speeds over the eSATA cable. This is an addition that makes SATA more useful in the datacenter.

Port Multipliers

SATA permits multiple disks to connect to a single SATA host adapter (Figure 8-3). SATA port multipliers are similar to USB hubs. A port multiplier will connect a single SATA port to up to 15 hard drives. The total bandwidth of the connection is limited to the bandwidth of the single port. Two forms of switching are available. *Command switching* switches from one disk to another like an A-B switch. This interferes with Native Command Queuing. The

---

[21] PCI replaced ISA as the common open PC bus. PCI also replaces the local bus.

[22] www.intel.com/content/www/us/en/io/serial-ata/ahci.html

[23] www.serialata.org/technology/esata.asp provides a fairly detailed description of eSATA.

alternative is Frame Information Structure (FIS)–based switching that permits the host controller to send and receive data to and from any drive at any time. FIS-based switching does not interfere with NCQ. Port multipliers can be important in enterprise computing where a single server may require many attached disk drives.

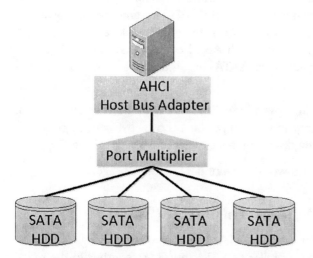

Figure 8-3. Connect multiple SATA hard disk drives to a single SATA port.

SATA 6Gb/s

SATA 6Gb/s is the latest version of SATA from SATA-IO. SATA-IO has released several versions. The earliest version was SATA 1.1Gb/s, followed SATA 3Gb/s. With SATA 6Gb/s, SATA is comparable to SCSI in several ways, both in throughput and in other ways.

SATA SCSI Tunneling

One of the most important aspects of SATA 6Gb/s is a feature of Serial SCSI (SAS). SATA devices can be plugged into a Serial SCSI domain by tunneling the ATA command set through the SCSI protocol. This makes it easy to plug relatively inexpensive SATA disks into a datacenter SCSI SAN.

Native Command Queuing (NCQ)

Native Command Queuing is also part of SATA 6Gb/s. NCQ is important when data transfer rates are high. The total throughput and performance of a disk depends on more than the theoretical number of bits that can be transferred in a millisecond. The data must be available to be sent. When data is received, it has to be used. If those conditions are not present, the line sits idle and data does not flow, no matter how high the transfer rate. This is one reason users are disappointed when a disk that doubles the transfer rate for short bursts of data only marginally improves performance. As the "Tagged Command Queuing" section described, time is lost while the heads shuffle around finding data. Reducing the shuffle time becomes a larger and larger factor as the transmission speed increases. TCQ attempted to solve the problem but was not satisfactory. NCQ is designed to address the problem with the aid of AHCI controllers. With AHCI controllers on the host side, the SATA NCQ commands give SATA an important boost in overall performance in many circumstances.

SATA 6Gb/s also provides improved power management. In large datacenters, optimized power consumption is important both by reducing power consumption and by cutting down the heat radiated from the drive.

Now it is time to look at the workhorse of datacenter storage.

Small Computer System Interface (SCSI)

SCSI has a richer architecture than ATA or SATA. The topology of typical SCSI implementations can be similar to SATA, but its strength is in the more complex and robust topologies that it is designed to implement. These topologies typically hold a wide variation of devices types. In addition, systems designers can implement SCSI on several different transports and interconnects. The SCSI standard is correspondingly more complex than the SATA standard, made up of many documents and incorporating standards from several different standards bodies.

SCSI Standards Groups

The SCSI Trade Association (STA) is the SCSI marketing organization.[24] They serve a similar role to the SATA-IO organization for SATA, except, unlike SATA-IO, the INCITS T10 subcommittee is in charge of the content of the standard. STA focuses on marketing SCSI, establishing market terminology, and promoting vendor interoperability. They sponsor plug fests for testing interoperability and publish white papers and other SCSI-related literature, but not the standards.

The content of SCSI standards is the responsibility of the NCITS T10 subgroup. ANSI publishes the standards. Several groups in addition to T10 are responsible for standards that have been incorporated into the SCSI standard.

---

[24] www.scsita.org

Two other NCITS committees play a role. T11 is responsible for Fibre Channel, which is an optional SCSI transport. T13, which was discussed in reference to ATA, also plays a part in SCSI because SATA disk drives can be plugged into a SCSI domain. IEEE is responsible for IEEE 1394 (FireWire), which is another SCSI transport. iSCSI is an Internet transport protocol for SCSI specified by the Internet Engineering Task Force (IETF). In addition, the InfiniBand Trade Association is responsible for InfiniBand, yet another SCSI transport. Finally, the Universal Serial Bus interconnect is under the USB Implementers Forum, Inc.

All of these standards are organized under the SCSI architecture document (Figure 8-4). The architecture provides a framework that ties together this diverse collection.

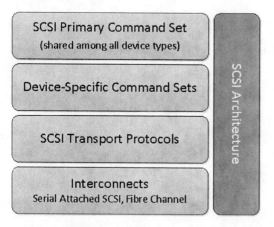

Figure 8-4. Overview of the organization of the SCSI standard

SCSI Architecture

SCSI architecture provides a flexible framework that will accommodate many different configurations. At the center of the architecture is the concept of a SCSI domain. A domain is a collection of SCSI devices linked together by a SCSI Service Delivery Subsystem (Figure 8-5). The Service Delivery Subsystem is an abstraction for the cabling and signaling by which SCSI devices communicate. Unlike ATA and SATA that always distinguish hosts from peripheral, SCSI treats both hosts and peripherals as devices in a domain.

Instead of hosts and peripherals, SCSI distinguishes between initiators and targets. A domain can consist of many initiators and many targets (Figure 8-6). SCSI devices may be nondisk drive data sources, such as tape drives and CD-ROMs.

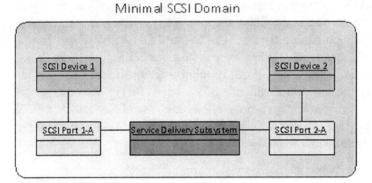

Figure 8-5. A minimal SCSI domain consists of two SCSI devices connected by a service delivery subsystem via SCSI ports.

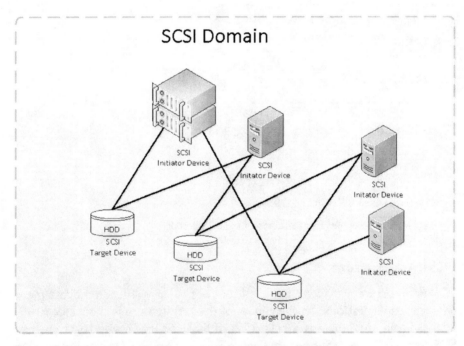

Figure 8-6. SCSI domains are interconnected initiators and targets.

An initiator issues requests and receives replies. A target receives requests and issues replies. This is the familiar client-server relationship in which clients request services from servers. Host computers are usually thought of as servers, but in this context, the peripherals, in other words, disk drives, are the servers, and the computers are the clients. In the SCSI architecture, a single device may be both an initiator and a host. This means that disks can communicate in the SCSI architecture. This allows for intelligent storage appliances to communicate with each other as well as data consumers in a SCSI domain.

The downside of SCSI flexibility is complication. The SCSI architecture is much more elaborate than the ATA or SATA architecture. In fact, SATA relies on SCSI to give SATA some architectural flexibility in datacenter installations by connecting SATA disks into SCSI domains. For the most part, SCSI abstraction is not needed for typical ATA internal desktop and laptop drive applications but is very useful in datacenter scenarios. As you will see, SCSI allows system designers to treat storage as a free-floating resource that many hosts can access. This is also possible with ATA disks, but it happens with NAS on the file system level, which can introduce unnecessary overhead and presents its own set of complications.

The Service Delivery Subsystem (SDS) resembles the lower levels in the OSI stack (Figure 8-7). The SDS is responsible for managing the transportation of data and commands between initiators and targets. From the viewpoint of the application and the target, the Service Delivery Subsystem is transparent. They appear to be communicating between each other without the presence of the subsystem. This allows for flexibility in implementing the subsystem without disturbing the upper layers of the stack.

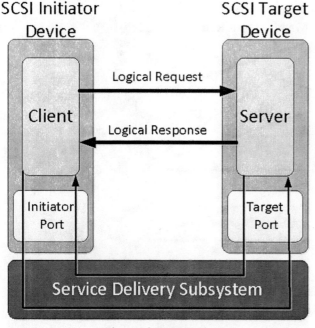

Figure 8-7. The SCSI client-server model resembles the OSI stack.

Logical units are one of the most frequently referred to elements in the SCSI architecture. Every SCSI target has one or more logical units. Initiators do not have logical units, unless the initiator is also a target, in which case at least one logical unit must be defined for the target aspect of the device but not the initiator aspect.

Most often, a logical unit represents a single peripheral—a disk drive, for example. However, a logical unit may also represent a grouping of peripherals, or a logical unit may be a portion of a single peripheral.

Logical units are often called *logical unit numbers* (LUNs) conflating the element with its identifier. Disk drives in a storage area network are casually called LUNs, although the name "logical" and the standard establish logical units as abstractions that are only sometimes related directly to a physical device.

The service delivery subsystem directs service and task requests to SCSI devices via SCSI ports. Target ports contain task routers. Task routers route commands to the correct logical unit (see Figure 8-8 and Figure 8-9).

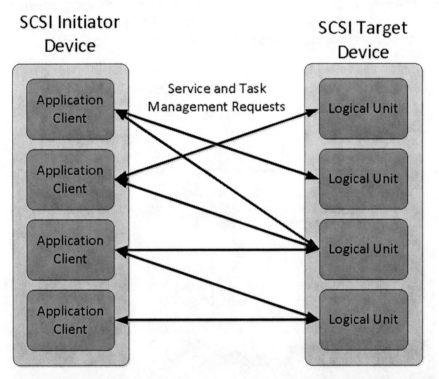

Figure 8-8. Applications in the SCSI architecture initiate service and task management requests with logical units.

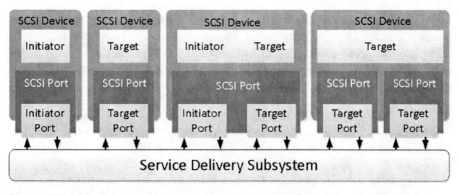

Figure 8-9. SCSI devices may have more than one port. Devices that are both an initiator and a target must have initiator and target ports.

SATA SCSI Comparison

SCSI is an older standard than ATA. SCSI followed a path similar to ATA, in that it has evolved from parallel to serial transfer, but it is different in many ways. The quintessential ATA disk is a single directly attached disk within a desktop PC enclosure. SCSI disks are more likely to be hot-pluggable units in rack in a datacenter.

SCSI topology differs from ATA, which is a reflection of their common usage scenarios. ATA is a disk-to-host, point-to-point topology. Until the SATA port multipliers appeared, an ATA host adaptor could connect with at most two disks. SCSI, on the other hand, not only permits one adapter to connect with many disks, but a single disk can appear to be many logical disks to SCSI.

SCSI flexibility makes it possible to configure disk storage as a resource rather than a device. That is an important distinction. Making use of the flexibility of SCSI domains, devices, and logical units, datacenter architects can treat storage as an abstract quantity they can distribute at will without giving thought to individual disk sizes or locations.

To understand how useful this property can be, consider a rack of a dozen servers, all connected in a simple Just a Bunch Of Disks (JBOD) configuration. Suppose the JBOD contains 24 individual disk drives, each with 250 gigabytes of storage. Thinking ATA-style, an architect might decide to distribute the storage evenly by attaching two disks to each server. But that is far short of ideal. Suppose, as often happens, some of the 12 servers have storage-intensive tasks, and others need little storage. If each server were attached to two disk drives, some servers would fill both disk drives and need more storage, and others would use only a small fraction of the storage on one of their disk drives. The configuration could be rearranged, taking drives away from the light users and moving them to the heavy users.

That would solve some problems, but it would be neither convenient nor a complete solution. The datacenter technicians would have to tinker with adapters—plugging, unplugging, and rerouting cables—activities that are time-consuming, often require down time, and error-prone. If the job distribution changes, the system has to undergo the same troublesome reconfiguration again.

In addition, the ATA granularity for storage assignment is constrained by disk sizes. The smallest increment of storage is a disk in this approach. If a server is assigned to compute intensive jobs and needs only 50 gigabytes of storage, the smallest increment in the JBOD is a 250-gigabyte drive; 200 gigabytes of space will be left vacant. That may not be a catastrophe, but it could be a substantial cost and waste of power.

Attaching storage directly to servers does not fit well in a cloud datacenter. Reconfiguration by swapping and pulling cables is too inefficient, and lack of flexibility results in inefficient use of resources.

In a SCSI system, several servers can attach to the same storage device. The storage device will appear to be a virtual disk for each of the attached server's exclusive use, freeing up other disks for the heavy storage users. Instead of swapping cables, software and automated processes assign and reassign storage quickly and accurately. This is virtualizing storage much like a virtual machine virtualizes computing resources, and many of the same benefits are realized. SANs take this approach much further, but the idea of a SAN is built into the SCSI architecture.

In the cloud, this ability to virtualize storage into an abstract resource is very important. Without it, clouds could barely exist. A virtual machine connects to virtual storage.

SCSI Hardware

SCSI disks are usually physically different from ATA or SATA disks. They are more expensive because SCSI logic requires more elaborate circuits than ATA disks, but more of the difference is derived from the mission-critical uses of SCSI disks. Enterprises are more willing to pay for performance and reliability in datacenters than they are willing to pay for these qualities in office desktops and laptops. Consumers are seldom willing to pay for datacenter-grade storage in home equipment.

SCSI purchasers place a premium on fast reads and writes and long mean-time-between-failure (MBTF) statistics. Performance and reliability are paramount because mission-critical processes and large numbers of employees rely on disks in the datacenter. Slow responses multiply in significance as critical processes and many users queue up for data, and a disk failure is much worse if hundreds of users and critical processes are affected instead of one or two users.

SCSI disks usually spin faster. This has nothing to do with the SCSI standard but everything to do with performance. Sectors arrive at the read-write head sooner when the disk spins faster, and data can be read and written in less time when the disk surface is moving faster under the head. Consequently, a typical SCSI disk drive spins at 15000–10000 revolutions per minute. A typical SATA drive spins at half that rate; 7200 revolutions per minute is common.

But faster spin has consequences. Speed introduces vibration into the disk housing, so the housing must be heavier and more carefully manufactured to suppress the vibration. Vibration affects a disk's neighbors as well as itself. And vibration causes failures and reduces the critical MTBF number. Greater speeds also tend to introduce vibration and instability into the movement of the read heads themselves, requiring more robust mechanisms and stronger activators for performance. Stronger activators are heavier and generate more vibration. All this adds up to a heavy and expensive housing manufactured to close tolerances.

In addition to rotational speed, SCSI disks generally have large caches. The SCSI protocol makes good use of cache for improving performance, so the cost of a large cache makes sense on a SCSI disk where improved performance is important.

For reliability, in addition to vibration-suppressing housings, disks that run 24 hours a day, 7 days a week must have more precise and durable bearings. The case must be sealed more tightly and filters added to stop the last speck of dust from entering.

SCSI disks tend to hold somewhat less volume of data than SATA disks. SATA disk sales are influenced by the cost per gigabyte of storage, so SATA manufacturers watch that ratio closely and design disks that keep that ratio low, which tends to mean larger-capacity disks. SCSI disks are sold more on performance and high MBTF, which does not equal high data volumes. In addition, and probably most important, high rotational speeds reduce the density of data on the disk. Of two disks with a head that reads or writes at the same rate, the one with the slowest rotational speed will lay down the most data in the smallest space. Vinyl record enthusiasts will point out that a 33-and-a-third rpm record holds more music than a 78 of the same size.

All these considerations taken, SCSI disks are heavier, spin faster, have lower seek times, hold somewhat less data, and cost more than SATA disks, but they also have longer lifetimes, are more reliable, and deliver data faster.

iSCSC

iSCSI is an abbreviation for Internet SCSI, a standard developed by the Internet Engineering Task Force in a series of Requests for Comments (RFCs) starting with RFC 3720 in 2004,[25] followed by a number of RFCs on specific topics, such as naming formats for iSCSI node names.[26] RFC 5048 in 2007 is a set of clarifications and corrections to RFC 3720.[27] RFC 3347 is not a standard, but it describes the requirements and considerations that drove the design of the iSCSI standard.[28]

iSCSI is an alternate transport for SCSI based on TCP/IP. It takes advantage of fast Gigabit Ethernet to transfer data over local area networks (LANs) and internets.

The iSCSI designers had a number of reasons for specifying iSCSI. Cost and performance were among the most basic. iSCSI uses the same network infrastructure that most other computing devices use. Instead of special cables, iSCSI uses ordinary Ethernet cables. iSCSI uses commodity Ethernet switching gear. Although special host bus adapters can be used for higher performance, an ordinary Ethernet NIC (Network Interface Card) can be used, and most operating systems have iSCSI drivers installed or available. The Ethernet infrastructure is already in place almost everywhere, and technicians are familiar with it. With the appearance of 40 and 100 gigabit/second Ethernet, the bandwidth available for data transfer is large, comparable to the data transfer rate of SCSI on a dedicated SCSI transport. All these factors add up to iSCSI as a cost-effective alternative.

However, cost is not the only driver. The demand for performance on SCSI systems is also formidable and growing, and iSCSI must perform well and be inexpensive.

Another part of performance is host CPU utilization. As you have learned in the discussion of ATA and SCSI, effective designs avoid interrupting and diverting the host CPU to processing data transfer. Software iSCSI drivers are a problem because they use the host CPU to manage the TCP/IP session and data transfer. This may be adequate for network traffic where data volumes are low compared to storage transfer, but when volume is high and performance is important, iSCSI has hardware alternatives. The alternative is some combination of Ethernet interface, TCP/IP offload engine (TOE), and a host bus adaptor.

---

[25] http://tools.ietf.org/html/rfc3270

[26] http://tools.iet.org/html/rfc3980

[27] http://tools.ietf.org/html/rfc5048

[28] http://tools.ietf.org/html/rfc3347

When the CPU manages TCP/IP as well as other computing tasks, TCP/IP transfer rates can be much lower than a SCSI bus, even when Gigabit Ethernet at the data link layer is fast. The bottleneck is opened by offloading TCP/IP processing from the host CPU to a TCP offload engine (TOE) implemented in hardware. The bottleneck can be opened further by combining the TOE with an Ethernet NIC and a host bus adapter. Therefore, iSCSI implementations often include at least TOEs on important initiators and targets.

Other considerations that shape iSCSI are related to flexibility. As datacenters become larger, the need to link together devices that are physically distant grows. At the same time, as data transfer rates increase, the standards limit cable lengths more and more because error rates increase. iSCSI and fast Ethernet offer the distances and flexibility of an Ethernet LAN and even a WAN to data storage.

iSCSI retains all of the command structure and initiator-target architecture of SCSI. iSCSI addressing also retains the same general structure as SCSI addressing, but because an Ethernet network is much more open than a SCSI domain and addresses on the Internet may be involved, the addresses are more complex and involve more elaborate conventions and address registration authorities.

Serial Attached SCSI (SAS)

SCSI has followed the same developmental pattern as ATA, moving from parallel to serial attachment for approximately the same reasons; namely, both reached the bandwidth threshold beyond which the parallel cable issues with length, noise, and signal synchronization became impractical to deal with.

Beyond improved data transfer rates, SAS adds a few features to SCSI. The topology and structure of a SAS domain are almost identical to a SCSI domain, except the SAS Service Delivery Subsystem is based on a different physical layer. The number of SAS devices supported in a domain is larger than a SCSI domain, and SAS includes "expanders."

SAS Expanders

A SAS expander is similar to a SATA port multiplier but more powerful. A SATA port multiplier is analogous to a network hub. It is capable of splitting an input line and distributing the signal to several devices instead of a single device. Like a physical layer network hub, the host bandwidth is shared between the devices. Unlike a port multiplier, an expander can fan out from a single initiator, and it can also receive from several initiators devices and route to multiple targets. In addition, an expander signal is switched, not split, so each device has full bandwidth, allowing for greater total throughput for the domain. This makes an expander closer to a router in its capabilities. Expanders can also act as bridges between a SAS HBA and a SATA device, which greatly adds to the usefulness of SATA in datacenters.

Expanders also increase the limits on the size of a SCSI domain. Using expanders, a single SAS domain can have up to 16,384 devices.

SAS PHY

SAS discussions include the PHY. The PHY is a chip that translates the encoding of data on the physical wire and the logical encoding of the upper layers. SAS specifies the behavior of a PHY chip in expanders and other SAS devices. Expander and SAS devices ports may have multiple PHY chips.

SAS Domains

Figure 8-10 illustrates the cardinality of SAS objects in the SAS architecture.

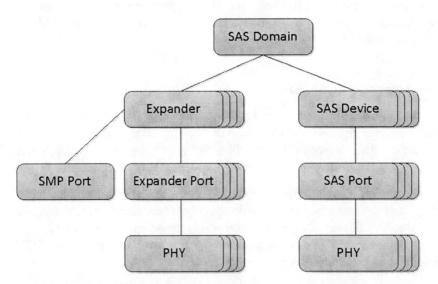

Figure 8-10. SAS objects include expanders, PHYs, and Serial Management Protocol ports, in addition to SAS versions of SCSI objects.

The SAS specification includes three protocols for communication in SAS. The primary protocol is Serial SCSI Protocol (SSP). This protocol is used between SAS devices and expanders and is a replacement for the SCSI protocol used in Parallel SCSI. The most important characteristic of SSP is that it preserves the SCSI command set.

The Serial ATA Tunneling Protocol (STP) connects ATA devices to a SAS domain and adds greatly to the flexibility of a SAS domain. With STP, low-cost ATA hard disks can be mixed in with more expensive SAS disks. The ATA disk is used for less critical storage that does not require the high performance and reliability of a SAS disk.

The third protocol is used to manage topologies. This is the Serial Management Protocol (SMP). As mentioned, expanders are similar to routers. Initiators use SMP to direct expanders to initiate discovery of the system and modify the system configuration (Figure 8-11).

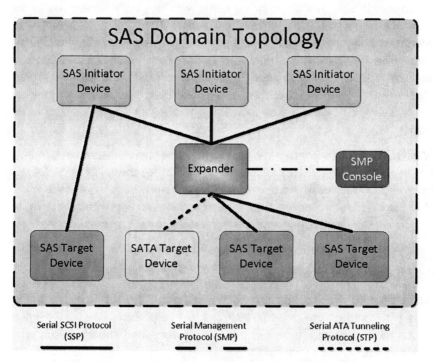

Figure 8-11. A SAS domain can include an expander and SATA devices.

SAS 12Gb/s

At this writing, the SAS 12Gb/s standard is not yet available, but it is expected in the second half of 2012.

Preliminary reports from SCSITA say that it continues to use the 8b/10b encoding that is also used by SATA 3Gb/s and SATA 6Gb/s. Even though the data transfer rate doubled, they are able to maintain the 6 meter (20 feet) length with their passive copper cable and longer lengths for cables with active signal enhancement. Connectors for plugging into backplanes (PCIe) remain unchanged.

Data Transport Protocols

Data transport protocols play a critical role in storage. One of the trends in storage has been to replace transports designed as part of a peripheral interface like SCSI with alternate transports that add to the capabilities of the interface. iSCSI is an example of replacing native SCSI (or SAS) with Ethernet and TCP/IP for greater flexibility. Other transports provide different benefits.

Fibre Channel

Fibre Channel is a network technology that was originally developed as an interconnect for high-performance computing (HPC). Fibre Channel was designed to transfer data rapidly in large quantities with high reliability. These qualities proved to be ideal for SANs, and Fibre Channel became the most common transport for SANs. The original specification for Fibre Channel was directed toward fiber-optic cables. However, later specifications include copper twisted-pair cables. Later specifications offer an option that replaces the Fibre Channel physical layer with Ethernet.

The INCITS T11 subcommittee maintains the Fibre Channel standard, similar to the T10 subcommittee for SCSI and the T13 subcommittee for SATA. There is also a marketing association, Fibre Channel Industry Association (FCIA).[29] The FCIA promotes the standard, sponsors interoperability plug fests, and maintains marketing artifacts such as uniform naming and logos.

Fibre Channel Architecture

The Fibre Channel architecture is in five layers, similar to the OSI layers (see Figure 8-12). The bottom-most layer, FC 0, is the physical layer. It includes specifications for Fibre Channel cables, connectors, and the PHY chips to produce and detect the signal on the wire.

The next layer up, FC 1, is the data link layer. FC 1 is responsible for translating digital data to the form suitable for FC 0 to translate to signals on the wire. FC 1 used 8b/10b encoding, until the 10 gigabit/second and the 20 gigabit/second standard switched 64b/66b encoding. The 64b/66b standards are not backward compatible with the 8b/10b standards. The change was made because 64b/66b encoding entails less overhead than 8b/10b encoding.

The FC 2 layer is called the *network layer*. FC 2 is where most of the Fibre Channel specification applies. FC 2 is roughly similar in function to TCP/IP, but it benefits from not being constructed over Ethernet. Ethernet is a lossy

---

[29] www.fibrechannel.org/

protocol that can drop or disorder packets. FC 2 maintains a session and routes messages to the appropriate endpoint like TCP/IP. The lower Fibre Channel layers do not lose packets or deliver them out of order. Losing packets and out-of-order delivery at the network level is acceptable for ordinary network performance, but it does not work well for low-level high volume transmissions. When TCP/IP receives packets out of order, the packets are buffered and reordered. At high volumes, the buffers must be larger, and the time for re-ordering is more intrusive. Low-level protocols like Fibre Channel usually aim to deliver data directly into system memory without ever requiring movement. This is difficult with lossy Ethernet. One of the basic goals of Fibre Channel is a lossless protocol with no dropped packets and no reordering.

FC 3 is the Common Services layer, similar to the OSI Presentation layer. Common services such as encryption would appear in FC 3.

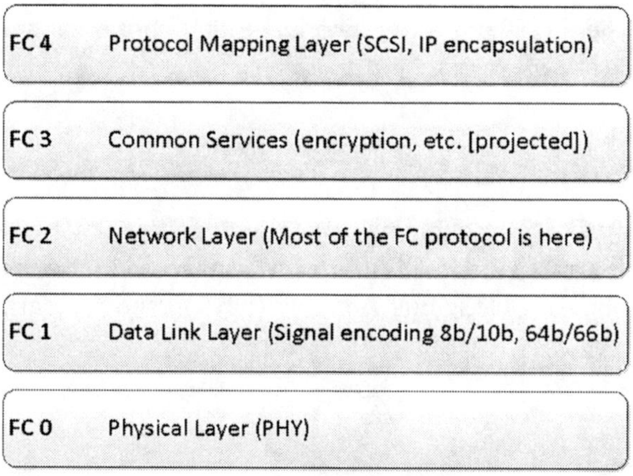

FC 4	Protocol Mapping Layer (SCSI, IP encapsulation)
FC 3	Common Services (encryption, etc. [projected])
FC 2	Network Layer (Most of the FC protocol is here)
FC 1	Data Link Layer (Signal encoding 8b/10b, 64b/66b)
FC 0	Physical Layer (PHY)

Figure 8-12. Fibre Channel layers are similar to OSI network layers.

The top layer, FC 4, is the layer containing application protocols such as SCSI.

Fibre Channel can be deployed in three topologies: point-to-point, managed ring, and fabric (see Figure 8-13).

Fibre Channel is no longer used often as an HPC interconnect. It has been largely supplanted there by Gigabit Ethernet and InfiniBand, but Fibre Channel is now used much more frequently as the underlying transport for SANs.

The coexistence of SANs for data transport and LANs for other internode communication requires two network infrastructures with separate cabling and switching and routing gear. Two networks double network costs and maintenance. Therefore, there is pressure to combine SANs and LANs into a

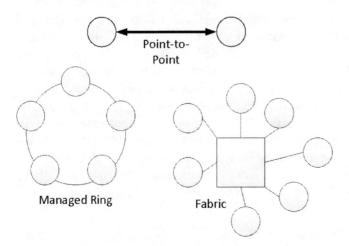

Figure 8-13. Fibre Channel can be deployed in three topologies.

single system. In response, the T10 Committee produced the Fibre Channel over Ethernet (FCoE) specification.

Fibre Channel over Ethernet (FCoE)

FCoE replaces the FC 0 and FC 1 Fibre Channel layers with Ethernet. There are several advantages to this arrangement. FCoE uses a Converged Network Adapter (CNA), which combines a Host Bus Adapter (HBA) used for data

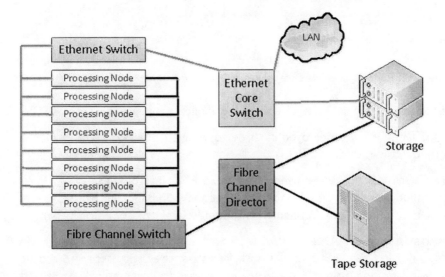

Figure 8-14. Unconverged Fiber Channel and Ethernet switches are used with separate NICs and HBAs on hosts.

transfer and a NIC used to connect to an Ethernet LAN. Converging the networks reduces the number of cables in the datacenter and simplifies the configuration and reconfiguration of the system (compare Figures 8-14 and 8-15).

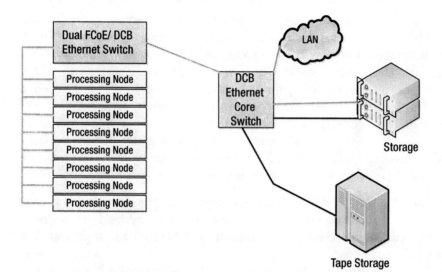

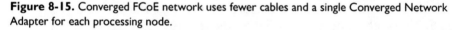

Figure 8-15. Converged FCoE network uses fewer cables and a single Converged Network Adapter for each processing node.

FCoE is designed to be compatible with both Fibre Channel and the Ethernet specification. A basic challenge to this effort was the lossy nature of Ethernet and TCP/IP. Fibre Channel designers built Fibre Channel to be loss-free. This is a requirement for a computer interconnect, but it is not as practical for a protocol stack like Ethernet and TCP/IP that was designed to transmit data through the wilds of the Internet where connections are unpredictable and sometimes unreliable.

The Ethernet that runs at FC 0 and FC 1 of Fibre Channel is not identical to standard Ethernet. It provides flow control, bandwidth allocation, and congestion notification to provide a more reliable transmission within the data center while converging data and LAN transmission.

InfiniBand

InfiniBand was designed as an interconnect for supercomputers and computer clusters by a consortium of manufacturers in 1994. The consortium became the InfiniBand Trade Association (IBTA). The trade association markets the InfiniBand standard, and they develop and publish the standard itself. The current version is release 1.2.1, which is available on the IBTA web site.[30] A road map for the standard, FAQs, and white papers are also available on the IBTA site.

The architecture of InfiniBand was driven by the requirements of a high-speed interconnect. The InfiniBand designers focused on high throughput and low latency. They also designed for controllable quality of service, ready failover, and scalability. No network designer would intentionally ignore any of these goals, but network designers have to be concerned with systems that are inexpensive and are compatible with a wide range of equipment. Networks must be scalable, but scalability for an interconnect is different from network scalability. A scalable interconnect performs well when connecting hundreds of thousands of nodes in a limited physical space over a well-maintained, reliable, and homogeneous infrastructure. A scalable network must perform while connecting millions of nodes over widely varying unreliable subnets with unpredictable performance characteristics.

As an interconnect, InfiniBand has been quite successful. Since 2009, among the world's top 500 supercomputers, InfiniBand and Gigabit Ethernet have been the clear interconnect leaders. Gigabit Ethernet has had a slight lead, but the two are very close.[31] In 2003, InfiniBand had a less than 1 percent share, and Gigabit Ethernet had 24 percent. In 2011, both InfiniBand and Gigabit Ethernet had more than 40 percent shares. Although Fibre Channel started as an interconnect, it does not appear in the top 500 supercomputer list.

InfiniBand is one of the transports that SAS uses, which is why InfiniBand appears in the storage standards section of this book, but it is likely that InfiniBand will be used as storage transport in a datacenter unless it is also the interconnect for the datacenter. InfiniBand is similar to a peripheral interface standard because it is designed for direct connection with processor memory like Direct Memory Access (DMA) in SCSI and ATA. Consequently, InfiniBand communication seldom interferes with the host processor, and it seldom has to wait for service from the host processor.

Topology

The simplest InfiniBand topology is a single-processor node and a single InfiniBand switch (see Figure 8-16). The InfiniBand host channel adapter (HCA) connects to an InfiniBand switch. The switch connects to target channel adapters (TCAs), which deliver and receive data from I/O nodes. I/O

---

[30] www.infinibandta.org

[31] http://i.top500.org/stats

nodes can be a wide variety of objects. InfiniBand does not specify I/O commands or cluster services. For example, the SCSI command set is not part of the InfiniBand architecture, although there are SCSI adapters for InfiniBand.

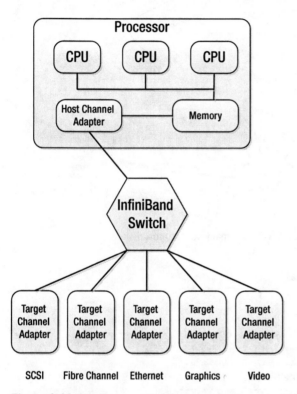

Figure 8-16. InfiniBand can interface a single processor node to many different targets.

Topologies that are more elaborate are possible. Thousands of processor nodes can be connected to tens of thousands of I/O nodes. In a cloud configuration, the I/O nodes are likely to be connections to the Internet and storage, providing the scale necessary for servicing large numbers of consumers simultaneously (see Figure 8-17).

Architecture

A basic principle of the InfiniBand Architecture (IBA) is to minimize the involvement of the host processor by performing I/O via direct access to processor memory (Figure 8-18). The IBA HCA has direct access to the

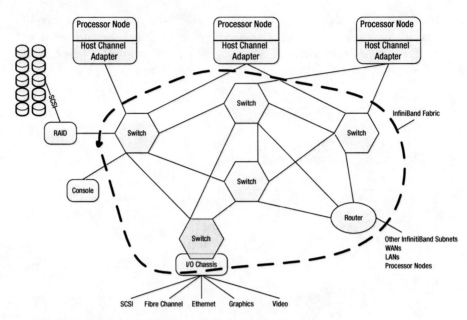

Figure 8-17. An InfiniBand fabric can connect many subsystems.

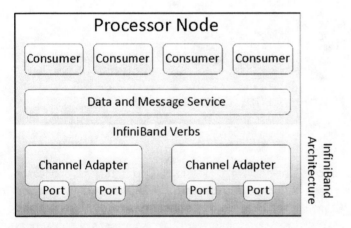

Figure 8-18. InfiniBand channel adapters are designed to work directly with processor memory.

processor node memory and is able to manipulate it without affecting the host CPU.

IBA includes five different classifications of devices: routers, switches, channel adapters, repeaters, and links. Links interconnect all the other devices in the architectures.

Links are cables and wiring on a backplane. The cables can be either copper or optical fiber. Repeaters extend the range of links on the physical layer by repeating signals. Higher levels are not aware of the existence of links.

Channel adapters generate and consume packets on processor nodes and I/O nodes. They come in two flavors: HCAs and TCAs.

A channel adapter is a direct memory access engine that can safely deal with memory operations initiated both locally and remotely. A channel adapter may have multiple ports that are capable of sending and receiving concurrently. Channel adapters have globally unique identifiers assigned by the channel adapter vendor. Channel adapter ports also have globally unique identifiers assigned by the vendor.

An IBA switch passes along packets based on the destination address in the packet's local route header and consumes packets for managing the switch itself. Thus, switches are the primary instrument for routing within an IBA subnet. They relay packets from one link to another, following the destination address of the packet and the forwarding table of the switch.

IBA routers consume packets for managing themselves, but their main job is to forward packets from one subnet to another following the packet's global route header. Often, multiple paths are deployed to maximize availability if a link fails.

IBA distinguishes two types of command semantics: memory semantics and channel semantics. With memory semantics, the initiator directly reads or writes to a virtual memory address on a remote node. Channel semantics include the traditional read and write commands that typify most peripheral interfaces. In an example described in the InfiniBand specification, a host initiates a write to a disk by issuing a channel write command. The disk responds by reading the data directly from the host memory using memory semantics, and then the disk uses channel semantics to return a completion notification. Thus, the write uses both types of semantics in combination.[32]

Processors and I/O nodes use IBA verbs to communicate with HCAs and the TCAs. These verbs are not the native commands of the I/O device or cluster service. Instead, they are commands issued to set up the communication. The native commands are then passed through the IBA subnet to the target. The channel adapters support multiple send and receive queue pairs that are communications interfaces between a host and target. The IBA verbs supported for a Send Queue are commands like Send Buffer, a channel

---

[32] InfiniBand Trade Association. "InfiniBand Architecture Release 1.2.1, Volume 1 – General Specifications," November 2007, p. 118, http://infinibandta.org/content/pages. php?pg=technology_download.

semantic that pushes a buffer to a remote queue, or Remote Direct Memory Access (RDMA) Read, which is a memory semantic that reads a virtually continuous buffer on a remote node and writes it to memory on the originating node.

This concludes the data transport protocol section. Gigabit Ethernet is also an important data transport protocol, but it will be covered in Chapter 9.

Other data transport protocols include serial data transports such as the venerable RS-232 standard used to connect personal computers to peripherals. RS-232 has been replaced by faster and more convenient protocols such as Universal Serial Bus and Apple Thunderbolt, which are robust enough for connecting storage media. These protocols are not discussed here because they do not play a large role in cloud implementation and usage although they do touch on the same technical subjects as datacenter protocols.

File Systems

File systems organize persistent data, data that is meant to be retained and reaccessed over time. File systems are usually implemented as a subsystem of an operating system. Most programming languages support interaction with file systems, and most programs interact with files rather than raw blocks of data. Files are an abstraction that represents an ordered sequence of bytes of data. The data maybe characters or arbitrary binary data. The file abstraction is logical and usually does not specify a physical organization or representation. The file abstraction includes opening, reading, writing, and closing the file. A closed file is assumed to be persistent. File systems also usually include a concept file organization, often hierarchical directories or folders. File systems also often limit file access to authorized users.

File systems present a contrast to peripheral interfaces. File systems operate at a higher level in the protocol stack. Peripheral interfaces work in the general neighborhood of the transport layer. Some parts of an interface like SCSI specify commands that are communicated via a transport protocol and are therefore close to being an application layer, but these same interfaces also go all the way down to specifying the electrical characteristics of the signal.

File system protocols are more clearly application layer entities. Their specifications designate protocols like TCP/IP, Ethernet, and InfiniBand, and they may suggest tweaks to the lower levels to make them more suitable for file system sharing, but they rely on lower-level protocols like TCP/IP and Network Basic Input/Output System (NetBEUI).

As mentioned previously, there is a certain amount of rivalry between block-structured data transport protocols like SATA and SCSI and network file systems like Network File System (NFS) and Server Message Block (SMB). File systems are used for NAS. Application layer protocols are generally easier to use by applications, but because they involve more overhead, they do not move data as fast. Block-structured protocols are fast, but block data may require resources to convert it to a useful form.

The file system protocol groups and vendors have striven to improve the performance of their products and take advantage of the new transports developed for the datacenter. Consequently, file systems have become more suitable for use in cloud implementations, making the benefits of an application-level protocol more attractive in a datacenter.

At the same time, the large amount of storage that the cloud has made available has inspired cloud consumers to store orders of magnitude more data. Scaling this mountain of data has prompted developers to write applications and utilities that skip file systems and operate directly on raw block data.

Network File System (NFS)

NFS is an old system, first developed at Sun Microsystems in 1984, that has evolved and is still widely used with UNIX and Linux. The original goals for NFS were characteristic of the time when NFS was developed. Networks were just beginning to become important, and the requirements for effective networking were only beginning to be understood. The requirements identified for NFS became part of the set of requirements that eventually became the requirements for cloud computing.

Some of the original NFS developers listed the NFS requirements in a paper the year after the first public release of NFS.[33] They expected NFS to be:

- Hardware and operating system independent.

- Easily recoverable from remote crashes.

- Transparently accessible. Remote files should be indistinguishable from local files.

- Reasonable performance. Remote file performance should be close to local file performance.

---

[33] Russel Sandberg, David Goldberg, Steve Kleiman, Dan Walsh, and Bob Lyon, "Design and Implementation or the Sun Network Filesystem." 1985, http://citeseerx.ist.psu.edu/viewdoc/summary?doi=10.1.1.14.473.

To meet these goals, they made use of two existing technologies: Remote Procedure Calls (RPCs)[34] and External Data Representation (XDR).[35] Both were defined by Sun Microsystems and later became standards. RPCs are a method of calling procedures on a remote machine. RPCs mimic the C local function call. XDR is a set of data representations designed to facilitate transfer of data between disparate sources that may represent the data differently.

These two standards provided a simple basis for the NFS protocol. A set of file manipulation verbs were implemented using RPCs, and the data was transferred using XDR representations. The challenge was implementation, not the specification.

The first versions of NFS were stateless. Each RPC contained all the information necessary to respond to the call. The server was not expected to cache anything. This meant that recovery from crashes was easy with no stacks to unwind or states to reconstruct, and the recoverability requirement was easily met.

The IETF published the current release of NFS, NFSv4 minor version 1, in January 2010 as RFC 5661.[36] NFSv4 became stateful. The main reason for becoming stateful was performance. Although stateless protocols are easy to recover, they tend to be chatty, exercising several stateless interchanges that can be replaced by a single stateful interchange. A stateful interface is usually more complicated, but an increase in performance often compensates for the complication. The stateful interface also made it possible to implement pipelining, sending commands before the previous command finishes. Pipelining speeds performance on slow connections because it can shorten the wait between pipelined commands for both the sender and the receiver. SATA and SCSI get similar benefits from their queued commands.

NFSv4 also includes support for Remote Direct Memory Access (RDMA), which has proven so important in SCSI, SATA, and InfiniBand.[37] NFSv4 does not directly use any RDMA facilities, but it operates over transports such as InfiniBand that can access memory directly. Even though it is not used directly, RDMA places requirements on the NFS system, such as the way caches are handled and, when retransmits are permitted, necessitating changes in the NSF standard.

---

[34] RFC 1831. http://tools.ietf.org/html/rfc181. The IETF RPC RFC was entered long after the de facto proprietary standard was established.

[35] RFC 1014. http://tools.ietf.org/html/rfc1014.

[36] RFC 5661. http://tools.ietf.org/html/rfc5661.

[37] RDMA is used in yet another data transport protocol, Internet Wide Area RDMA Protocol (iWARP), which is not discussed here.

Server Message Block (SMB) and Common Internet File System (CIFS)

SMB/CIFS is the proprietary Microsoft Windows remote file system. Microsoft has called the system both SMB and CIFS at different times, but for the majority of the system's lifetime, it has been called by both names. The latest Microsoft specifications call it SMB. Microsoft still owns SMB and CIFS, but it has made the specifications public.[38] It encourages free use of the specifications in implementations, although Microsoft warns that it retains patent rights.

SMB has gone through many changes and permutations since it was first developed by IBM and later modified and extended by Microsoft. It was altered to run on a number of different transports, and the functions supported have been stretched and modified many times, resulting in a complex protocol with overlapping, unused, and undocumented features.

Microsoft addressed these problems with SMB2 in 2006. The command set was reduced and rationalized, improving performance and resiliency. Data widths were increased to improve scalability and capacity.

SMB2.2 is linked to the Windows 8 release.[39] A preliminary specification has been published. Possibly the most interesting feature of the Windows 8 release is the addition of support for RDMA, like NFSv4. The two implementations are different because the basic architecture of NFS and SMB are different. Since NFS is a layer on top of RPCs, NFS support of RDMA depends more on RPC support of RDMA than it does on anything in NFS itself. That architecture certainly made the NFS implementation easier, but, as is often the case with layering, lack of direct contact with RDMA in the underlying transport may hinder optimization.

SMB was a more difficult job because SMB has no such separation. Microsoft's changes for RDMA had to reach higher in the stack. However, sometimes an implementation that reaches further can be a better implementation that takes more advantage of the low-level enhancement. It is possible that SMB will prove to perform better in the datacenter than NFS, but it is also possible that the difference will be negligible. Since neither NFSv4 minor version 1 nor SMB2.2 is widely deployed, there can be no decision yet.

Other File Systems

NFS and SMB are not the only file systems. IBM independently developed several file system for its products, including the Integrated File System (IFS),

---

[38] http://msdn.microsoft.com/en-us/library/gg258393%28v=prot.13%29.aspx
[39] http://msdn.microsoft.com/en-us/library/cc246482%28v=prot.13%29.aspx

which IBM developed for the AS/400 OS/400 operating system. IFS is notable for integrating several different types of files and storage, including relational databases and files with differing physical organizations, into a single file system.[40] Coda is a system under development for a number of years at Carnegie-Mellon University.[41] Extended File System (ets) ships in several versions with many Linux distributions.[42] These are a few among many other file systems that have been developed.

Conclusion

Storage standards have evolved steadily to support higher volumes of data and more rapid and reliable data transfer. Configuration has become simpler and more automated. Slower and less expensive storage has become easier to combine with faster and more reliable premium storage. These tiered storage architectures economically support volumes of data that were unimaginable not too long ago. In addition, the data and network infrastructures appear to be converging, making datacenters easier to cable and maintain. All of this is part of the rise of cloud datacenters.

---

[40] See http://publib.boulder.ibm.com/infocenter/iseries/v5r3/topic/ifs/rzaax.pdf. The AS/400 is now called the iSeries.

[41] See www.coda.cs.cmu.edu/ www.coda.cs.cmu.edu/.

[42] See http://e2fsprogs.sourceforge.net/ext2intro.html. This document deals with ets up to ets2. Current Linux distributions ship versions up to ext4. The citation was chosen because it was written by the original ets designers and implementers.

9

Network and Internet Standards

Connecting the Dots

The cloud is inseparable from the network. If data cannot be transported to and from remote clouds, clouds are remote islands in the sky that might as well not exist for most consumers and enterprises.

Bandwidth—the volume of communication—must be ample to connect a cloud to its users. Without copious bandwidth, the pooled resources of the cloud can perform only the few useful tasks that can be contained inside the cloud perimeter.

Some big data analysis is contained within the cloud perimeter and can be performed without much network activity. Analyzing ten years of accumulated astronomical data for cosmic ray patterns, for example, involves the slow transmission and storage of the data over a long period; the analysis uses many cloud processors working in parallel with little interaction with the outside world. Eventually a report is produced and delivered to the consumers of the analysis, but the transfer of data in and out of the cloud for the job is minor. A task like that does not require much network bandwidth.

But contained and isolated tasks are rare in clouds. Analyzing astronomical data may change our view of the universe, but it will not change commerce. Contrast that task to a CRM SaaS application or a social networking application that handles hundreds of thousands of interactions an hour. End users are interacting in real time. Anything slower than subsecond response is an annoyance to most users. Social networking applications like Facebook or LinkedIn thrive on storing and playing back sound, photographs, and videos. The volume of data transfer for those kinds of applications is very large. These applications are more typical of cloud applications than near stand-alone batch jobs, and they have an unquenchable thirst for bandwidth.

It is a chicken-or-egg question: have we expanded the available bandwidth because applications demand it, or do we create applications voracious for bandwidth because the bandwidth is there to be used? It's an unanswerable question, but undoubtedly the pressure exists in both directions.

This chapter is divided into three sections. The first section covers wide area networks (WANs). These networks are, for the most part, operated by public telecommunications companies. They are almost all related to voice networks. The second section covers local area networks (LANs), which are usually private. The final section covers the protocols of the Internet suite.

Someone once said that the good thing about standards is there are so many to choose from.[1] That is certainly true for networking standards. This chapter cannot cover all networking standards either in depth or in breadth. You will find a sampling of standards here, but many are missing. There are some official standards that are never used, but most are important somewhere. I hope no one is disappointed that I missed his or her favorite. The choices here are based on an importance in supporting the cloud and those that yield the best insight into the functioning of the cloud.

Wide Area Networks (WANs)

WAN standards are probably the least visible to the cloud consumer, but in some ways, they are the most important. WANs transport data great distances, like the long-distance telephone services that prevailed when electronic communication meant telephone service. Although WANs are usually reliable, possibly more reliable than LANs, they still have great potential for disruption. A request sent from North America to a European site is likely to travel through half a dozen routers in North American and as many in Europe, passing through the WANs of four or five different service providers. If any one of these hand-offs is not executed correctly, performance will

---

[1] Exactly who said it first is a subject for discussion and Internet searches. Grace Hopper and Andrew S. Tanenbaum are the leading candidates. Tanenbaum made the statement in *Computer Networks*, Second Edition (Prentice-Hall, 1988), in reference to the data link layer standards, but there are hints that Tanenbaum was not the first to use the trope. Network engineering is not the only discipline where the thought applies.

suffer. Examining some of the protocols used by these WAN providers will help you understand long-distance network communications.

Asynchronous Transfer Mode (ATM)

The ATM Forum–developed Asynchronous Transfer Mode (ATM) is a protocol for combined voice and data transmission on the same network. Telecommunications providers needed a standard protocol that could handle both bursty data, such as file transfers, and voice, which is less bursty but requires low latency over a longer period. *Bursty* is a networking term that refers to data transmitted in clumps of high volumes interspersed with periods of relative quiescence. As you will see as this chapter progresses, the distinction between bursty and nonbursty data is a recurrent theme that is important for satisfactory network performance.

ATM Standards

The ATM standard began in the ATM Forum, a consortium of telecommunications providers and network equipment manufacturers. The forum was founded in 1991. In 2005, the ATM Forum merged with the organization that eventually became the Broadband Forum. The ATM standards are available on the Broadband Forum site.[2] In the mid-1990s, the IETF became involved in the standardization of the use of ATM in the Internet, especially as a WAN transport. This resulted in several RFCs on transmitting Internet TCP/IP traffic over ATM networks.[3] Eventually, interest in ATM as a vehicle for future networks waned, and interest in writing new standards disappeared in both the Broadband Forum and IETF. RFC 4454[4] is a late-appearing IETF specification that is dated 2006.

Voice and Data

As awkward as it seems today, early computer-to-computer wide area networking tapped into the voice network with acoustically coupled modulator-demodulators (modems). The modem translated digital signals into sounds and played them into the telephone handset microphone. The modem listened to the speaker in the telephone handset with its own microphone and translated the tones into a digital signal for the computer. The modem mixed digital signals into the voice stream on the telephone

---

[2] www.broadband-forum.org/technical/atmtechspec.php

[3] RFC 1577, www.ietf.org/rfc/rfc1577.txt, describing IP over ATM is a good example. There are several more.

[4] http://tools.ietf.org/html/rfc4454

network. Computer networks based on the reliable and far-reaching telephone network could connect computers almost anywhere. However, there was a drawback: voice and digital data do not mix well on a single network. The next several decades of wide area networking would deal with this problem in various ways, transforming a voice-only system to one that handles many different types of data efficiently.

Data

Data traffic is bursty. Users typically see a file that downloads in a reasonable time and without errors as good network performance even if the amount of data transferred per hour is low, but any errors in the data are usually readily apparent and unacceptable.

When packets are variable length with a high maximum, a single packet may encapsulate an entire file. These large packets eliminate the overhead of transmitting many individual packets, and the transmission of a single packet ordinarily is not interruptible. This is an ideal pattern for bursty data. Bursts blast through in a few packets. Then the network is available for other uses until the next burst.

Fewer packets reduce the chance that packets will be lost or delivered in the wrong order. If packets are lost, at some point in the transmission the protocol orders a replacement and waits for its arrival. The protocol must reorder out-of-order packets. Resends and reorders are slow and can affect performance as much as overall low bandwidth. As long as the bursts are not so frequent and long that they begin to collide, long packets promote good performance while consuming minimal bandwidth.

When a data transmission is interrupted while the network takes a few seconds to retransmit a bad packet or re-order out-of-order packets, there may be a pause, but the users will barely notice if the overall download is fast. Even in the interactive context of reading pages in a browser, pauses are annoying but tolerable because the task is eventually completed; in other words, the page eventually refreshes, and the download completes. The viewing experience may be marred but not ruined.

Voice

Voice transmission is different. Continuous media do not demand the bursts of bandwidth that data requires, and they tolerate some errors in the transmission, but they do require predictably spaced deliveries, and a packet out of order can be as disruptive as a lost packet.

The voice has to be delivered in real time, or it is unintelligible. The codec that translates the digital signal to analog sound must have data at a real point in time. If the data is not there, the codec must go silent or guess an approximation. Retransmission of bad data is not useful because late data is useless to the codec and the codec must discard it. Intelligent codecs are capable of correcting and interpolating bad and missing data as it is translated to analog sound, but if too much data is missing or late, the reassembled voice is unintelligible. A large delayed packet is a disaster. A codec can repair a damaged signal easier than it can compensate for a missing packet. An unintelligible voice conversation is a failure, which is more serious than a delay in data delivery.

Jitter is the name given to unpredictable variability in the delivery of packets. Reduced jitter is an important indicator of a high-quality voice connection. Low-jitter connections are easier to understand and sound more natural because codecs do not have to drop packets often or make approximations that degrade quality. A bad cell phone connection is often the result of network jitter.

Short packets reduce jitter. If a packet has to wait for transmission of a long packet, jitter will result, but a short wait for a small packet presents less variability and less jitter. Therefore, data-oriented networks tend to have variable-length, long packets. Voice and continuous media networks tend toward short packets.

ATM Voice vs. Data Solution

ATM was designed to combine data and voice on the same network. The solution chosen by the ATM engineers was a short, 48-byte packet with a 5-byte header, making a total of 53 bytes. This is a relatively small packet. For comparison, a Gigabit Ethernet jumbo frame can have as many as 9,000 bytes of payload. On a 10 gigabit/second line, 9,000 bytes can be transmitted in micro seconds; on a 10 megabit/second line, the technology of the mid-1990s, a single jumbo packet could take more than 7 seconds. A 53-byte ATM packet would take less than 50 milliseconds, which was enough to keep jitter down to reasonable level.

In addition to small packets, ATM is based on virtual circuits.

Circuits and datagrams are two basic modes of network communication. In circuit mode, when a message is sent, the first step is to set up a path between the sender and receiver. With a circuit in place, data flows over the circuit until the session ends and the circuit is taken down.

Datagrams, on the other hand, are individually addressed. Each datagram contains all the information necessary to direct it to its destination. Each datagram in a message follows its own route through the network. There is nothing equivalent to a session end to designate the beginning or endpoint of a message sent via a series of datagrams, and therefore it may not be possible to determine when a message is complete.

There are advantages and disadvantages to datagrams over circuits. Datagrams are more subject to jitter because each route through the network adds unpredictable latency to delivery. On the other hand, datagrams are likely to be more resilient to network congestion and failures as the datagrams find their way around the blockages. Circuits can take time to set up, adding to the overall latency, but when latency occurs only at the beginnings and ends of long transmissions, it is less significant. Therefore, the latency of circuit establishment and takedown is likely to be especially apparent when traffic consists of short messages, as in bursty traffic.

Sometimes circuits are temporary; other times they are set up permanently and taken down only by exception. Circuits can be physical or virtual. A physical circuit reserves specific units of hardware for the circuit. A virtual circuit uses a pool of equipment, but the actual hardware used for the circuit may vary over time.

ATM is based on virtual circuits and supports both temporary and permanent circuits. The combination of small packets and a circuit-based communication was a compromise to provide support both for data and for voice. ATM allows for the adjustment of quality of service (QoS), which can mean adjusting the type of service provided to different classes of customers, including voice and data.

Many of the characteristics of ATM are reflected in its packet layout (Figure 9-1). The packet header contains the payload type and the cell lost priority, both of which reflect quality-of-service considerations. Packet addressing is in terms of virtual paths and channels, which taken together identify the session on the circuit that the packet is part of. The Header Error Control is a simple CRC calculation to ensure the integrity of the header. Generic flow control defaults to all zeros, but it was designed to allow several terminals to share the same network connection.

ATM does not guarantee reliability. Packets may appear out of order or duplicated, and they may disappear. This does not mean that messages carried over ATM are unreliable. A reliable system can be built on an unreliable system, which you will see with Transmission Control Protocol (TCP) later. As a WAN technology, reliability may not be desirable because reliability may

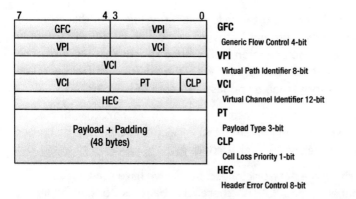

Figure 9-1. ATM has two package layouts. This is the user-network packet, the most used.

hinder performance. This is especially true if a higher layer in the stack requires reliability checks and corrections even if the lower level is reliable.

ATM and WAN

The ATM Forum designed ATM to support both data and voice for telecommunications providers in the period when the Internet was developing rapidly and campus and enterprise LANs were connecting into larger interconnected networks. ATM was one of several technologies used to connect distant LANs. These technologies gradually formed the Internet backbone. Eventually, ATM became one of the critical technologies of the Internet. Telecommunications providers implemented it in many cases to provide WAN services to their customers as part of their leased line services.

WANs were not the only users of ATM. It was also used to connect distant LANs. For example, a large enterprise with several large offices might use ATM to connect LANs in each office together into a single network, or a city government might use ATM to connect their police, fire, and city hall networks.

Current Use of ATM

Although ATM is still in use, the Broadband Forum has not released a new standard since 2005.[5] The cloud still depends on ATM as a WAN technology, but advances in hardware have made ATM less attractive than it once was.

When ATM was conceived, layer 2 protocols such as Ethernet and layer 3 protocols like Internet Protocol (IP) were not as fast or robust as ATM, largely

---

[5] The IETF RFC 4454 specification mentioned earlier was published shortly after the last Broadband Forum specification.

because of their dependence on software for executing logic, but that situation has changed. Ethernet now communicates via optical fiber as well as copper twisted-pairs. Ethernet communication has reached speeds that were scarcely thought of in the mid-1990s. In addition, with the addition of fast switches, Ethernet has become more reliable and less susceptible to collisions.

Layer protocols have also become faster. Routing algorithms that had to be executed in software have been implemented in silicon. Packets can be routed in layer 3 at speeds equivalent to layer 2 routing.

All this has transformed the network landscape. As we have seen with storage networks, interconnects, and LANs, there are benefits to consolidation. Clouds are complicated enough. When two technologies can be replaced with one technology, the job of maintaining the cloud gets easier, and the cost of designing and manufacturing equipment to support the cloud decreases. One can certainly debate the merits of Ethernet or any of several other standards, but unless there is an outstanding advantage to a unique technology, the common technology is likely to prevail.[6]

Fiber Distributed Data Interface (FDDI)

Fiber Distributed Data Interface is a protocol designed to occupy the physical and data link layers of the OSI stack. FDDI was specifically designed to operate over optical fiber. It can run on both long-distance, narrow single-mode fibers and thicker and less expensive multimode fibers. Later, a specification for FDDI over copper twisted-pair cables also appeared. FDDI often replaced Ethernet for campus backbones and in wide area networks. FDDI had superior bandwidth for its time, 100 megabits/second. A later version doubled the bandwidth to 200 megabits/second. It was also designed redundantly to survive various kinds of failures, and it could extend over relatively long distances. For these reasons, it was used often as the backbone for citywide and larger networks.

FDDI still is used as a backbone for many legacy systems, but it has been replaced in many cases by faster and more flexible protocols.

---

[6] The forces that ultimately drive adoption of a given technology are often complex. Economics is a powerful force that is blind to fine points of engineering. Economics will favor a technology that can drive down cost over a more elegant technology that achieves the same goal at greater cost. Cost is more subtle than cost per unit. Readily available components and trained technicians reduce maintenance and operations cost. Increasing the number of units installed will drive manufacturing costs down. These factors and more influence adoption.

FDDI Standards

FDDI standards began to appear in the late 1980s. ANSI and later ISO/IEU published the standards. Sections of the standard correspond to the sections in the FDDI architecture (Figure 9-2).

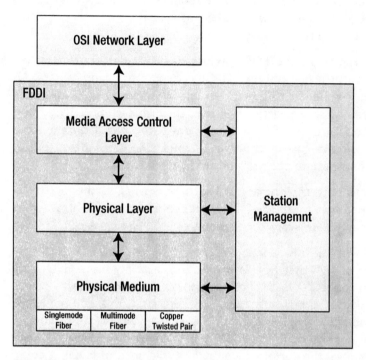

Figure 9-2. The FDDI architecture occupies the bottom two layers in the OSI stack.

FDDI can be a replacement for Ethernet in the Internet TCP/IP stack. The IETF produced a number of standards for IP over FDDI. An example is "Transmission of IP and ARP over FDDI Networks," RFC 1390, published in 1993.[7]

Architecture

FIDDI architecture is similar to IEEE 802.5 token ring LAN. Nodes in a token ring LAN pass a token, a special signal pattern, from node to node in an endless loop. To use the token ring for data transmission, a node captures the token, which gives the node exclusive access to the ring for an interval. Unlike

---

[7] https://datatracker.ietf.org/doc/rfc1390/

Ethernet, the token ring protocol performs predictably when the ring saturates with data.

FDDI is similar, but it uses two rings, each traveling in an opposite direction. The two rings are for resiliency and fault tolerance. Ordinarily, one ring is quiescent and prepared to take over if the primary ring is disabled. In a later version, both rings run simultaneously to double the bandwidth to 200 megabits/second. In this version, when one ring fails, the surviving ring takes over transmission for all the stations.

In additional to the rings, the FDDI architecture includes single attached stations (SAS), dual attached stations (DAS), concentrators, and routers. An FDDI concentrator connects to both the primary and secondary rings. SASs attach to a concentrator. The active ring goes through each SAS. Without a concentrator, the failure of a SAS will bring down the ring. Concentrators automatically close the gap in the ring when a SAS goes down. Thus, concentrators contribute to the resiliency of FDDI networks.

A DAS attaches to both the primary and secondary rings, further adding to system resiliency. Important devices, like mainframes, can be dual attached to a DAS to provide a fault-tolerant connection to the FDDI ring. A FDDI router is usually a DAS.

The combination of high-speed performance and reliability made FDDI very attractive as a backbone. A typical configuration placed servers directly on the FDDI ring. End user stations were usually on Ethernet LANs, and the LANs connected to the FDDI ring. This avoids the cabling and hardware cost of connecting each user station to the FDDI ring. If a node on an Ethernet LAN later began to require the performance or fault tolerance of FDDI, it could connect directly to the FDDI ring with the appropriate connectors and cabling.

Frame Relay

Frame Relay is a protocol designed to occupy the physical and data link layers in the OSI stack. It uses packet switching with variable-length packets and statistical multiplexing. Frame Relay can transport many different upper-level protocols in wide area or metropolitan area networks. The protocol is simple and stripped down, which is possible because it assumes that the physical infrastructure is reliable enough that most error correction can be left to the upper layers. Frame Relay simply drops detected faulty packets. It also drops packets when congestion occurs, although there is some provision for quality of service and congestion avoidance.

Standards

Frame Relay was presented to the Consultative Committee on International Telephone and Telegraph (CCITT)[8] in 1984. The CCITT standard was incomplete and not often implemented. In 1990, a vendor consortium consisting of Cisco, Digital Equipment Corporation, Northern Telecom, and Stratacom developed a number of extensions to the CCITT Frame Relay standard. ANSI and CCITT both eventually accepted the specification from this forum. The forum specification received wider acceptance, and Frame Relay began to be used in WANs and metropolitan area networks (MANs).

Architecture

Frame Relay distinguished two types of equipment: Data Terminal Equipment (DTE) and Data Circuit Terminating Equipment (DCE). The classification reflects the fact that Frame Relay is primarily a protocol for service providers. DTEs are located on the customer premises. DTE consists of terminals, PCs, routers, and bridges. DTE is often customer-owned, although providers may supply DTE also.

DCE is always provider-owned and resides on the provider premises. DCE transmits data through the WAN or MAN. It provides clocking and switching. A DCE is usually implemented by a packet switch.

Many variations are possible in the architecture of a WAN or MAN implementation. Figure 9-3 depicts a WAN using Frame Relay to connect two remote sites to a private cloud located at the company headquarters. A LAN at the headquarters is shown connected directly to the private cloud without an intervening WAN.

An important concept in Frame Relay is the data link connection identifier (DLCI). The DLCI is the basis for Frame Relay addressing. It works differently from Ethernet and IP addressing. An Ethernet Medium Access Control (MAC) address uniquely identifies an Ethernet network adapter. An IP address uniquely identifies a network node. Each Ethernet packet contains the source and target MAC addresses. An IP packet contains source and target IP addresses. A Frame Relay packet contains a single identifier, the DLCI. The DLCI identifies a virtual circuit rather than a node on the network. The DLCI is an instruction to send the packet over a certain circuit. The circuit has both a starting point and an endpoint, so the DLCI implicitly identifies a source and target, but it is a single identifier.

---

[8] CCITT later became the International Telecommunication Union Telecommunication Standardization Sector (ITU-T).

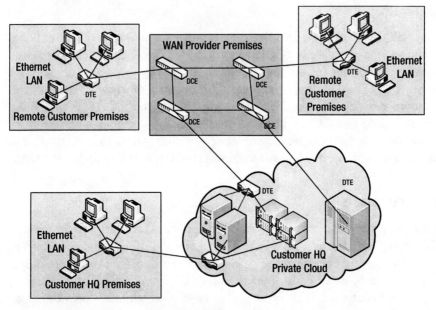

Figure 9-3. Frame Relay can be the WAN transport between remote offices and a headquarter's private cloud.

Virtual Circuits

Frame Relay supports both Switched Virtual Circuits (SVCs) and Permanent Virtual Circuits (PVCs). SVCs are constructed and taken down as needed. PVCs have a much longer lifetime. Both have advantages. SVCs consume resources more efficiently, but they have additional setup time when a connection initiates. PVCs avoid the setup time but require more resources.

When considering Frame Relay virtual circuits, it is important to keep in mind that they are virtual. The existence of a virtual circuit does not mean that physical resources are in use. The virtual circuit may be multiplexed with other virtual circuits over the same physical connection, and a virtual circuit may shift from physical connection to physical connection. This implies that the distinction between SVCs and PVCs is not as crisp as may be apparent. Virtual PVCs may not require physical resources when they are not in use, so the advantage to SVCs may not be as great as it appears. Conversely, connecting over an unused PVC may require a certain amount of virtual setup, so its start-up may not be as quick as expected.

Frame Relay Packets

The minimum size for a Frame Relay packet is six octets (bytes): one octet of user data and four octets of header and footer (Figure 9-4). The beginning and end of the packet are marked by a flag bit pattern, represented by a hexadecimal 7E.

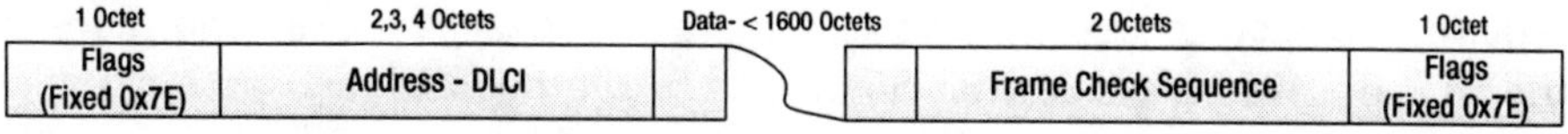

1 Octet	2,3, 4 Octets	Data- < 1600 Octets	2 Octets	1 Octet
Flags (Fixed 0x7E)	Address - DLCI		Frame Check Sequence	Flags (Fixed 0x7E)

Figure 9-4. Frame Relay packets are variable length.

The address section contains the DLCI and several bits used for quality of service and congestion response. (See the next section.) The data section is variable length. The standard recommends 1,600 octets or less, but the data size can be configured above the limit. The Frame Check Sequence can be used to check data integrity.

Quality of Service

Frame Relay packets have three bits that are used for quality of service. The Forward Explicit Congestion Notification (FECN) and the Backward Explicit Congestion Notification (BECN) are set by DTEs when they encounter congestion in the Frame Relay network. The FECN is set when moving to the target; the BECN is set when the packet is moving in the opposite direction. When the packet arrives at a DCE with an FECN or BECN set, the DCE may notify upper layers of congestion, and the upper layer can institute flow control (slow down sending data) or some other response to congestion.

The third bit, the Discard Eligibility (DE) bit, is set to indicate that a packet is low priority and a first choice for discard.

In use, Frame Relay is used similarly to ATM, as a transport for WAN and MAN installations.

Multiprotocol Packet Label Switching (MPLS)

Multiprotocol Packet Label Switching is an important protocol among MANs and WANs. Although ATM and Frame Relay are still used, MPLS often replaces them. MPLS has goals similar to ATM but is different in implementation. Like ATM, MPLS is a unifying technology for telecommunications providers offering a range of services on the same physical network. The ATM strategy chose small packets and virtual circuits. The MPLS resembles ATM in its approach, but MPLS is also different.

MPLS permits large packets. If you recall, the ATM design favors small packets because large packets can interfere with the timely delivery of voice data. Interference of that type declines in significance as the speed of transmission and switching increases. Transmission speeds have increased greatly, and switching has gotten much faster since ATM was designed and greater packet size has become an option. Data that is broken into many small packets requires more switching than the same data in one large packet, and there is the cost of splitting packets up on ingress to the network and putting them back together at egress. The ATM small packet advantage has diminished.

MPLS is well-suited to the Internet age where IP is clearly the predominant layer 3 protocol. MPLS is at its best when it is a transporting IP packets through WANs and MANs. ATM can be used in the same way, but MPLS does it with less complication. In fact, MPLS often is an intermediate between ATM and IP. ATM switches can usually be configured to act as MPLS routers, even to run as ATM switches and MPLS routers at the same time. Frame Relay is also compatible with MPLS, and MPLS is able to carry real-time media like voice. This flexibility and overall high performance has made MPLS an attractive choice.

History and Standards

MPLS began with RFC 1953, published in 1997.[9] Engineers from Ipsilon Networks and Sprint authored the submission. It was not called label switching, but contained parts of the kernel of label switching. Later, Cisco embraced the concept and called it *tag switching* when it first released an augmented specification in 1998 as a proprietary protocol. Cisco presented the tag switching specification to the IETF. The IETF changed the name to Multiprotocol Packet Label Switching and published RFC 2547 in 1999.[10] RFC 2547 fouses on MPLS VPNs, which is a frequent application of MPLS. The IETF has modified and extended the specification more than 150 times, most recently with RFC 6515 in February 2012.[11] As a comprehensive introduction, the best of the MPLS RFC is probably RFC 3031, "Multiprotocol Label Switching Architecture," published in January 2001.[12]

Architecture

The Label Switching Router (LSR) is the workhorse of MPLS. There are two roles for LSRs: core and edge LSRs: core router switch packets internal to the MPLS network and edge LSRs interface between external networks and the core. Edge LSRs have two subroles: ingress LSRs and egress LSRs. Ingress

---

[9] http://tools.ietf.org/html/rfc1953

[10] http://tools.ietf.org/html/rfc2547

[11] http://tools.ietf.org/html/rfc6515

[12] http://tools.ietf.org/html/rfc3031

LSRs insert a MPLS label into entering packets based on the destination address of the entering packet; egress LSRs strip off the labels.

The labels identify circuits through the MPLS network. The labels act as a Forwarding Equivalence Class (FEC). The router treats every packet with the same FEC in the same way and directs the packet through the same virtual circuit.

When a packet enters an MPLS network, the ingress LSR reads the destination address of the packet and looks into an internal table to find the label and port that will direct the packet to the correct core LSR that will eventually lead to the correct egress LSR. The ingress router then puts the label on the packet and sends the packet out on the designated port. Each core LSR has its own table that maps entering labels to actions. The most common action is to swap in a new label from the lookup table and push the packet out the designated port. The packet continues from core LSR to core LSR following the circuit to the proper egress router. The egress router does its own lookup, which tells it to strip off the label and send off the packet from the proper port to the external network.

The labels are a fixed 32 bits long. In addition to the circuit identifier, there are the 3-bit Traffic Control field; Priority of Service bit; and the 8-bit TTL, a checksum (Figure 9-5). The early MPLS RFCs called the TC field EXP for experimental, although the field was for traffic control almost from the beginning. The field changed officially from EXP to TC in RFC 5462.[13] RFC 3270[14] described the use of the EXP field for traffic control seven years earlier in 2002. Some documentation still refers to the TC field as EXP.

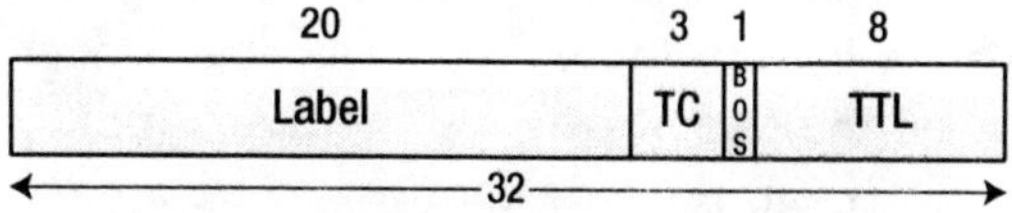

20	3	1	8
Label	TC	B o s	TTL

$\longleftarrow$————————————32————————————$\longrightarrow$

Figure 9-5. The label identifier occupies the first position in an MPLS label.

The MPLS label is actually a stack; there may be more than one label assigned to the packet. This occurs, for example, when the path directs the packet to a subpath. Instead of swapping the label for the new label, the LSR pushes the old label and puts the new label on the top of the stack. The pushed old label remains on the stack, but it is not operational. When the subpath is complete, the LSR does its lookup, which directs it to pop the old label. The popped

---

[13] http://tools.ietf.org/html/rfc5462

[14] http://tools.ietf.org/html/rfc3270

label is directly from the LSR where the subpath started. The LRS then does a lookup on the popped label, and the packet proceeds on the main path.

MPLS does not encapsulate packets and add a header like Ethernet or IP. Instead, the MPLS label is a shim—it is inserted between layer 2 header and the layer 3 header in the packet it is transporting (Figure 9-6).

Figure 9-6. An MPLS label stack is shimmed between the layer 2 and layer 3 headers.

If the packet entering the MPLS network has a virtual circuit identifier, like ATM or Frame Relay, the MPLS label stack is encapsulated in the circuit identifier (Figure 9-7).

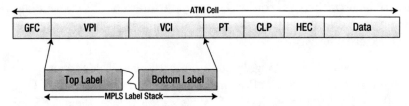

Figure 9-7. The MPLS stack is contained in the ATM VPI and VCI fields.

Benefits

MPLS circuits are embodied in the lookup tables in LSRs, which are maintained with a chosen routing algorithm. The algorithm does not matter as long as it can map the needed path. Because the ingress router sets the path through the network, the core routers pass on the packet with a single direct lookup rather than a complex calculation. Early on, this was thought to be a great advantage to MPLS because it eliminated slow software by the core routers. However, hardware developments such as Application Specific Integrated Circuits (ASICs) have moved route calculation from software to hardware, and the switching speed advantage of MPLS has effectively disappeared. Nevertheless, devices can be used as core LSRs that are not capable of executing complex routing algorithms, like ATM routers. This means that under the right circumstances, designers can convert an ATM network into an MPLS network using legacy hardware instead of requiring new hardware.

There are more advantages to MPLS. It is source routing; the path through the network is set at the source, rather than calculated by the routers as the packet traverses the network. In practice, manual source routing is not difficult, but it is hard to automate and scale beyond a few short routes.

Nevertheless, source routing has strengths. Source routes can be changed at the source, which is easier than modifying tables on the core routers. This is valuable in responding to router failures, traffic changes, congestion, setting up arbitrary paths for testing, and similar exceptional changes to routing patterns. Perhaps most important, paths can be changed to accommodate quality-of-service decisions. This ease of management is an advantage to MPLS.

The focus of MPLS is on the edge, the ingress LSRs. The algorithms for choosing the FEC can be as complex as needed without affecting the core LSRs. The contents of a packet are examined only at the edge. Consequently, packets can be encrypted differently depending on properties such as the origin of the packet or the quality of service.

Possibly the most important property of MPLS is the odd place it occupies between layer 2 and layer 3 in the network stack. Because it is a shim between the two layers, it is independent of both and enables integration of networks with mismatched layer 2 and layer 3 protocols.

Local Area Networks

LANs are the networks familiar to end users. They are the last link in the chain between the end user and the cloud. If two end users with similar equipment have different experiences with the same cloud service, the first place to look is the LAN. Without an effective LAN, the cloud is inaccessible.

Ethernet

The amazing aptness of the Ethernet name in the cloud has only begun to become evident. For cloud computing to be significant, the cloud must be accessible. It must be like the ether, the fluid that ancient philosophers posited to pervade the entire universe and later was theorized to be the vehicle of light and electromagnetic waves. Ethernet is now the medium on which the cloud communicates but has evolved far from the 10 megabit/second Ethernet described in the IEEE specification of 1983.

In 1983, Ethernet was a slow, low-bandwidth, indeterminate[15] protocol, prone to collapse during heavy traffic and painfully limited in physical distance between stations, not at all suitable for the many roles it now plays. In 1983,

---

[15] An indeterminate protocol is one with points of unpredictable behavior. Token ring, for example, is determinate—there is a predictable point to which a token ring may slow, but unless there is an exceptional hardware failure or other catastrophe, performance is certain. Classic Ethernet was indeterminate because there is no predictable minimum speed.

suggesting that Ethernet might be used as a backplane interconnect for supercomputers would have brought rolled eyes rather than agreement. Yet today, Ethernet is the leading supercomputer interconnect[16] and is used in WAN backbones as well as in enterprise networks and tiny home LANs.

History

Ethernet is arguably the single most successful standard in the cloud. It began as a proprietary standard for linking desktop computers at Xerox PARC, at the center of distributed personal computing from the beginning. It has evolved to play an important role in large high-volume systems. In the course of its growth, it has changed, to the point that Ethernet LANs seldom use the basic protocol that characterized Ethernet at its inception.

The roots of Ethernet are in the ALOHA protocol developed at the University of Hawaii to connect remote island campuses to a central computer. The ALOHA protocol was modified and adapted at Xerox PARC to local networks of personal computers. The first Ethernet installations were heavy coaxial cable. An alternate lighter coaxial cable appeared later. Eventually much cheaper and easier-to-handle unshielded twisted-pair copper cable became the norm.

Xerox collaborated with Digital Equipment and Intel to produce the DIX (Digital, Intel, Xerox) specification. The DIX specification was the basis for the 1983 IEEE 802.3 specification.

The tug-of-war that can go on between industry and standards groups shows in the Ethernet frame layout. The DIX frame has a 2-byte "Ethertype" that was intended to indicate the upper-layer protocol encapsulated in the payload of the frame. The IEEE group replaced the two bytes of the DIX type field with a length field. The encapsulated protocol type was contained in an additional 803.2 Logical Link Control (LLC) header. The industry continued to use the DIX-style frame, and eventually, almost 15 years later in 1998, the DIX-style frame was included in the 802.3x addition to the standard. The DIX-style frame, which may be used more than the 802.3 frame, was finally accepted as part of the standard.

In the years since the release of IEEE 802.3 in 1983, IEEE has released 802.3 specifications at close to one specification per year, showing the steady interest in Ethernet. In 1983, the transmission speed was 10 megabits/second. In 2010, 802.3ba included specifications for 100 gigabits/second transmission.

Congestion can bring it to a halt. For early Ethernet installations, the risk of a network crash was a reasonable trade-off for low overhead and easy implementation.

[16] See www.top500.org/charts/list/38/connfam.

Carrier Sense Protocol

On the remote island campuses of the University of Hawaii, wired connections to the central campus were expensive and unreliable. The ALOHA protocol was developed to connect the remote campuses to the central computer on the main campus. Instead of wires, the ALOHA protocol was transmitted on radio signals. The origins of Ethernet trace to the ALOHA protocol. Therefore, Ethernet began as a wireless protocol.

The Aloha protocol was simple. Messages were split into packets each with header information. The ALOHA system was full-duplex. That is, one frequency transmitted all packets from the remote campus stations to the central computer station; another frequency broadcast packets back from the central computer to the campuses. If a station was ready to transmit, it simply transmitted without regard for activity on the channel. When the central computer received a message, it broadcast an acknowledgment on the return channel. The main occasion for central not sending an acknowledgment was when two nodes transmitted at the same time and the collision garbled the packets. When the wait time for an acknowledgment expired, the sending station sent the packet again. This worked, but collisions were frequent.

The Ethernet protocol added elements to ALOHA. First, it is, or was for many years, a half-duplex system; frames are sent and received on the same wire, implying that frames[17] could not be sent and received at the same time. Second, before sending a frame, an Ethernet controller senses the wire and does not send until the wire is clear. This is the "carrier sense" aspect of the protocol. Third, an Ethernet interface has collision detection; it is aware when a collision starts on the line. When the interface senses a collision, it halts sending immediately, sends a jam signal (a distinctive 32-bit pattern) and waits a random interval to avoid sending at the same time as other stations that detected the collision, and begins testing again for an opportunity to seize the wire. This is the Carrier Sense Multiple Access with Collision Detection (CSMA/CD) protocol. CSMA/CD characterized Ethernet for many years. In fact, the formal name for the 802.3 standard is "Carrier Sense Multiple Access with Collision Detection (CSMA/CD) Access Method and Physical Layer Specifications."

The pattern of states on the wire shown in Figure 9-8 influences the design of Ethernet networks. Detecting collisions is an analog process. Unlike some

---

[17] Packets, frames, cells, and datagrams are all the same thing: a delimited stream of data sent as a unit on the network. Packets, frames, and datagrams all have headers with information such as source and destination and other indications of how to handle the contents of the packet. Ethernet packets are customarily called *frames*. ATM packets are called *cells*. Usually, *packet* refers to a data unit from a higher-level protocol like IP, but usage varies. IP and TCP packets are frequently called *datagrams*. In practice, the four terms are often interchanged.

other collision control techniques, the controller must sense the wire and make an analog comparison of voltages to detect a collision. The Ethernet interface detects a collision when the signal on the wire is not the same as the signal transmitted. That implies that the encoding supports collision detection. For example, a 0-voltage signal colliding with another 0-voltage signal will not be detectable as a collision. An encoding that permits this would not work well with CSMA/CD. This places limits on encoding methods. This lack of separation between the data link and physical layers places constraints on the design of the physical layer.

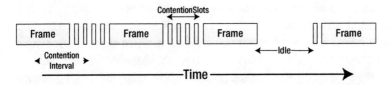

Figure 9-8. CSMA/CD has three states: contention, transmission, and idle.

Ethernet Congestion

A collision domain is a group of stations whose signals can collide. In a collision domain, the time it takes for a signal to travel between the two most distant stations on the wire determines the time it takes to verify that there is no collision occurring. When a station transmits to a clear wire, the frame may collide with a frame that was on its way but had not arrived when the sending station sensed the wire (Figure 9-9).

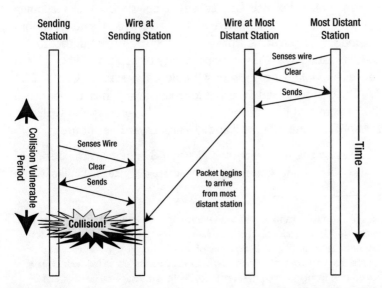

Figure 9-9. A frame sent from a remote station cannot be detected until it arrives.

A collision can also occur when a remote station starts to send before the frame from the sending station arrives and is detected by the remote station (Figure 9-10). Therefore, the period when a frame is subject to collision is twice the maximum travel time between two stations.

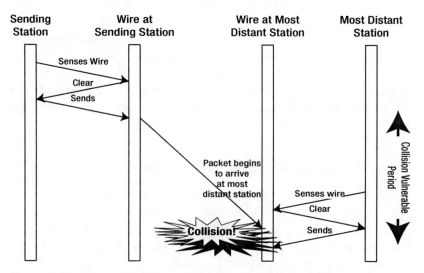

Figure 9-10. A frame may collide with a frame transmitted from a remote station.

This implies, perhaps counterintuitively, that collisions are more likely when the maximum distance on the wire between stations increases. The travel time for a signal between the most distant stations depends on both the distance between the stations and the transmission speed. LANs with widely dispersed stations on a single bus are proportionally more vulnerable to congestion than LANs that limit the geographical spread of stations. Therefore, the standard limits the physical size of a collision domain.

Congestion is constant consideration for networks. There are two main strategies for dealing with network congestion. One approach is to eliminate congestion with techniques such as token passing that grant permission to transmit. Token ring and token bus, IEEE 802.5 and 802.4, respectively, take this strategy. These are called *determinant protocols* because they guarantee that a station will always be able to get its message to its destination under a designated maximum time. Under these protocols a station always will be granted permission to send according to a predictable allocation algorithm. These protocols deal with the problem, but the solution uses precious network bandwidth. When the system is lightly loaded, the overhead for negotiating transmission privileges can be significantly greater than an indeterminate protocol like CSMA/CD. However, heavy traffic affects performance less on these networks. Where there are many traffic cops, travel is slower, but it is predictable. Ethernet is faster and makes better use of available bandwidth when collisions are few, but when the network is saturated, the CSMA/CD protocol will choke.

In the past, when Ethernet was less sophisticated, token ring and token bus were favored in situations where determinate performance was critical like controlling assembly lines. Special embedded applications are the only common users of token ring and token bus now. This is because many of the issues around CSMA/CD collisions are no longer as vexing as they once were. Increasing transmission speeds reduces the window of collision vulnerability as well as decreasing latency and increasing throughput. Also, new hardware such as Ethernet switches has decreased the number of stations that are contending for slots on the wire.

Collision Domains and Ethernet Switches

Assuming the similar volumes of traffic per station and constant geographic spread, the fewer stations in a collision domain, the fewer collisions. A typical Ethernet collision domain consists of several stations connected to a hub. The hub connects the stations as if they were sharing a single wire (Figure 9-11). One way to reduce vulnerability to collisions is to reduce the size of collision domains.

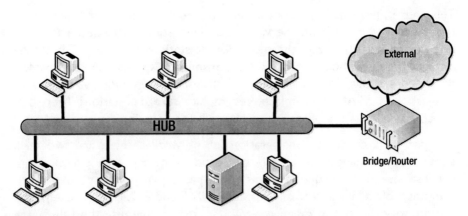

Figure 9-11. A classic Ethernet LAN has several stations connected to a hub, forming a collision domain.

Replacing a hub with an Ethernet switch reduces the size of the collision domain. A hub is a way to connect a group of stations to the same wire. Each frame in the domain passes to each of the other stations. Each station plucks the frames addressed to it from the wire and sends on the wire, following the CSMA/CD protocol. Frames can and do collide.

A switch, as the name implies, switches traffic so that stations connected to a port only receive frames addressed to stations connected to the port. In Figure 9-11, eight stations, including the router, contend for time on the wire in a single collision domain. In Figure 9-12, only one station connects to each port. The only possible collisions occur when a station and the switch start to send at the same time. The CSMA/CD protocol now only mediates between the switch and each station.

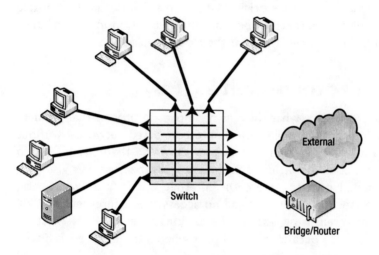

Figure 9-12. A switch separates stations into individual collision domains.

Ethernet switches are made possible by solid-state technology, such as Application Specific Integrated Circuits, which switches traffic at high speeds. Layer 2 switching, another name for Ethernet switching, began to appear in the early 1990s.

There is another Ethernet innovation yet to be mentioned. Switching greatly reduces contention, but it also makes possible full-duplex communication, which eliminates the last bit of contention in Ethernet and eliminates the CSMA/CD protocol.

Full-duplex communication separates send and receive channels. With full-duplex, the switch sends frames to the station on one channel, and the station sends to the switch on the other channel. Neither the switch nor the station needs to sense the line because each owns its send channel. Contention is completely eliminated. The CSMA/CD protocol is no longer necessary with full-duplex Ethernet. Segmenting collision domains with switching and full-duplex also removes size limitations that derive from CSMA/CD collision detection. Full-duplex was added to 802.3 in 1998 in the same revision that sanctioned the DIX frame, 802.3x.

Currently, half-duplex Ethernet, which amounts to CSMA/CD Ethernet, is still supported because there is a legacy of hardware that supports only half-duplex, but Gigabit and faster Ethernet is not deployed in half-duplex because the size limitations for collision detection are too restrictive to be practical.

Ethernet without CSMA/CD is more flexible than classic Ethernet. It removes distance limitations for collision detection and increases reliability by eliminating congestion because of collisions. With the addition of hardware that handles functions that were originally done in software and that enable high-speed switching, Ethernet has become the foundation for the massive volume of data and communication that the cloud requires.

Internet Protocol Suite (IPS)

The Internet protocols are what their name implies: protocols that connect networks. The Internet is a collection of interconnected networks; without protocols for moving data from network to network, there would be no Internet. Ethernet could be included in this category, because it is also part using the Internet. However, before the Internet was in use everywhere, Ethernet was connecting LANs that had no access to the Internet. It is still used in that way, often in high-security situations where a LAN must be isolated or during those occasional dark hours when Internet access is down.

Ethernet is an IEEE standard. The Internet protocols are IETF standards. This is a further distinction between Ethernet and the Internet protocols. IEEE is involved in software, but hardware is the heart of its focus. The IETF occasionally addresses hardware, but its main concern is software. Ethernet straddles the physical layer and the software layers. These standards correspond to OSI layers 3 and 4.

Internet Protocol (IP)

Internet Protocol is the layer 3 protocol of the Internet. It is everywhere. IP is the protocol that understands the structure of the Internet. Ethernet is everywhere also, but Ethernet is like a mole burrowing under a lawn. It has tunnels that connect everywhere, but the Ethernet has no conception of what goes on above its underground tunnels. It takes IP to provide a map of the sprawling reaches of the Internet and lead data to and from the clouds where it is stored and processed.

It is astounding how far IP has extended. Sprawl of the Internet used to refer to the exploding numbers of networked desktop computers all over the world, each with its unique IP address. Now, not just computers have IP addresses. Your car may have an IP address. The vending machines in the break room probably have IP addresses. The controller on the generator at the dam that is producing the electricity to keep the lights on has an IP address. The gas meter outside your house is likely to have an IP address. Smartphones have IP addresses. It may not be long before heart implants have IP addresses. They are everywhere, growing in number, and likely to fall under the control of processes running on clouds in the not-too-distant future.

History

IP is tied to Transmission Control Protocol (TCP). IEEE published the original proposal, "A Protocol for Packet Network Interconnection," by Vint Cerf and Bob Kahn in 1974.[18] The paper described the "Transmission Control Program," which contained elements of both TCP and IP. Later, the design split into a connection-oriented service over a connectionless service. The rationale for the split are discussed in the "Transmission Control Protocol (TCP)" section.

The IPv4 version of the protocol, which is still the most commonly used version, was published in 1980 in RFC 760.[19] RFC 760 was replaced by RFC 791 in 1981.[20] There were versions of IP before IPv4, and IPv4 is being replaced by IPv6, mostly because the address space of IPv4 is approaching saturation. The process is not complete, but it accelerates every year.

Addressing

The main job of IP is to move data from one host on the Internet to another. The data link layer, Ethernet usually, takes care of local data movement within a local network, but IP moves data from one network to another. When IP moves data, it relies on lower layers to manage the signals on the wire. Often the lower layer is Ethernet, but for long distances, IP directs the data to WAN data transfer services such as MPLS, which takes the place of Ethernet for managing the lower levels in the network stack.

IP uses routable addresses to make this possible. Ethernet addresses, MAC addresses, are not routable. MAC addresses are, for the most part, globally unique. They consist of a manufacturer identifier and a serial number. In theory at least, that combination ensures that no two Ethernet interfaces have the same MAC address. But MAC addresses are not very useful for moving data from network to network because a MAC address does not have

---

[18] http://ieeexplore.ieee.org/xpl/login.jsp?tp=&arnumber=1092259&url=http%3A%2F%2Fieee xplore.ieee.org%2Fxpls%2Fabs_all.jsp%3Farnumber%3D1092259

[19] http://tools.ietf.org/html/rfc760

[20] http://tools.ietf.org/html/rfc791

any clues to a path from the source MAC address to the destination MAC address. This is what it means not to be routable.

IP addresses are routable. An IP address has a network part and a local part. The local part identifies a host within a network. The network part represents a network, which is hierarchical. Routers use the hierarchy and their routing tables to make decisions. They decipher the network part of the address and match it against their tables. Either a router sends a packet to the target network, or it passes the packet to another router for further routing.

Routing Considerations

The routing table tells the router the appropriate output port for the packet. From the output port, the packet sometimes travels directly to its destination host or, more likely, to a LAN that will direct the packet to its destination host or to another router. Routing tables are usually generated algorithmically, and maintenance is much lower than it once was, but routing tables are an important concern of network administrators in the face of varying loads and equipment faults. There are many algorithms for calculating and updating routing tables.

The contents of routing tables determine the path a packet takes when it arrives at each router. Although a best-effort protocol, IP allows for some variation in handling packets. Some networks have Maximum Transmission Units (MTUs) that restrict the size of packets that can pass through the network. When a packet must go through such a network, packets may have to be broken up into smaller units. If a packet must not be fragmented— perhaps a real-time requirement that all the information in the packet must arrive simultaneously or the destination cannot reassemble packets—then the Do not Fragment (DF) bit can be set in the header. An intelligent router can route the packet away from a network that requires fragmentation. If it cannot find an alternate route, the router will drop the packet and send an error message to the destination.

The Type of Service (TOS) byte was intended to represent specialized handling of the requirements for types of service such as voice, video, streaming music, and so on. This did not catch on well, and the meanings of the bits were changed several times. Current usage, RFC 2474,[21] splits the TOS byte into a six-bit Differentiated Service (DS) field and 2 bits for Explicit Congestion Notification (ECN) defined in RFC 3168.[22] Setting the ECN bits is another

---

[21] http://tools.ietf.org/html/rfc2474
[22] http://tools.ietf.org/html/rfc3168

way for routers to indicate congestion other than dropping the packet. The DS bits are a relatively coarse-grained designation of service levels.

IPv4 and IPv6

Although there were earlier studies and proposals, in 1995 IPv6 was defined in RFC 1883.[23] This RFC was replaced by RFC 2460 in 1998.[24] Since that time, there have been numerous RFCs.

Chapter 6 discussed the depletion of the IPv4 address space and some of the routing improvements that IPv6 provides. The problem with address depletion is subtler than it may appear. IPv4 has more than 4 billion possible addresses, but in early 2011, only 14 percent of the total was estimated to be in use.[25] Even allowing for headroom for management, that does not look like a crisis.

Unfortunately, depletion is still a crisis for two reasons. First, IP addresses must be routable. Most MAC addresses are assigned at the factory without regard for where they may be installed. Manufacturers receive a unique prefix from IEEE, and then they usually fill up their address space sequentially with no gaps. This uses the address space efficiently. The MAC address space is larger than the IP address space since MAC addresses use 48 bits compared to an IPv4 address's 32 bits, but they are also are easier to assign efficiently. IP addresses are not so easy. They must be assigned with regard for the routing location of the host. This limits the ways addresses can be allocated.

Second, although the addresses allocated exceed addresses in use, the reallocation of allocated but unused addresses is not trivial. The early adopters of the Internet received huge blocks of addresses, many of which are almost certainly not in use. The usual way of allocating addresses within an organization is to hand them out in hierarchies that facilitate internal routing. This practice tends to distribute addresses over the address space, not leave large blocks of easily reassigned addresses. Thus, even though there is no absolute shortage of addresses, the addresses available for allocation are dwindling fast. Estimates vary on when the day is coming, but all the estimates point to the near future.

Converting from IPv4 to IPv6

The issue with converting from IPv6 to IPv4 is that the two protocols do the same job, but they are not compatible. Network nodes can handle both

---

[23] http://tools.ietf.org/html/rfc1883

[24] http://tools.ietf.org/html/rfc2460

[25] Shankland, Steve. 2011. "Moving to IPv6: Now for the hard part (FAQ)." CNET News. http://news.cnet.com/8301-30685_3-20030482-264.html

protocols simultaneously with the proper hardware and software, but a native IPv6 node cannot deal with IPv4, and vice versa, without special steps. There are many RFCs on specific methods for interoperation.[26]

There are two core methods: dual stacks and tunneling. A dual-stack implementation supports both IPv4 and IPv6. Most current operating systems support dual stacks. Since Windows 2000, for example, Windows has supported both IPv4 and IPv6. Most often, Dynamic Host Configuration Protocol (DHCP) supplies IPv4 addresses, and IPv6 address auto-configuration assigns IPv6 addresses based on the MAC address of the device.

Tunneling methods send IPv6 addressed packets through domains that only support IPv4 by encasing the IPv6 packet in an IPv4 packet. IPv4 packets tunnel through IPv6 domains by similar means.

The important consideration for the cloud is that IPv6 portends to be an improvement. The IPv6 auto-configuration using the MAC address of the host as the local identifier, for example, promises to be quite efficient, and IPv6 routing seems to be an improvement, not to mention the ample address space.

Transmission Control Protocol (TCP)

TCP is the connection-oriented transport layer protocol for the Internet. The transport layer provides end-to-end communications services for applications. The most important characteristic of the transport layer is that it goes a step beyond the network layer in its addressing. An IP address directs a message to a host, but hosts run more than one application. For application-to-application communication, sending a message to a host identified by an IP address is not enough. In some way, the programmer must specify the application on the host to which the message is directed.

Transmission Control Protocol vs. Internet Protocol

TCP and IP split early into two separate layers. This happened for good reason. TCP as originally defined was a connection-oriented protocol that guarantees delivery and maintains a connection between processes.

---

[26] "The China Education and Research Network (CERNET) IVI Translation Design and Deployment of the IPv4/IPv6 Coexistence and Transition" (http://tools.ietf.org/html/rfc6219), "IPv6 Rapid Deployment on IPv4 Infrastructures (6rd) – Protocol Specification" (http://tools.ietf.org/html/rfc5969), and "IP/ICMP Translation Algorithm" (http://tools.ietf.org/html/rfc6145) are all interesting examples.

Why were the two separated? The answer lies in the differences between best-effort and connection-oriented protocols.

A best-effort protocol makes no guarantees. The service may only partially deliver the data or deliver packets out of order. However, if occasional lapses are tolerable, best-effort protocols can out-perform protocols that promise more service because a best-effort protocol operates with less overhead. Establishing and taking down connections, error-checking, resending, and reordering packets all take time and resources. A best-effort protocol can direct those resources to using bandwidth more efficiently, deliver more data in a shorter period, and be easier to implement.

Some uses of a network require more than best-effort service; others do not. Some networks are unreliable and cannot provide more than best-effort service. TCP provides a connection-oriented service running on top of IP. For example, TCP keeps track of sessions to provide a connection-oriented service. The IP layer of the Internet will support other protocols in addition to TCP. Designers can tailor these protocols to specific purposes. Without this flexibility, instead of services like sound, video, and data all transmitted over one Internet, separate networks for each of these services might be required. The concept of a cloud utility that provides many services would turn into a collection of specialized services, resulting in redundancy and inefficiency as well as inconvenience.

Layering TCP over IP also helps with the diversity of the networks that make up the Internet. Levels of reliability vary widely from network to network. IP assumes little and will operate on all of them. TCP adds the level of service required for activities such as file transfer and transaction processing.

TCP Standard

The origin of TCP was in the same paper by Vint Cerf and Bob Kahn in 1974 that started IP (discussed earlier). RFC 761[27] in 1980 articulated TCP as a separate protocol from IP. In 1981, a second RFC, 793,[28] replaced 761. Since 761, there have been many additions and emendations to the specification.

When discussing cloud application development, it is hard to mention IP without TCP. For application programmers, TCP/IP is almost synonymous with networking. Programmers say "TCP/IP" more often than they say "TCP" or "IP" separately. Application developers seldom program against raw IP, but TCP without IP is scarcely imaginable. On the other hand, Universal Datagram

---

[27] http://tools.ietf.org/html/rfc761
[28] http://tools.ietf.org/html/rfc793

Protocol (UDP), an alternative to TCP, over IP comes up often. (More on UDP later.)

Developers connect to processes on hosts connected by the network. The word *process* is important. A process is an instance of a single computer program in execution. It is a more exact term than *application* because applications are often made up of interacting processes. A process can have many threads of execution, but threads are usually invisible from outside a process. When hosts have many running applications, applications have many processes, and processes have many threads, simply sending and receiving messages from one host to another host is not adequate. Even a server dedicated to supporting a single service may have an FTP application for transferring files and a Telnet application for externally logging in. A web server will also have an HTTP process for sending and receiving structured documents and probably other processes. Effective communication requires some way of directing data to processes on hosts, not just hosts.

Ports and Sockets

For application-to-application communication, TCP adds the concepts of ports and sockets. Ports and sockets are two sides of the same construct. Externally, a host has many ports that can receive messages. Internally, an application interacts with sockets bound to ports that send and deliver messages to and from the application. In use, a socket is always bound to a port.

Ports are numbered. Some port numbers are always bound to the same application; others are temporarily assigned as needed. Organizations can register the ports used by their applications. The same organization that manages domain names, the Internet Assigned Numbers Authority (IANA),[29] registers port numbers. IANA manages port numbers in ranges. The lowest range is for well-known ports that never change their binding to well-known applications (Figure 9-13). For example, ports 20 and 21 are assigned to File Transport Protocol, and port 80 is assigned to Hypertext Transfer Protocol. The next range up is reserved for not-so-well-known but registered ports. The upper range is for temporarily assigned ports that are usually assigned arbitrarily by the TCP/IP stack.

Using the concepts of ports and sockets, an application can communicate directly with another application on a remote host. The connection orientation of TCP is important.

---

[29] RFC 6365 (http://tools.ietf.org/html/rfc6335), published in 2011, defines the IANA process for assigning port numbers.

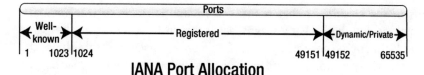

IANA Port Allocation

Figure 9-13. IANA assigns and registers ports.

TCP Programming

A TCP/IP client creates a socket and calls "connect" on the socket using the IP address and port of the server application (Figure 9-14). Behind the scenes, the TCP stack does a three-way handshake with the TCP stack on the server: the client sends a request to the server, the server replies, and the client acknowledges the server's return. These steps establish the connection between the client and server.

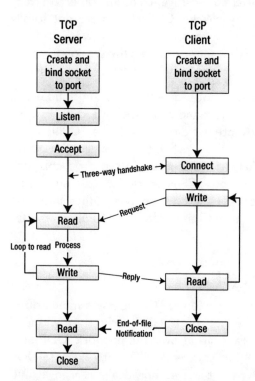

Figure 9-14. The TCP programming model usually involves a looping by both the client and the server to complete the transaction.

From the viewpoint of the client process, "connect" is a single call to the TCP/IP stack. When the session is established, both the initiating and the responding processes are bound to sockets that are the internal representation of the two ends of the circuit. At that point, the session is ready to transfer data. The session is full-duplex—messages are sent and received on the same socket and through the same port. For some servers, establishing the connection is the prompt to send data to the client. In other scenarios, the client and the server may exchange information as peers, and the distinction between client and server may be arbitrary. Often, for concurrency, the server process will start a separate process to handle the communication with the client while the server returns to listening for new connections.

As a connection-oriented protocol, the TCP/IP stack takes care of the housekeeping. Before the application receives data, the stack eliminates duplicate packets, waits for resends on missing or damaged packets, and places packets in the correct order. The stack also strips the packets of extraneous headers and concatenates the data into a single contiguous message, which is an exact reproduction of the message the sender passed to the TCP/IP stack at the sending end. When TCP delivers a message, transmission errors very seldom get through the TCP integrity checks; CRC checks are not totally infallible, but errors are highly unlikely. If a server failure or network problem disturbs a session to the point that TCP cannot maintain the session to repair a message, the stack returns an error rather than faulty data.

Passing messages between clients and remote servers makes the cloud work. Most message passing between consumers and processes in a cloud is over TCP/IP. Many enterprise applications interact directly with the TCP/IP stack, although applications usually run in a browser when they interact with cloud-based back ends. These are more likely to use application-level protocols such as HTTP. Nevertheless, HTTP uses the TCP/IP stack for communication between browsers and other web services and web servers. Other interfaces less familiar to consumers, such as FTP and Telnet, also use TCP/IP to transfer data.

User Datagram Protocol (UDP)

UDP is a connectionless, best-effort companion to TCP. UDP was standardized in 1980 in RFC 768.[30] Like TCP, UDP runs on IP. UDP packets are wrapped inside an IP packet when they are transmitted over the network. UDP uses the same sockets and ports as TCP but somewhat differently because UDP has no concept of connection. Each packet arrives individually as a single unit.

---

[30] http://tools.ietf.org/html/rfc768

UDP Characteristics

UDP datagrams are independent units, and there is nothing in UDP designed to help programmers connect data spread over several datagrams. Like IP, when a process sends a datagram, there is no certainty that the datagram will arrive at its destination. If the datagram is sent to a nonexistent IP address, a down server, or a port that is not accepting messages, an Internet Control Management Protocol (ICMP) message will usually be sent, but not to the UDP stack.[31] The UDP send function sends a datagram and immediately returns to send another. The error returned from send tells the programmer only that the send was executed successfully, nothing about what happens to the datagram after it entered the network. Receive only waits and will accept any datagram addressed to the port. This makes programming simple and execution fast, but error checking is minimal.

If a datagram is lost because the network was congested, the datagram was misrouted, or there is a hardware failure, the sender will never know and neither will the receiver, unless extra programming detects errors.

Although UDP does not guarantee that datagrams will arrive or that they will arrive in the order they are sent, it does have a checksum that checks that the header and data sent is the header and data received.

Surprisingly, for some applications, this checksum is a disadvantage. Audio codecs that translate digital messages to analog sound often have circuitry and software to fix damaged signals by interpolation and other means of bridging over bad segments. The patched output sounds better than missing the packet entirely. For uses like this, there is another protocol, UDP-Lite, RFC 3828.[32] This protocol is identical to UDP except an application can designate a section of the data insensitive so it will not be checksummed. Accurately addressed but otherwise damaged datagrams will be delivered.

UDP Programming

When developers design programs that will communicate directly over the Internet, one of the decisions they make is whether they will use TCP or UDP.

The typical pattern for a UDP server is a loop (Figure 9-15). The server opens a socket bound to a port. The server then waits for a request to arrive. Clients must know the port and address of the server to connect with the service. A client creates a socket and sends a datagram to the server port.

---

[31] Some UDP implementations do help with handling asynchronous errors, but traditional implementations do not. This is another part of UDP that can be programmed around.

[32] http://tools.ietf.org/html/rfc3828

The server then replies with a datagram. On receiving the server's datagram, the client closes its socket. The server's socket remains open, waiting for another request.

This skeleton example illustrates the UDP style. Unlike TCP where servers and clients typically exchange a series of datagrams over a connection, UDP datagrams are independent. The server may receive datagrams from many clients on the same socket. When the server replies to the sender, it must use the address and port of the sender extracted from the inbound datagram. If the server carries on a stateful conversation with the client that requires the server to keep track of previous messages, the UDP stack provides no help. The next incoming datagram may be from anywhere. In TCP, until the connection closes, the stack assures the server that all the incoming data is from the same client.

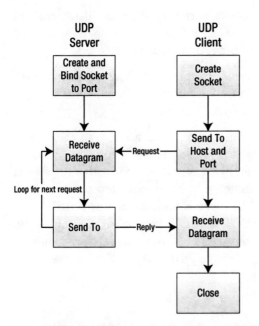

Figure 9-15. A UDP server usually loops waiting for new requests. Each datagram received may be from a different client.

This is not to say that UDP cannot be used for multistep transactions that require keeping track of what has happened. It can be, and it can also provide a reliable service, but there will be programming required—programming that TCP supplies. One reason for building a stateful or reliable service with TCP might be that all features that TCP supplies may not be required, or TCP does not supply exactly the right feature for a specialized purpose. In general, UDP is best suited to short interchanges that exchange single datagrams where a connection is not helpful or voice-like applications that can tolerate missing and disordered datagrams better than pauses. An important use of UDP is multicasting, in which a single packet in broadcast simultaneously to many different receivers. A single packet is sent out to a range of addresses. Network hardware, often routers, replicate the packet as needed to direct it to all the receivers. A protocol that does not correct errors like UDP is simpler for this purpose.

Internet Control Message Protocol (ICMP)

ICMP is a protocol in the Internet Protocol suite that does not transfer data from host to host on the Internet. Instead, it is a messaging system that is used by networking equipment to keep the Internet working smoothly. ICMP is used to spread information about datagram delivery issues such as unreachable destinations and expired hop limits.[33]

ICMP Standard

RFC 792,[34] published in 1981, is the standard for ICMP. An IP packet encapsulates the ICMP message. The protocol field in the IP header is set to the code for ICMP, and all other fields are used normally. The first byte of the ICMP message is an 8-bit ICMP message type followed by an 8-bit subtype. The subtype is not always used. An identifier used for matching requests with replies, a sequence number, a checksum, and a data area follows these two fields. The type code determines the content and layout of the data area.

RFC 792 ICMP CONTROL MESSAGES

- Destination unreachable
- Time limit exceeded
- Parameter problem
- Source quench
- Redirect
- Echo
- Timestamp

---

[33] The hop limit is the Time To Live (TTL) in the IP header.

[34] http://tools.ietf.org/html/rfc792

- Timestamp reply

- Information request

- Information request reply

RFC 792 defined 12 control messages. The list has since more than tripled in length in a number of additional RFCs, but the original 12 are still heavily used. The message types and codes are managed by IANA, which maintains a current list.[35]

User ICMP Commands

The exceptions are the network utilities ping and traceroute. These utilities are tools for detecting hosts on the network and analyzing the connection to a host. Both use the ICMP echo command. When a host receives an ICMP echo packet, it is expected to echo the packet back to the source. The ping command sends a packet to a host and tracks the time from sending to the return of the packet. The user then knows whether the host is reachable and an estimate of the quality of the connection from the elapsed time.

The traceroute[36] command is more elaborate, although it uses the same ICMP echo message as ping. Traceroute makes use of the hop limit. Traceroute starts by sending an ICMP echo with a hop limit of one. The first router the message hits will discard the expired packet and send back an expired hop limit message to the source address. Traceroute writes out the name of the router that sent the expired message and the time. Then it sends another packet with a hop limit of two, which will expire at the second router on the route. Traceroute continues to send packets, incrementing the hop limit in each packet, writing out the time and router until the packet reaches its destination. At that point, the target host issues an ICMP echo message. Then traceroute assembles the returned messages into a report that shows the path and timing of the packet through the network.

ICMPv6

ICMP for IPv6 is similar to ICMP for IPv4, but ICMP is associated closely with IPv4, and IPv6 is enough different from IPv4 to require a new standard, RFC 4443,[37] published in 2006. The ICMPv6 message is similar to the ICMPv4

---

[35] www.iana.org/assignments/icmp-parameters/icmp-parameters.xml

[36] tracert on Windows.

[37] http://tools.ietf.org/html/rfc4443

control message but a little simpler. The ICMPv6 message consists of the type, the subtype code, and a checksum. The data area follows. Like the ICMPv4 message, the type determines the contents of the data section. RFC 4443 divides message types into errors and information. Error types are numbered 1 through 126; informational messages are numbered 127 through 255. The message types and codes are managed by IANA, and many informational messages have been added since the original RFC.[38]

Domain Name System (DNS)

DNS is not formally part of the Internet Protocol suite since it is system rather than a protocol, and the Internet could get along without it, but it does influence the popularity and ease of use of the Internet.

DNS mediates between human and machine capabilities and requirements. Humans remember and reproduce names more accurately than sequences of arbitrary digits. IP addresses, as 4 or 16-byte sequences of data, make sense to a few engineers, but they are opaque to most people and difficult for humans to reproduce correctly. Humans remember domain names, like google.com or spiegel.de, more accurately, and they enter them correctly more often.

The job is not as easy as it may appear. IP addresses must translate into routes from one IP address to another on the Internet, but domain names provide a memorable clue to the content of the domain. Those goals are not the same. DNS meets that challenge, and its continued existence for close to three decades of explosive growth of the Internet proves its success.

History

The DNS began its development not long after the IETF standardized IPv4 in 1980. The first manifestation of what was to become DNS was a single text file that listed host names and IP addresses. This host file was copied around the then tiny Internet (or Arpanet as it was called then). As the number of hosts and locations grew, this mechanism progressively became harder to maintain. Improvements were needed. The result was the DNS. When thinking about the DNS design, it may help to keep that original text file in mind.

---

[38] www.iana.org/assignments/icmpv6-parameters

The first round of standardization of DNS appeared in 1983 with RFCs 882 and 883.[39] Four years later, RFCs 1034 and 1035 appeared.[40] These RFCs specified the fundamentals of DNS. Since then, DNS has expanded with many RFCs as the system expanded and scaled to support the burgeoning Internet. As cloud computing expands and the number of devices with IP addresses continues to expand, DNS will expand and scale also.

Domain Names

Domain names are the familiar names seen in Uniform Resource Locators (URLs). All hosts connected to the Internet have a Fully Qualified Domain Name (FQDN) that corresponds to their name in the DNS. FQDNs are seen less often than the domain names in URLs, but they unambiguously identify a host in the context of the entire Internet.

Structure

Unlike IP addresses where, as they are usually written, the highest level in the hierarchy appears at the left, the highest level in a domain name appears at the right. The highest levels in the domain name hierarchy are the familiar .com, .org, .net, and the country domains like .uk, .de, and so on (Figure 9-16). The root of the domain tree does not have a name. FQDNs are often written with a final dot (.) to indicate the root of the domain tree.

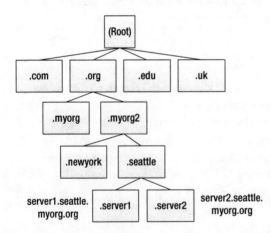

Figure 9-16. This diagram traces one branch of a domain name tree.

---

[39] http://tools.ietf.org/html/rfc882 and http://tools.ietf.org/html/rfc883

[40] http://tools.ietf.org/html/rfc1034 and http://tools.ietf.org/html/rfc1035

There is no limit to the depth of the domain tree, and it has been widened several times by adding new top-level suffixes. One of the important characteristics of the DNS is that it is designed to be expanded.

Internationalization

DNS limits the characters in domain names to the letters a–z and A–Z, the digits 0–9, and hyphens. That limitation eases processing, but it does not support international domain names such as those expressed with ideographs or non-Western alphabets. To support international domain names, the standard includes a system that maps Unicode (an international character set that encompasses almost all characters used anywhere) to the DNS name character set. Processing in the name servers does not change.

Registration

Domain names are regulated. Distinct domains with the same name would cause intolerable confusion. Individuals or enterprises cannot pick domain names out of the air and claim them as their own without names eventually colliding and causing ambiguity in a system that must remain unambiguous.

To cope with the number of applications, domain names and IP addresses are managed with a multilevel system of registrars and subregistrars. The primary registrar is the Internet Corporation for Assigned Names and Numbers (ICANN), a nonprofit organization incorporated in 1998. ICANN took over domain registration from Internet Assigned Numbers Authority (IANA). Previously, IANA operated under a contract from the U.S. Department of Defense. IANA still exists, but now it is a subsidiary of ICANN.

Although ICANN and IANA maintain overall responsibility for the domain name structure and the top-level name servers, a single registrar is not scalable. At the rate that the Internet has expanded, ICANN would have been overwhelmed within a few years of its establishment if the DNS had been based on a single registrar.

As the top-level registrar, ICANN accredits subregistrars to manage the registration of subareas of the domain tree. These subregistrars further delegate registration.

At the lower levels of the domain tree, local unofficial authorities assign names. In Figure 9-16, an accredited registrar registered myorg.org, but seattle.server1 was assigned locally. In all likelihood, a corporate network administrator managed names at the .seattle and .newyork levels, and a technician in Seattle named the host server1.

Implementation

The DNS implementation has two parts: the resolver that is implemented on a host and name servers queried remotely by resolvers.

Resolvers

Resolvers are usually libraries implemented on a host and linked into programs that use the TCP stack. The stack itself accepts IP addresses, not FQDNs. The programs that use the resolver commonly make two calls: gethostbyname and gethostbyaddr.[41] Gethostbyname takes a domain name as input and returns an IP address. Gethostbyaddr takes an IP address as input and returns a name.

The exact input and output of these calls depend on a number of factors. For example, gethostbyname might accept a bare host name without a domain and default to the local domain. A server might return an IPv6 address if one is available and default to an IPv4 address, or it might return an error if an IPv4 address is not available. These, and other variations, depend on local configuration and setting made in the calling program.

Each resolver has a list of a few DNS name servers that the resolver calls when attempting a resolution. An administrator usually sets the list of DNS servers, or the system sets the list automatically when the host joins the network. The resolver issues a query to the first server on its list, usually sending a UDP datagram. UDP works well for DNS requests because each request is a single datagram with a single datagram reply. Using UDP saves the extra traffic of setting up and taking down a TCP connection.[42]

When the host sought is part of the local or enterprise network, resolution will be possible without leaving the enterprise or local network. When seeking a foreign host, the process can become more complex.

Resolvers are iterative. When a resolver sends a request to a DNS server, there are two kinds of answers. The first is a simple reply with the information requested. The second is the address of another DNS server to try. The server to try is the first server's best guess at a server better prepared to answer the query. The resolver executes a query against the second name

---

[41] Gethostbyname and gethostbyaddr are the traditional Unix names for the functions. Names in other implementations may vary. DNS can supply other information. For example, DNS can store mail hosts used by e-mail systems. Those DNS functions are not covered here.

[42] DNS name servers usually will accept either a UDP or a TCP query, but UDP appears to be prevalent.

server. This process may repeat several times until a name server responds with the information requested. However, the resolver library does all this, not the caller of a resolver function.

DNS Servers

The network of DNS servers implements a distributed hierarchical database. The design does not expect a single server to contain all domain names, and all domain names are expected to be contained in more than one name server. This serves two purposes. No single name server should be overwhelmed with queries that it alone can answer, and the failure of a single server should not cause unanswerable queries. The design establishes this level of redundancy by periodically transferring data to other name servers and maintenance of caches. One of the consequences of this distributed approach is eventual rather than constant consistency. When a record changes in the DNS, it may take time for the change to migrate throughout the system. Users of the DNS must consider this latency when they use the system.

Conclusion

What we now refer to as the Internet with a capital *I* is the product of the Internet Protocol suite (IPS). The Internet is a collection of interconnected networks that has become both dense and widespread. The Internet covers the entire globe, and smaller and smaller embedded computing devices everywhere are connecting the Internet. The IPS passes messages from processes on computers in one network to computers on other networks, no matter how remote or how differently implemented. When connected to networks that comply with the IPS, supercomputers, smartphones, and networked industrial controllers all can use the global Internet.

The concept of a network stack, exemplified by the OSI stack, makes the IPS possible. The isolation of layers of the stack means that networks that work with the IPS operate independently of other networks as long as they continue to support the IPS.

In earlier sections, WAN and LAN protocols were discussed. These protocols evolve independently of the IPS. The IPS does not restrict LANs or WANs to any particular protocol. A LAN using token ring or half-duplex Ethernet can connect to the Internet as easily as a LAN based on InfiniBand. Consequently, the Internet does not advance in lockstep. As new protocols and networking equipment are developed, networks are not forced to roll out the new technology simultaneously to maintain. Instead, by both supporting the IPS, the new technology communicates with the old.

Increasing power and miniaturization of computing components has pushed networking forward. Mention was made earlier of the influence of Application Specific Integrated Circuits (ASICs) on router and switch design. The increasing sophistication of processing on network equipment has opened the way for advances like Software Defined Networking (SDN) and the related OpenFlow protocol.[43] Under SDN, software controls routing. This is more dynamic and flexible than traditional routing algorithms. SDN helps in cloud implementations because the dynamic flexibility of SDN permits greater separation between the virtual networks offered to users and the physical network in the cloud datacenter. This is especially important in IaaS where virtual networks are part of the services offered.

The Internet Protocol suite and networks, both wide area and local, are entering into a new phase with cloud computing. Networking and the Internet have grown immensely in the last 30 years. The scope and utility of distributed computing today are a tribute to the foresight of engineers and the standards committees that created this vast structure.

Cloud computing will bring changes, new strains, and new challenges. Looking at how distributed computing has scaled and how well the standards have encouraged rather than stifled expansion, however, we have every reason for optimism.

---

[43] See http://openflow.org for discussion and specifications for OpenFlow. The Open Networking Foundation, https://www.opennetworking.org/, is pursuing SDN.

The Internet Application Layer and the Cloud

Where Code Does Business

The applications in the Internet application layer are the face of the cloud. When an enterprise user records a sales contact in a SaaS customer relations management application, they use a browser. The browser interacts through the Web with a back-end application in a cloud. In Chapter 9, I talked about how applications can make use of Internet and network protocols to establish remote communications between applications. In this chapter, the focus is on how applications are structured to make use of the Internet and the infrastructure that makes this possible.

In review, the IPS consists of three layers: Internet, transport, and application. These layers are similar but more flexibly defined than the corresponding OSI layers. The Internet layer is characterized by the Internet Protocol (IP), which connects networks. The transport layer sits on top of the Internet layer and manages connections between ports. Ports correspond to processes on a network node. Transport Control Protocol (TCP) is the most common transport protocol. The third layer, the application layer, is the subject of this chapter. The World Wide Web, for example, is implemented with application-layer protocols. Application-layer protocols assume that basic communication from process to process has been established by the lower layers, leaving the application layer free to concentrate on structuring data and transactions for efficient implementation of applications.

From one viewpoint, the application-layer protocols and technologies discussed in this chapter are unnecessary for cloud implementation, but it is improbable that clouds could exist without them. For many years, using basic network protocols like TCP/IP, developers have built applications that communicate over the Internet. Cloud applications that rely on application-layer standards do not inherently have more functionality than these hand-coded TCP/IP applications, but application-layer standards reduce the effort required to build applications that match or exceed the performance and reliability of these older-style applications. This is because prewritten utilities and modules have replaced independently designed and hand-written code. These standard utilities and modules, such as hypertext transmission servers like Apache, are intensively tested for performance and reliability. They are reusable because they conform to public standards that developers can follow with assurance that they will be able to work with this reusable functionality.

An added benefit of application-layer standardization is a dramatic decrease in the application-specific code on the end user's device. Instead of multimegabyte client installations, applications share ubiquitous browsers. This saves hours of tricky installations and provides a pleasingly predictable user interface.[1]

The TCP/IP stack is the foundation of all these standards. A well-built application constructed directly on the TCP/IP stack is carefully designed and elegant, but elegance is no advantage if engineers and IT practitioners with minimal experience and training cannot reproduce and modify the elegant design easily and reliably to reuse it in future projects.

The Internet application layer is an easier way to conduct interactions over the Internet because it standardizes interaction on a higher level. Typical application-layer interactions over the Web, and the clouds connected in the Web, are more organized and accessible than a connection between two sockets via ports and IP addresses. One of the most important technologies for achieving this organization is Hypertext Transmission Protocol (HTTP), the first protocol in our discussion of the Web.

---

[1] These are not the only benefits of cloud implementations. Portability, elasticity, and efficiency all derive from the cloud model and would be present even without the benefits of application-layer standardization. However, without the application layer, delivering those benefits to consumers would be more difficult.

World Wide Web (WWW)

The World Wide Web and the Internet are closely related, but they are not the same thing. The WWW (or the Web) is a very large distributed application. The Internet is a collection of interconnected networks. End users interact with applications that use networks to communicate, but they do not interact directly with networks. The Internet is the network that connects the components of the WWW application.

The WWW application consists of many intercommunicating components in which an entire set of standards make the communication possible. Perhaps the most surprising result of this complex application is the number of components from diverse sources that work together well. Users from small children to grandmothers can traverse the Web and access well-presented data from every corner of the globe with confidence. The standards that make all this possible are agreements, not international laws or government treaties.

The decisions made by Berners-Lee and his colleagues early in the design of the Web are the root of its simplicity.[2] The design of Uniform Resource Locator (URL) addresses and HTML move functionality out of HTTP that a less prescient design would lump into a complex and inflexible protocol that would have required repeated redesigns.[3] HTTP relies on the standard TCP/IP protocol for communication, which is built on lower-level network standards. The entire WWW is the result of careful layering and reliance on standards. Instead of disruptive changes to a monolithic protocol, the World Wide Web has evolved with relatively minor and nondisruptive changes to independent technologies that each occupies its place in the WWW architecture.

Without the establishment of standards for the Web, the Web would have been impossible. The Web is far-reaching, and its implementers are diverse. The standards established by the IETF and the W3C are a single handbook that implementers can rely on. Following this handbook is the ticket to entering the Internet. Free access from every corner of the Internet to cloud implementations is one of the key building blocks to the value of cloud computing.

---

[2] The simple beginnings of the WWW appear in Tim Berners-Lee's original formal proposal for the WWW (www.w3.org/History/1989/proposal.html).

[3] URLs were replaced later with Uniform Resource Identifiers (URIs). More on the distinction in the "Addressing" section of this chapter.

Protocols

Protocols set the rules for interaction between communicating processes. One protocol predominates on the World Wide Web: Hypertext Transmission Protocol. HTTP is not the only protocol on the Internet; I have discussed an entire stack of protocols that HTTP depends on. TCP, UDP, and IP are used directly in cloud implementations as well as acting as a lower layer to HTTP. Nevertheless, HTTP is the most common protocol used both on the Internet and in cloud computing.

Hypertext Transmission Protocol (HTTP)

When Tim Berners-Lee conceived of the World Wide Web, there were three essential concepts. The first was a protocol for exchanging documents. The second concept was a universal, uniform way of addressing documents and anything else that consumers might want to share on a computer. The third concept was a way to indicate how a document should appear that would not depend on the means available for displaying the document. The result was HTTP, Uniform Resource Locators (URLs), and Hypertext Markup Language (HTML). This section is devoted to HTTP. Later sections address URLs and HTML.

History

Tim Berners-Lee's first version of the HTTP specification, HTTP 0.9,[4] is dated 1991. It documents only the GET operation, but it represented principles that continue to be important. The stateless nature and simplicity of HTTP are already prominent, and the document declares GET to be idempotent.[5]

The IETF published the first RFC for HTTP 1.0, RFC 1945, in 1996.[6] The first implementations of HTTP were around 1990 from Tim Berners-Lee's original design. The IETF HTTP working group was established in 1994.[7] The working group was chartered to document current practice and extensions and go on to improve the protocol.[8]

---

[4] www.w3.org/Protocols/HTTP/AsImplemented.html

[5] Idempotence and statelessness will be discussed in detail later, especially in the context of Representational State Transfer (REST). Repeating an idempotent operation has the same effect as performing it once. The behavior of a stateless system does not depend on its history.

[6] http://tools.ietf.org/html/rfc1945

[7] http://ftp.ics.uci.edu/pub/ietf/http/hypermail/1994q4/0000.html is the first recorded e-mail of the HTTP working group.

[8] http://datatracker.ietf.org/wg/http/charter/

RFC 1945 aimed at the first goal of the group, documenting current practice. The authors of the first RFC were Tim Berners-Lee, Roy Fielding, and Henrik Frystyk Nielsen, who are all still prominent in the development of the Internet.[9]

RFC 1945 documents HTTP 1.0. HTTP 1.0 documents three methods: GET, HEAD, and POST. HEAD is a variation of GET that returns only header information. It is a quick way to check whether a full GET is worthwhile. POST takes a different vector from GET and HEAD. Neither safe nor idempotent, POST sends data to the server from the client.

The addition of POST in RFC 1945 could be the most significant step in the development of the World Wide Web and eventually the cloud. With POST, HTTP was no longer a one-way protocol that imitated a reader picking up a newspaper from the newsstand. With POST, the reader could write news items and post them to the paper. We often talk about the Internet being a paradigm shift from the printed word. If the shift could be concentrated into a single event, the appearance of POST in RFC 1945 could be it.

RFC 1945 was the beginning of the World Wide Web as a two-way street. The Web did not change overnight when the specification was made public, but with the transformative addition of POST, the transition from a Web of static pages of information to the Web of interactive communication had begun.

The next major event in the history of HTTP was HTTP 1.1. The first version of HTTP 1.1 was RFC 2068 published in 1997.[10] Two years later, in 1999, a revision was published as RFC 2616. [11]

RFC 2616 remains the HTTP 1.1 standard document. RFC 2616 contains a number of emendations and clarifications to RFC 2068, but the features are the same. Perhaps the most interesting difference between the versions is in the PATCH operation.[12] RFC 2068 contains a section that documents protocol elements not implemented universally or consistently at the time. The PATCH method was included, defined similarly to RFC 5789 in 2010.[13] RFC 2616 dropped the additional features section, and PATCH disappeared from view in

---

[9] Tim Berners-Lee has been head of the W3C for many years. Roy Fielding is now well-known for his formulation of the REST architectural style, and Henrik Frystyk Nielsen went on to develop the Arena Browser and SOAP.

[10] http://tools.ietf.org/html/rfc2068

[11] http://tools.ietf.org/html/rfc2616

[12] The PATCH operation performs a partial update to a resource. It is similar to PUT, except PUT replaces a resource entirely rather than a partial update. PUT is idempotent; PATCH is not. More on PATCH later.

[13] http://tools.ietf.org/html/rfc5789

the standard for 11 years, although the subject of PATCH is still a point of contention today.

HTTP 1.1 is a more elaborate and sophisticated protocol than HTTP 1.0. A rough measure of the elaboration is the number of pages in the standard. HTTP 1.1 nearly triples the length of the standard from 60 to 176. Between HTTP 1.0 and 1.1, the number of methods rose from three to eight. The methods are detailed in the "Operations" section of this chapter.

The Protocol

HTTP is remarkable in its simplicity. It consists of simple stateless transactions that use a limited set of methods.

Statelessness

One source of simplicity is statelessness. A stateless protocol treats each transaction without regard for any previous transaction. For example, if a client requests the first element in a series, after the server responds, a stateless protocol allows the server to forget that the client ever made the request. The client cannot expect the server to respond with the second element in the series on its next request. Instead, the client must keep track of what it wants from the server and explicitly request the second element.

Statelessness is wonderful for programmers. When a protocol is stateful, precious memory must be allocated to recording state when it could be spent on more interesting tasks such as improving performance. Programmers write tortured conditional logic to implement intricate state transitions. A stateless protocol avoids all this and therefore can be lean and efficient.

When communications break down, often a network fault, the state has to be unwound, carefully returning the system to some determinate consistent point in the transaction. Recovery operations like this typically require some of the most difficult code to write and adequately test.

Statelessness resembles an unreliable transport like IP. IP is unreliable, but a reliable protocol like TCP can be built on top of it. Similarly, the HTTP protocol does not require state between clients and servers, but applications built on HTTP can maintain state. This is important because developers can implement some cloud applications more easily with awareness of state. There are strong reasons for avoiding state, but there also strong reasons for stateful applications.

Life is not stateless. The quality of the code I write this morning depends on the breakfast I ate when the sun came up. Statelessness can be a hindrance as well as a help. If my head is swimming from a donut carbo-load, I can ignore state and force myself to write suboptimal code or accept state and return phone calls and attend meetings until after lunch. Similarly, some applications require a stateful dialogue between the client and the server. For example, filling out a service desk ticket often is more than entering a few details and getting a ticket number back. To speed resolution of the ticket, the server may issue a series of questions, each of which depends on previous answers. That kind of application can be implemented without state using techniques that will be described in the "Representational State Transfer (REST)" section, but those techniques are not everyone's choice. For some applications, they can be awkward and as difficult to implement as server state.

Different approaches to state exist, and debates that hinge on where state is to be kept are often critical in standards discussions. One side of the debate argues that applications designed with all the state kept on the client are simpler and more reliable. This belief leads to highly resilient and efficient systems. Proponents argue that every application can be built this way. The downside is that this can increase client complexity and more data must reside on insecure clients, at least temporarily.

The stateful server side argues that state on the server side may present some problems, but the benefits in rich functionality and simple clients outweigh the problems. This is the essential argument between remote procedure call (RPC) versus representational state transfer (REST) designs. I will discuss this battle in more detail later.

HTTP Message

There are two types of HTTP messages: requests from a client to a server and responses from a server to a client. An HTTP message consists of a header and a message body. A message body is not always required. For some requests and responses, for example, informational error messages, HTTP 1.1 specifically prohibits a message body.

The message header consists of a request or response line followed by any additional header fields that may apply. Header fields are attribute-value pairs. The standard classifies header fields as general, request, response, and entity header fields.

General header fields include date, caching directives, connection, and other fields that apply to both requests and responses. General header fields extend some control over the way servers, clients, and intermediary proxies and gateways pass HTTP messages (Figure 10-1).

```
GET http://example.com/data/info-text HTTP/1.1
```

```
HTTP/1.1 200 OK
Cache-Control: private
Content-Type: text/html; charset=utf-8
Expires: Sun, 21 Feb 2010 20:39:08 GMT
Server: Microsoft-IIS/7.5
Date: Sun, 21 Feb 2010 20:39:07 GMT
Connection: close
Content-Length: 208969
```

Figure 10-1. Sample GET message and reply

Request Messages

The request line and headers transmit information about the request and the client to the server. A request is similar to invoking a method in a programming language like Java or C++. HTTP 1.1 specifies eight methods and allows extension methods. A simple request line consists of a method, followed by a request URI and the HTTP version.[14] The request URI identifies the targeted resource. When the request is routed to a proxy, the request-URI will still include the host address of the targeted resource.

Request header fields add to the information about the method and target in the request line and provide additional information about the client, such as acceptable character sets and encoding. They may also include authorization information and when to respond or not respond to requests based on the disposition of the target resource. For example, the request header might indicate not to respond if the target resource has not changed recently.

When a client sends an HTTP request message to an HTTP server, the client sends the message to the HTTP port on the server. Typically, this is port 80, but others may be specified, thus allowing more than one HTTP server on the same host.

The HTTP standard does not require TCP, only a reliable network service, that is, a service that guarantees accurate delivery rather than best effort. However, other services almost never appear in practice. The default behavior

---

[14] Uniform Resource Identifier is a more technically correct term for what is usually called a Uniform Resource Locator (URL). A URL is an address where a resource can be accessed. A URI identifies a resource uniquely but may not locate the resource. URL was used early in the development of the Web, but as the Web evolved, URI became the prevalent term. More on URIs and URLs in the "Addressing" section of this chapter.

for HTTP 1.1 is to keep the connection open between the client and server unless a party sends an explicit close connection.[15]

Response Messages

Response messages begin with a status line. The status line contains the HTTP version, a status code, and a brief text description of the status. Status codes are in five classes.

HTTP 1.1 STATUS CODES

- Informational. These messages acknowledge that the request was received and the server is processing the request.

- Success. The request was received, understood, and accepted.

- Redirection. Request was not completed. Further action is required.

- Client error. The request was badly formed or erroneous in some way, detectable by the server.

- Server error. Server acknowledges valid request but is unable to fulfill it.

The statuses appear as three-digit numeric codes. Informational statuses start with 1, success statuses start with 2, and so on. The status codes in the standard are extensible, and clients may not understand the subtleties of individual status codes, but the standard demands that clients respond reasonably to the class of the status. Servers often place detailed information on the status in the message body of responses. Clients are encouraged to display these responses to human end consumers.

Response header fields add to information in the status line. Response header fields convey information like the cacheability of the response, the willingness of the server to accept requests for ranges of data from the requested

---

[15] Occasionally the question comes up why HTTP does not to avoid the overhead of setting up and taking down the TCP connection by using UDP instead of TCP and inserting its own mechanism for reliability. This argument was strong under HTTP 1.0 where default behavior was closing the connection after each response. However, HTTP 1.1 keeps the connection open by default, which considerably weakens the argument for UDP.

resource, where to query for moved resources, and other information to help proxies and clients process the response properly.

For example, in Figure 10-1, the response declares that cache-control is private. This means that the message is for a single client. If the message is cached, it must not be placed in a shared cache that is accessible to other clients. The content type provides clues to interpreting the message. The MIME type, which is discussed later, tells the client that the message is HTML text, not some other format like JSON. HTML and JSON are also explained later. The content type also declares the encoding for the text, in this case a form that supports Western and non-Western characters.

Message Body

The message body is for bulk data transport. The headers contain metadata, data that describes the data. You can think of the headers as the paperwork that tells where the data came from and how it is packed, but all this is packaging, which is very necessary but seldom exciting. The interesting material is in the message body.

Not all requests and responses have message bodies. Among requests, POST, PUT, PATCH, and TRACE include a message body in their request, and they may have message bodies in the response. OPTIONS, GET, HEAD, and DELETE do not have message bodies in their request. A GET response always has a message body. The response to a HEAD request specifically does not have a message body. The presence or absence of a message body with other responses is response-dependent. Most error responses will contain detailed error information in the message body. Successful responses usually contain either requested information or details on what the server performed.

The concept of transfer coding brings in the term *entity body*. A message body is an entity body, but an entity body may be encoded for transfer in various ways. The terms *message body* and *entity body* distinguish between the message content and the message content plus the encoding.

Transfer coding is a property of the entity body, not the message content. Transfer coding ensures the "safe transport" of the message over the network, but it has no effect on the contents of the encoded message body. The transfer coding resembles a plastic bag slipped over a package to protect it until a package service picks it up. The service can remove the plastic bag or keep it, as it suits them. The package is intact, no matter what happens to the plastic bag after the package is out of the rain. In the same way, transfer coding is not a property of the message content, unlike JPEG coding of an image, which a client, server, or intermediary cannot strip off and replace without affecting the content.

One form of transfer coding is called *chunking*. One of the uses of chunking is to allow a form of full-duplex communication over HTTP. Latency decreases if a server can begin sending before it has completely filled a request. Suppose a client has requested a large file. It may take a long time for the server to read the file and package it up in the message body of a single HTTP response. However, many servers can send a partial message to the client without waiting to read the complete file. A succession of partial messages will take less time than waiting to construct a single full message. Chunking breaks single large messages into smaller chunks. Other forms of transfer coding are zipped, compressed, and deflated. Identity means no transformation whatsoever, which is useful for some types of messages, such as medical images, which must be transmitted with total accuracy.

Entity Header Fields

Since both requests and responses can have message bodies, entity header fields apply to the message body of either a request or a response and are present only when a message body is present. An entity header field, CONTENT-TYPE, declares the MIME type of the entity body.[16] There is more discussion of MIME types in the "Internet Media Types (MIME Types)" section. The entity header fields also include the length of the message, the encoding method (usually a compression method), and the expiration and last modified dates.

Operations

HTTP also preserves simplicity by judiciously limiting the operations it implements.

HTTP limits itself to four basic operations: GET, POST, PUT, and DELETE. The other operations, OPTIONS, HEAD, TRACE, and CONNECT, are more administrative than functional. RFC 5785[17] added PATCH to the four basic operations.

Safety and Idempotence

Both the HTTP 1.0 and 1.1 specifications discuss two important concepts: safety and idempotence.

Safe Methods

A safe operation does not significantly change resources on the server. The exact meaning of "significant change" can be confusing. The standard points

---

[16] Mime types will be discussed later. They describe the format of the message.

[17] http://tools.ietf.org/html/rfc5785

out that the important distinction between safe and unsafe methods is that when calling a safe method, the client does not request a change to a resource on the server, and no one can hold the client accountable if a change takes place.[18] This allows for housekeeping operations on the server such as performance tracking that may take place when a safe operation occurs.

Safety has important implications for security and caching. Safe methods will not endanger the integrity of the server, if properly implemented. Web crawlers, for example, use only safe methods to avoid disturbing data on the sites they crawl. Although safe methods might unintentionally reveal private data to the crawler, the site will not be modified. Servers are free to implement safe operations to act unsafely in response to a safe operation, but they do so at their peril.

Perhaps more importantly, a properly implemented safe operation will not invalidate caches. This is important because the World Wide Web depends on caching for performance. Many HTTP transactions do not reach the target server, because a cache intercepts the transaction and returns the requested data. Caching improves performance, but it depends on the integrity of caches that exist throughout the World Wide Web. Safe operations help control when caches have to be renewed.

Idempotent Methods

All safe methods are also idempotent. Idempotent methods can be repeated as many times as you like, and the effect will be the same as if you executed the method only once. Deletion is an example of idempotence. No matter how many times you delete an object, its end state is always the same: deleted.

Idempotence, or its lack, appears on some storefront web sites. When you click the "order" button on some of these web pages and a message warns you not to press the button again, the web developer is telling you that the order operation is not idempotent. If you press the button again, you may get a duplicate line in the order. An idempotent order button can be pressed many times without producing duplicates in the order.

GET

POST and GET were the only methods defined in HTTP 1.0.[19] GET is the most familiar and most used of the HTTP methods. It was the only method

---

[18] When HTTP is referred to as stateless, it means that the server is not aware of the state of the client. A client may, and frequently does, change the state of the server, and the server is always aware of its own state.

[19] PUT and DELETE were discussed as additional features that were documented but not part of the RFC 1945 HTTP 1.0 specification. See http://tools.ietf.org/html/rfc1945#appendix-D.1.

documented in Tim Berners-Lee's 1991 specification.[20] GET is used in two ways depending on what the resource addressed in the message header happens to be. When the resource is a static object, HTTP returns a representation of the resource. When the resource is a process or factory that generates data, the server returns the output of the factory. A URI that reads a sensor and returns the temperature at a location is an example of a factory resource. Query strings are strings the follow the resource path in a URI. When the resource addressed by a URI is static, the server ignores query strings and returns a representation of the resource, but when the resource is a process or a factory, the query string is passed on to the process.

Query strings are useful, especially when they restrict the return from a query, but they also offer an opportunity to compromise the safety of GET. A server process can, and some do, use query strings to trigger actions, including unsafe actions such as creating, updating, or deleting. This practice is an innovative use of HTTP, but it can be dangerous and is generally not considered good practice, especially by REST practitioners.

POST

POST is a powerful method. It is the only HTTP 1.1 method intended to be unsafe and not idempotent. Consequently, it is usable for many different purposes that require violation of safety or idempotence. The request URI in the POST message header can be either an existing resource for the server to manipulate or something like a factory that will create or modify other resources. Often, a POST will add a subordinate to the resource in the request URI. For example, to add a line to an order, a client might POST to the URI of the order with the line to be added in the body of the message. This POST would not be idempotent, since each repeat POST message would add another line to the order.

The POST method is versatile. If a site were so inclined, it could use POST exclusively because a server can simulate the other methods (GET, PUT, and DELETE) with POST, sometimes to good effect. For example, extremely long query strings may exceed the allowable length of a URI. This limits GET to shorter queries. A POST avoids that limit by placing the query string in the message body that can be much larger.[21]

---

[20] www.w3.org/Protocols/HTTP/AsImplemented.html

[21] Using POST to accommodate long query strings has a downside. The POSTing client has performed an idempotent and safe operation, but intermediaries like proxies will not be able to detect this easily. This unnecessary lack of transparency will mean that an opportunity for caching is lost, and caches may be invalidated and refreshed unnecessarily. In addition, unsafe operations require greater security; the system may invoke security strictures without real cause, generate annoyance, and waste effort. Critics of long query strings point out that their

Using POST for everything is usually not a strong design. It constrains clients to treat all operations on the site as unsafe and not idempotent. This puts unnecessary barriers in front of clients that use assumptions of safety and idempotence in their interaction with the server and makes caches more difficult to manage.

PUT

The PUT command completely replaces the resource addressed by the request URI with one described in the body of the message. When used correctly, PUT is unsafe but idempotent. If PUT performs partial updates, it is not idempotent. For example, if a client were allowed to replace a single line in a document and a second client replaced a different line and then the first client executed its PUT a second time, the resulting document would not be the same as the document that resulted from the first PUT (Figure 10-2a and Figure 10-2b).

The requirement that PUT execute complete replacements can be frustrating. Everyone is familiar with the PUT style when a word processor replaces a several megabyte file when only a single letter was changed. Replacing an entire document on a laptop or desktop where bandwidth between memory and disk is relatively plentiful is not a big problem, but sending megabytes of data over a network connection to correct a few bytes wastes precious resources.

The idea of a partial PUT, called PATCH, that would allow replacement of only a portion of a resource was floating around with RFC 2068 in 1997, but it was not made a formal part of the standard until RFC 5789 in 2010.[22] The current difficulty with PATCH is that although it has been around and understood for well over a decade and officially part of HTTP 1.1 for several years, it is not yet widely implemented, especially in browsers, and many developers are hesitant to include it in their code.

DELETE

The DELETE method is a request to the server to remove the resource addressed in the request URI. The specification warns that a server may override a DELETE and not delete the resource. Frequently, DELETEs are implemented to inactivate rather than remove a resource. The client has no guarantee that a true delete has occurred, even if the return message from the server indicates successful completion.

---

presence may point to a resource structure on the server that is not sufficiently granular. HTTP works more easily if every important resource has its own URI.

[22] http://tools.ietf.org/html/rfc5789

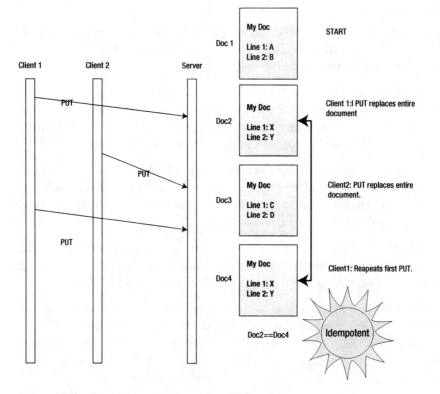

Figure 10-2a. Properly executed complete PUT is idempotent.

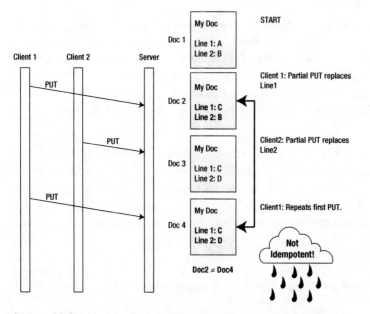

Figure 10-2b. Improperly implemented partial updates with PUT can be nonidempotent.

Other Methods

In addition to GET, POST, PUT, and DELETE, HTPP 1.1 defines OPTIONS, HEAD, TRACE, and CONNECT. These commands are not as common as the popular four and have an administrative character.

The OPTIONS method queries the server or a specific resource for its capabilities without triggering any action or data retrieval. When the request URI is an *, the client is asking for information about the server. When the URI is present, the request applies to the resource addressed by the URI.

The HEAD is a GET that does not return a message body. The method retrieves information about a request without transferring data. Typically, it is used to gauge the volume of data to be returned. If the volume is too great, the client might respond with a more restricted query.

The TRACE method is similar to an ICMP echo. The server, or the proxy, that receives a TRACE message is expected to return a copy of the entire TRACE message in the return message body. TRACE is mainly used for testing.

The CONNECT method is not defined in HTTP 1.1, but some forms of HTTP tunneling use the CONNECT method. HTTP tunneling uses the HTTP protocol and servers to communicate where ordinary network communication is impossible. For example, HTTP tunneling can pass through firewalls or proxy servers that would ordinarily block communication.

Internet Media Types (MIME Types)

An Internet media type identifies file formats. They first appeared as Multipurpose Internet Mail Extensions (MIME) in four RFCs: 2045, 2046, 2047, and 2048 in 1996.[23] When first defined, the MIME type standard described a type system that could support a wide range of document types for e-mail services. This design met requirements that were similar to the requirement of HTTP to transport a rich set of documents from server to client.

The first version of HTTP 1.1 in January 1997 was only months behind the publication of the MIME type RFCs in November 1996, so the specification of MIME types and their use as HTTP content types was almost simultaneous. The final HTTP 1.1 specification, RFC 2616, has a detailed discussion of the differences between MIME types as defined in RFC 2045 and HTTP 1.1.

---

[23] See http://tools.ietf.org/html/rfc2045, http://tools.ietf.org/html/rfc2046, http://tools.ietf.org/html/rfc2047, and http://tools.ietf.org/html/rfc2048.

The most important difference is that HTTP provides for transfer coding, coding that is external to message content and not part of the content MIME type. MIME includes similar coding as part of the MIME type. This difference may seem trivial. It is not. By specifying transfer coding as external to the message, HTTP gives servers and proxies freedom to use transfer coding as needed for the demands of the network links they must cope with. Transfer coding that is part of the MIME type cannot be changed in response to circumstances. This is important flexibility in the variable reaches of the Internet.

MIME types consist of a type, subtype, and optional parameters. Types and subtypes are registered with IANA. There are nine types: application, audio, example, image, message, model, multipart, text, and video. Under each of these types, especially application, there are many subtypes registered. Vendors often register subtypes to describe formats used in their software.

HTTP over TLS (HTTPS)

HTTPS replaces TCP/IP with Transport Layer Security (TLS). TLS, and its earlier form, Secure Socket Layer (SSL), is a layer over TCP/IP that provides a reliable and secure transport using cryptographic methods. In Chapter 4, the HTTP authentication mechanisms, Basic Authentication and Digest Authentication, were discussed. Authentication, affirming the identity of an agent, is an important part of security, but a system with robust authentication may not be secure. HTTPS goes much further toward secure Internet communication.

History

HTTPS started at Netscape in the mid-1990s and was later published by the IETF. RFC 2818, published in 2000, describes HTTP over TLS.[24] In its early form, HTTPS used the Secure Sockets Layer (SSL), and developers still occasionally call HTTPS Secure Sockets.[25] Netscape developed SSL. When security issues appeared in SSL, the IETF designed TLS to replace SSL. TLS has gone through several versions as flaws have appeared and more secure techniques evolved. Until recently, a standard compliant TLS connection could negotiate the level of security down to SSL if that was the highest level

---

[24] http://tools.ietf.org/html/rfc2818

[25] RFC 6061 is a historical document, not a standard, that is an authoritative statement of SSL 3.0 for reference (http://tools.ietf.org/html/rfc6101). RFC 6061 was published in 2011, but its contents were originally published in 1996.

of security supported by either the server or the client. RFC 6176[26] prohibits using SSL. The current version of TLS is in RFC 5246, published in 2006.[27]

Implementation

The implementation of HTTPS replaces TCP/IP with TLS (Figure 10-3). The use of TLS begins with a handshake before HTTP enters the picture. After the TLS connection is established, the HTTP protocol communicates over the TLS secure connection exactly the same way it communicates over an unsecured TCP/IP connection. To indicate a TLS connection request, HTTPS uses a different port than HTTP.[28]

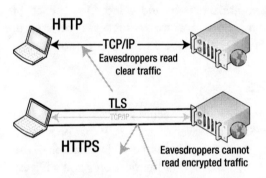

Figure 10-3. HTTPS protects messages with encryption.

The TLS specification describes the TLS record protocol and the TLS handshake. TLS record protocol governs data transfer. It uses symmetric encryption[29] to ensure the privacy of the data passing to and from the server.

The handshake verifies the identities of the client and server and sets up the TLS record protocol. The client and server negotiate a security level in the handshake. Asymmetrically encrypted certificates from certification authorities establish verification. Usually only the server offers a certificate to verify its authenticity, although the protocol allows for both client and server to present certificates. The client can verify the certificate with the issuing certification authority. The client and the server then establish a shared secret that will be the basis for encryption of the messaging.

---

[26] http://tools.ietf.org/html/rfc6176

[27] http://tools.ietf.org/html/rfc5246

[28] The default port for HTTP is 80. HTTPS typically uses 443. HTTP uses http: as the address scheme; HTTPS uses https:.

[29] Symmetric encryption uses the same key to both encrypt and unencrypt the message.

An issue that is specifically warned against in the RFC is that a man-in-the-middle attack can negotiate the level of security downward, using less secure encryption for example, by interposing between the server and the client. Clients and servers should be aware of the security of the connection and not accept connections that do not meet their required level of security.

Not using HTTPS has been pointed out as a danger in many circumstances. For example, sending private information over HTTP on a public network such as in a coffee shop or other public place is dangerous. The information can be read relatively easily. Although flaws are occasionally found and fixed, HTTPS provides an impressive level of security for web communication in a convenient form. Nevertheless, consumers should be wary. Security is always a contest; the malefactors sharpen their methods all the time. When privacy is paramount, consumers would do well to keep aware of security issues by consulting authorities such as US-CERT.[30]

Addressing

The World Wide Web is an enormous collection of resources that web users read and modify by sending HTTP messages to resource addresses. It depends on a robust and flexible addressing system to function. The IETF and the W3C have continually faced a challenge in balancing readability against unambiguous addresses that programs can accurately and efficiently interpret.

Browser users are familiar with Universal Resource Locators that point to web sites on the Internet. URLs were the first form of Internet address; according to the W3C and the IETF, the proper name is now Universal Resource Identifiers. There are two other acronyms associated with World Wide Web addressing: Universal Resource Name (URN) and International Resource Identifier (IRI). Most of the time, IRI is the most correct, although it is not used often. In addition, many people, even those who know the official preference, still call network addresses URLs. All the addressing variants and the reasons for moving beyond URLs are discussed in detail in the following section.

Universal Resource Identifier (URI) and Universal Resource Locator (URL)

All World Wide Web addresses are URIs. A URI uniquely identifies a resource, but a resource may have more than one URI. For instance, an International

---

30 www.us-cert.gov

Standard Book Number (ISBN) may identify a book, and at the same time, an HTTP address may identify the same book.

URL is an older term. In past usage, a URL was a URI that provided a path for access to a resource on the Web. Since the path to a resource identifies the resource, a URL is also a URI. In current standards documents, the term *URL* is seldom, if ever, used, and an effort has been made to change *URL* to *URI* in older standards.

This happened for several reasons. First, the standards seldom apply only to URLs. Most of the time, *URI* is a better term because the statement applies to all URIs, not just those that are a path. When referring to a partition of the address space, it is usually more useful to point to a URI scheme rather than bring up URLs. Schemes, such as http, ftp, or mailto, are more precise than URL.

Further, the distinction between URIs and URLs is not as crisp as it may appear. Addresses that appear to be paths cannot necessarily be resolved to a network location from which an HTTP GET will elicit a reasonable response. Extensible Markup Language (XML) namespaces are a good example of the ambiguity. XML uses URIs to identify namespaces. http://example.org/my-schema/ is valid as a namespace identifier, but XML namespaces do not require an XML schema document or anything else to be accessible at a namespace URI. Frequently, a GET on a namespace URI will return a document, but that is only a courtesy from the owner of the namespace domain, not a requirement. A namespace URI is a pure identifier that may incidentally also be a locator. Calling a namespace URI a *URL* would be deceptive, even though its expression is indistinguishable from a path. In XML documents, namespace identifiers are not the only constructs that look like locators but may not be locators. Sometimes these locate a resource; sometimes not.

When an unambiguous identifier is needed, a URI is a convenient way of creating one because URIs are limited to domains. Identifiers that are designed to be unique over all time and space and not require a central registration authority are useful in many contexts. But long hexadecimal identifiers, like Universally Unique Identifiers (UUIDs), are hard for humans to remember and work with. On the other hand, identifiers like URIs that are specific to a domain and organized hierarchically are easily grasped, and uniqueness is easily managed by the domain. Using URIs as global identifiers has been adopted readily. These identifiers act as addresses for abstractions that do not have physical locations. Since these abstract addresses are intermingled with locatable addresses, the distinction between the two is often arbitrary and of little use. Using the term *URI* for all addresses has become the best practice.[31]

URI Syntax

RFC 3986[32] defines a generic syntax for URIs. The generic syntax contains both requirements for all URIs and descriptions of common features that appear in almost all URIs.

All URIs begin with a scheme name. The initial *http* in Internet addresses is a scheme name. IANA registers URI schemes. About 70 URI schemes are registered.[33] Scheme examples are http, ftp, mailto, ietf, and so on. Each scheme sets its own syntax within the framework of the generic syntax.

The generic URI character set is limited to ASCII uppercase and lowercase letters, digits, hyphens, periods, underscores, and tildes. There is also a set of reserved symbols. If a URI requires a reserved or excluded character, the encoded ASCII numeric value of the character substitutes for the character.

A generic URI can contain five components: scheme, authority, path, query, and fragment. The components are hierarchical from left to right, each narrowing the scope of the component to its left. Both the scheme and path are required, although the path can be empty. The other components are optional. Figure 10-4 dissects two URIs into their components.

Comparing URIs presents some issues because a given URI can be written in different ways. The scheme and host parts of URIs are not case-sensitive, but other parts of the URI are case-sensitive, unless the scheme specifies otherwise. Usually, URIs are translated to the canonical form defined by the scheme before comparison. URI comparison is important to the Web when a client or intermediate attempts to identify cached versions of a resource. It is also worth noting that clients often apply ad hoc heuristics to URIs. Browsers that automatically prepend *http://www* to a bare domain name are applying heuristics that are not in the standard. The standard cautions that these heuristics may change as practices change. For URIs that are recorded and expected to be used for a long time, it is best to avoid reliance on heuristics.

---

[31] On the other hand, seeing how the URL usage has stuck, the definition of URL could have been extended to include abstract identifiers, and all this lexical fuss would not exist.

[32] http://tools.ietf.org/html/rfc3986

[33] www.iana.org/assignments/uri-schemes.html

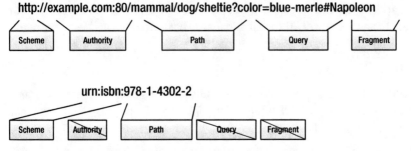

Figure 10-4. The scheme and path are required for all URIs, but other components may be optional or not used.

Universal Resource Number (URN)

URN is a special URI scheme that has close to 50 subschemes registered with IANA.[34] URNs are persistent, location-independent, and precise names for objects. An example URN is the ISBN URN displayed in Figure 10-4.

The syntax for the path portion of the URN following the second colon is specified in the RFC for the subscheme. For example, RFC 3187[35] describes using ISBNs as URNs and cites NISO/ANSI/ISO 2108:1992 as the authority for ISBN. RFC 3187 discusses the precise meaning of an ISBN and ways in which bibliographic information can be derived from an ISBN. It discusses when an ISBN may need to be encoded to meet URI generic syntax requirements.[36] RFC 3187 all defines ISBN lexical equivalence, stating that before comparing two ISBN URNs, all hyphens must be removed, and any appearances of the letter X must be converted to uppercase.

Other URN subschemes are similar to ISBNs. The IETF defined a URN subscheme for IETF documents. In that case, RFC 2648 fully defines the IETF URN.[37] Recently, the Open Grid Forum (OGF) requested a URN subscheme for their documents in RFC 6453.[38] This RFC is very similar to RFC 2648.

International Resource Identifier (IRI)

URIs are constructed from the basic ASCII character set. If a URI contains a non-ASCII character or symbol, the character must be encoded. In this way, the specification allows non-Western characters, but reading URIs with

---

[34] www.iana.org/assignments/urn-namespaces/urn-namespaces.xml

[35] http://tools.ietf.org/html/rfc3187

[36] Never, since allowable ISBN characters are a subset of the URI set.

[37] http://tools.ietf.org/html/rfc2648

[38] http://tools.ietf.org/html/rfc6453

encoded characters is often inconvenient for those more familiar with characters in the extended international set. Since many operating systems and applications support international characters, expressing URIs in international characters has become a requirement that the original creators of the WWW did not anticipate.

RFC 3987 (2005)[39] addresses this deficiency by specifying IRIs, which are syntactically the same as URIs, but they support a full Unicode character set.[40] Every URI is an IRI because the URI character set is in the Unicode character set. All IRIs have an equivalent URI that the standard mapping specified in RFC 3987 will generate. IRIs with no characters outside the URI character set are already valid URIs and are not changed by the mapping, A consequence of this is that the IRI to URI mapping is idempotent; after an IRI is mapped to a URI, future mappings of the resulting IRI (that is also a URI) will not change the representation. Figure 10-5 illustrates an equivalent URI and IRI.

URI containing the encoded UTF-8 character "%C3%BC"

```
http://www.example.org/D%C3%BCrst
```

Equivalent IRI using the actual "U +00FC LATIN SMALL LETTER U WITH DIAERESIS":

```
Http://www.example.org/Dürst
```

Figure 10-5. URI and equivalent IRI

The relationship between URIs and IRIs often generates confusion. Are IRIs a special form of URI? No, the reverse is true. URIs are a special form of IRI. Every URI is an IRI, but some IRIs are not URIs until the mapping is applied. Consequently, URIs are a subset of IRIs. This is probably confusing because IRI and URI sets have the same cardinality; in other words, both sets have the same number of elements. This is a classic enigma of transfinite numbers. It is just like the argument that the cardinality of natural, non-negative integers is the same as the cardinality of all integers (both positive and negative).[41]

The practice in standards groups now is to use IRIs rather than URIs unless there is a specific reason to limit the discussion to URIs. However, just like the general population tends to use *URL* instead of *URI*, *URI* is often used when *IRI* would be a more accurate choice.

---

[39] http://tools.ietf.org/html/rfc3987

[40] Unicode (STDREF) aims to represent all international character sets in use. It comes close to succeeding.

[41] Or maybe I am a little too much taken with transfinite numbers.

Data Transfer Languages

The World Wide Web and applications built on HTTP use data transfer languages to transfer data between clients and servers. Servers often exist in a cloud rather than on the premises of the client. The efficient transfer of data to and from servers in the cloud can easily become the central issue of application design and performance.

One approach to improving application throughput is to compress the data into as few bytes as possible. Compression of data can increase throughput compared to uncompressed data, but other aspects of application design can also affect perceived performance, sometimes much more than the number of bytes on the wire. For example, a "chatty" application that indulges in unnecessary back and forth exchanges between the client and the server can be less responsive from the accumulated latency of client-server round-trips than an application that transfers quantities of data. Flexibility and ease of interpretation can be more important than compactness.[42]

It is hard to decide which is more important to the World Wide Web and the cloud: Extensible Markup Language (XML) or Hypertext Markup Language (HTML). Both are common. HTML is probably a bit better known because it is used in conventional web sites, but it is difficult to imagine serious web

---

[42] An important lesson for practical application builders is not jump to conclusions on performance improvements. Once, I was working on an application that transferred a large volume of data over the Internet between client and server. Performance was not what we expected, so we jumped onto the idea of compressing the data for transmission. We snooped the data and saw that it was mostly nulls imposed by the way strings were loaded. We decided to implement a very simple form of "run-length encoding" in which a series of the same character is replaced with a count. It is probably the simplest form of data compression.

The compression algorithm worked perfectly, and the amount of data on the wire dropped dramatically, but performance did not change. After putting several man-weeks into the effort, someone pointed out that the uncompressed messages were still contained in a single packet and arrived at the same time as the compressed messages. Compressing the messages helped performance only if the uncompressed message spilled into multiple packets or packets had to be broken up to traverse a network segment with a low maximum transmission unit (MTU).

The real cause of poor performance was a series of queries and responses to and from the server that preceded every real data transmission. When the team eliminated the chatter, the effect was dramatic and much more effective than compression. The reduced chatter removed the latency of several full round-trips from client to server and yielded a substantial performance improvement.

The important point for the cloud is that verbose data transmission languages like XML are not necessarily the cause of performance issues.

development without XML. Since XML is more general than HTML, we will begin there.

XML

XML was originally devised as a simplified data markup language for electronic publishing. It is a subset of Standard Generalized Markup Language (SGML), specified in ISO 8879:1986(E).[43] Some current electronic publishing formats, such as EPUB format for electronic books,[44] are based on XML, but XML is used for more than publishing. XML has become an everyday workhorse in computing for expressing structured read by both humans and computers. Figure 10-6 is an example XML document.

```
<<?xml version="1.0" encoding="UTF-8"?>
<bookList>
   <book id="98-101">
      <author>Samuel Clemmens</author>
      <pseudonym>Mark Twain</pseudonym>
      <title>Adventures of Huckleberry Finn</title>
      <genre>Masterpiece</genre>
      <publishYear>1883</publishYear>
      <description>Rafting down Mississippi.</description>
   </book>
</bookList>
```

Figure 10-6. Simple XML document

Standards for the World Wide Web use XML for many purposes. Markup languages are related to traditional proofreader and printer marks on manuscripts. These marks assume that a document exists and is being prepared for printing. XML, and most markup languages, starts with a similar scenario in mind. XML approaches markup hierarchically. A document begins as an outer set of begin and end tags that surround the full document. Then further pairs of tags delineate sections, subsections, sub-subsections, and so on. The inner sections of the document may vary widely. They can repeat, nest deeply, and form elaborate structures. The contents between begin and end tags are elements. Tag names suggest the semantic significance of the elements they surround. Tags may have attributes that further refine the significance of the tags and provide information on the content of the element.

---

[43] www.iso.org/iso/iso_catalogue/catalogue_tc/catalogue_detail.htm?csnumber=16387
[44] EPUB is a standard from the International Digital Publishing Forum (http://idpf.org/epub).

The capabilities of XML go beyond document markup. XML also has the ability to represent structured information that differs materially from publishers' manuscripts. Structured business documents such as invoices or balance sheets all fit naturally into XML form.

XML can represent data from a relational database well, which leads to one of the strengths of XML that is also a source of criticism. The contents of a relational data in XML take many more bytes than the database itself because the XML representation is filled with tags, and these tags, following good XML practice to use explicit and easily understood names, are often long. These tags are written out for each element, both at the beginning and at the end of the element.

Explicit tags make XML comprehensible to human readers and parsable by computers, but the documents are verbose. Some argue that XML is not easy to read or work with. The frequent use of XML editors that depict XML graphically rather than textually tends to support this contention. Although storage has become much cheaper, network bandwidth is still a constrained resource, and cost is not the only constraint on storage volume.[45] Bandwidth is significant because XML is probably the most prevalent format for transporting web service data over the wire inside of and in and out of clouds, and the total quantity of XML data is immense.

History

ISO published the SGML standard in the late 1980s. SGML documents can be complex and difficult to parse, although they are also expressive and flexible. In the mid-1990s, the W3C recognized the need for an SGML language tailored to the World Wide Web. A working group formed with the goal of specifying an SGML language that was easy to read, parse, and write; contained a minimum of optional features; and was usable on the Internet. Although XML has critics, the release of XML 1.0 in 1998 was outstandingly successful, if only by the number of books published on XML and projects based on XML.[46] Five editions of XML 1.0 have appeared, the last in 2008.

---

[45] For example, fast directly attached storage on blade servers is often constrained by physical space.

[46] www.w3.org/TR/2008/REC-xml-20081126/ (fifth edition, released in 2008)

XML 1.1

XML 1.1 was published in 2004. XML 1.1 and 1.0 are largely compatible, and editions of 1.0 continued to be issued after 1.1 was issued.[47]

The advancement of the Unicode standard was the primary driver behind XML 1.1. In 1998 when XML 1.0 appeared, Unicode 2.0 was the current standard, and XML 1.0 is based on the Unicode 2.0 character set. By 2004 when XML 1.1 appeared, Unicode had gone through several minor and major releases and many characters were added to the Unicode 2.0 character set. Unfortunately, 1.0 enumerated the characters from Unicode allowed. This meant that characters added to the Unicode character space in subsequent releases of Unicode were prohibited in XML 1.0–compliant documents without explicit changes in the specification and changes to 1.0 validators. XML 1.1 addressed this problem with a significant change in XML name rules. Instead of enumerating the characters allowed in names, 1.1 enumerates the characters not allowed. Thus, the new characters in Unicode's expanding character space could appear in XML names without constantly changing the specification.

The 1.1 specification also added support for additional end-of-line handling to accommodate the conventions of a range of operating systems and expanded the ways in which non-ASCII characters, such as EBCDIC,[48] could be expressed in XML.

Similar to many other structured documents, XML permits alternatives in expressions. For instance, some whitespace is not meaningful in a document, and processes can remove or augment it without changing the meaning of the document. This flexibility is useful, but it can make it hard to determine that two documents or document segments are the same or only insignificantly different. XML 1.1 overcomes this obstacle with instructions for converting documents to a canonical form. Documents converted to a canonical or fully normalized form can be compared accurately.

The XML 1.1 additions to XML 1.0 have no effect on most documents. If a document has no extended Unicode or is not concerned with newly permitted line endings, an XML 1.1 processor is not likely to act differently from a 1.0 processor. If comparing documents is not important, full normalization to 1.1 canonical form is also unimportant.

---

[47] www.w3.org/TR/2006/REC-xml11-20060816/ (second edition, released in 2006)

[48] Extended Binary Coded Decimal Interchange Code is a character encoding used on IBM mainframe and midrange computers. EBCDIC is considerably different from ASCII.

XML users did not accept XML 1.1 as readily as the W3C expected.[49] There is some speculation that XML 1.1 is a dead end and will never supersede XML 1.0, even though there is now significant tooling for XML 1.1. The fifth edition of XML 1.0 accepts characters included in later releases of Unicode. This move in the XML 1.0, fifth edition, reduces the reason for using XML 1.1 and means that XML 1.0 largely supersedes 1.1.

Namespaces

Namespaces are among the most confusing aspects of XML, although they are simple in concept. Namespaces prevent collisions between tags when valid XML documents are combined. Often, especially in large enterprises, XML documents form a complex referential web. Changing one document to avoid a conflict can affect many other documents. Namespaces avoid endless chains of modifications or convoluted prefixes.

The problem arises because tags from different valid XML documents may be indistinguishable but have different meanings. Instead of changing the tags in the source documents, namespaces can be assigned to the documents. A namespace prefix then designates tags that come from specific documents, and the tags are distinguishable. The confusion with namespaces often stems from the scoping rules for namespaces within a document, which can be complex.

The W3C chose URIs as namespace identifiers because URIs with IANA registered sites ease choosing unique identifiers. Namespace identifiers are not URLs. Even though an HTTP GET on a namespace identifier looks like it should return a useful document, the specification says nothing. A 404 Not Found error message is perfectly acceptable to the specification. Most namespace identifiers do return documents of some kind, but this is a courtesy, not a requirement.

The third edition of XML Namespaces 1.0 was published in 2009,[50] and the second edition of XML Namespaces 1.1 was published in 2006.[51] The namespace documents parallel XML 1.0 and 1.1.

---

[49] http://lists.w3.org/Archives/Public/xml-editor/2008OctDec/0017.html talks about some of the controversy.

[50] www.w3.org/TR/REC-xml-names/

[51] www.w3.org/TR/2006/REC-xml-names11-20060816/

Schemas for XML

XML 1.0 and XML 1.1 specify the structure and syntax of all XML documents. Parsers use these rules to determine whether an XML document is well-formed. If a document does not conform to XML structure and syntax, it is not XML, and standard-compliant XML parsers must reject the document, unlike HTML parsers that often make a best-guess rendering of incorrect documents.

Schemas go beyond well-formed XML to validation. Many useful XML documents do not have schemas, but a well-formed document still may be far from the designer's intent. For example, an XML invoice with an "itemQuantity" subelement placed in the invoice total section instead of in a line item section could be well-formed according to XML rules but still far from a correct invoice. Schemas specify structures and data types tailored to a document. In the invoice example, a schema might declare that "itemQuantity" defaults to one and must appear only as a subelement of "Item."

XML does not require a schema, and XML documents do not always need a schema. Schemas are good for checking compliance, but compliance checking is not always desirable. For example, computer programs often write XML output. After initial debugging of the output program, the program may not be capable of making schema-type errors. Schema validation, which can be slow, is then extraneous and can be eliminated. Since schema writing is more difficult than writing straight XML, some development shops skip the step.

When schemas for XML are mentioned, W3C XML Schema is often the first thought, but there are alternatives to XML Schema. The XML standard itself discusses Document Type Definitions (DTDs).

Document Type Definition (DTD)

SGML defines DTDs, and DTDs apply to non-XML SGML documents as well as XML documents. An example is Hypertext Markup Language (covered shortly), which is related to XML but not an XML language. Part of the HTML specification is a DTD. A DTD describes the elements allowed in a document and the structure of subelements and character data. A DTD can also limit the allowable sets and types of values for attributes and elements.

DTDs may be included in the XML document or be a separate document. Unlike XML Schema Definition Language, DTDs are not written in XML. The SGML specification governs DTDs. Therefore, DTD syntax and features cannot be changed without going to the ISO. Consequently, DTDs have not kept up with features of XML. For example, DTDs do not recognize XML namespaces. DTDs do not specify content and data types in as great a detail as XML Schema.

XML Schema Definition Language (XSD or XSDL)

XSD was designed to duplicate and extend the XML DTD capabilities in an XML-based language. XSD is more complex than DTD. Data types in DTD are very simple. XSD specifies many data types and provides for restrictions on the basic types. For example, XSD strings can be restricted with regular expressions. XSD also defines powerful rules for specifying structure for XML documents.

History

XML Schema 1.0 was first published in 2001,[52] with an error correction edition in 2004.[53] A second version called XML Schema Definition Language (XSD) 1.1 parts 1 and 2 were published as a W3C recommendations in April 2012.[54]

The formal name for XML Schema changed slightly between 1.0 and 1.1. Unadorned XML Schema is ambiguous because *XML schema* can refer to any of the XML schema languages, of which XSD is only one. The longer name and the XSD acronym clarify the ambiguity.

XSD 1.1 has a long list of small changes to 1.0, but the 1.1 authors tried to make all valid XSD 1.0 documents also valid XSD 1.1 documents. In addition, with a few exceptions, XSD 1.1 documents should be valid 1.0 documents. The spec describes its goal as clarifying and simplifying the standard rather than making changes in compliant documents. The specification also accommodates XML 1.1.

Regular Language for XML Next Generation (RELAX NG)

OASIS published the RELAX NG standard shortly after the W3C published the first edition of XSD. RELAX NG has goals similar to XSD. Like XSD, a RELAX NG schema is an XML document, but RELAX NG also has a compact form that is not XML-based. The compact form is popular for its readability. OASIS published the compact form specification in 2002.[55] Backus-Naur Form (BNF)[56] productions and regular expressions influenced the compact RELAX NG form. The compact form translates to and from the XML form of RELAX NG without loss of information.

---

[52] www.w3.org/TR/2001/REC-xmlschema-1-20010502/

[53] www.w3.org/TR/xmlschema-1/

[54] www.w3.org/TR/xmlschema11-1/

[55] www.oasis-open.org/committees/relax-ng/compact-20021121.html

[56] For those unfamiliar with BNF, Wikipedia has a useful summary at http://en.wikipedia.org/wiki/Backus%E2%80%93Naur_Form Retrieved 2012-05-14. Wikipedia is useful but not definitive.

RELAX NG and XSD are alternative ways of specifying the allowed elements and structure of XML documents, but they are not exactly equivalent. Each has advantages. RELAX NG has a dependency on XSD; it allows implementations to define their own data types, but most implementations rely on the XSD data types.

XSD is powerful and expressive, but it is also formidable to read and understand easily. Many developers prefer to work with the more readable syntax of RELAX NG, especially in the compact form. Recent standards have tended to express schemas in both compact RELAX NG and XSD to satisfy developers who prefer the simple form.[57] Despite its simplicity, XSD still has wider acceptance among development tool makers. There are more parsers and validators available for XSD than RELAX NG, and there is a general lack of tools for automatically generating interface code from RELAX NG. However, interest in RELAX NG appears to be rising, and the situation could change.

Schematron

Schematron is a schema validation language for XML that is based on a different principle from XSD or RELAX NG. The former two languages are grammars that describe what is allowed in a schema-compliant XML document. Schematron is a rule-based language that states rules that a schema-compliant XML document must follow. Consequently, a Schematron schema with only a few rules will accept any document constructed with any valid XML entities as long as the rules are not violated. Conversely, an XSD specifies a limited set of elements, attributes, and structures and will accept only those documents constructed with those few entities and none other. Thus, the more an XSD or RELAX NG schema will accept, the larger the schema.[58] The more a Schematron schema will accept, the smaller the schema.

Schematron rules can specify constraints that are based on combinations of several elements and attributes using XPATH.[59] Combined constraints are

---

[57] See the Oasis, Topology, and Orchestration Specification for Cloud Applications (TOSCA), currently in progress, at http://docs.oasis-open.org/tosca/TOSCA/v1.0/csd02/TOSCA-v1.0-csd02.doc. Appendix C is in compact RELAX NG; Appendix D is in XSD. TOSCA is an important emerging cloud standard that will be discussed in the next chapter.

[58] XSD has xs:any that drops XSD grammar checking, but the more constructs an XSD schema has to check for compliance, the larger the schema grows.

[59] XPath is an XML language not covered in this book. XPath constructs point to nodes in an XML document. See Wikipedia at http://en.wikipedia.org/wiki/XPath for a general but not authoritative introduction. www.w3.org/TR/xpath20/ is authoritative but less readable.

more limited and difficult to express in XSD. Schematron has been implemented as an XSLT transformation and is often combined with XSD.[60]

Schematron is an ISO standard, ISO/IEC 19757-3:2006(E).[61]

JavaScript Object Notation (JSON)

JSON is a data language that often appears as an alternative to XML. JSON and XML are now commonly specified as acceptable MIME types for HTTP data transfer. JSON is simpler than HTML. It does away with explicit markup tags and replaces them with a simple attribute-value pair[62] syntax for expressing data structures. The syntax is taken directly from the JavaScript language, which makes handling JSON in JavaScript easy. Most browsers support JSON, and many programming languages also support JSON. With fewer rules and less verbosity, many programmers prefer JSON to XML.

A JSON schema validation language exists but is not used as often as XSD or RELAX NG. XML can often express the same data structure in different ways. A value can be expressed as an attribute or an element, for example. This kind of choice is not available in JSON's simple syntax. JSON's simplicity reduces the need for schemas. Perhaps more important, JSON's best quality is its simplicity and ready understandability. Schemas make JSON more complex, and therefore developers often decide not to use them.

History

JSON is a subset of JavaScript. It is based on the ECMA-262 Standard 3d Edition, 1999.[63] The application/json media type is described in RFC 4627.[64] The application/Jason+schema media type is described in 2010 IETF Internet draft.[65]

---

[60] Extensible Stylesheet Language Transformations (XSLT) is another language written in and inspired by XML. XSLT transforms XML documents into other documents. The output of an XLST transformation may be another XML document or some other format.

[61] The Schematron specification (http://standards.iso.org/ittf/PubliclyAvailableStandards/c040833_ISO_IEC_19757-3_2006(E).zip) is one of the few ISO/IEC standards available without charge.

[62] Attribute-value pairs are a common data structure. { "Name": "Martin" } is a JSON attribute-value pair in which "Name" is the attribute and "Martin" is the value. In XML, this might be expressed with markup tags as <name>Martin</name>.

[63] See www.ecma-international.org/publications/files/ECMA-ST/Ecma-262.pdf. http://json.org/ has an easy-to-follow description of JSON.

[64] http://tools.ietf.org/html/rfc4627 is informational.

[65] http://tools.ietf.org/html/draft-zyp-json-schema-03 expired in 2011.

Hypertext Markup Language (HTML)

HTML is the language that most people associate with the World Wide Web. If provides the format for semantic descriptions of documents. Originally, Tim Berners-Lee and his colleagues designed the first version of HTML for describing scientific documents at European Organization for Nuclear Research (CERN).[66] The uses of HTML quickly expanded as interest in the World Wide Web grew. Web users and designers began to use HTML to describe all forms of hypertext, including e-mail, online documentation, and database query results in hypertext.

Ownership of the HTML standard transferred several times, first to the IETF and then to the W3C. The HTML4 specification was published in 1998. The sentiment of the W3C at that time was that HTML had reached its limits and would be replaced by XHTML. The users of HTML and the browser vendors went in a different direction, continuing to expand HTML, producing an HTML5 specification. The W3C soon realized that XML and HTML were continuing to go separate ways. In 2004, W3C resumed work on HTML, accepting the vendor draft of HTML5 as input to a W3C standard. In May 2012, the W3C published a "Last Call for Comment" draft of HTML5. Last Call W3C drafts are close to official adoption, although a number of formal objections and open issues remain at this writing.[67]

HTML is not as important for cloud computing as it has been for the World Wide Web. That is not to say that HTML is unimportant. Whenever data from the cloud is displayed to users or user interfaces communicate with the cloud, HTML (or XHTML) is almost certainly being passed back and forth in HTTP message bodies. On the other hand, when communication occurs that is not intended to be directly displayed, which happens often in cloud computing, XML (or other data transfer languages like JSON) is almost certainly in use.

XML and HTML are both derived from SGML and are similar yet fundamentally different. HTML from its beginning was specifically designed for displaying information in a browser. The types of documents to be displayed has expanded, and some goals have been refined and modified, but the basic goal of describing a document independently from the implementation of the browser displaying the document has never changed.

---

[66] www.w3.org/History/19921103-hypertext/hypertext/WWW/MarkUp/Tags.html is an early document by Tim Berners-Lee preserved in the W3C archives. It shows HTML in an early form.

[67] W3C. 2012. Working Draft of HTML5. www.w3.org/TR/2011/WD-html5-20110525/. The Last Call Working Draft has 3 formal objections and 10 open issues.

XML is a more formal language than HTML. HTML browsers, for example, are tolerant of errors and ambiguities. If the HTML is not well formed, an HTML browser will usually guess at what the author intended and display something. XML rules compel an XML parser to stop parsing and declare an error when the XML grammar is violated. This is a decidedly unfriendly action where the input is from untrained authors trying their best and hoping that their document will display. This describes a large segment of the web community. When humans see a display that has been patched up by the browser, they usually can gather the author's intent or at least identify it as an error, but computer programs are seldom able to make sense of malformed data. For program-to-program activity, which is important for cloud implementations, the causes and implications of malformed input are more significant, and halting processing is a better response.

XHTML is an effort to bring the benefits of XML to HTML. XHTML documents are intended to be the equivalent of HTML documents. XHTML documents conform to XML rules and can be parsed with XML parsers. Some developers and browser builders embraced XHTML; others did not, leading to typical compatibility issues. There may be long-term benefits of an XML-based browser markup language. By combining the efforts of the XML and HTML development communities, both will benefit from richer tools and innovations. However, the vast store of HTML documents and the hordes of HTML-trained web site designers will change only slowly. For designers who strive for presentable pages rather than verifiable documents, the looseness of HTML has important benefits.

The decision of the W3C to return to developing HTML5 acknowledges the fundamental need for two kinds of communication on the World Wide Web but acknowledges the need to support the HTML community. The HTML5 specification combines both HTML5 and XHTML5 into a single specification suggesting that HTML and XHTML can coexist. The influence of the cloud is apparent in this move. Program-to-program web service communication is becoming a more important element in programming for the World Wide Web as cloud computing becomes more prevalent. Although web services do not use XHTML often, XML is often used, and experience with XML may build acceptance for XHTML.

Cascading Style Sheets (CSS)

Cascading Style Sheets are a side note to cloud computing, but they have become important in the display of data in a browser, which is vital to effective use of cloud services. They address the need for a solution to the rising complexity of HTML documents with more and more complex tags for detailed control of the appearance of HTML documents in various competing browsers.

HTML originally had two purposes. One was to identify the logical parts of a document and the relationships between them. Browsers use these logical relationships to lay out the data on the screen. The second purpose is to provide hints to the browser on how to display those parts. Combining these two purposes in a single HTML can be simple and compact, but as documents become more complicated and web designers want to specify more of the final appearance of documents, these HTML files become more complicated and harder to manage.

When logical relationships and display hints are intermingled, changing one without the other can be difficult. Also, between the hot competition of browser builders and the voracious appetite of web designers for display features and control of behavior, extended, nonstandard HTML tags proliferated. Writing robust HTML became even more challenging because it had to either descend to the lowest common denominator or resort to different versions for different browsers. In addition, a given browser may not have the resources to display everything specified in standard HTML. This left HTML authorship in a chaotic and challenging position.

CSS separates the appearance part of HTML and provides a layer of abstraction so that the designer can apply a single style (font, size, color, border style, and so on) in many different logical segments of the document. This abstraction also separates appearance from logical document relationships and simplifies the HTML. The web page author can place style sheets in a separate file or embed them in the HTML file. CSS is also usable with any XML document, as well as HTML. CSS is a W3C specification.[68]

Although it is not a complete solution, CSS has made writing HTML documents somewhat easier.

Programming

Most of cloud programming is almost identical to distributed enterprise programming, because the direction of enterprise programming has been toward a model like the cloud for a long time. Is the cloud the result of this trend? Or is it a coincidence that the technology has appeared at the moment it is needed? These are unanswerable, but the convergence is clear.

---

[68] See http://w3.org/Style/CSS/Overview.en.html. CSS is divided into several specialized specifications.

The pattern for a cloud programming model is a back-end server running in a cloud that communicates with clients via HTTP. Distributed enterprise applications often follow the same pattern but locate the back-end server on their own premises. The main difference between the enterprise model and the cloud model is in the amount of separation between the server and the client. Except occasionally in private clouds, cloud clients are seldom in the same location as the server or even on the same network.

The trend for the last decade has been to use HTTP for communication between servers and clients, even inside an enterprise network. This might be surprising because the diverse and unpredictable nature of the Internet drove the HTTP design with its stateless servers and support for caching.

Thin vs. Thick Clients

The move to HTTP and the browser is associated with a move from "thick" to "thin" clients.[69] In typical thick client architecture, much of the processing and business logic occurs on the client. The server is primarily a supplier of raw data. In the thinnest of thin clients, the only processing that occurs on the client is the display and exchange of HTML pages. The client does not perform any logical or data transformation (Figure 10-7).

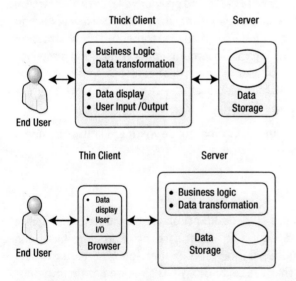

Figure 10-7. Thick clients perform business logic and data transformations. Thin clients leave this to the server.

---

[69] Thick clients can be built to use HTTP, and thin clients can be built without HTTP, but HTTP is an effective and most frequently used protocol for thin clients, so the two are closely associated.

Perhaps in reaction to the earlier time-sharing model in which all processing occurred on the central mainframe or mini-computer or from experience with stand-alone applications running on isolated desktops, developers in the early days of distributed computing tended to use the processing power of the client as much as possible and minimize activity on the server. This also made better use of resources when the processing power of distributed servers was more limited and expensive than today.

The thick client approach has challenges in large enterprises. Upgrading thick clients in enterprises with thousands of desktops can create challenges that last for months. The problem begins because thick clients and their servers are typically closely coupled. Servers and closely coupled thick clients must be upgraded at the same time. Usually, if an upgrade is significant, the old client will not work with the new server, and the old server will not work with the new client. In other words, both clients and servers have to be upgraded at the same time.

Upgrading a server is usually not hard, but simultaneously upgrading a few thousand desktops can be a logistic nightmare. Even finding all the desktops with installed clients can be difficult. In the days prior to network installs, installation disks or CDs had to be distributed. The humans sitting in front of the desktop were likely to need help with even simple installations, which leads to a prolonged upgrade as IT personnel go from desk to desk upgrading. If the application is at all mission-critical, a second shadow server will have to be set up to service the old clients until they are all upgraded. When the upgrade is complete, data from the old server has to be migrated into the data on the new server, which often ends up being a painstaking manual process.

Although distributing processing to the desktop provides some scalability by decreasing the incremental load on the server as new users are added, the cost in loss of productivity for upgrades is high, perhaps highest for managed service providers where desktops are in the control of the provider's clients, not the provider.

On the logistical side, thick clients are not optimal for other reasons. Patching thick clients can be almost as big a logistical problem as installation and upgrades. Defects and security issues are an inevitable reality in IT. The code installed on desktops today tends to be only a browser, a few common office utilities like word processors and mail clients, and an operating system. Since these are widely distributed products, they can be supported by large staffs, searching for defects and security flaws and fixing the quickly and dispatching patches. A small staff with additional responsibilities usually supports enterprise applications, especially custom applications developed in-house. Therefore, fixes to thick client code tend to take much longer and the patch cycle much longer. This can lead to unacceptable application behavior and even security issues.

There are other problems with the thick client architecture. Not all clients are equal. Clients often must run on the cast-off desktop relegated to the stockroom for printing labels as well the best and most recent machine sitting in an executive office. Performance expectations in the stockroom may not be high, but the thick client at least has to work. If it will not, the application upgrade gets another black mark and another reason to delay installation.

Browsers, HTTP, and thin clients provide a solution to the challenges of thick clients. With logic and other processing removed from the desktop, upgrades become a server-only issue. The client is only a common browser with no special application code that is not downloaded from the server. The only time the browser must be updated for the application is when a new version of the browser is needed to support a new feature. Even this problem is easier for the IT department because the browser vendors already have the problem of creating upgrades and patches suitable for the most naïve users, taking the pressure off IT. As a bonus, upgrading a browser typically has more benefits than upgrading a single application; users accept the inconvenience of an upgrade more readily.

All these factors have impelled enterprise applications to move to thin client architectures, most based on HTTP and HTML browsers.

Thin Clients and Clouds

The move from thick to thin clients has paved the way toward cloud implementations. By placing HTTP between the client and the server, the way is paved for cloud implementation. Clients and servers can be widely separated, and they can make use of the robust architecture of the Internet to provide connectivity between clients and servers. Applications no longer have to be limited to the boundaries of the corporate network. Relying on HTTP, which was designed from its beginning to operate over the Internet, distributed application designers and managers have choices. They can place servers on remote clouds. These clouds can be reached via private networks or the public internet.

Until recently, enterprises have not structured their datacenters as servers running on a cloud, either public, private, or hybrid. The difference between a conventional distributed enterprise application and an enterprise application hosted on a cloud lies more in the way the IT department administers the back end rather than the programming and code. A well-designed, HTTP-based thin-client application is likely to work well with the application and enterprise information system tier implemented in a cloud rather than on dedicated servers in the datacenter.

Moving an application back end to a cloud can be a test of quality of an enterprise application's design. An application that is difficult to upgrade, is hard to scale, demands frequent and challenging maintenance, and forces inconvenient downtime will be at least as bad and more likely worse deployed in a cloud. On the other hand, an enterprise application that has been built to follow architectural best practices and does not have the issues just described will probably work well deployed on a cloud.

Security is occasionally an issue because a cloud implementation, particularly a public cloud implementation, makes the back end more accessible than servers protected behind enterprise firewalls and cipher locks. However, these issues usually do not affect the core design of the system, and most enterprise applications are now designed with much more substantial security than the early days of distributed computing.[70]

When a cloud hosts applications, the datacenter pools hardware back-end servers into a single resource that is available to all the processes running in the cloud. Pooled resources are more efficient because a stressed process in need of resources can be allocated slack resources from idle resources. Resource balancing and reallocation takes place on a level below the application, and the application developer does not see the allocation process.[71]

When developing a cloud-hosted application, developers see a cloud-hosted resource, usually virtual but not always, the same way they see a remote resource on a private or public network. One reason enterprises have so readily adopted clouds is developers can use techniques and programming models that have been developing since the beginnings of the Internet. Cloud implementations are more exposed to security assaults because they generally rely on the public Internet for communication, but the requirements for cloud security actually do not differ much from the requirements of a banking application that is exposed to remote customers on the Internet.[72]

---

[70] There are security problems that are unique to cloud computing. These are discussed in Chapter 4. Most of the issues discussed there are not directly related to the architecture of an enterprise application. They have to do with making security less apparent to the user, keeping data encrypted, and assuring auditors that data and systems are properly cared for.

[71] Nevertheless, some application designs are more readily balanced than others. For example, an application that runs as a single unthreaded process is more difficult to balance than a multithread, multiprocess application.

[72] Cloud governance is another issue, which is generally a matter of identifying the appropriate security measures and verifying that it has been properly implemented and is in

A cloud application that is accessed via a public network may require encryption and authorization that would not be needed behind a firewall, but the same programming techniques are used when implementing a client-server application distributed over a public network. The difference between a cloud-hosted application and other forms of distributed client-server applications is administration, not architecture; some architectures are more natural and are more prevalent for cloud implementations.

Gateways

The core problem in creating cloud applications is connecting the application server in the cloud to clients on the consumer premises. Remote connections are often an issue for all distributed applications, but the ramifications are more pressing for clouds. This is most evident in SaaS implementations where cloud-hosted applications compete with applications installed on the consumer premises. The SaaS implementation must provide services comparable in performance and reliability to the consumer premises application even though the application on the premises may be on the same LAN as the clients. The pressures only differ slightly for installations on IaaS and PaaS clouds, which are a little more likely to host applications that are not competing with an alternative installed on the consumer premises.

There are alternative ways to communicate with the cloud. One alternative is to use TCP/IP or UDP/IP directly. At the furthest extreme, although not likely to occur often, an application can be coded on raw IP sockets without the benefit of TCP, UDP, or other transport protocols. Before the rise of the Web, programming on the TCP/IP stack was the only good alternative for designing distributed applications. Although TCP/IP is still occasionally a good choice, programming on a protocol above TCP/IP, particularly HTTP, is a better choice because it is so common and users are so used to the Web.

The World Wide Web brought HTTP servers and browsers. Programmers could begin to rely on HTTP for a communication protocol, a browser for a UI, and an HTTP server, such as Apache.

The advantage in using HTTP comes from the frequency with which HTTP is used and the infrastructure that has developed for using it. Corporate networks, independent service providers (ISPs), and Internet backbone providers implement proxies and caches that help make HTTP reliable and fast. HTTP servers are easily obtainable, and an abundant selection of

---

operation. There may be issues with cloud security, but they generally differ from noncloud scenarios because ownership and responsibility have shifted, not because the security mechanisms are different.

infrastructure eases building of applications on HTTP. In addition, firewalls are typically configured to allow HTTP to pass through, making that much easier to deploy distributed applications.

Building on lower-level protocols is sometimes necessary to meet special requirements, but developers must be careful not to fool themselves that development on low-level protocols is required. For some developers, creating their own protocol stack is a great temptation. HTTP is not a panacea, but there is strength in the number of implementations working with it. Managers have to keep in mind that developers familiar with HTTP are abundant, but competent TCP/IP coders are relatively rare.

Early in the evolution of the Internet, web deployment was only a browser requesting documents from an HTTP server. The browser requests a file identified by a URI with an HTTP GET, and the server returns the file. The user might modify the file and return it with a POST or PUT. From the user's point of view, this interaction is largely visual, and interaction is limited. Developers soon realized that the interaction did not have to be visual and the resources did not have to be physical files on the server. One of the consequences of these realizations was the concept of "web services."

Web Services

Web services are an important part of current application architectures and critical to cloud implementations. Web services are not required to use HTTP, but they are most often implemented on it. They are a means of communication between differing software applications running on a wide variety of platforms on a network or internetwork. Web services do not require that developers be aware of the internals of the applications with which they communicate. An application coded to interact with a web service protocol will be able to connect with all services that have the same interface and follow the same protocol, no matter how they are implemented.

There are many possible architectures for web services, but two dominate. Both are usually based on HTTP because it is prevalent, but neither architecture demands HTTP. These two architectures are Representational State Transfer (REST) and remote procedure call (RPC), which is usually characterized as SOAP.

Remote Procedure Call (RPC) and SOAP

RPC is an older architecture than REST and seems more natural to many application designers.

RPCs derive from one of the fundamental constructs of programming: the function call. A function call is an exit from a command sequence that performs a specific action and returns to the original sequence. Function calls are among the most powerful concepts in programming because functions isolate capabilities that can be reused in other contexts. They also separate implementation from functionality. In straight-line code, each line depends on preceding lines for its meaning. When a program calls a function, the code in the function body does not depend on the lines of code preceding the call. It depends only on the values passed to the function.

Independence from calling context is important to both the function caller and the author of the function body. A functions called from C++ can be implemented in C, even Fortran or Algol. The caller never needs to know the language of the implementation. The function implementation may even change as runtime circumstances change.

Consequently, the caller can use the function anytime and anywhere without concern.[73] As long as a function does what it promises, the caller is unconcerned. At the same time, the implementer of a function does not need to be aware of the context of the function call and can concentrate on a correct implementation, without fretting over the context of the call.

Developers leverage the separation between the caller of a function and its implementation in many ways. The basic concept of a service, the separation of consumer and provider, is the same separation as the divide between the caller and implementer of a function. In the simplest scenario, developers implement functions in the main program or in linked-in libraries, but scenarios can be more complicated. One possibility is to implement a function in another process. For example, a program devoted to a user interface might call a "login" function implemented in a process devoted to controlling user logins.

The next step is the remote procedure call. Instead of implementing a function in the same process as the function call, the developer implements it in another process, and that process may be on another node on the network.

Remote procedure calls (RPCs) are a simple logical extension for a local function that makes distributing applications conceptually easy. To distribute an application, pick some functions and implement them remotely, turning them into RPCs. *Voilà!* A distributed application.

The mechanics of remote implementation present difficult challenges, but the core design of a stand-alone application is preserved. Standard implementation

---

[73] This is an idealistic picture: not all programs practice good code hygiene. When good code practices are not followed, promises can and are broken.

methods take over the repetitive and exacting work of constructing remote implementations. These standard implementations do much to mitigate the challenges of distributed RPCS. One such standard that eases RPC implementation is SOAP, discussed in the next section. With the help of standards like SOAP and HTTP, using RPCs becomes an effective way to distribute applications without changing the basic design of the application.[74]

In the cloud, the developer implements RPCs in the cloud that consumers call from the consumer premises. The difference between the cloud design and a noncloud distributed design is the placement of the implementation in a cloud with all the administrative advantages of cloud implementations. RPC-based distribution is a proven design that developers use repeatedly. It leverages legacy applications and the experience of application designers who have designed applications to run as a single process or a collection of local processes.

SOAP

SOAP is one of the standards that apply to the implementation of RPCs. SOAP is a W3C standard that was originally an acronym standing for Simple Object Access Protocol, but the W3C working group responsible for SOAP decided that the long form for the name no longer applied, and it changed the official name for the standard to SOAP. The SOAP standard applies to more elaborate interactions than simple message-reply RPCs, but the heart of the standard and most of the implementations deal with RPCs.

Web services and SOAP were almost synonymous until REST began to generate interest. The SOAP standard specifies a uniform way of serializing RPCs and their results in XML. When the SOAP standard was first developed, object-oriented design was on everyone's mind. The SOAP authors naturally thought in terms of objects, and the pressing requirement was to implement remote access to object data and methods. In an object-oriented design, most activities manipulate an object through its methods. In that orientation, web services are calls to remote objects on the server. Thinking has evolved since then, and the emphasis has shifted toward implementing services, which may involve accessing objects, but a service implementation is not obliged to be object-oriented. This helps explain why SOAP no longer uses an acronym that implies that SOAP is limited to object access. Object-oriented design is still part of the software architect's tool set, but requests can made to SOAP web

---

[74] This is a simplification. Designing distributed applications with RPCs is not picking functions at random and implementing them remotely. There are many considerations in effective distributed designs. Nevertheless, they are increments to the principles of stand-alone design, not a new set of principles.

services without the sense that object manipulation is the point of the call. For example, SOAP calls can start workflows without reference to an object.

The W3C publishes the SOAP specification in three documents: Primer, Messaging Framework, and Adjuncts.[75] The Messaging Framework and Adjuncts are normative; the Primer is informative. The latest version of the documents is 1.2 (Second Edition) released in 2007.

The basic SOAP message structure is not complex (Figure 10-8). It consists of an envelope that contains a header and a body. The body contains the call to the implementation and its parameters. The header, which is optional, is for additional information that is not part of the application request but may be useful for processing. The header may contain information for passing the SOAP request on to other SOAP nodes and message interaction patterns. Complex interaction patterns are possible in SOAP as well as a simple message reply. These patterns can involve many SOAP nodes acting in coordination.

```
POST /GasPrices HTTP/1.1
Host: www.example.org
Content-Type: application/soap+xml; charset=utf-8
Content-Length: 299
SOAPAction: "http://www.w3.org/2003/05/soap-
envelope"

<?xml version="1.0"?>
<soap:Envelope xmlns:soap="http://www.w3.org/2003/
05/soap-envelope">
  <soap:Header>
  </soap:Header>
  <soap:Body>
    <m:GetLocalGasPrice xmlns:m="http://
www.example.org/gasprices/local">
      <m:Location>Bellingham</m:Location>
    </m:GetLocalGasPrice>
  </soap:Body>
</soap:Envelope>
```

Figure 10-8. Sample SOAP HTTP POST

Web Services Description Language (WSDL)
WSDL is an important standard associated with SOAP. WSDL provides a formal abstraction for describing web services in a standard way using XML. Although WSDL is primarily associated with SOAP, the WSDL designers did

---

[75] Primer: www.w3.org/TR/2007/REC-soap12-part0-20070427/ ; Messaging Framework: www.w3.org/TR/2007/REC-soap12-part1-20070427/ ; and Adjuncts: www.w3.org/TR/2007/REC-soap12-part2-20070427/ .

not intend to limit WSDL to SOAP, although SOAP is the only specific binding discussed in the standard.

The current, 2.0 version of WSDL is specified in three W3C documents, published in 2007.[76] The original 1.0 specification was published in 2000 by a group of vendors.[77] The W2C published a more formal 1.1 version in 2001[78] and another 1.2 version in 2002.[79]

WSDL provides an XML abstract language for describing the functionality and details of a service without reference to the underlying implementation of the service.

A WSDL service description consists of four parts: types, interface, bindings, and services. The types section describes the message types used in the service. These are usually expressed in XSD. The standard does not designate a schema language, but XSD is the most likely to be supported by WSDL processors. Types can be described directly in the types section, or they can be included with an import capability. This is important for complex collections of interrelated services. The section describes the message signature and the types of the data passed in the basic type system of the schema language.

The interface section describes the operations performed by the service. An operation uses message types. The section also describes the message pattern of the operation. A simple inbound-only operation needs only one message type. Operations with replies and other complexities may need more message types.

The bindings section describes the underlying protocol that will deliver the messages of the service and the message format such as SOAP. HTTP is the protocol usually bound to WSDL. The section is concerned with the communication of the service. The section names the endpoint for the service, the binding for the endpoint, and the address of the endpoint.

Representational State Transfer (REST)

REST is a different approach to building web services. It is an architectural style, not a standard. The closest thing to a REST standard is Roy Fielding's PhD dissertation.[80] Fielding was one of the key architects of the Web and one

---

[76] Primer, Version 2.0: www.w3.org/TR/wsdl20-primer/; Core, Version 2.0: www.w3.org/TR/2007/REC-wsdl20-20070626/; Adjuncts, Version 2.0: www.w3.org/TR/2007/REC-wsdl20-adjuncts-20070626

[77] http://xml.coverpages.org/wsdl20000929.html

[78] www.w3.org/TR/wsdl

[79] www.w3.org/TR/2002/WD-wsdl12-20020709/

[80] www.ics.uci.edu/~fielding/pubs/dissertation/top.htm

of the authors of HTTP. In his dissertation, he described the characteristics he felt constituted an architecture that would take full advantage of the Internet and HTTP. As one of the key authors of the HTTP specification, his statements are generally accepted as authoritative.

However, the Fielding dissertation and the REST style have been interpreted in diverse ways, engendering acrimonious battles in forums and blogs over what is true REST. Controversy also rages over the merits of SOAP, representing the RPC architectural style, and REST.

The REST style is based on the architecture of the Web and especially the concept of resources with durable addresses. Durable means that a resource address can be stored (bookmarked) with a reasonable expectation that the stored address will be usable for accessing the resource in the future. This is in effect a working definition of a resource, something with a durable address.[81]

HTTP works with addressed resources. The HTTP methods GET, POST, PUT, and DELETE are all directed to resource addresses, which are often thought of as referencing documents. Addresses can also reference factories that produce resources. For example, POST a latitude and longitude to a temperature resource, and the return message might contain the current temperature at that location.

Now, a question to ask is, "Is the temperature for a location a resource?" The address of the factory is not the same as an address for the temperature at a location. The addressability of the temperature at a location is up to the designer.

To a REST designer, the call to the temperature service should return a durable address of the temperature resource for the location. An RPC temperature service, on the other hand, is a function that knows how to derive the temperature from a location value. To repeat a lookup in the REST scenario, the client performs a GET on the resource URI. With an RPC, the client passes a location to the temperature service endpoint.

A REST durable address for the temperature at a location is useful for the user of the service. They can bookmark the address and check the temperature with a GET to the bookmark. There are also benefits to the service provider. If most service users do not know their latitude and longitude, they might urge the service provider to drop the latitude and longitude lookup and switch to a ZIP code lookup. If the old lookup is not preserved, the bookmarks and links that pass a latitude and longitude to a temperature function will fail. These bookmarks and links may have proliferated all over the Web, and their

---

[81] Tim Berners-Lee wrote a classic article on the subject in 1998: "Cool URIs don't change." Find it at www.w3.org/Provider/Style/URI.

failure will annoy the users of the service who succeeded in using the old service. The RESTful durable addresses that directly reference the temperature-location resources are not affected when the method for calling the temperature changes.

On the other hand, the designer might decide that implementing the location temperature by assigning a URI to every possible location is not feasible. Although assigning URIs may be beneficial to users, the investment required to maintain a large number of URIs could be too much to bear. Or addressed resources may interfere with other required functionality. And finally, the benefits of durable addresses might be deemed trivial.

There are many differences between REST and RPCs, but their treatment of addresses is one of the most important. REST style surfaces functionality by exposing durable addresses of resources. RPC implementations do not assume that all significant resources are addressable. RPC endpoints are gateways to methods that return data. The data returned may have addresses, but the addresses are usually from an address space that is determined by the implementation of the RPC, not a web address that can be accessed from anywhere via a general protocol like HTTP.[82] An RPC-based incident management service may return incident numbers, a form of unique address, but these incident numbers are not URIs accessible directly with an HTTP GET. The service probably does provide an operation that accepts incident numbers and returns incident documents. Thus, incident numbers are in a private address space.

The RPCs reveal addresses of functions (endpoints) that execute methods that will modify the state of the server or return data. The function usually does not reveal direct addresses of the resources it accesses—if the addresses are revealed as URIs, the RPC is approaching the REST style.

REST is a simple style. Although REST as Fielding described it does not require HTTP, REST and HTTP were designed together and combine naturally. A popular conception of REST equates REST to pure HTTP. In this view, an application that relies only on the HTTP verbs (GET, POST, PUT, and DELETE) and follows the HTTP usage rules (such as GET is always safe) is RESTful.

Purists take issue when a supposedly RESTful application "tunnels RPCs," a somewhat pejorative term for an application that restricts itself to HTTP methods but supports RPC-like operations. This usually means that an application has a set of significant addressable resources (like our temperature locations or incidents) behind a function endpoint URI.

---

[82] A URI that can be accessed from anywhere is not necessarily accessible to everyone. Resource owners are always free to restrict access to their resources.

The purists have a point, but as discussed with temperature-location resources, assigning URIs to every resource sometimes does not make sense. An application designer may be porting a legacy object-oriented application to the cloud and does not want to redesign the application to reveal addresses. Or the designer of a greenfield application may have good reasons for not revealing addresses. For example, compatibility with authorization systems can complicate designing addressable resources.

Beyond the addressability issue, REST has many advantages in the cloud, not the least of which is that WSDL and SOAP stacks are difficult to implement, and the learning curve to using them effectively is steep. REST has its own set of learning obstacles because the resource-oriented approach to design is often poorly understood, but the technology is generally simpler and more congenial to developers not trained intensively in SOAP web services.

Currently, REST—at least loosely defined REST—has momentum in cloud implementations. Most new standards, such as those discussed in the next chapter, are REST-oriented. Whether this trend is good or bad is beyond prediction.

Cloud-Specific Standards

A Tide to Raise All Boats

Fundamentally, cloud consumers and providers have both coinciding and opposing concerns. Clouds present advantages to both providers and consumers, so both have an interest in standards that promote healthy and robust growth of cloud computing, but each group also has distinct business goals; those goals sometimes complement and reinforce each other, but they can also be antagonistic. Therefore, it is not surprising that consumer and provider interests in cloud standards are similar but not identical.

Consumers are eager for standards that will lessen the effects of vendor lock-in and reduce the total cost of computing in their enterprise. Providers are less so, although most providers recognize that standards that decrease lock-in promote customer acquisition as well as loss. Providers also see that decreasing costs equal more business for them. On the other hand, vendors are above all eager to develop competitive cloud offerings that they can develop and operate to the advantage of their own stakeholders. Consumers have their own stakeholders to worry about.

Historically, providers have prospered from standards. Many of the great fortunes of the late nineteenth and early twentieth centuries were made after railroads standardized track widths, car couplers, and braking systems, enabling transcontinental rail shipments. Standardized voltages, frequencies, wiring, and connectors made possible electrical grids and an electrical appliance industry. In both cases, standardization enlarged markets and opened up opportunities for providers of the standardized services.

Good standards simplify designing solid cloud technology. When a committee sets out to design a horse, conventional wisdom says the result is a camel.

That is amusing but not realistic. First, in defense of the camel, it works rather well in its arid environment. Second, committee products are often effective and reliable, even forward-looking. There are many examples among committee-developed standards, for instance Ethernet, that show remarkable efficiency, flexibility, and durability stemming from decades of thoughtful contributions from "camel designers."

Not all standards are as apt and durable as Ethernet, but many are. The standards discussed in this chapter are new because cloud computing is a new discipline. Some are not yet published as standards. We do not know how these nascent standards will endure or flourish over time. All we can do is examine the standards themselves and the process followed in their development and then look as intelligently as we can toward the future.

Interface Standards

The standards in this section specify uniform interoperable management interfaces to Infrastructure as a Service (IaaS) clouds. The interfaces apply equally to public and private clouds. However, these standards do not apply directly to Software as a Service (SaaS) or Platform as a Service (PaaS) clouds.[1] Interface standards for SaaS and PaaS are a subject for the future.

Cloud Infrastructure Management Interface (CIMI)

CIMI is a standard in progress from the Distributed Management Task Force (DMTF)'s Cloud Management Working Group (CMWG). The CMWG began as an incubator group that set out to develop informational specifications on the cloud computing environment focusing on IaaS. The DMTF accepted the group's charter in April 2009. The incubator produced several deliverables including two white papers on cloud architecture and a set of detailed use cases.[2]

---

[1] IaaS, SaaS, and PaaS are discussed in detail in Chapter 5.

[2] Public deliverables from the incubator are:

"Interoperable Clouds" (http://dmtf.org/sites/default/files/standards/documents/DSP-IS0101_1.0.0.pdf)

"Architecture for Managing Clouds" (http://dmtf.org/sites/default/files/standards/documents/DSIS0102_1.0.0.pdf)

"Use Cases and Interactions for Managing Clouds" (http://dmtf.org/sites/default/files/standards/documents/DSP-IS0103_1.0.0.pdf)

The CMWG has published several work-in-progress versions of the specification. Version one of CIMI was published by the DMTF as a standard in September 2012.[3]

The main CIMI document focuses on a REST-style protocol, but the interface design separates the interface from the communications protocol in order to support the same interface with different interaction styles. The group has concentrated on a RESTful interface, but a significant subgroup is working on a SOAP-oriented version of the interface based on the CIMI resource model. This interface will appear in a separate standard document and is likely to be released after the main REST specification.

The appearance of the interface in both REST and SOAP versions is important. Although REST has a vigorous following and has captured the interest of many developers, SOAP and RPCs are by no means a forgotten or irrelevant architecture.

Service providers often offer a choice between REST and SOAP to their consumers, and it is likely that at least some providers will want to offer CIMI in the same way. Therefore, the CIMI working group did not constrain CIMI to a single style of interface. The provider can implement CIMI as a single core infrastructure and layer on REST, SOAP, or other interface style of their choice.

This choice differs from other cloud standards like Open Cloud Computing Interface (OCCI) and Cloud Data Management Interface (CDMI); both will be discussed in detail later in this chapter. Although these standards maintain a separation between the protocol and the data model, preserving the possibility of alternative interfaces, the respective working groups have expressed less public interest in standardizing a SOAP or RPC-style interface.

The CIMI working group charter projects three protocol-mapping specifications: a REST mapping, a SOAP mapping, and a WS-MAN mapping.[4] At this writing, the CIMI working group has not published work-in-progress protocol mappings for SOAP or WS-MAN, but there are firm plans for additional mappings that are likely to have appeared at least as works in progress by the time this book is published.

CIMI's architectural flexibility may prove useful to both implementers of CIMI servers and clients, which are groups that correspond roughly to providers

---

[3] http://dmtf.org/news/pr/2012/8/dmtf-releases-specification-simplifying-cloud-infrastructure-management

[4] www.dmtf.org/sites/default/files/DMTF%20Cloud%20Management%20WG%20Charter%20VI_1g_03-10-11.pdf

and consumers.[5] Providers of public clouds and those who implement or supply tools for implementing private clouds can choose an interface to offer or supply both REST and SOAP. To meet specialized requirements, they could also develop custom interfaces with different protocols but still based on the CIMI.

Consumers will benefit also from this flexibility. If CIMI is widely accepted with the current enthusiasm for REST, the REST interface will most likely be the most commonly implemented. Some development groups familiar with REST will welcome REST, but not all development groups are eager for REST interfaces. If an enterprise has standardized on SOAP-based web services and has a common platform such as an application server framework like J2EE or .NET,[6] REST may not be an agreeable choice. In that case, a SOAP or RPC interface will be more desirable.

Time will determine the direction.

The CIMI Model

At the core of the CIMI interface is a set of resources that represent the key entities in IaaS, derived from the studies performed by the DMTF cloud incubator on the requirements of an interoperable cloud infrastructure service and the experience of the members of the CMWG. The characteristic entities in the model are machines, storage volumes, networks, and cloud environment monitoring artifacts such as events, meters, and event logs.

Model Pattern

Most of the CIMI model follows a similar pattern. The CIMI specification, unlike the OCCI specification discussed later in the chapter, is not described as a formal structure. Instead, it is described as part of the process of a consumer choosing a configuration they want and deploying it.

The standard is not a formal set of object superclasses from which instances may be derived. Instead, it is a simple implicit pattern that the resources in the standard follow and extensions to the standard are expected to adhere to.

---

[5] The correspondence is not exact because some providers will build clients for their consumers, and some consumers of private clouds will build their own servers.

[6] J2EE refers to Java Platform 2, Enterprise Edition. Later versions have superseded Java Platform 2, but the name, J2EE, is still often used. .NET is Microsoft's application server platform.

Each type of resource has a template resource, a configuration resource, and the resource specification itself (Figure 11-1).

A CIMI template is a preexisting description of a resource that becomes a blueprint for creating a resource in the future. The CIMI design makes it easy for a provider to offer a catalog of templates to their consumers. Instead of designing their own virtual machines and other infrastructure, a consumer chooses prefabricated designs from the catalog. A typical computer system template would list a CPU type and speed, amount of available memory, and disk and networking capabilities such as number and types of network interfaces. If consumers can specify their own variations on what is available in the template, then another entity, a configuration resource, is used. For example, if a provider offers an option for extra memory or more processor cores for a machine template, the consumer can request these in a configuration resource supplied with the template. The provider combines the template and the configuration into the specification for the instance, which the provider then instantiates.

This skeleton allows for variation. A cloud provider might supply all their own templates for their consumers. Or they could allow their customers to create their own templates. The specification allows providers to accept templates entered into a resource "by value." In other words, instead of pointing to an existing template, the consumer can insert the relevant properties and values directly into an instantiation request instead of using a template.

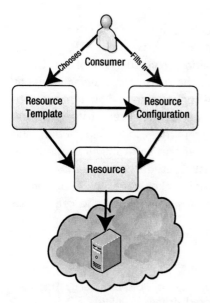

Figure 11-1. Each resource has a template, a configuration, and an instance.

Resources

CIMI resources are resources in the REST sense. They are addressable resources that are designed to be accessed, created, modified, deleted, and operated on using basic HTTP methods on URIs discoverable through links embedded in the resources.[7] The design of the CIMI resource model reflects the working group's interest in a REST interface, even though the model is also intended to support other interaction styles like SOAP.

Cloud Entry Point

The Cloud Entry Point entity reflects the REST orientation of the first interface protocol specification for CIMI. In robust discoverable REST style, the Cloud Entry Point resource contains lists of the resources that exist in the provider's cloud. Although the CIMI standard does not address resource-level security, providers will undoubtedly scope the visible contents of the Cloud Entry Point to the role of the user in the consumer's organization, and when the provider is supporting a multitenant environment, resources will be scoped to those accessible to the consumer-tenant.

Machines

CIMI Machines are abstractions of a single computer system. Although Machines are usually thought of as virtual machines, the notion of a Machine is not limited to virtual machines. A provider could implement Machines as physical computers, but that will undoubtedly be when special cases require isolated hardware.

The pattern for instantiating a Machine is common to most CIMI resources. The CIMI primer[8] describes the process in detail with sample HTTP messages. The process begins, as do most CIMI activities, from the URI of the Cloud Entry Point that the provider has supplied to the consumer. Gaining access to the Cloud Entry Point probably will involve registration and an account with the provider, although the CIMI specification does not extend to registration and the process is provider dependent. From the Cloud Entry Point, the consumer retrieves a list of available machine images and configurations. From the image and configuration, a machine is instantiated. Templates may also be available, although the CIMI primer example takes the simple option of entering the template information directly "by value" into the request to create the Machine.

---

[7] IRI is technically more accurate, but the CIMI specification uses URI consistently. There seems to be nothing in the specification that would preclude the use of IRIs.

[8] http://dmtf.org/sites/default/files/standards/documents/DSP2027_1.0.0d.pdf

Creating a new Machine in a cloud presents an interesting security issue that was discussed earlier in Chapter 5 on implementation. On the consumer premises, the operating system is usually installed on a physical machine without any security. The administrator immediately uses the functional interface for the machine to create a password for an administrator with control of the system. From that point on, the functional interface may be presumed to be secured by the password. This scenario might have breaches because of system flaws or human failure, but, in theory, the process is secure because it takes place within access-controlled premises isolated from threats until the machine is locked down. This will not work for a public cloud if the administrator's first access to the machine is over a public network. In some way, the management interface must provide for the safe transfer of control of the functional interface to the consumer. This necessitates some interaction between the functional and management interface. The details of this scenario will change with different security schemes, but the basic problem of securing the functional interface of the system remains the same.

CIMI provides a solution to this problem with the Credentials resource that can be used when creating a Machine. Because security schemes are likely to vary between providers and over time, the Credential resource is dependent on the consumer discovering the security extensions of the provider. One simple mechanism is for the provider and the consumer to negotiate a Credential that will permit the consumer to establish root access to a newly created machine. The consumer-administrator uses this Credential to access the machine via a protocol like Telnet.[9]

The request to create a Machine, if successful, returns a Machine resource URI. The consumer can bookmark this URI or obtain it by returning to the Cloud Entry Point and querying the list of instantiated Machines. A GET to the Machine URI returns a representation of the Machine resource. The provider will have filled in some properties, including the start-stop state of the Machine.

The Machine start-stop state is an example of a consumer-managed property. If the Machine is stopped, the consumer can start it with a POST to an URI in the operations array of the Machine. The presence of a start action URI in the operations array indicates that the action is available; in other words, the user can start the Machine.

A GET to the Machine URI will then show the new state of the Machine, which will be in "started" or some other starting state if the operation is successful.

---

[9] The process for working with vendor extensions is not described here, but the CIMI primer works through an example that obtains metadata for creating credentials.

This is the general pattern of operations in CIMI. Most resources have an operations array to query to find actions. If the action appears in the array, the action may be taken. Actions appear and disappear in the array depending on the state of the resource.

The main variation on this pattern is when a provider returns the URI of a Job resource instead of a simple success or failure of the POST to the action. The Job entity is helpful for long-running actions that the consumer is likely to want to treat asynchronously. Consumers can track Jobs to determine which actions are pending and follow their status. You can find more on Jobs in the "Jobs" section.

Volumes

CIMI Volumes represent storage. They are similar to Machines in the way they are created and used. Like Machines, the consumer starts at the Cloud Entry Point and selects a Volume image and configuration and uses them to request an instantiation of a Volume. Like creating a Machine, a template can be used to create a Volume.

When a Volume is first instantiated, there is no way to use it because there is no way to read or write data to it. To make it usable, it must be associated with a Machine or perhaps a Network. The process to associate a Volume with a Machine is an operation like starting or stopping a machine, although the intermediate steps differ. To associate a Volume with a Machine, the consumer looks at the representation of the Volume collection resource of the Machine, which holds the URI for the add operation. The consumer then POSTs the Volume URI to the Volume collection "add URI" resource. If the POST is successful, the tie between the Machine and the Volume is established. The consumer can verify the successful add operation by performing a GET on the Machine's Volume collection, which will return the new Volume on the list.

Network

The CIMI Network resources are more complex than other CIMI resources. Fundamentally, they are an abstraction of a transport network, and they are concerned with network interfaces, addresses, and routing for connectivity, but they do not deal with the physical implementation.

The resources that specify a CIMI Network are Network, Network Port, Address, and Forwarding Group (Figure 11-2).

A CIMI Network is an abstraction of a transport-layer broadcast domain. In other words, machines on a CIMI network are reachable in a single broadcast. The CIMI Virtual Switch Port is an abstraction of a port on a switch. A

Network can have many Virtual Switch Ports. A CIMI Address represents an IP address requested by the consumer or assigned by the provider. Addresses are associated with other resources, often Machines. A Routing Group is the group of Networks that route to each other. A Network participates in at most a single Routing Group, but other entities, like Machines, may be in several Routing Groups. The standard cautions that multiple Routing Groups can result in security anomalies if not administered carefully.

The Cloud Entry Point is the starting point for accessing the CIMI networking resources. It has URI collections for Networks, Ports, Addresses, and Forwarding Groups.

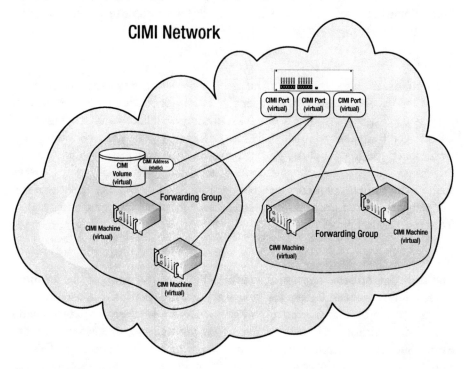

Figure 11-2. A CIMI Network

Monitoring

The CIMI monitoring resources are Job, Meter, and Event.

Jobs

Jobs are, as mentioned earlier, related to CIMI operations. Consumers can query Job resources to determine the state of an operation. They are optional for providers, but if a provider does support Jobs, CIMI requires that the provider support them uniformly. That means the provider must expose a Job for every state-altering operation.

The existence of a Job does not carry any requirement that resources be left in any particular state when the Job completes. For instance, a Machine create action could terminate, leaving a Machine instantiated but not fully conformant to the supplied configuration. To help with the potentially problematic system state after a failed Job, the Job resource has a list of affected entities. The provider is obliged to fill this list completely and correctly no matter how the Job terminates. From the affected entity list, the consumer can assess the state of the system.

Jobs may have a complex structure with parent and child Jobs. The Cloud Entry Point has a Job collection that the consumer can use to find Jobs and check their status.

Meters

CIMI Meters monitor the health and performance of the system. Meters have targets and aspects. Aspects represent what aspect of a resource to measure, such as CPU usage. Aspects are represented by qualified names expressed as URIs.[10] CIMI supplies a small collection of aspects, such as www.dmtf.org/cimi/aspect/cpu, for CPU usage, but providers are anticipated to add to this list. Meters also have properties that detail the characteristics of the meter such as the sample frequency, sample duration, and so on. The results of the sampling are stored in the Meter resource. Meters are managed and created from the Cloud Entry Point.

Events

The provider, not the consumer, creates CIMI Event resources, unlike most other CIMI resources. Events can represent any information that the provider tracks and may want to expose to the consumer. An Event contains a time stamp, an indication of severity, a type, contents, and an outcome of the Event. Suggested outcome values range from Pending to Success to Failure. The Cloud Entry Point has a collection of Event Logs where Events are accessed and tracked.

System

The CIMI System and System Template resources are potentially the most complex and powerful resources in CIMI. They touch on but do not exactly coincide with the Open Virtualization Format (OVF) system and the Topology

---

[10] *Qualified name* is a technical term for a name that is made unambiguous by including the scope in which the name is defined. A URI is qualified by its domain.

and Orchestration Specification for Cloud Applications (TOSCA) service template. (See the "Topology and Orchestration Specification for Cloud Applications" section.) A System resource represents a group of resources. The resources in a system are seldom random; service architects design the resources to work together for planned purposes. Some systems support a department or organization. Other systems implement a service, such as a product information system, that serves many departments in an enterprise.

A System aggregates the core CIMI objects: Machines, Volumes, Networks, and Monitoring. System Templates are patterns that can describe the infrastructure of a complex service composed of multiple machines, networks, routing groups, storage, and monitoring apparatus. Templates are then used to reproduce the system repeatedly. Service providers could manage System Templates in a catalog of complete off-the-shelf services for their consumers.

Security

Security is a difficult subject for standards. It is on everyone's mind, but it changes rapidly as the security experts contend with new technology and security assaults. Consequently, what is considered secure one day can be declared unacceptably insecure the next day. Standards writers are in a quandary. If security is spelled out too precisely, an insecure practice may inadvertently become a mandatory part of the standard. On the other hand, leaving security too vague may decrease interoperability or encourage insecure implementations.

The CIMI working group has been cautious about requiring security mechanisms that could be overtaken by events and discredited before a revision of the standard could be published. Instead, CIMI specifies the aspects of the interface that must be secured and points out areas where security may be necessary.

CIMI divides security into two domains: API security and resource security. API security deals with the security of the CIMI cloud management interface. API security is fully within the scope of CIMI. Resource security is only partially within the CIMI scope.

Resource Security

Resource security affects the resources that are running on the cloud, in other words, the resources that interact with the cloud functional interface. For the most part, resource security is outside the scope of CIMI and is the responsibility of the IaaS consumer.

For example, if a consumer installs an application in a provider's cloud, the consumer must build into the application the security necessary to prevent unauthorized users from accessing the application. CIMI API security will prevent unauthorized users from using the CIMI management interface to interfere with the managed infrastructure, but the consumer is responsible for the functional interfaces of the infrastructure. System security and application security is a similar distinction made on the customer premises. IT departments deal with system security. The IT department prevents unauthorized intruders from tampering with servers, networks, and the rest of the infrastructure. Application security is left to the administrator of the application. Only when the IT department happens to be the application administrator is it responsible for application security.[11] Similarly, CIMI addresses API security but passes on resource security.

There is one exception to the exclusion of resource security from CIMI. That is the problem of authorizing a first user of the functional interface to a CIMI Machine discussed earlier. The CIMI credential resource addresses that single resource security issue. If, for example, similar issues were to arise with Volumes that require passwords or other authentication and authorization, the Credential resource would also apply to that case.

API Security

CIMI identifies five areas of API security for attention: Authentication, Message Integrity, Message Confidentiality, Authorization, and Multi-Tenancy. Of these five, CIMI uses the strongest language, SHALL, for authentication. CIMI insists that the consumer of the system must always be securely identified. The specification urges implementers to provide for message integrity and confidentiality but does not require it. One way of assuring integrity and confidentiality is to use the secure HTTPS protocol, although CIMI does not specifically require HTTPS nor does it provide guidance on how HTTPS should be used.

Authorization is also important. Unauthorized users, users who may be securely authenticated but are not authorized to interact through CIMI, are usually undesirable—just as enterprises block authenticated employees who have no system privileges from tampering with system management. It is ordinarily not enough to know who is performing an action; the system must also know that the person or agent has authorization to perform the action or view the data. CIMI encourages but does not require a mechanism for authorization.

---

[11] IT departments often are application administrators and do get involved with application security. SaaS providers also are concerned with the security of the applications they offer, but CIMI is not a SaaS standard.

When multiple tenants use the provider's CIMI, tenants should not have access to the infrastructure of other tenant-consumers. CIMI assumes that a consumer's view of the system is limited to entities provisioned for or created by the consumer. For example, the provider may offer a number of Machine Templates to all tenants, but a particular consumer should see only the Machine Templates that are shared, provisioned specifically for that consumer, or created by them. CIMI leaves more detailed control of tenant access to data to other standards such as CDMI, discussed later in this chapter.

Extensibility

The model is extensible. Sufficient detail appears directly in the standard to support many important use cases, but both providers and consumers can extend it to cover special features. Entities in the model have property-value pairs. Consumers can put any properties and values they care to in these pairs. The provider is not obligated to understand or respond to these properties, but they are required to return the properties to the consumer unchanged. The consumer might use these properties to associate their own information directly with the resource on the consumer. For instance, a consumer might add "asset-tag : ENG-20120606-A" to a machine resource to identify the machine in an asset inventory of a department. The tag may have no meaning to the provider, but the consumer's administrative procedures may need to retrieve this tag from the virtual machine itself sometime after the machine has been instantiated, similar to checking the inventory tag on the case of a physical machine.

CIMI also has an extensibility facility tailored to the needs of providers. All clouds are not equal. Different providers offer different features and limitations. One provider might provide only a limited range of memory configurations, one processor architecture, and one attached disk size. Another might offer more processor architectures and several disk alternatives. Yet another might offer a completely unanticipated network configuration that the CIMI model does not accommodate. In all of these situations, the provider can extend the interface to accommodate these features and limitations using the CIMI metadata description resource that describes additions to the base schema. The consumer can discover this metadata and make decisions about using the features described in the metadata.

Extensions may hinder interoperability. Both providers and consumers should pay attention to the extensions they offer and the extensions they use. When designed and used with care, extensions do not hinder interoperability. A consumer that uses an optional extension from one provider may be able to stand up a service on another provider's cloud using CIMI with exactly the same input. For example, a provider might supply a special metric on virtual network traffic as an extension. A consumer might prefer to have the metric, but their cloud installation will probably work without it. In that case, the consumer could stand up the same service on a second provider that does not support the metric, with identical CIMI input. The second provider would ignore the request for the unsupported metric, but the service would still stand up. If for some reason the service was dependent on the metric, the service would not stand. Consumers must be aware of their dependencies on extensions if they want to change providers readily. Providers who want to provide interoperability must design extensions carefully to avoid forcing their customers to construct services that do not interoperate.

Scope

Compared to general models for the IT environment, the CIMI model is straightforward and tailored to the needs of a cloud management interface. It is not a general model of everything deployable in an IT infrastructure implemented on an IaaS cloud. General models such as the DMTF Common Information Model (CIM)[12] or the TM Forum's Frameworx Shared Information/ Data Model (SID)[13] are better suited to general modeling of IT. However, those models are necessarily complicated and daunting to a consumer who never has occasion to use them.

The CIMI model represents the entities that are needed for cloud infrastructure management with adequate detail to be useful but remains simple and straightforward.

The distinction between cloud management and functional interfaces, discussed at length in Chapter 5, is important in understanding CIMI. A management interface model does not need to model everything in the IT infrastructure that can be deployed on IaaS because most interaction with the deployed interface occurs through the functional interface.

---

[12] See http://dmtf.org/standards/cim. An appendix to CIMI does indirectly provide a mapping to CIM. The appendix discusses the use of Open Virtualization Format (OVF). OVF resources are explicitly mapped to CIM resources. By discussing the mapping of CIMI resources to OVF, CIMI is mapped to CIM. For more details on CIMI and CIM, we have to wait for the SOAP-oriented addition to the CIMI specification.

See www.tmforum.org/InformationFramework/1684/home.html for the TMF SID. SID is an end-to-end service model that includes the IT infrastructure.

[13] The TM Forum was formerly the TeleManagement Forum and, before that, the OSI/ Network Management Forum. As the name implies, the TM Forum is primarily made up of telecommunications providers.

A scenario will help explain this. Operating systems, for example, are not modeled in CIMI because operating systems are not directly managed in the CIMI management interface. Virtual machines (VMs) and other entities are instantiated through CIMI, and while it is true that virtual machines are usually instantiated with operating systems installed, the operating system is managed by logging on to the running VM and making whatever adjustments are necessary or using automated installation tools, like those that could be supported by OVF or TOSCA. The job of the cloud management interface is to do the work that is ordinarily done before a system administrator logs on to the machine with Telnet, SSH, or RDP and begins to make adjustments, starts depositing files with FTP, or uses other mechanisms to load databases and perform the work that the cloud infrastructure is meant to perform.[14]

The CIMI interface can instantiate a virtual machine with a configured operating system and preinstalled software, easing the system administrator's post instantiation job, but CIMI only directs the deployment of the preconfigured machine image; it does not perform the functions of a logged-on administrator or their automated agents. Installing an image requires only the image to install. The image itself is opaque to the management interface. The CIMI machine template references an image to install and can designate arbitrary data to pass to a newly instantiated machine, but it does not go beyond that. Similarly, CIMI has no models for installed applications, and the CIMI network model is abstract and does not manage physical networking gear beyond the external operations that correspond to switching off or reconfiguring the system.

CIMI Status

CIMI is now an official standard of the DMTF, released August 29, 2012. It is difficult to predict the future of a newly minted standard. CIMI is an ambitious effort with great promise. It addresses the problems of IaaS management in remarkable detail, which is not surprising given the participants in the CMWG. Many of the contributors have been actively working with the construction of production or management of IaaS clouds, both public and private. This experience is a significant contribution to the standard, which reflects the experience of the working group in pragmatic attention to detail.

---

[14] Telnet is an insecure Unix application for remote logging in to Unix or Linux systems. Secure Shell (SSH) is a more secure version of Telnet. Remote Desktop Protocol (RDP) is a Windows protocol for remote access to Windows machines. RDP clients have been developed to run on some non-Windows machines. File Transfer Protocol (FTP) is a protocol that runs on both Unix and Windows operating systems for transferring files.

Open Cloud Computing Interface (OCCI)

OCCI is a community-specified standard published by the Open Grid Forum in three documents published in 2011. Its goals are similar goals to those of CIMI, although the two differ in many ways. Both aim at an interface for IaaS clouds. Two of the three OCCI documents focus on a REST-style interface to IaaS management.

The first of the three documents, the Core document, is a high-level description of the interface. The abstract system described in the core document does not address any specific domain. The document points out that it could apply to PaaS and SaaS as well as IaaS. Nothing in the Core document limits OCCI even to clouds. It could be the core of a management system in almost any domain.

Core OCCI

The fundamental element in the OCCI model is the Resource. Links define Relationships between Resources. Both Resources and Links are derived from an abstract class called Entity. Because they are derivatives of the same abstract class, Resources and Links share the characteristics of Entities (Figure 11-3).

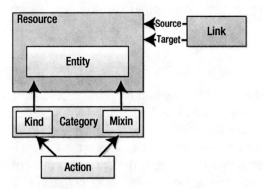

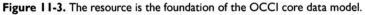

Figure 11-3. The resource is the foundation of the OCCI core data model.

Entities

The abstract Entity class is common to both Resources and Links. Several other OCCI classes are associated with Entities: Kinds, Mixins, and Actions. Because Entity is their abstract parent, both Resources and Links inherit connections with these classes from Entity.

Kinds

Kinds define the type for descendants of the Entity class. The properties unique to a descendant of Entity (either a Resource or a Link) are properties from a Kind class. For example, if the Kind is Computer, it might have a property to indicate the quantity of memory. A Kind for software probably would not have such a property. A Resource must be associated with one and only one Kind.

Kind in the OCCI structure is the repository of type-specific information. The properties of a resource are not specified in the description of the resource itself. Separating the Kind from Resource is an elegant and efficient model that will no doubt lead to flexibility in OCCI models.

Mixin

Another OCCI concept is the Mixin. Mixins are used to insert functionality into Entity descendants. Like interfaces in Java, Mixins provide some of the benefits of multiple inheritance without permitting the confusing complexity that full multiple inheritance sometimes creates. A Java interface defines a set of methods that can be added as a group to any class. All classes with the same interface included have an identical set of methods that can be called in exactly the same way. A single OCCI class can share in many Mixins without formally inheriting the Mixin from many parent classes.

For example, a modeler might define a speed control interface that has methods for gradual acceleration, maintaining a fixed speed, and controlled deceleration. The modeler could apply the speed control interface to jet airliners, automobiles, and kitchen blenders, making it easier for jet pilots to learn to drive cars and whip up lime daiquiris. In the same way, a "shutdown" Mixin could shut down a computer and a router with an identical set of calls. Mixins are a little different from Java interfaces because the methods in a Java interface are abstract—they have to be implemented for each class they are included in. Mixins have their own implementation and are not abstract, although they are always implemented as part of another class.

As an example, the OCCI standard Infrastructure document describes IP network Mixin that includes properties like IP network addresses and gateway addresses. The Mixin provides a uniform definition of IP network properties that can be used to build up other resources that have IP network properties.

Actions

Actions are the verbs of OCCI. They represent operations that may be performed on a resource. The example of a shutdown operation for computers and routers are examples of Actions can be associated with both Mixins and Kinds.

Categories

The final OCCI structure is the Category. The Category brings together Kinds, Mixins, and Actions into a single entity. The Category of an Entity (which can be either a Resource or a Link) determines its Kind, Mixins, and Actions. Thus, the Category ties together all the characteristics of a Resource into a single package.

CIMI and OCCI

Unlike CIMI, OCCI has been published as a standard long enough to have some implementations. It has been incorporated into the Open Stack open source cloud project.[15] The OCCI web site lists a number of other implementations, especially among the scientific community.[16]

For the implementer deciding between OCCI and CIMI, they should realistically look at the flexibility they need. The need for flexibility and abstraction in an interface is easily over- or underestimated. Generally, flexibility is the enemy of interoperability. The more flexible an interface, the more unique interface elements are possible and the more difficult it is to accommodate interoperability. On the other hand, a detailed and specific interface may not be malleable enough to meet the requirements of a situation.

Unlike OCCI, CIMI defines each Resource completely and independently instead of inheriting properties. Extensions to resources are provided for in CIMI, but consumers are offered predefined resources that are intended to meet most consumers' needs. CIMI does have an implicit core model that is apparent in the resources defined in the standard, but the model is shown in the consistency of the resources defined in the standard, not in an abstract structure like OCCI. The CIMI working group has tended to emphasize simplicity for consumers over difficulty for the provider. The use of structurally simple predefined models is an example of this tendency.

In contrast, OCCI uses an explicit class structure that imposes an elegant model for resources. The use of the Kind class for resource-specific properties is a sophisticated approach that imposes a structure on resources with few constraints.

---

[15] http://openstack.org/

[16] http://occi-wg.org/community/implementations/

CIMI has no concept like Mixin. Instead of building blocks like Mixins, CIMI defines complete structures. For example, CIMI provides a Network resource that provides for IP addresses. CIMI has traded flexibility for consumer simplicity.

The OCCI core model is a blank slate. A feature that could not be described in the OCCI model is hard to imagine. However, for an object to be effective, the implementer has to model the object well and explain to the consumers how to use it. Without agreements outside the current OCCI standard, other providers may not easily support another provider's extensions. The browser standard dilemmas of a few years ago illustrate this. CIMI, on the other hand, offers concrete models. The CIMI models will be relatively easy to use, but only if the CIMI working group has included the right set of properties and structures. The CIMI models are extensible, but they are not blank slates like the OCCI core.

The second and third documents of the OCCI standard do go into more details, providing examples of implementing the basic entities of a virtual system and providing a REST-style interface. The documents are not laid out with the specificity of CIMI. Programmers will probably find CIMI rigid, perhaps prohibitively rigid, compared to OCCI, but rigidity often removes choices that may be wrong.

Will CIMI, OCCI, or some other yet unknown standard become the single predominant standard for IaaS? It is impossible to predict. Although CIMI has not yet become a ratified standard, both are sure to be adopted by some sites, and both will be tested under harsh conditions in production.

The upshot may not be the triumph of one standard over the other. Consider Ethernet vs. token ring. Although Ethernet is by far the most prevalent standard and has been for at least a decade, token ring hardware still has a market. OCCI and CIMI may each find their niche and coexist for decades to come, one may disappear entirely, or a new technology may replace both.

Cloud Packaging Standards

Packaging complex services is an important adjunct to cloud computing. Deployment flexibility, balancing IT capital expenditures and operational expenditures, and the efficiency of large cloud data centers are important reasons for cloud implementations, but the cost of the service deployment procedure can interfere with these benefits.

Deploying a large and complex system is a maze of details. There are often hundreds, if not thousands, of configuration file entries that must be exactly right for the system to work properly. Software must be installed on the correct machine, and each machine has to be connected properly to the network. Installations like this are error-prone, expensive, and typically anything but agile.

The cloud brings an important new quality to the IT environment: uniformity. Traditional IT environments grow over time and are subjected to evolving requirements. The demands of the moment determine server configurations, and the network grows in continuous response to changing user demands and hardware capabilities. When an installation team stands up a new service in a traditional environment, the team either modifies the environment configuration to accommodate the installation or adjusts the installation to fit the environment. Both involve time and effort and are open to costly errors and side effects on previously installed systems.

Clouds are different. The variation in the physical environment is abstracted away into a uniform virtual system. The underlying physical system of a cloud is usually a systematically designed, uniform set of servers, but consistency or inconsistency of the underlying physical infrastructure does not affect the consumer as long as the provider conforms to service level agreements. The consumer sees only a uniform and predictable virtual environment governed by the cloud service level agreements and objectives.

That uniformity is an opportunity for consumers and providers. The trouble required to install a system or transfer it to a new platform is an obstacle to progress. One reason companies do not install new and more efficient systems is that the effort to change is too daunting. They pass up business opportunities because the cost of installing new IT services threatens to consume the benefits. The uniformity of cloud resources is a chance to reduce the trouble and cost with prefabricated packaged services. These packaged services offer the possibility of quick and reliable installations that may also be used to transfer entire services quickly and transparently from cloud to cloud, moving transparently from private to public, thus protecting the consumer from vendor lock-in and becoming a rising tide to raise all boats in the cloud arena.

The standards groups are addressing the problem with service package specifications.

Open Virtualization Format (OVF)

OVF is a standard from the DMTF that has been accepted as an ISO/IEC standard. OVF 1.1[17] was released in 2010 and was accepted as an ISO/IEC standard ISO/IEC 17203:2011[18] in 2011.

---

[17] http://dmtf.org/sites/default/files/standards/documents/DSP0243_1.1.0.pdf

[18] www.iso.org/iso/iso_catalogue/catalogue_tc/catalogue_detail.htm?csnumber=59388

OVF is not specifically a cloud standard. It takes on the challenge of distributing virtual machines to different virtualization platforms. Although OVF takes explicit aim at virtualization and packaging virtual services, not clouds, it can be important in cloud implementations, most of which are built on virtualization platforms.

Portability of services between clouds influences the practical value of clouds. One of the pillars of cloud value is competition. Public clouds compete for consumers. Other vendors compete to implement private and community clouds for enterprises and enterprise groups. The vigor of this competition is dampened when consumers are forced to rebuild services in order to change public clouds or their cloud implementation. Vendors of service packages want to avoid building a different package for each flavor of cloud that their customers may prefer.

Packaging standards like OVF interact with interface standards like CIMI and OCCI. Although CIMI and OCCI standardize the interface, they are not designed to specify packages that can be installed on different clouds. A CIMI or OCCI interface simplifies the construction of a deployment platform for standard packages like OVF and provides a standardized management interface for services installed from a package like OVF.

If a provider implements both CIMI or OCCI and an OVF deployment platform, consumers could deploy OVF packages, or they could use the lower-level management interface to develop and deploy services piece by piece. They could also use the management interface to manage services previously installed via OVF. In all cases, they have the advantage of using uniform packages and interfaces that do not force a new implementation and learning curve for each cloud provider or implementation.

OVF is not the only service package standardization effort. An OASIS technical committee is developing the Topology and Orchestration Specification for Cloud Applications (TOSCA). TOSCA's orientation is somewhat different from OVF. TOSCA will be discussed in a later section.

OVF, as mentioned before, aims at virtualization. This focus influences the way OVF works. Virtualization on the customer premises often starts with the hardware. Existing servers are replaced with virtual servers running on a pool of physical servers. The virtual servers have the same software and data as the old physical servers and perform the same function. The initial virtual model begins close to the physical model and then eventually evolves to a less constrained virtual design. When developers design and construct packaged services, they often follow a similar path. They start from a plan for a physical model and then devise a plan for virtual deployment; even though the initial prototype of the service is likely to be implemented on an IaaS cloud, they stay close to their physical experience.

Both when virtualizing a system and designing a service, the infrastructure model is derived from the service model, and then the infrastructure model is expressed in the package model. The plan for the service is certainly present in the package, but there is an intermediate step that postulates a physical model. The package model is derived from the physical model. An alternative is to skip the physical intermediate model and go directly from service model to package model.

This difference may seem subtle, but it is significant because going from service to physical to virtual package means that the package is only indirectly influenced by the service design. The package designer tends to work around the limitations of the postulated physical model. Instead of thinking of services that require a physical implementation, the thought process starts with a physical implementation and tailors the service to it, like the old process of installing a service to conform to the resources on a customer premises. The designer tends to think of a service as a set of machines, storage, networks, and software in a specified relationship, not as a set of functionality directed toward a consumer.

OVF reflects this orientation. The foundation of an OVF package is a set of virtual machines structured as hierarchical collections. This is fundamentally an infrastructure model to support a service. Creating an OVF package is fundamentally defining an installation of a set of VMs and other infrastructure that will support a service. This service has already been designed, and the infrastructure for running the service may have already been tested. The service design, implementation, deployment package sequence is a frequent practice and can be very effective. OVF fits into this pattern and provides some flexibility with support for alternate implementations and consumer choices at deployment time, but it is not the only way to approach a structure package.

OVF Package Structure

An OVF package is a collection of files: virtual machine and installation images and an XML document that fits all the pieces together. Specifically, there are four types of files in an OVF package.

- The descriptor, which is an XML document that ties together all the pieces in the package.

- Disk images, which consist of zero or more disk images to be deployed on the virtualization platform.

- Resource files, which consist of zero or more resource images (often .iso files) that will be installed with the package.

- An optional manifest file that contains a cryptographic digest of the descriptor and each of the disk images and resource files in the package.

- If a manifest is included, an optional certificate file may also be included. The certificate contains a cryptographic digest of the manifest file plus a digital certificate from the issuer of the package.

The image and resource files can be in any format, as long as the format is published and freely available. The files in the package may be collected into a single file with a "tar" command.

The OVF Descriptor

The OVF descriptor is a single XML file that describes many aspects of an installation from an OVF package. The packages themselves are not limited in their complexity. The number of virtual machines and software in an OVF package has no formal limit.

The OVF descriptor encourages reuse and reduces complexity with a recursive structure. There are there two core entities in an OVF package: VirtualSystem and VirtualSystemCollection. Both contain similar elements derived from the same root, but a VirtualSystem represents a single virtual machine, which may include both virtual hardware and software. Naturally, VirtualSystems can appear in VirtualSystemCollections, but VirtualSystemCollections may also appear in parent VirtualSystemCollections, permitting rich structures that reflect services made up of systems and subsystems with subsystems (Figure 11-4).

For example, consider a database VirtualSystemCollection with several servers and a complex backup VirtualSystemCollection embedded within the database VirtualSystemCollection. Databases do not stand alone; they are used by applications. This database may be a component of a storefront system. One model of a storefront is a flat, single VirtualMachineCollection of machines and software all tied together with a network. OVF permits that kind of package, but a storefront package could alternatively be composed of a storefront application system with a database subsystem and a backup subsystem embedded in the database system. Each system and subsystem could be modeled as a VirtualSystemCollection in an OVF package.

The components in the package are reusable. A package designer could reuse the backup component in several different database systems without

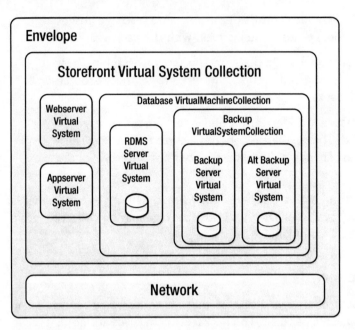

Figure 11-4. OVF packages support hierarchical components.

redefinition. The database system could be used in many different packages, including storefronts and inventory control—there are many possibilities. Packages structured as collections of components save effort and promote the use of proven modules.

OVF gives system designers the option of packages that reflect a component design. In addition to reusability, a component system is easier to understand, deploy, and maintain. Ultimately, a well-structured and maintainable system is more reliable, it can be more easily tuned for performance, and the total cost of ownership goes down. A component system can require a greater effort in design, but it has long-term benefits that often outweigh the initial cost.

Descriptor Structure

The OVF descriptor is an envelope composed of sections. The first segment of the descriptor is the references section in which the image and resource files in the package are inventoried and assigned identifiers. The section is first so that the integrity of the package can be determined before the rest of the descriptor is parsed and a damaged package can be rejected before any real work commences.

The next sections are content sections. The schemas of content sections are all derived from the same XSD Content element. At least one content section is required in a descriptor. Content sections are divided into Virtual Systems, which are in turn collected into Virtual System Collections. Virtual System Collections can contain Virtual System Collection themselves, forming a recursive structure permitting great complexity.

OVF defines a number of additional useful content sections. These include a section for describing the products installed as guest software, disks, hardware, and licenses.

OVF also provides for extensibility in the form of elements and sections that describe aspects of the package not covered in the standard. Extensions can often jeopardize interoperability. Extensions recognized by one deployment platform may not be recognized by another deployment platform. OVF mitigates this somewhat by defining three levels of conformance for OVF packages:

- *Level 1*: Only elements and sections defined in the standard are used.

- *Level 2*: Custom elements or sections appear, but they are optional.

- *Level 3*: Custom elements or sections are required.

Level 1 is the most interoperable. Level 3 requires deployment platforms to support the same extensions in order for both to support the package. A level 2 package will work on any compliant deployment platform, but only deployment platforms that support its extensions will deploy the package completely. The compliance level of the package helps users make choices when interoperability is a factor.

The OVF Environment

The OVF Environment manages the interaction between the guest software installed with the virtual machine images and the deployment platform. The environment makes it possible for configuration activity to take place after a virtual machine boots. This could be in the form of user-configurable properties that are set in the course of deployment.

The environment has two parts: the protocol and the environment.

Protocol

The protocol is the format of an XML file made available to the guest software on a virtual machine. Environment files are unique to each virtual machine for which the deployment engine creates a file. The XML targets a single machine and contains only those entries that apply to the target machine, although information about siblings and parents may also be included when it is useful.

For example, a parent VirtualSystem may have properties that a child virtual machine must have to complete its configuration. A virtual machine may have to be aware of properties of a sibling in order for guest software to interact correctly between the siblings.

The main section of the environment XML file is the properties section. This is a flat list of key-value pairs abstracted from the package descriptor. The list is simple and flat to make parsing easy for software on the virtual machine. The properties apply to the virtual machine and its parent virtual system collection.

Another section of the environment file, the entity section, contains key-value pairs that apply to siblings of the target virtual machine.

Transport

The environment transport is the way the deployment platform communicates the environment XML file to the virtual machine. If the target virtual machine has a virtual CD-ROM drive, the platform must create an ISO CD-ROM image containing the environment file for the virtual machine. This image is usually expected to be created by the deployment platform in response to the installation of the package. The image is placed in the virtual CD-ROM drive of the virtual machine before the virtual machine is booted. The guest software accesses the file and configuration proceeds. See Figure 11-5 for the full life cycle of an OVF package.

OVF Security

The OVF manifest and certificate files are intended to guarantee the integrity of an OVF package.

The manifest contains a cryptographic digest of the other files in the package. Users can verify the integrity of files in the package by calculating the digest of each file and comparing it to the digest in the manifest.

The certificate file is another layer of verification of the integrity of the package. Users can verify that the digests in the manifest were not tampered with by calculating the digest of the manifest and comparing it to the digest of the manifest in the certificate. Finally, they can verify that the package came from its ostensible source by checking the public key digital certificate in the certificate file. OVF 1.1 calls for SHA-1 digests.[19] The recommended algorithm in the standard will undoubtedly change as newer algorithms are certified and older algorithms are deemed insecure.

---

[19] For more on the SHA series, see Chapter 4.

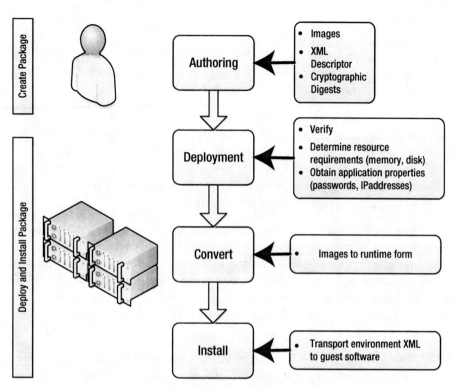

Figure 11-5. Creation and deployment of an OVF package

The OVF manifest and certificate are only for integrity; in other words, assurance that the source of the package is not an impostor and that the package received is exactly the package sent. Conceivably, the installation of a service that a malefactor has tampered with could catastrophically affect an entire cloud. The OVF integrity checking mechanism is therefore important.

The OVF specification does not address other security issues, such as authorization or privacy. There is a provision for placing password protection on designated values in the package, but the specification cautions that it does not provide full protection.

Topology Orchestration Specification for Cloud Applications (TOSCA)

TOSCA and OVF both are standards for packaging services, but they have different goals and orientations. Compared to OVF, TOSCA is a newcomer and at this writing is moving toward becoming an established standard. TOSCA was developed by a group of vendors and then moved to OASIS.

OASIS published a charter and call for participation in 2011.[20] A technical committee began to meet early in 2012. The TOSCA charter calls for delivery of a standard approved by the technical committee within nine months of the first meeting of the technical committee, which implies an OASIS TOSCA standard before the end of 2012.

TOSCA approaches service packaging from the design of the service rather than the infrastructure that supports the service. This is a business-oriented methodology. In recent years, business has increased the urgency of requests for IT services that are more exactly tailored to the business systems they support. These are serious demands for IT to deliver more value, and IT must pay heed or fail to align with enterprise goals.

Rising interest in industry best-practice guidance such as the IT Infrastructure Library (ITIL) is one indication of this trend. ITIL recommends that IT departments continuously examine the business motivation and implications of every IT activity. This scrutiny has become a prevalent attitude. Today, IT tends to look more at business requirements as the starting point for IT decisions rather than the older practice of proposing projects to business based on the latest technological developments.

TOSCA may become a significant tool in the quest for IT-business alignment. To align business and IT, the process usually begins with compiling a prioritized set of business requirements and goals with the help of business managers and analysts. IT planners and architects then design systems to meet the business requirements. After the design is established, they optimize the designs to match the resource budget for the project. The reverse approach begins with the resource budget and designs systems to use the available resources efficiently, meeting as many business requirements as they can. In reality, neither of these extremes is practiced often, but the trend has been to shift away from resource-oriented designs to service-oriented designs. System design can be more constrained by technology budgets than business requirements, but meeting business requirements is always important.

The increased resource flexibility of cloud computing may shift the balance, but the challenge of service design has always been to counterpoise business requirements with resource budget restraints. The cloud may change the dynamics of this situation. Nevertheless, working from business requirements to service designs that drive technology requirements is still widely accepted as a best practice.

TOSCA embraces service-oriented designs by making the service design the primary structure of a TOSCA package. To begin a TOSCA Service Template,

---

[20] https://www.oasis-open.org/committees/tosca/charter.php

the designer must look at the overall structure of the service, which TOSCA calls the *Service Topology*. The OVF structure, on the contrary, emphasizes on what must be installed and how.

TOSCA's approach is higher level than OVF. An OVF package is built around the virtual systems and virtual system collections that make up the package. It is hard to imagine an OVF package without them. A TOSCA Service Topology, on the other hand, can contain virtual machine specifications, but a Service Topology can define a service without reference to any implementation. See Figure 11-6, and compare it to Figure 11-4. The OVF storefront package depicts the virtual systems to be instantiated, while the TOSCA template shows the logical relationships between the entities. Both describe the same logical entities to support the same service. High-level TOSCA templates are useful because a service designer can lay out the components of a service and their relationships without awareness of the resources available on any specific site, and the implementation of the service can change without affecting the design of the service.

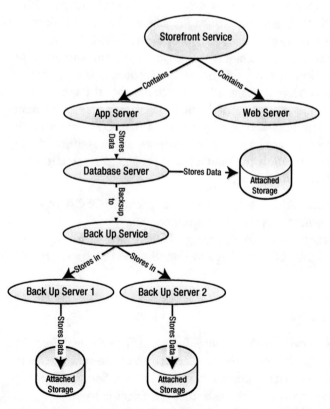

Figure 11-6. A TOSCA Service Template is a directed graph of the logical structure of the service.

Contrast this with an OVF package in which the service design and the virtual system design are the same thing. The designer cannot change the implementation without changing the service or change the service without changing the implementation. Since the service is characterized by the nested VirtualHardwareSystems, modifying the implementation of the service implies a change to the service design, and the only way a change to the service design can be shown is through a change to the implementation.

A TOSCA service designer can leave many decisions to the implementers, who probably know the resources available far better than the designer does. The deployment environment may be in the unknowable future. When the time comes, the implementers might decide a given component should be implemented as hardware on the consumer premises, virtually on a private or community cloud, on a public cloud, or as a managed service from a service provider. In any case, TOSCA embodies the service design directly derived the business requirements for the system.

OVF also supports implementation flexibility with multiple hardware sections and deployment plans that are chosen at deployment. In fact, it probably is possible to devise OVF packages that are as flexible as TOSCA services will be. The decision between OVF and TOSCA is not easy. TOSCA emphasizes service design. This has definite advantages. However, no one should forget that careful representation of the implementation resources is often critical to success. No matter how well designed a service may be, the quality of its implementation determines the quality of the delivery of business requirements and user experience. The details of implementation that OVF brings to the forefront are crucially important to a quality implementation. A methodology that defers these decisions until the end of the project threatens to turn implementation into hasty afterthoughts.

The TOSCA draft specification mentions OVF explicitly. TOSCA refers to OVF packages as *deployment artifacts*. A component of a TOSCA service can be implemented by deploying an OVF package. TOSCA acts as a higher-level framework that places the OVF package within the overall structure of a TOSCA service template.

TOSCA Structure

The root of a TOSCA service is the Service Template. The Service Template contains a directed graph that represents the structure of the service called a Service Topology. Every Service Template has at least one Service Topology. The topology graph is composed of nodes and edges. Edges in a directed graph are links with a direction from node to node. The edges in a Service Topology graph are binary relationships between nodes. The nodes represent the logical components of the service. These nodes and relationships are templates that are patterns for the real nodes and relationships instantiated in a deployed service. These templates are derived from TOSCA Node Types and Relationship Types that are also part of the Service Template (Figure 11-7).

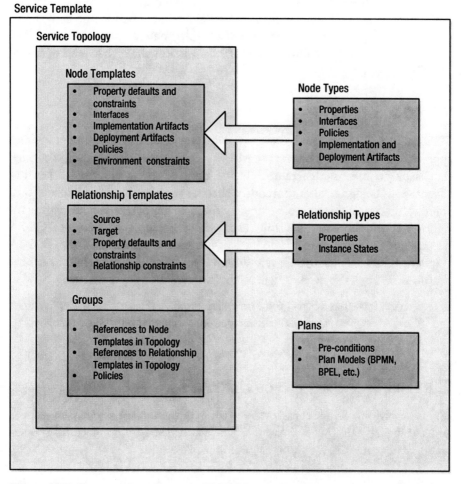

Figure 11-7. The central structure of a TOSCA Service Template is the Service Topology.

One additional element completes the top level of a TOSCA Service Template: Plans. Plans orchestrate various aspects of a service life cycle. The TOSCA specification defines build Plans and termination Plans. Build Plans orchestrate the deployment and installation of a service. Termination Plans orchestrate decommissioning a service. Designers of TOSCA services can add plan types as needed.

Plans use established workflow notations such as BPMN or BPEL to specify the plans.[21] The use of standard workflow such as BPMN taps into the expertise in the business process design that has already developed around these standards.

TOSCA nodes have additional characteristics. Node Interfaces describe methods for interacting with a node, such as REST or SOAP interfaces. Implementation and Deployment Artifacts aid in implementing or deploying a node. An OVF package is an example of a Deployment Artifact. Using an OVF package as a TOSCA Deployment Artifact illustrates the higher-level design of TOSCA.

TOSCA and OVF

TOSCA and OVF are two standards with very similar goals but divergent approaches. Eventually, one standard may overshadow the other, although that is by no means a certainty. At the time of this writing, OVF has the advantage of being a published standard that has been ratified as an international standard, and it enjoys support from a number of important vendor platforms. There will undoubtedly be some cases where implementers reject TOSCA because an OVF implementation is already present. However, if the TOSCA standard is as useful at the service design level when it is published as it now promises to be, its service design orientation will be very attractive.

One possibility is that both standards will prevail, OVF controlling deployment and TOSCA orchestrating OVF packages into coherent services designed to suit business requirements.

Cloud Storage Standards

There is only one cloud storage standard currently, unlike cloud IaaS interfaces and packaging, but the one standard is distinguished among cloud-specific standards because it was the first published. [22]

---

[21] Business Process Model and Notation (BPMN) is a standard maintained by OMG. See www.bpmn.org/. Web Services Business Process Execution Language (BPEL, also known as WS-BPEL) is also a language for specifying workflow. BPEL is an OASIS standard. See https://www.oasis-open.org/committees/tc_home.php?wg_abbrev=wsbpel .

[22] OVF was published before CDMI, but when it was published, OVF was described as a virtualization standard, not a cloud standard, even though it is important to the cloud. CDMI was clearly published from the beginning as a standard for cloud management.

Cloud Data Management Interface (CDMI)

CDMI is a standard for managing data on a cloud from the Storage Networking Industry Association (SNIA). The storage faces special problems in the cloud. Management of storage in the cloud is a major obstacle to cloud adoption, particularly of public clouds where economies of scale have the greatest potential. Chapter 4 on security and governance discussed these obstacles in detail. They boil down to a group of related problems: consumers must be sure that providers will handle their critical data in compliance with regulations and laws, not lose their data, and not expose it to unauthorized users. CDMI addresses many of these issues.

CDMI also addresses cloud storage complexity. Cloud storage can be bewildering. The range of technology, the geographical spread, and the array of requirements employed in a cloud storage implementation can be daunting. Data management is unique because the quality of other cloud computing resources can usually be judged nearly instantaneously by monitoring errors, performance, and events, but lapses in storage quality may not appear until an anomaly such as a compromised file surfaces days, even years after the data is stored. Perhaps the greatest achievement of CDMI is that it has established a set of concepts that captures this complexity in a uniform framework that manages these factors comprehensibly.

History

CDMI is part of the Storage Network Industry Association (SNIA)[23] Cloud Storage Initiative (CSI), whose goal is to advance cloud storage as a mode of delivering storage services that expand and contract with changing demands and are billed according to metered service usage. The CDMI international standard was written to advance these CSI goals.

SNIA approved the 1.0 release of CDMI as a Technical Position in 2010. A Technical Working Group (TWG) of the Cloud Storage Initiative developed the standard. Revision 1.01 was published in 2011. CDMI is also an ISO/IEC international standard: ISO/IEC FDIS 17826.[24]

Data Storage Service Challenges

Data storage as a service challenges system designers on several levels. Many of the obstacles that prevent enterprises from moving mission-critical services to the cloud stem from data storage issues. These are often legal or regulatory

---

[23] www.snia.org

[24] www.iso.org/iso/iso_catalogue/catalogue_tc/catalogue_detail.htm?csnumber=60617

issues. For example, some enterprises must control the geographical location of their stored data because laws and regulations limit where data of some types can be stored. Some countries in the European Union prohibit storage of personal data outside designated national boundaries. Some enterprises hesitate to store data in the United States because anti-terrorist legislation permits government inspection of private data under some circumstances. These regulatory strictures contradict some of the logic of the cloud, but they still must be followed, especially in public clouds. For cloud data management to thrive, these issues and many others require managed compliance.

In other cases, consumers may be concerned with the auditability of data in cloud storage. Some consumers have data retention rules and data destruction policies that are best implemented at the architectural level of the physical storage. Others require automated data encryption. On the consumer premises, the IT department typically implements and enforces these and many other restrictions and policies. When storage moves to a cloud, these requirements do not disappear, and consumers expect cloud providers to help with, or take over, the implementation.

Multitenancy, several consumer organizations using the same installation of a provider application, presents complications that often stem from storage issues. In a multitenant installation, data must be partitioned to prevent a tenant from gaining access to data owned by different tenants. Breaching multitenant data partitions may expose the provider to severe penalties and damage their reputation. Multitenant data partitions can be supported in application code and in the structure of data storage. Multitenant data partitions also apply to backups and data management policies. The policies may be as private as the data itself.

Multitenancy appears somewhat differently depending on whether the service is IaaS, PaaS, or SaaS.[25] For IaaS, multitenancy primarily involves marking off the storage of each consumer and preventing other consumers from accessing the data. This may include preventing or controlling access to the data by the provider's personnel. For SaaS, the problem becomes somewhat more complex because some application data may be shared among tenants. When SaaS takes the form of a managed service in which provider personnel become active agents in delivering the service—for example, when the provider supplies technicians to respond to incidents in a SaaS service desk—access rules become even more tangled. PaaS straddles the roles of the IaaS and SaaS provider, sometimes entering into the problems of the SaaS managed service provider if the services provided by the platform become complex.

---

[25] IaaS, SaaS, and PaaS are discussed in Chapter 3.

Storage management is complex, but storage technology is also physically complex. Many technologies and protocols are available. From manually mounted tapes to solid-state drives, they all have their place, and they all could be deployed in a single service. Nevertheless, the consumer usually expects to be oblivious of the kind of device that stores the data.

In addition to management and technology, storage configuration can also be complex. A single IT service can require a combination of storage on the consumer premises along with storage on public, private, and community clouds. The processes the use and create the data may run on an equally complex combination of clouds and consumer premises.

Confronting this complexity with vendor-specific interfaces challenges everyone. Vendors are hesitant to use another vendor's interface because they justifiably hesitant to relinquish control of interface release schedules and defect stabilization to an uncommitted third party or competitor. Therefore, they often feel forced to develop their own proprietary interfaces to avoid using another vendor's published and widely accepted interface, even though they are aware that every variant proprietary interface is another thick manual on the mountain of expertise that it takes to design, deploy, and maintain complex systems (Figure 11-8).

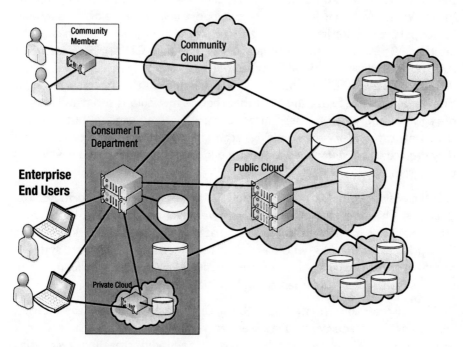

Figure 11-8. Storage implementations can be geographically complex.

These complex situations lock everyone in. The vendor locks the customer into the vendor's proprietary interface. But the vendor is equally locked in to their own interfaces and the proprietary interfaces of other components of the system, which may be from other hardware or software vendors or service suppliers or even the system vendors' own products from a few revisions back. Complex systems like this are staggeringly difficult to evolve to new modes of operation like the cloud.

CDMI Structure

The CDMI standard does not solve every storage related problem, but it does take a hard look at the challenges and confronts them with an interface that applies three main concepts: REST, containers, and metadata. The result is a single interface that meets the issues head-on. Each of these concepts in CDMI requires explanation.

REST

The CDMI interface is RESTful. That choice is not surprising with the current preference among developers for RESTful interfaces, but the choice is still significant. REST was designed as a discipline for document exchange on the World Wide Web that has evolved to support a wide range of transactions. It is popular today for its simplicity and its natural fit with interaction over the Internet. These are also requirements for the CDMI interface. The straightforward simplicity of the REST usage of HTTP GET, POST, PUT, PATCH, and DELETE methods is a welcome step up the abstraction ladder from interfaces like SATA and SCSI that require meticulous setup and reading of registers and buffers. These interfaces are fast and precise, but they are also as intricate and uncompromising as the underlying hardware. Consequently, they require detailed knowledge and are difficult for inexperienced developers to program.

CDMI hides the complexity of lower-level interfaces under its uniform RESTful interface. This does not eliminate the lower-level programming, but it does make it easier to isolate the parts that require specialized knowledge. Enterprise programmers, who have to deal with dozens of different systems, benefit from the CDMI interface treatment of storage as a uniform set of services rather than a fragmented and specialized set of devices.

REST is also an appropriate choice because it works well over the Internet with cacheable resources and stateless servers. Although REST is popular, it is not everyone's choice. Statelessness is an advantage for recovering interrupted transactions, which is important for data integrity, and it simplifies server design. Statelessness also complicates managing transactions; for example, transactions that involve transmission of data that is calculated or accumulated over time are somewhat easier to optimize if the server is aware of each client's previous requests for data.

The CDMI choice of the REST style is a commendable simplification. The relative importance or unimportance of REST advantages and disadvantages will influence the overall acceptance of the CDMI standard.

CDMI defines only JSON[26] payloads. This choice is similar to the REST choice. Standards now tend to define both XML and JSON forms for HTTP message payloads, permitting the client and server to negotiate a choice of data exchange forms. JSON is generally simpler and less verbose than XML and appears well-suited to CDMI needs. Many developers prefer simple JSON to XML, which can be very complicated and hard for humans to read. There are programming languages that consume JSON directly, notably JavaScript, but XML tooling is still more abundant, especially tooling to convert XML and XSD directly into procedure code, such as Java, for processing the XML data. JSON tooling seems to be growing rapidly, so this consideration will probably become less significant over time.

Containers

Although REST simplifies interfaces, without an effective underlying resource model, REST can be as chaotic and difficult to use as any other architectural style.

Containers are a key element in the CDMI resource model. The word *container* can have various meanings in software architecture. Most of the meanings stem from the notion of one structure being a subset of another structure. The superset is a container for the subset. For example, a computer contains a processor chip just as a peach contains a pit. The computer and the peach are the respective containers of the processor and the pit.

Some containers only physically surround the contained object; other containers also provide the means to use the contained object. A processor chip makes a nice fob on a key chain, but it has few other uses outside a computer. However, plug the chip into a socket on the motherboard of its container, the computer, and software engineers can put the chip to work. Without a computer to contain it, an electrical engineer might be able to use the chip directly, but it would take specialized skills of an electronics technician and engineer like soldering, voltages, and frequencies. Most software engineers do not have these skills. In software engineering, containers often refer to smart containers like the computer that provides an environment for the

---

[26] JavaScript Object Notation. See Chapter 10.

contained object to operate and interfaces that make the object useful in a wider context.

CDMI introduces storage containers. A CDMI storage container resembles a computer containing a processor. The processor inside the computer can vary greatly. The uses of a computer vary, but most computers have keyboards and some form of cursor control that are all used a similar way. CDMI containers can contain many different storage devices like SCSI and SATA disks configured as storage networks and other arrangements, but they all provide the CDMI management interface to the storage capacity that they contain.

The CDMI container is similar to a traditional file directory. Traditional file systems implement all directories in a similar way, and all directories contain objects that are dealt with as files. The CDMI equivalent of a file is a data object. Data objects are not limited to files, and CDMI containers can contain diverse storage objects. A traditional directory of files is only one variety of CDMI container.

Like directories can contain directories, CDMI containers can contain other CDMI containers. Recursive systems like this that contain versions of themselves have both extensibility and elegant uniformity. End users can manage the storage of their personal backups in CDMI containers that aggregate into CDMI-manageable departmental storage containers. The departmental container can be part of an enterprise cloud container.

Although each of these containers can hold different kinds of storage objects, they are all managed using the same CDMI interface. In addition, the departmental and individual containers inherit policies through controlled metadata inheritance that are set at the level of the enterprise cloud. For example, a file designated for storage within the EU only at the individual level can retain this characteristic in the enterprise cloud storage. This nested structure promotes uniform storage management policies without requiring uniform storage technology.

CDMI containers reduce data management to a uniform set of containers that represent the data management interface to a number of different logical and physical configurations.

Like CIMI and OCCI, CDMI does not try to replace functional interfaces, but it does provide a uniform management interface. The CDMI management interface helps simplify the functional interface. Systems that have gradually developed over time often intertwine management and functional interfaces. The lack of separation can be unnecessarily complicated and hinder integration, modification, and migration of systems. When changing systems that intermingle management and function, modifications to a system can force functional changes when only management changes are needed, and needed functional changes can forced unneeded management changes. When the systems are as complex as cloud systems can easily become, an approach like CDMI containers becomes valuable in keeping the system modular and therefore maintainable and agile (Figure 11-9).

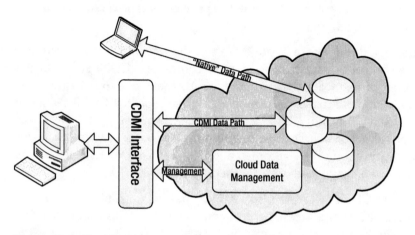

Figure 11-9. The CDMI interface supports data transfer as well as management.

Metadata

Data storage entitlements, prohibitions, and policies can be hard to keep straight and administer even without the consumer-provider separation of a cloud implementation. The cloud consumer-provider separation increases the difficulty. On the consumer premises, changing or adding a data policy ordinarily involves an executive decision and an internal discussion in the IT department on implementation. For example, a new regulation may demand an audit log of changes to a transaction system. After executive management establishes the need for compliance to the regulation, the IT compliance manager and an operations group that maintains the transaction system join in a conference and form a plan for implementing the log. The resulting implementation could range from an adjustment to an automated policy system to a completely ad hoc, paper-and-pencil, manual system.

In a complex cloud, such a change is not so simple. First, the requirements can be much more difficult to understand because cloud storage is an abstract and unknown quantity instead of a tangible group of physical storage devices in a company datacenter. Instead, the data is probably stored in an enormous storage bank in a remote datacenter that enterprise personnel may never have seen. Instead of hands-on experience, a consumer-provider contract and provider policies govern most aspects of the management of the data. There is seldom a collegial relationship between management and operations under the governance of a single group of enterprise business executives. There is no sharing lunch in a conference room to hash out a new compliance plan.

The lines of communication in a cloud consumer-provider relationship are much more formal and constrained. Consequently, the cloud consumer may slide into positions where proper governance of their data is difficult and either lax or overly constrained. This entire problem was discussed concerning security in Chapter 4.

A solution to this impasse is for the provider to offer transparent and extensible control of data storage to their consumers. CDMI supports this with a range of metadata that is extensible to meet new requirements. In addition, CDMI metadata is discoverable. In other words, a CDMI client can discover what a CDMI storage service has to offer through the CDMI interface rather than relying on sources outside the API. Discoverability is desirable for interoperability because an automated process is able to use discovered capabilities to configure itself to a new service automatically.

One aspect of CDMI metadata is ACLs. Most people are familiar with access control lists (ACLs) and access control entries (ACE). ACLs are usually lists of what an individual or group can do with a file. Typically, these are the familiar read, write, and execute privileges. UNIX System V parceled these rights out to the system administrator (root), the owner of the file, and everyone else. ACLs can be much richer and varied, depending on the operating and file system used.

CDMI applies metadata, including ACLs, at several levels in their model. The most granular element is the data object. As mentioned, a data object is similar to the file in other systems, although CDMI data objects are a more general concept than files and include almost any structure that can be stored as a unit, such as data blocks and table entries similar to rows in a relational database.

CDMI specification mentions metadata on several levels: HTTP, data systems, users, and storage systems. HTTP metadata is concerned with the HTTP transport. Data systems metadata is associated with objects and is specified by CDMI clients. Data systems metadata specifies data handling requirements to the storage system. User metadata is arbitrary user-defined data from the client and is associated with data objects. The storage system generates storage system metadata, which is useful information such as creation dates, creator identifiers, and so on.

CDMI Adoption

CDMI is the most mature of the cloud standards. It has advanced to the point that a reference implementation[27] and conformance testing is available.[28] A critical point is approaching when a large number of potential implementers of CDMI have evaluated the appropriateness of CDMI and how well it can be implemented with the available resources. Like all cloud-specific standards, it is not clear whether it will be accepted or left by the wayside.

Cloud Governance and Security

Chapter 4 discussed cloud security and governance. Security and governance is often cited as leading obstacles to cloud acceptance. Security and governance have received increasing attention as interest in cloud installations has grown. The Cloud Security Alliance has published guidelines for cloud security and governance, but its publications have not been in the form of computing standards. There are standard practices for security that apply to the cloud but are not specifically directed toward cloud security and governance. These were examined in Chapter 4. Here, I review an emerging audit standard aimed specifically at cloud.

Cloud Auditing Data Federation (CADF)

CADF is a product of the DMTF Cloud Auditing Data Federation Working Group, which was chartered in 2011.[29] In 2012, the group published a work-in-progress white paper that describes the use cases the standard will address. It also describes the goals, scope, and direction of the group.[30]

The CADF has chosen to focus on audit events, logs, and report information. It has begun to describe a standard event data model. A uniform event model is the foundation for audit event federation. When an enterprise works with a diverse range of cloud applications and providers, reports and summaries that combine audit events from different sources are often required for an adequate audit. If audit data from each source is in a different form, federating

[27] www.snia.org/forums/csi/programs/CDMIportal

[28] www.tcs.com/news_events/press_releases/Pages/TCS_CDMI_Automated_Test_Suite_Cloud_Storage_Interoperability.aspx

[29] www.dmtf.org/sites/default/files/DMTF_Cloud_Auditing_Data_Federation_Charter%20v1.0.8.pdf

[30] http://dmtf.org/sites/default/files/DSP2028_1.0.0a.pdf .

the information coherently into a combined report can be difficult, and the results may be of questionable value if there is no uniformity. This is the problem that the CADF has chosen to solve.

Identifying applicable use cases is the first step in this effort. The CADF has analyzed a wide range of audit use cases identifying the reporter, initiator, action, target, and outcome of the event.

An example use case involves the encryption of credit card information when transmitted over public networks. This involves a standard from the Payment Card Industry Data Security Standard (PCI DSS) and Control Objectives for Information and Related Technologies (COBIT).[31] CADF events are tagged with the governing controls and standards so that the events can easily be identified and reported. The white paper analyzes the requirements for the use case, such as that cardholder data must be tracked from entry to the system to the secure storage of the data and audit events must record the progress of the data through the system.

The group has not yet published a specification, but the group's charter estimates delivery of event model and API specifications for DMTF approval in late 2012.

The State of Cloud Standards

Cloud standards are new, and none of them has reached a stage of maturity that anyone can truly estimate the value of each to the cloud computing industry. Probably the most successful of the standards is OVF, which predates the current interest in cloud computing. Even OVF, which was first released in 2009, has received wide interest, but it has barely begun to be adopted widely enough to declare it more than very promising. The unreleased standards, CIMI and TOSCA, are even more difficult to evaluate. They have certainly generated interest, and both are technically interesting, but they are far from being influential. OCCI and CDMI have begun the path toward wide acceptance, but none has arrived. At this time, no standards have appeared that apply specifically to SaaS and PaaS, although TOSCA and, to a lesser extent OVF, could be applied to provisioning SaaS and PaaS installation. OpenID and OAuth help with authentication on SaaS services, but the proliferation of accounts and poorly managed passwords is a problem that cries out for a solution. This problem threatens to become a hindrance to the expansion of consumer SaaS. Standards could address the intervendor issues

---

[31] PCI DSS is available at https://www.pcisecuritystandards.org/security_standards/. COBIT is published by ISACA (formerly the Information Systems Audit and Control Association). See https://www.isaca.org/Pages/default.aspx.

that a consistent solution demands. Although CADF will be a stride forward in auditing cloud services, cloud security remains a concern. Standards designed to address cloud-specific security issues would be welcome. For example, a multitenancy security standard might assure prospective tenants that their interests will be protected.

Cloud standards will undoubtedly grow and become more significant as time goes on.

Conclusion

Service Management, Cloud Standards, and the Future

This book has covered a lot of ground, and yet many readers will insist that crucial subjects are missing. I sympathize. They are probably right. Many choices went into limiting the scope of this book to a reasonable length. For example, HTTP implementations and application servers could have been discussed in more detail. Language standards were almost completely ignored. There may have been too much discussion of networks and data transport, yet important protocols may still be missing.

Nevertheless, there is much to learn from the selection of standards and concepts in this book.

Clouds promise to be a new phase in the evolution of computing. Computers began in cloistered research centers and moved to a limited number of large datacenters devoted to a few large businesses and government organizations. From there, computing expanded, adding flocks of smaller minicomputers, and then exploded to millions of personal computers. The microprocessor placed the power of an earlier datacenter into the hands of individuals. These personal computers linked together, first in local area networks that tied together offices and small groups of personal computers. Eventually these local networks were connected into the global Internet. With the advent of the Internet, the stage was set for a full range of large public, community, and private clouds. At each phase of this evolution, standards played a role, and standards became more significance as their effect accumulated.

There are three great trends in computing that are converging and blending: cloud computing, service-oriented computing, and the continued minia-turization of computing equipment into handheld and even more compact mobile and embedded devices. These trends are independent but comple-mentary and synergistic. Together, they are changing the way computing is designed and delivered. These three trends are likely to change society and business in fundamental and important ways. These changes are dependent on widespread adoption of cloud utility computing, which depends, in turn, on the acceptance of standards of interoperability.

Cloud

Early in Chapter 1, the Information Technology Infrastructure Library (ITIL) definition of *service* appeared, which is a business-oriented definition that describes a service as a method of delegating costs and risks from the service consumer to the service provider. Cloud computing is a highly technical subject that depends on the most sophisticated computer engineering available, but it is also a fundamental change to the business foundation of information technology, not the technology itself. Cloud computing could not exist without the technology, but cloud computing is a business and ownership pattern that uses the technology, not the technology itself.

The consumer of a SaaS customer relationship management (CRM) service delegates the costs and risks of purchasing hardware and deploying, maintaining, and administering a CRM application on their own site to a SaaS provider. The SaaS provider accepts the costs and risks by implementing and maintaining the CRM service in their datacenter. In return, the consumer pays the provider a fee proportional to the consumer's use of the CRM service. The consumer no longer has to worry about system failures, application upgrades, or the cost of maintaining hardware to handle the peak usage that occurs rarely but at critical times when performance must not falter. Cloud computing is a technical means for the CRM provider to offer a CRM service to a consumer.

Offering CRM as a service instead of a purchased and locally installed application is primarily a business decision. The CRM application may not be identical to an application installed on the customer premises, but it will be similar to a site-installed version. The software techniques and hardware necessary for the SaaS implementation is not much different from techniques and devices that have been available for more than a decade. New software and hardware has been and will continue to be designed and built for SaaS, but the technical changes are minor compared to the change of ownership and responsibility on the business side. The innovation is in the choice of the provider to offer a metered service instead of a product for purchase and the choice of the consumer to contract for the service rather than purchase and install an application.

Services are not a new way of doing business. Businesses have long relied upon external services, possibly as long as there have been businesses. The reasons for resorting to purchased services have not changed. Sometimes the service provider has special skills that the consumer cannot obtain with their limited experience in the subject area. In other cases, the service provider is prepared to supply the service for less than the consumer's local cost. Sometimes the consumer has no appetite for the risks, even dangers, involved in providing the service and uses the service provider as a hedge against loss. These reasons apply as much to a farmer choosing to hire out the harvesting of his wheat crop as they apply to a particle physics laboratory joining a consortium of similar laboratories to use computers in a community cloud datacenter.

If the delegation of services is so basic to business, why has the cloud suddenly become so important? Businesses have been delegating IT services to service providers for a long time. In earlier chapters, the old concept of timesharing was discussed. What makes the early twentieth century special for cloud computing? Part of the answer is that computing technology can now support clouds more efficiently. But efficiency alone is seldom persuasive. The businesses seldom run to the cheapest supplier unless the supplier offers more than the lowest price. Without more incentive than price, the significance of clouds would be slight.

Are there reasons other than technical efficiency for the ascendance of cloud service implementations? What are they?

For several decades, IT has shaped many aspects of business, especially businesses like banking and insurance that deal with numbers and information rather than tangible things. Products like online bill payment are available today that could not exist without computing systems. Information technology has revitalized productivity in old lines of business and created entire new products and industries. Industries that deal with physical objects have been influenced also. Manufacturing industries rely on just-in-time inventory and computer-aided design to produce products at lower cost and with design flexibility that would not be possible without IT. Today, IT is essential to efficiency and profitability.

Service Management

IT has become a bountiful cornucopia for business and industry, but IT also has a reputation for unruliness. IT project costs regularly overrun estimates and fail to meet completion deadlines. The functionality delivered by projects often falls short of expectations. The shakedown after a new solution is up and running can drag on for years instead of days. Oversold IT solutions tantalize executives with their potential and then sink into a dispiriting medley of unintended consequences: defects, hidden costs, and unmet promises.

Some of these failings stem from hyperbole designed to generate enthusiasm at the beginning of a project, but more often, failures derive from fundamental misunderstandings between business planners and technologists. Business enters into IT ventures to gain competitive advantage, and instead they stumble into unanticipated costs and perils because they do not understand the technology they rely on. They frustrate technologists by both misunderstanding what the technology can do and insisting on what appear to be unreasonable demands. Technologists, on the other hand, misinterpret business requirements and are unaware of the pressures that determine the lives of their business counterparts. The result is mistrust and outright antagonism on both sides.

Skirting the pitfalls of IT has become an important part of successful enterprise management. A discipline called *service management* has come to the fore as an important instrument for successful IT management.

Both the business and technical sides of the house have largely endorsed a service management approach to IT. ITIL is a widely accepted set of practices that exemplify the service management approach. ITIL includes an extensive apparatus of education and certification. However, service management has grown beyond ITIL and become a pervasive attitude that has broader acceptance than strict certification and adherence to canonical ITIL practices.

Service management maintains that IT is a provider of services that happen to be implemented with information technology. This approach advocates evaluating IT on how well it meets the obligations laid out in an explicit service level agreement (SLA). The service level agreement describes the expectations and requirements placed on both the service provider and the consumer when they agree to enter the consumer-provider relationship. Service level agreements may be formal documents or casual verbal exchanges, but they work best when they are translated to clear metrics for judging the success of services.

A service level agreement may not be formal, but to be effective it must express the rights and obligations of both the consumer and the provider of the service. In addition to rights and obligations, an effective SLA also expresses what the service is, how it will be used, and what it will deliver. Without agreements like this, a service-provider relationship is difficult to maintain.

Service management manages the relationship defined by the SLA between a provider and consumer. Like private and public cloud providers and consumers, service providers and consumers may be segments of the same company or enterprise, or they may be from entirely different organizations.

The service management process includes the business strategy that directs high-level decisions, the design of services to carry out the strategy, and the structures necessary to deploy the service and support its operation. Service management usually employs a Deming continual improvement cycle, which begins with the strategic planning of services and proceeds through design, deployment, operation, and analysis. At every stage, the cycle relies upon a clear identification and measurement of the mutual obligations of the consumer and the provider.

Traditional IT management concentrates on IT department efficiency and project management. Hardware and software choices, metrics like total cost of ownership (TCO) and mean time between failure (MTBF), and project delivery dominate traditional IT management discussions. These considerations emphasize the technology itself over the fitness of the services delivered. The service management approach does not ignore these aspects of IT but places new emphasis on the services IT provides rather than the means for delivering the service.

Cloud computing fits well into the service management paradigm. Service management emphasizes the design of the service rather than its implementation. Cloud computing gives organizations the opportunity to shift more of the technical implementation of services either to an implementation specialist group in the organization or to an outside cloud provider. As enterprises become more aware of the service requirements that are independent of the underlying technologies, the benefits from delegating the technical implementation to a provider become more evident.

The cloud's logical and physical separation of consumer and provider corresponds to the concept of business as the consumer of services provided by IT. The service management framework for planning and managing services readily accommodates cloud services and provides a structure for deciding between private and public clouds and use of IaaS, PaaS, and SaaS; evaluating cloud contracts; and even managing the services after deployment. ITIL, for example, defines the roles for service performance and capacity managers for deployed services.

The confluence of cloud technology and service management is not surprising. Both are the result of the perennial pressure on IT and business to wring every bit of performance from the available resources, aided by the continual progress and evolution of the technology. The rise of the service management perspective and the development of cloud technology were certainly mutually synergistic.

Consumerization of IT

Cloud plays a significant role in the consumerization of IT. The relationship between IT and the consumer has changed from the mainframe days when the average person had never seen a working computer. Then, only a select group of engineers and technicians ever touched computer operation.

One way of looking at IT is a progression of human interfaces that have become easier to understand and more foolproof. The progression is evident. When you look around in almost any gathering of people today and count the number of smartphones, you see that people are contentedly absorbed in the Web, playing games, reading and responding to their e-mail, updating their calendars, and exchanging text messages. Some may even talk on their phone. Thinking back a decade or two, even if a personal computer could have been shrunk to smartphone size, interacting with the computer in the casual way we see today was still too difficult and frustrating for an untrained user.

The increasing ease of use was the result of the growing relationship between IT and the individual consumer. Hardware and software manufacturers could tap into a consumer market hungry for innovation, but only if the products could be made to appeal to the skill levels and tastes of the market.

Cloud computing is closely tied to tailoring computing to consumers. Consider an automated cloud backup service. Why is it desirable? To the consumer, desirability derives from the simplicity and convenience of a wireless utility that silently backs up to a cloud repository. Just like a SaaS CRM system frees an IT department of setting up and maintaining a large software and hardware installation, a consumer cloud backup service has freed users from the bother of remembering to back up and from fussing with easily lost or damaged DVDs and thumb drives. This is even more important when the computing devices go everywhere. No one has time to go back to home base to perform backups or other maintenance tasks.

Many consumer cloud services follow this pattern. Document services serve up a user's documents to any device anywhere. Music services that deliver wirelessly from cloud repositories that keep track of the user's collection follow the same pattern. Cloud services like accounting services are more complex, but they deliver the same convenience to users.

Consumers are receiving the benefits that businesses get from the cloud: convenience, flexibility, and better service. In addition, the cloud simplifies human interaction with their computers by moving much of the maintenance from the user's hands to the cloud. Instead of worrying about disk configurations and connecting peripherals, the smartphone user only has to be sure to recharge their battery.

Cloud and IT Progress

IT has gone through a series of stages that have each been necessary steps toward cloud computing as we know it today. It is impossible to say that the progression to the cloud was inevitable or even that cloud computing represents some sort of technical pinnacle, but it is clear that each of these computing developments is essential to cloud computing. With each phase, new kinds of standards have been involved.

IT PROGRESS TO CLOUD COMPUTING

- Programmable mainframe computers
- Distributed computers
- Networks
- Global Internet
- Clouds

IT has a rather short history. Prior to World War II, nothing existed that would be recognizable as a computer today. Many people in today's generation still pre-date the computer era that began to pick up steam and reached a crescendo with the dot-com crash at the turn of the century. The crash scarcely caused progress to miss a beat as computing moved on following the crash and business became comfortable with doing business on the Internet and World Wide Web.

Programmability

Each important aspect of IT has built upon the previous achievements. IT as we think of it began with the concept of the programmable computer. Special-purpose calculators designed to solve a single problem have existed in the West at least since the Renaissance. The Chinese abacus and counting boards are much older.

These devices are not programmable. The input to a programmable computer includes instructions for processing data as well as the data itself. In retrospect, this step may seem obvious, but it changed everything. Programmability means that a new device does not have to be designed and built for each problem to be solved. It is a first step in separating problems from the underlying hardware that executes the solution.

Electronics and digitalization are closely related to programmability. Analog and mechanical calculators preceded the electronic programmable computers, and they had some elements of programmability, but nowhere near the ease with which a new program could be developed and loaded onto an electronic computer.

Digitalization, the concept that all significant tasks can be represented as discrete sequences of combinations of digits,[1] rather than continuous quantities, is also an important foundation of electronic computers.

The first programmable computers came from the pressure cooker of world war. One of the first uses of programmable computers was cracking wartime codes and ciphers. Other important uses were calculating trajectories for projectiles and complex defense research such as the Manhattan Project. Resources are always in short supply, but they are scarcer and more critical during wartime. The pressure to conserve resources undoubtedly contributed to the invention of computers that did not have to be scrapped and rebuilt when an encryption method changed or a new problem cropped up.

Programmability is more significant than it may seem. It does more than economize on hardware. Most programmers are familiar with the driving sense that arises when one programming problem yields the insight to solve yet another more difficult problem. When this happens, the urge to write the code to solve the new problem is nearly irresistible. This onward flow of solution and insight is one of the profound motivations behind the advance of IT. The stimulus glues programmers to their seats in front of computer screens far longer than their job demands and causes purveyors of caffeinated beverages to thrive.

Without programmability, profluent development is much more difficult to attain. If a new computer had to be built for each problem, computing innovation would be similar to mechanical engineering where painstaking physical models or prototypes have to be built. The cost and time required interrupts the enthusiasm and flow of ideas. The creative energy dissipates, and the programmer goes on to some other subject.

Although the programmable computer grew from wartime necessity, it unleashed a flood of creativity that has yet to crest. The first computers were large and expensive. Opportunities to program were rare. If there is a calculus of creativity that dictates that the total sum of creative advances will be

---

[1] As everyone knows, electronic computers work entirely with binary 0s and 1s. Hardware that we use now uses only binary, but there is no theoretical reason f\or binary. If the hardware could support it as efficiently, another base would do just as well. Quantum computers, which may be the hardware of the future, are likely to use more states, but that is a long way off.

directly proportional to the number of those attempting to advance, then those isolated early computers were a hindrance to progress in the field.

Standards did not play a big part at the beginning of the computing era. Generally, large computers, mainframes, and their peripheral equipment all came from a single vendor whose products were internally consistent, but software and hardware were compatible only with products from the same vendor.

Distributed Computing

Distributed computing brought computing out of the datacenter and expanded computing to departmental-level mini-computers and then to the desktop and home. When computers became small and cheap enough to appear on desktops and in homes, new opportunities for innovation appeared. Computing moved out of the glass house datacenter and onto desktops. The image of the lone programmer inventing and enhancing the word processor, spreadsheet, relational database, and all the basic programs that are now standard equipment on desktops became almost iconic as distributed computing began to play a larger and larger role.

Distributed computing did more than abolish the typing pool and teach nonsecretaries to type. Knowledge of computer programming flourished and with it, a greater recognition of the potential of computing for individual consumers. Public recognition of the potential of personal computers was the first step toward some of the largest uses of cloud computing today, including massive Internet search engines and social networking designed for mass audiences of individual consumers.

Personal computers that are not connected to a network are rare now, but isolated computers still forced standards for interoperability. To sell computers to the new audience of computer users, manufacturers discovered that consumers were not satisfied with software that ran on only one model of device. They sought and obtained interoperable machines from different manufacturers that would all run the same software. This was the result of architectural standards such as the *de facto* IBM PC standard and internal standards such as the SATA standard for disk drives.

The Network

Networking, connecting computers together to share data and provide remote interfaces into other machines, appeared with mainframes and mini-computers. Distributed desktops were soon networked. When this happened, it meant two other kinds of standards became important—network communications standards and management standards like Simple Network Management Protocol (SNMP). The need for standardized computer-to-computer communication gave rise to one of the most basic network standards that has remained a mainstay of computing, the Ethernet standard, which has proved to be efficient and extensible through many changes and revisions of hardware and escalations of demand. As standardized networks expanded, the need for management standards like SNMP soon followed.

Network standards are important to the cloud. Without uniform methods of connecting computers, the whole idea of providing remote computing from a cloud would be impossible.

The Global Internet

The Internet and distributed computing are roughly contemporaneous, although the Internet was primarily restricted to mini-computers in universities and other research institutions until personal computers were well established. The Internet has required an enormous number of standards. The IETF RFC series has nearly 7,000 entries. Not all these RFCs are standards, and many RFCs represent revisions of previous standards; however, that number of standards devoted to the Internet is still large.

Internet standardization has been remarkably successful. For example, when traveling between North America, Europe, and Asia, a traveler has to pack a selection of converters to use their laptop with the local electrical system, but no converter is necessary to connect to the Internet. The Internet is a standard global system, unlike power grids, which are standard within their own domains, but travelers still have to pack a selection of converters and be careful what they plug into.

A lot has been said about Internet standards in the previous pages. The Internet, as a communication system, depends on *interoperability*, the ability of computer users over the globe to connect with the network and interchange information using their own equipment. This interoperability would not be possible without interoperability over the entire network stack.

The genius of network design is that although data link layers must interoperate with network layers, the network is still interoperable if two data link layers do not interoperate. As long data link layers interoperate with network layers and so on up and down the stack, communication can occur. A consequence is that localities can implement layers to suit their requirements and still maintain interoperability. Physical point-to-point connections can be wireless or wired and fiber or copper, and WANs can be ATM or MPLS, and end-to-end communication will continue. Communication is still only as robust as the weakest link in the chain, but the links can vary drastically.

The robustness of the Internet, which is the result of an overall design that promotes variation and preserves intercommunication, is central to the technology behind the cloud services. Without the ubiquitous presence of the Internet and its rapid, generally reliable, high-volume data path, the utility of cloud computing would be limited to private and community cloud services, similar to earlier stand-alone mainframe installations. Although these services are useful, as many implementers of private clouds are finding, they do not equal the mass impact of services like Google searches and Facebook social networking.

The Role of Cloud Standards

Up to this point, I have been discussing the past, which has already been implemented and works today. Cloud standards apply to what will work tomorrow.

The present set of cloud standards covered in the previous chapter is a new layer to the cloud computing stack (Figure 12-1). Earlier standards were primarily aimed at removing obstacles and improving communication over the Internet. Cloud standards address the work that is done with the communicated information rather than the communication itself.

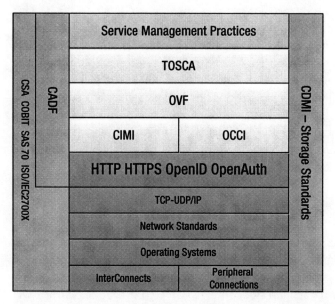

Figure 12-1. TOSCA, OVF, CIMI, and OCCI are at the center of cloud computing.

CIMI and OCCI describe standardized ways to set up and manage IT infrastructure over the Internet. In comparison, the HTTP standard lays out the requirements for building and operating HTTP servers and browsers that will transfer data and instructions between applications, but HTTP does not go beyond a communication protocol. CIMI and OCCI use HTTP communications protocol to install and manage services remotely. Instead of enabling communication, they use it.

TOSCA and OVF provide ways to define and configure complex services that are communicated via HTTP to cloud services. CDMI is an interface, in some ways similar to CIMI and OCCI, which is specialized for managing storage and data as a service.

TOSCA, OVF, and CIMI or OCCI could all work together in a cloud service-management stack. To begin, a service architect designs a TOSCA service template concentrating on business requirements for the service. The TOSCA architect must be certain that the service template can be implemented but does not decide how to implement the service. An OVF designer analyzes the concrete specifics of possible implementations and reduces them to a few detailed virtual machine configurations. When a service consumer decides to implement and use the service, they choose among the options in the OVF package, which is then fed to CIMI or OCCI. The CIMI or OCCI implementation does its job, and the service begins working on a cloud.

The beauty of this stack is that any cloud that implements CIMI or OCCI and supports the required resources can implement the service. The consumer can choose between cloud providers that implement CIMI or OCCI. This prevents rewriting the entire service when a lower level changes. Changing a service provider does not have to force rewriting a service of every level, only up as far as the implementation changes. If two providers provide the same resources and they both use CIMI or OCCI, there will be little or no change. If the resources are different, changes on the OVF level may be required, but not in the service template. Although enterprises have trained technologists to rewrite their services for each provider, rewriting is expensive and time-consuming and discourages moving from provider to provider in pursuit of the provider that will be their best partner.

The Future of Cloud Standards

Competitive cloud computing could easily cause computing to become an even larger part of individual and enterprise life. The computing power of laptops, tablets, and smartphones today is staggering compared to a few decades ago. As giant datacenters become available to everyone, as they will if current trends continue, the resources available to everyone—giant corporations, governments, research institutes, and lone individuals—will expand by orders of magnitude. We have no more idea today of what those new resources will make possible. In 1960, no one predicted that in 50 years, online searches would replace trips to academic libraries, and social networking would fuel revolutions.

It is intriguing to project some current trends into the future. We have already mentioned the service approach to managing IT. Other important trends are highly portable tablets and intelligent phones replacing desktops and laptops. Various forms of wireless networking that provide connections to the global network from anywhere will enhance this portability. As a result, information workers are no longer tethered even to home offices. Cloud services add to this freedom by increasing the resources available.

Cloud resources eventually will be available to anyone with the proper credential as hardware increases in power and decreases in price. A modest prediction is that computing will become more individualized. Constructing computer applications is not more difficult than other project-oriented problem-solving disciplines such as cooking or home repair, but the tools of programming are not as commonly available as saucepans and claw hammers.

That could change. Utility computing providers may offer convenient and easy-to-use tools for combining prefabricated functionality. These tools could make functionally individualized computing services as common as personal web sites are today. The popularity of these services would be greatly enhanced if a cloud service stack based on the current crop of cloud standards made moving individualized services from one provider to another as easy as it is to move a web site from one Internet service provider to another.

These tools could make the data and processing power of the cloud as accessible as the Internet is today. No one accurately predicted how near-universal Internet access would change the way we approach information today and how it has influenced personal and world events. It is equally unclear what kind of knowledge and capabilities will be unleashed from the cloud, but the potential is astounding. If the cloud follows the pattern of the Internet, we are likely to see changes as profound as the revolution in retail and communications that we have experienced in the last few years. We are on a cusp, we don't know what awaits us, but we have every reason to expect to be delighted.

Index

I

P, Q

R